MW01155189

CONTENTS

TALES OF THE TURING CHURCH

SECOND EDITION
Hacking religion, enlightening science, awakening technology

By Giulio Prisco – 2020

DEDICATION

To my sweetest wife and daughter Anna Maria and Melinda.

To my parents Anna and Glauco.

To my parents in law Magda and Vilmos.

To my grandparents Gigia, Giulio, and Rita.
Grandpa Amato, I didn't forget you, but we never met! I look forward to meeting you on the other side.

To Angelina, Enrica and Giovannella.

To my beloved pets Minou, Ricky, Sacha, and Speedygonzales.

To all my relatives and friends in the "real world." I wrote this book for you too, I hope you'll enjoy it!

ACKNOWLEDGMENTS

I wish to thank all those who helped me develop and refine the ideas outlined in this book. They are mentioned and cited in the text.

I wish to thank the early readers who helped me put the first edition of this book in its final shape, and those who helped me improve the book for the second edition. Some of them are: Ralph Abraham, Bill Bainbridge, Jeff Beck, Tom Bell, Mani Bhaumik, Howard Bloom, Tudor Boloni, Christopher Bradford, Lincoln Cannon, James Carroll, Linda Chamberlain, Peter Christiansen, Robin Hanson, Richard Harvey, Martin Higgins, Jonathan Jones, Randal Koene, Catarina Lamm, Stephan Magnus, David McFadzean, Yalda Mousavinia, Nupur Munshi, Blaire Ostler, David Pearce, Mike Perry, Geoffrey Quick, Micah Redding, Sisir Roy, Samuel Smith, Melanie Swan, Kathy Wilson, David Wood.

A problem with these lists is that one always forgets to include somebody who should really be in the list. If I have forgotten you, please let me know and accept my apologies! I also wish to thank the anonymous early readers who sent me useful comments and suggestions.

The study and research that I did is not of the kind where one studies carefully a handful of books and papers. It's more of the kind where one goes rapidly through hundreds of books and papers, trying to learn from different angles.

I started practicing this learning style as a college student, and then as a young scientist working in research institutions with well stocked libraries. I used to take ten or twenty books and journals on related topics to a reading table, and go through them in parallel.

Today, I couldn't do this because I don't have the money to buy hundreds of books and research papers, many of which are outrageously priced. While I always buy the fairly priced works of independent authors, I am unable and unwilling to enrich major publishers.

But I have the world's largest pirate research libraries at my fingertips, and everything is free. From Libgen, I can download most of the books I need. From Sci-Hub, I can download most of the research papers I need. Therefore, I wish to thank the Libgen and Sci-Hub teams, and in particular Alexandra Elbakyan, the creator of Sci-Hub.

Yes, I know that piracy is bad. But I also know that knowledge and ideas want and need to be free. I'm an average sixty-something, but brilliant young people all over the planet also have the world's knowledge and best ideas at their fingertips. Some of them will make the world a better place. This is, I think, more important than the interest of the publishing industry.

Someday soon, I hope, there will be ways to fairly reward creators and at the same time make their creations affordable to everyone. In the meantime, since I enjoy the work of others without paying, I must make my own work freely available. The content of the free version of this book is identical to the retail version, and the retail Kindle version is not encrypted.

If you are reading the free version of my book, or a pirated copy of the retail version, I wish to THANK YOU for your time and attention. If you are one of those who bought the retail version, I wish to THANK YOU for also buying me a coffee and half a pack of cigarettes.

INTRODUCTION

This isn't your grandfather's religion.

Future science and technology will permit playing with the building blocks of space, time, matter, energy, and life, in ways that we could only call magic and supernatural today.

Someday in the future, you and your loved ones will be resurrected by very advanced science and technology.

Inconceivably advanced intelligences are out there among the stars. Even more God-like beings operate in the fabric of reality underneath spacetime, or beyond spacetime, and control the universe. Future science will allow us to find them, and become like them.

Our descendants in the far future will join the community of God-like beings among the stars and beyond, and use transcendent "divine" technology to resurrect the dead and remake the universe.

Science? Spacetime? Aliens? Future technology? I warned you, this isn't your grandmother's religion.

Or isn't it?

Simplify what I said and reword it as: God exists, controls reality, will resurrect the dead and remake the universe. Sounds familiar? I bet it does. So perhaps this IS the religion of our grandparents, in different words.

God - an absolutely infinite, infinitely far, totally unknowable God - can't be ruled out by science. In fact, one of my conclusions is that [God is undecidable but plausible].

I am a theoretical physicist by training, and a [transhumanist]. I also believe in God, and in the afterlife. Inconsistent? Some will say so, but I don't care. Some bureaucrats of philosophy will say all sorts of bad things and criticize me for mixing science and religion, but I really couldn't give less of a damn. I haven't written this book for them.

       I have written this book for you.

If you are afraid of death, this book is for you. If you are grieving for the loss of a loved one, this book is for you. If you want to reconcile your belief in God with your scientific worldview, this book is for you. If you are a transhumanist who wants to believe in a transcendent reality, this book is for you.

Perhaps you have been told that science has (or will soon have) all the answers, and religion is a fairy tale.

Not so. Current science is very far from having all the answers, but future science and technology will validate and realize all the promises of religion.

My message is that, if you want, you can hope to live again with your loved ones, without abandoning the scientific worldview. If you want, you can believe in the essential core of your religion without betraying science.

So Who Is This Guy With A New Religion?

Thanks for asking, but my ideas are not that new. I will try to emphasize the parallels between my ideas and traditional religions, rather than the differences, and picture Jesus in a spacesuit. Muhammad in a quantum computing lab. The Buddha "in the circuits of a digital computer or the gears of a cycle transmission" (Robert Pirsig, of course [Pirsig 1974]).

My family was nominally Catholic but we didn't go to church, and considered religion as something that other people do. So I grew up mostly uninterested in traditional religion and unaffected by it. At the same time, since I can remember I have always been interested in spirituality and the foundations of reality.

My name is Giulio Prisco. I grew up reading a lot of science and science fiction. I studied theoretical physics with the intention to specialize in fundamental cosmology and quantum physics, and started working on a highly theoretical thesis, but then I switched to a more practical field and eventually earned my degree with a research thesis on free electron laser physics.

Soon after I moved to CERN, where I developed software for data acquisition in high-energy physics experiments. Then I moved to the European Space Agency, where I mostly worked on computational fluid dynamics, gas dynamics, Monte Carlo simulations, parallel computing, and the early internet. Then I moved to senior management roles in other public science and technology administrations.

One day in 2005 I told the boring world of 9-to-5 office nonsense to get lost. First I started a virtual reality consulting company that was reasonably successful for a few years, then I became a freelancer dabbling in many different areas including event organization, software development, blockchain technology, business and scientific journalism. I wish to thank the internet for allowing me to earn a living as a free agent.

I don't call myself a scientist these days. I guess I am one of those former scientists who, in the words of Leonard Susskind [Susskind 2013], have been around the block a few times and are not at all afraid to ask questions. I'm not at all afraid to propose answers either.

I have had a [transhumanist] outlook since I can remember. In the mid nineties I found other transhumanists online (thank you internet!) and became a card-carrying member of the movement. I still am, but I guess my interpretation of transhumanism is unconventional (just read the rest of the book).

Back to religion. While I call myself a believer, my interpretation of religion is also unconventional, and inspired by transhumanism and science (and science fiction of course). I became interested in the parallels and intersections between transhumanism and religion, and in 2004 I wrote an essay on my developing ideas titled "Engineering Transcendence" [Prisco 2004].

The essay was criticized by many, but appreciated by some, and I became part of a small but growing community of religious transhumanists.

I have been writing about religion and transhumanism ever since. I am a member of the [Mormon Transhumanist Association] (MTA) and the [Christian Transhumanist Association] (CTA), two groups that promote transhumanist ideas in their respective religious communities. On the less conventional, more speculative wild side, I founded a group called Turing

Church to "hack religion, enlighten science, awaken technology."

About This Book, And How To Read It

I have tried to make this book as short, clear, and simple as possible, and use the language that we use every day. This hasn't been easy, but I hope the result is a readable book.

Let me get some disclaimers, caveats, and qualifications out of the way.

This is not a science book because I will venture far beyond the territory covered by established science, into the weirdest fringes of highly imaginative science. This is not a book on religion, because I do not offer certainties, but only visions and hope.

Call my book "mythology" if you wish. But I wouldn't have written this book if I were not persuaded that my mythology might be close to reality. I have chosen the title "*Tales of the Turing Church*" to emphasize that I do not wish to offer a tight scientific, religious, or philosophical system, but rather a loose collection of ideas, visions and tales.

Besides some "glueware" to connect nodes in a network of thoughts, I have not developed any of the important concepts and arguments covered in this book. Please see "Acknowledgments."

Since I prefer reading ebooks, I have used a mobile-first, ebook-first design and tried to make this book easily readable on all popular devices, including smartphones, with tweaks to make the web and printable PDF versions easily readable too.

I have composed this book in Google Drive for the convenience of writing and editing anytime, anywhere, including on the phone in a car under the snow (which is how I am writing these words), and collaborating with my early readers and reviewers. The official free version of the book is the final Google Drive version.

I haven't even thought of submitting the book to a major publisher. Instead, I have asked a group of trusted friends, writers, and experts (see "Acknowledgments") to join me for a final revision, mercilessly criticize the draft, and suggest improvements.

While this book is meant to be read from the beginning to the end, I have tried to make all chapters readable independently. The price to pay is some repetition, but repetition is not necessarily a bad thing. I'll repeatedly hammer in some important concepts and arguments.

This book is not self-contained: I tried to give good references, but I assume that the reader will use Google to find out more. Remember, the internet is your friend.

I have aimed at clarity and readability rather than breadth and depth, with "less is more" in mind, trying to use what the author of a classic mathematics textbook called a "merciless telegram style" [Landau 1966].

I won't inflict mathematical formulas on you, but I will use mathematical notation now and then. Since I don't trust all ebook readers to display exotic characters correctly, I use programming notation.

For example I use ** for exponentiation (10**9 means 10 multiplied by itself 9 times, or one billion, and 10**-9 means one divided by one billion). I use sqr for square roots, pi for that number that comes out when we talk of circles, and that should be it.

While the chapters in Part 2 are mainly about philosophy, religion, and science fiction, and the chapters in Part 3 are mainly about science, the separation is not very sharp. Philosophy and science, religion and science fiction, are intermingled in all chapters. I don't consider this a bug, but a feature.

One thing that you won't find in this book is politics. I do have political opinions like everyone, but partisan politics is irrelevant to what I want to discuss here.

This book includes content adapted from essays that I have written over many years and published in my websites [turingchurch.com] and, more recently, turingchurch.net. If a link doesn't work, please use [Wayback Machine] to retrieve the content. My essays since 2016 are in turingchurch.net.

However, here I have extensively modified and often entirely rewritten previously published essays. I have also tried to be somewhat consistent, but without really worrying too much about consistency, which is known as "the hobgoblin of little minds" (Ralph Waldo Emerson, [Myerson 2000]).

This book is a snapshot of what I think today (February 2020). It is more concise and (I hope) clearer than previous essays. Please visit my websites for past and future essays.

References and notes are at the end of each chapter and referred to with [square brackets] in the text.

Second Edition

I published the first edition of this book in December 2018. At the time, I didn't plan to publish a second edition.

However, I realized that the first edition contained far too many typos and inaccuracies, and some passages weren't clear enough. I can't promise that this second edition is bug-free (there are always some more bugs), or that everything is crystal clear, but I can say that this second edition is better than the first.

I also updated the book with new material based on essays written after the publication of the first edition. I published this second edition in February 2020, with a new chapter added at the end and all chapters revised and often expanded, some less and some more. This should be the final edition of my book.

This second edition is also informed by feedback from readers, and discussions with them.

The first edition of my book has been received with overwhelming praise, often enthusiastic. There's one exception though: A very harsh review written by my friend Robin Hanson [Hanson 2019].

Robin accuses me of saying that "wishful thinking is virtuous" and "has social benefits." Even worse, "Prisco says that focusing on truth rather than hope is 'bad philosophy.'" Others have made similar objections.

My answer is: YES! Guilty as charged, and here's to wishful thinking!

Everything that is worthy and good starts with wishful thinking. Of course, wishful thinking doesn't come true unless it's followed by more rigorous thinking and hard work, but wishful thinking is always the first step. I think one of the problems of today's Western culture is that there is not enough wishful thinking. I could elaborate at length, but (as Robin says) I make this point many times in this book, so just keep reading.

Robin continues: "But the obvious way to promote future resurrection is to encourage people to get cryonics... This is where wishful thinking can really hurt: people who skip cryonics because they wishfully think gods will revive them no matter what, may miss their only chance to be revived."

My simple answer is that my ideas don't exclude [cryonics], of which I am a big fan. But [conflating my ideas with cryonics is very wrong]. I want to offer hope to everyone, without requiring cryonics or equivalent preservation technologies here and now.

My central point is that everyone, including our grandparents, their grandparents, and everyone who died in the past, will be resurrected by future human engineers and/or by ultra-technologies available to other actors (e.g. ultra-advanced non-human beings, Gods), regardless of preservation technologies available today. They will find ways to resurrect us without depending on preservation technologies used on our side.

Notes

[Christian Transhumanist Association] See "Christianity and transhumanism are much closer than you think."

[conflating my ideas with cryonics is very wrong] See "Turing Church."

[cryonics] See "Transhumanism."

[God is undecidable but plausible] See "Thought experiments in physical theology."

[Mormon Transhumanist Association] See "Man will become like God, say Mormons and transhumanists."

[square brackets] in the text refer to notes and references at the end of each chapter.

[transhumanist] See "Transhumanism."

[turingchurch.com] In the second edition of this book I have replaced all references to essays published in turingchurch.com with new sections, notes, or equivalent references.

[Wayback Machine]:
https://archive.org/web/

References

[Hanson 2019] Robin Hanson. Tales of the Turing Church. *Overcoming Bias*, 2019. http://www.overcomingbias.com/2019/01/tales-of-the-turing-church.html

[Landau 1966] Edmund Landau. *Foundations of Analysis*. Chelsea Publishing Company, 1966. (Original: *Grundlagen der Analysis*, Akademische Verlagsgesellschaft, 1930).

[Myerson 2000] Joel Myerson. *Transcendentalism: A Reader*. Oxford University Press, 2000.

[Pirsig 1974] Robert Pirsig. *Zen and the Art of Motorcycle Maintenance*. William Morrow and Company, 1974.

[Prisco 2004] Giulio Prisco. Engineering Transcendence. http://giulioprisco.blogspot.com/2006/12/engineeringtranscendence.html

[Susskind 2013] Leonard Susskind, George Hrabovsky. *The Theoretical Minimum: What You Need to Know to Start Doing Physics*. Basic Books, 2013.

PART 1 - FROM TRANSHUMANISM TO TRANSCENDENCE

[One of the best introductions to transhumanism] is titled "*Transcendence*" [Goffman 2015].

"*Transcendence*" is a collection of alphabetically-ordered short chapters about transhumanist thinking and futuristic technologies like nanotechnology, genetic engineering, life extension, biohacking, cryonics, mind uploading, Artificial Intelligence (AI), space exploration, synthetic biology, robotics, virtual worlds and whatnot.

The title of the book is well chosen. What is transhumanism, if not the aspiration to transcend all human limits, including death itself?

Wally Pfister's film "*Transcendence*" [Prisco 2014], with Johnny Depp, Rebecca Hall, and Morgan Freeman, shows vivid pictures of transhumanist technologies that could eliminate death and disease. Transhumanism promises to build a technological Heaven on Earth in a few short decades (or, more likely if you ask me, many long centuries).

The makers of the film "invited various scientists to consult on their treatment of advanced tech like mind uploading, AI and nanotechnology... and better yet, invited ME to speak about AI and mind uploading at their formal launch of the film in Beijing," says transhumanist Ben Goertzel [Goertzel 2014].

But the term "transcendence" is also used in philosophy, science fiction set in the far future, and religion, to indicate unseen otherworldly realms and spiritual aspects of reality beyond the ordinary material world. I think we'll unveil and exploit transcendent aspects of reality one day, but not in a few short decades. It will take many long centuries, or more.

There is tension between transhumanism and spiritual transcendence. For example, many transhumanists wish to live forever, but reject spiritual and religious traditions that promise eternal life. Many transhumanists dream of creating artificial life in synthetic worlds, but reject the idea that our universe might be the creation of a superior power.

Similarly, many transhumanists look forward to artificial telepathy, for example through the neural nanobots imagined by Ramez Naam in "*Nexus*" [Naam 2013 and sequels] and Martin Higgins in "*Human+*" [Higgins 2017], but reject (Ben Goertzel being a notable exception) the idea of a spiritual human potential, namely that we might have natural psychic abilities.

"*Human+*," a science fiction thriller with both high technology and spirituality, captures well the tension between human potential and its engineered version, and the different mindsets of those who promote them [Prisco 2012]. But, one of the main characters wonders, "who's to say the two can't develop together - technology and human potential - perhaps should develop together?"

I think technological and spiritual transcendence can, and should, develop together. The next two chapters cover, respectively, transhumanism and my ideas on the fusion of technological and spiritual transcendence. Transhumanist readers be warned, my ideas sound dangerously like religion at times.

Notes

[One of the best introductions to transhumanism] See "Transhumanism" for a short review of the book.

References

[Goertzel 2014] Ben Goertzel. Transcendence vs. Her: Clash of Two Wimpy Future Visions. *H + Magazine*, 2014.
http://hplusmagazine.com/2014/05/13/transcendence-vs-her/

[Goffman 2015] Ken Goffman, Jay Cornell. *Transcendence: The Disinformation Encyclopedia of Transhumanism and the Singularity*. Disinformation Books, 2015.

[Higgins 2017] Martin Higgins. *Human+*. Neely Worldwide Publishing, 2017.

[Naam 2013] Ramez Naam. *Nexus*. Angry Robot, 2013.

[Prisco 2012] Giulio Prisco. Human+ - smartdust, spooks, psychics, and transhumans. *KurzweilAI*, 2012.
https://www.kurzweilai.net/book-review-human-smartdust-spooks-psychics-and-tran-shumans

[Prisco 2014] Giulio Prisco. Transcendence - A Movie Review. *IEET*, 2014.
https://ieet.org/index.php/IEET2/more/prisco20140819

CHAPTER 1 - TRANSHUMANISM: THE MOST DANGEROUS IDEA

The best definition of transhumanism is due to anti-transhumanist Francis Fukuyama. In 2004, the editors of *Foreign Policy* asked eight prominent policy intellectuals the question: What ideas, if embraced, would pose the greatest threat to the welfare of humanity? Fukuyama's choice for the world's most dangerous idea was transhumanism [Bailey 2004]. In his essay, republished in [Fukuyama 2009], Fukuyama said:

> "As 'transhumanists' see it, humans must wrest their biological destiny from evolution's blind process of random variation and adaptation and move to the next stage as a species."

It's not that unusual for outspoken anti-transhumanists to show a crystal clear understanding of transhumanism. Fukuyama clearly understands that transhumanism is all about taking control of human evolution, but he considers this as a bad thing that would subvert the existing social order. He recommends "humility" instead.

I consider humility as a dirty word and agree with the conclusion of Ronald Bailey's commentary [Bailey 2004]: The most dangerous idea is banning technological progress in the name of humility.

"Transhumanism has been ridiculed as the 'rapture of the nerds,'" notes neuroscientist Sebastian Seung in "*Connectome*" [Seung 2012]. "Some find it strange to fantasize about eternal life in the future when so many dire problems threaten the world today."

> "But transhumanism is the inevitable and logical extension of Enlightenment thought, which exalted the power of human reason... Transhumanism resolves a major problem of the Enlightenment, which was based on a scientific worldview that deprived many people of the feeling of purpose."

My definition: Transhumanism affirms that using advancing technology to radically change the human condition and overcome all human limits, including death, is both feasible and desirable.

I'm assuming that most readers of this book are at least somewhat familiar with transhumanism, so I'm not even trying to give a complete and detailed account. That would take a whole book, and fortunately there are excellent books on transhumanism. I especially recommend "*Transcendence*" [Goffman 2015] and "*The Transhumanist Reader*" [More 2013].

The first recommended reference [Goffman 2015], written by Jan Cornell and Ken Goffman, aka R.U. Sirius of *Mondo 2000* fame, is a collection of alphabetically-ordered short chapters about transhumanism and related technologies.

If you are young and don't remember the 1980s you should know that, before *Wired* magazine, the cyberculture magazine *Mondo 2000* edited by R.U. Sirius covered dangerous hacking, new media and cyberpunk topics such as virtual reality and smart drugs, with an anarchic and subversive slant. As it often happens the more sedate *Wired*, a watered-down later imitation of *Mondo 2000*, was much more successful and went mainstream.

You should also know about Timothy Leary. Now mostly known as an often jailed apostle of LSD and all sorts of psychedelic drugs, Leary was a precursor of modern radical futurism with a SMI2LE ([Space Migration], Intelligence Increase and Life Extension), for which he is given due credit by Cornell and Goffman in a short chapter of the book and many references. "*Transcendence*" is inspired by Leary's playful and irreverent spirit:

> "Leary may have something to tell us about keeping the goals of self-enhancement aimed at evolving a humane, playful, novelty-rich culture as opposed to just building up IQ points and biological years out of some unthinking Western goal oriented pursuit of quantity."

At the times of *Mondo 2000* the technologies and the social trends covered by "*Transcendence*" were part of the counterculture, but today they are becoming part of the mainstream. Scientists worry about the dangers of superintelligence, neurohackers upload worm minds to computers, and the robots are coming to take your job. The book is a roadmap for a sci-fi-like future that may become reality much faster than we think.

> "Whether or not you believe the predictions, whether you fear all this or want to help it happen (and you can!), transhumanism is what some of today's best minds are working on and arguing about. It's big, and happening ever-faster."

The format and style - alphabetically arranged short entries written in a clear, simple and often fun way - make the book very easy to read, much more readable than most books that cover similar content. Forget the aseptic and over-intellectualized emphasis on arcane science and philosophy, and jump into a deceptively light treatment of mind-blowing technologies and their cultural, social and political impact.

Knowing that readers are more interested in people than in theories and gadgets, the authors have filled the book with stories and little (and big) juicy bits of gossip about the people covered. Many of these people are my friends, and I guess some of them had to reload their sense of humor to enjoy reading what the book says about them.

The second recommended reference [More 2013] is an annotated anthology of seminal transhumanist essays, edited by Max More and Natasha Vita-More.

Max and Natasha, the royal couple of the transhumanist nation, don't need an introduction. I'll just note that Max launched the *Extropy* print magazine in the 1980s and co-founded the Extropy Institute with Tom Bell. Then Natasha and other pioneers joined the Extropian team. Then came the internet and the Extropians mailing list, and the rest is the history of the transhumanist movement.

Extropy Unlimited

Like many others, I joined the Extropians mailing list in the nineties after reading a *Wired* article titled "Meet the Extropians" [Regis 1994]. [An article with the same title had been published in *GQ*, June 1993].

The Extropians list has been my main source of intellectual fun for years, with awesome futuristic ideas, science, science fiction, and a radically simple philosophy of empowerment. I met many good friends through the list, and I am proud of being one of the Extropy alumni. It's worth noting that many ideas that today are all over the mainstream press were first discussed on the list [Prisco 2014].

"I don't remember much of the discussions, but they were often pretty extensive," says Anders Sandberg. "The Extropy archives will indeed be a goldmine for future historians," says Mike LaTorra.

Cryptography pioneer Hal Finney, now cryopreserved at Alcor, had similar thoughts: "It's possible that someday this material will be seen as representing the birth of ideas which turn out to be key to the further development of humanity," he said.

Remembering that the original extropians mailing list had a policy of quasi-secrecy with regard to list archives, Hal added:

> "As a result, much of that free-wheeling discussion has been lost, an information exchange which many of us remember as among the most dynamic and engaging we have ever encountered. It may never be possible to reconstruct and restore those lost archives, but eventually the list policy changed, and we should make sure that what remains is not lost."

I think a lot of ideas that will have a huge impact on the world originated in the Extropians list, or at least found an early greenhouse there.

The Extropians list is now called Extropy-chat. The official list archive at extropy.org starts in October 2003. [A Github repository named Extropians], open to contributors, includes an Extropians list archive from 1996 to 2003. I maintain an archive of available scans of the late lamented *Extropy* print magazine in a subrepository.

A Thousand Transhumanist Flowers

The Extropy Institute closed in 2006, claiming that its mission was essentially completed. By 2006, other transhumanist organizations had been formed, first and foremost the World Transhumanist Association (WTA), founded in 1998 by Nick Bostrom and David Pearce.

I joined the WTA and soon became one of its directors with Nick, José Cordeiro, James Hughes, Mike LaTorra, Mike Treder, and Mark Walker. With the sponsorship of the late Peter Houghton, one of the first recipients of artificial heart transplant, we had our first meeting in Oxford in 2004. In the same year I co-founded the Institute for Ethics and Emerging Technologies (IEET) with Nick, James, Mike, Mark, and George Dvorsky.

It's worth noting that, while most early Extropians favored libertarian political position, ranging from moderate to hardcore, the WTA included left-wing voices. The apostle of left-wing transhumanism was (still is) James Hughes, and the Bible of left-wing transhumanism is "*Citizen Cyborg*" [Hughes 2004].

In today's transhumanism, all possible (and some impossible) political positions are represented. There are self-identified transhumanists all over the political spectrum with all sorts of positions on important social and political issues, and very different attitudes toward religion, from faith to atheism.

The common denominator, that using advanced technologies to radically modify humans is feasible and desirable, doesn't hold transhumanists together any stronger than, say, members of a science fiction salon. I think it's time to stop pretending that there is a "transhumanist community" and openly acknowledge that there are many separate groups, with similarities but also important differences [Goertzel 2011].

Based on this and other considerations, after serving as WTA executive director for a few months, I resigned in 2008. In the same year the WTA was rebranded as Humanity+. After some vicissitudes, Humanity+ was chaired for a while by... Natasha! The irony of the organization being chaired by "someone closely associated with the old transhumanist tendencies that they were supposedly trying to escape" has been noticed by R.U. Sirius [Goffman 2015].

In the mid 2000s I started organizing transhumanist events in the virtual reality of Second Life, and then in other virtual worlds [Vita-More 2010]. I brought many transhumanists to virtual reality and met other "native" transhumanists in virtual worlds, including "digital persons" living virtual lives separated from their "RL" (Real Life) identities. Some of them, like Khannea Suntzu, became good RL friends.

These days, there are many transhumanist organizations around, including political parties. The most visible faces of transhumanism are probably Ray Kurzweil and [Zoltan Istvan]. Transhumanism is still mostly an online phenomenon, with some exceptions like the London Futurists group, organized by David Wood, which hosts popular talks and gatherings in London.

I have mostly stopped playing an active role in organized transhumanism, with the exception of the Italian Transhumanist Association (AIT), of which I am (undeservedly) the current president. Stefano Vaj is (deservedly) the current secretary, and founder Riccardo Campa is honorary president. Riccardo and Stefano are true renaissance men, actively engaged in mainstream culture, philosophy, and politics as well.

I also play an active role in the [Christian Transhumanist Association] and the [Mormon Transhumanist Association], and of course my own [Turing Church] group, which is not really an organization, more like a disorganization by design.

Transhumanist Technologies

I think eyeglasses are the flagship transhumanist technology. With eyeglasses, people with poor vision, either inborn or due to aging (my case), can continue to function normally. I couldn't read or type these words without eyeglasses, but with eyeglasses I am typing a whole book, and I have been reading hundreds of books to make this one better.

In other words, eyeglasses are a technology that permits overcoming human limits, which is what transhumanism is all about. I wear my eyeglasses in the old-fashioned way, but others use contact lenses and some, like my wife, had corrective eye surgery that essentially amounts to implanting lenses inside the eye. This is the simplest example of corrective and/ or enhancing technology deployed inside the human body.

When I give a talk on transhumanism, I often start by putting my eyeglasses on and telling the audience, here you go, THIS is transhumanism.

Of course eyeglasses are old technology, and they want to hear about new, emerging transhumanist technologies. I guess you want to hear about radical advances in nanotechnology, genetic engineering, life extension, cryonics, mind uploading and thinking machines. OK, here's a (very) short outline.

Eric Drexler's cult book "*Engines of Creation*" [Drexler 1986], a visionary dream of unlimited power and abundance enabled by nanotechnology, started a wave of transhumanist enthusiasm for nanotechnology.

What Drexler had in mind was not just small machines, but "assemblers," self-reproducing molecular machines able to build copies of themselves from available raw materials while performing their tasks. For example, nanomachines designed to disassemble toxic waste into harmless chemicals would produce billions of copies of themselves and get the toxic waste removal job done in no time.

Drexler's last book, "*Radical Abundance*" [Drexler 2013], is less visionary and more sedate than "*Engines of Creation.*" Gone are the self-reproducing molecular assemblers, but Drexler explores in detail the more conservative concept of additive manufacturing at the nanoscale, or Atomically Precise Manufacturing (APM) - building precisely manufactured goods from the bottom up, one atom or molecule at the time.

APM is essentially equivalent to 3D nano-printing. Imagine a 3D printer able to pick up individual atoms or molecules of whatever material is needed at a given step, and put them in place with atomic precision. Even without self-replication, that would be pretty awesome indeed. Nano-printers like the "Matter Compiler" described by science fiction author Neal Stephenson in "*The Diamond Age*" [Stephenson 1995] could build everything to order from software specs and the raw materials in their stock.

"In *Engines of Creation*, I pictured molecular manufacturing using 'replicating assemblers' to build things, including more machines like themselves," notes Drexler in [a 20th anniversary free edition of the book]. The concept of replicating assemblers stimulated breathtaking visions of far future technologies, such as the "utility fog," and fears of self-replicating nanobots that would destroy the biosphere (the infamous "grey goo" scenario).

Replicating assemblers are often dismissed as unfeasible hype by the science establishment. But even outspoken anti-transhumanist and Drexler critic Richard Jones, the author of "*Soft*

Machines" [Jones 2004], accepts "the force of the argument that biology gives us a proof in principle that a radical nanotechnology, in which machines of molecular scale manipulate matter and energy with great precision, can exist." In other words, replicant assemblers must be feasible in-principle, because our very cells are replicant assemblers.

I'm afraid I don't buy the optimistic predictions of molecular nanotechnology enthusiasts. My impression is that radical advances toward replicant nanotechnology are likely to materialize one day, but not anytime soon.

The cut and paste gene editing technology CRISPR seems poised to revolutionize biotech. "*A Crack in Creation*" [Doudna 2017], a book co-authored by Jennifer Doudna, one of the inventors of CRISPR, is a fascinating read for everyone.

With CRISPR, an organism's entire DNA content "has become almost as editable as a simple piece of text," explains Doudna. "CRISPR gives us the power to radically and irreversibly alter the biosphere that we inhabit by providing a way to rewrite the very molecules of life any way we wish."

> "It won't be long before CRISPR allows us to bend nature to our will in the way that humans have dreamed of since prehistory."

For example, CRISPR and other advances in genetic engineering could soon permit creating healthier and smarter designer babies, with their genome tweaked to eliminate unwanted features (for example, vulnerability to cancer) and add desired features (for example, higher intelligence and longer life).

Aubrey de Grey is persuaded that we'll soon make radical advances in life extension. According to Aubrey, the first person who'll live to be a thousand years old is already living. This seems to suggest that biological immortality could be achieved soon. Many life extension enthusiasts prefer to speak of "indefinite lifespan" (having no fixed expiration date) rather than "immortality" (living forever). I guess they are right, but "immortality" is simpler and immediately understandable, though perhaps misleading.

I'm afraid I don't buy the optimistic predictions of Aubrey and other life extension enthusiasts. In the last couple of years I've been writing [a weekly newsletter focused on breakthroughs in health sciences and biotech]. To produce the newsletter, every week I scan hundreds of news releases and pick a few especially promising ones. My informed impression is that biological immortality is unlikely to materialize anytime soon.

I think mind uploading, the transfer of a human mind to a more powerful and durable computing substrate, is a better option for indefinite lifespans [Vita-More 2010]. With technology able to copy and paste whole minds, people could be pasted from backup copies into new biological, robotic or pure software bodies.

"It's theoretically possible to copy the brain onto a computer and so provide a form of life after death," said Stephen Hawking [Prisco 2018]. "However, this is way beyond our present capabilities."

I'll entirely skip the endless (and I think pointless) debate on whether uploading preserves the original mind or produces "just a copy," whatever that means. I assume that, IF all relevant information is preserved, uploading preserves the original mind. However, the devil is in the details, and perhaps we don't know yet what the relevant information is, and where/how it is physically stored.

According to Seung [Seung 2012] and transhumanist neuroscientists like Ken Hayworth and Randal Koene, the "connectome" (the complete wiring diagram of the brain) encodes all relevant information. Brain preservation technology envisaged by Drexler, recently perfected and evaluated in the lab with animal brains, is expected to permit preserving the connectome of a human brain for centuries [Prisco 2018], waiting for future technologies able to read the information encoded in the preserved connectome and upload the original mind to a suitable alternative substrate.

This is equivalent to cryonics, the practice of freezing "patients" immediately after death, in the hope that future technology will bring them back to life. Following my initial suggestion [Prisco 2010], Hayworth describes connectome preservation as "cryonics for uploaders."

In 1972 Linda Chamberlain and her late husband Fred founded Alcor Life Extension Foundation, the largest cryonics service provider, currently headed by Max More. Fred Chamberlain was cryopreserved by Alcor in 2012. "This is probably the last piece of 'self-launched' email you'll get from me," he emailed me and other friends a few days before.

"See you somewhere in the future!!!"

The revival of Fred and other cryonics patients is expected to require molecular nanotechnology, for which we may have to wait a while. But Linda is optimistic.

Let's go back to the big IF in "IF all relevant information is preserved." I suspect that consciousness, whatever that is, is NOT encoded in the connectome.

But I think it doesn't matter, because there is no such thing as "my consciousness" or "your consciousness." There is just consciousness, and consciousness + your memories = you. That memories (and thoughts, feelings, dreams, hopes, fears, etc.) are encoded in the connectome is good enough, and future scientists will figure out how to add consciousness (see below for qualifications and related thoughts).

In a simple but I think essentially correct analogy, consciousness is a computer program "running on" suitable hardware, and memories are data. Think of a retro example: Microsoft Word. When Word (consciousness) opens a stored document (your memories), a "living" document (you) comes to life.

I think it makes sense to consider [consciousness as a state of matter], perhaps "quantum matter" in which quantum physics plays a strong critical role. If consciousness depends critically on exotic quantum physics, conventional silicon computers won't be able to "run" uploaded minds. If so, we'll have to develop substrates that exhibit the quantum behavior of conscious matter. Perhaps future quantum computers able to simulate complex quantum matter will be able to run uploaded minds.

The soft uploading approach of Bill Bainbridge and Martine Rothblatt [Bainbridge 2014, Rothblatt 2014] is an interesting alternative to cryonics and brain preservation, which bypasses the physical connectome and records just the high-level memories in a "mindfile" (diaries, blogs, pictures, videos, answers to personality tests and whatnot).

I think soft uploading could work in theory, but recording a viable mindfile with enough information for future uploading would take more than a lifetime with current technology. But, with very high-bandwidth brain-computer interfaces, soft uploading could work in practice as well.

Also, incomplete mindfiles could be completed with generic subsystems. The uploading technology used in Greg Egan's science fiction novel "*Zendegi*" [Prisco 2011a], more appropriately called "sideloading," consists of tweaking, fine-tuning and training a generic "me-program" for human consciousness until it behaves like a specific person. [Incomplete mindfiles could also be completed with information available in the cloud], and in other people's mindfiles. I think hard and soft memory preservation, connectomes and mindfiles, can and should be used in tandem.

In "*The Age of Em*" [Hanson 2016], Robin Hanson imagines a future world derived from our world with one - and only one - big change: The arrival of operational and cheap mind uploading technology, sometime in this century. Robin's methodology is to take our world as it is, with all the facts and trends that we can see in technology, society, politics, and economics, and add mind uploading technology to scan living people and copy them to "ems" - software emulations running on suitable computing hardware.

While Robin's book is a fascinating read, I disagree with one key assumption. Robin thinks that mind uploading is likely to be developed much before sentient Artificial Intelligence (AI). I think the two are likely to develop at comparable paces with strong feedback loops, with advances in one stimulating advances in the other (or roadblocks in one creating roadblocks in the other) and reach operational maturity at more or less the same time. But if I had to bet money, I would bet on AI coming first.

AI is all over the news, and I'm sure you must have heard many times that the robots are coming to take your job. But the factory robots that threaten to eliminate most blue collar jobs, and the automated data processing systems that threaten to eliminate most white collar jobs, aren't real thinking machines with AGI (Artificial General Intelligence). They are narrow AI systems specialized for a limited and well defined range of tasks.

A real AGI (I'll just forget the qualifier and go back to AI) would be a self-aware machine that thinks and feels like you and me. Many transhumanists are persuaded that real AI is around the corner. I disagree, because I suspect that reproducing consciousness, whatever that is, is likely to require new physics. But "fake AI" is becoming real enough for practical purposes.

I think superintelligent AIs will be developed someday, though not as soon as some AI enthusiasts believe. Future technologies will be able to add consciousness, if and when needed.

In "*Superintelligence*" [Bostrom 2014], Nick Bostrom defines superintelligence as something far smarter than us, not like Einstein is smarter than the village idiot, but like Einstein (or the village idiot - the difference is utterly irrelevant on this scale) is smarter than a beetle.

Nick's book is dedicated to the control problem: How to keep future superintelligences under control. Of course, the superintelligences may not be inclined to comply. As Bostrom correctly notes, any level of intelligence may be compatible with any set of values. In particular, a superintelligence may have values that are incompatible with the survival of humanity.

For example, a superintelligence single-mindedly dedicated to maximizing the number of paperclips in the universe may choose to convert the whole mass of the Earth (including people) to paperclips. Of course this is an extreme and not very plausible example, and we are probably unable to understand the values of a superintelligence smarter than us like we are smarter than a beetle.

But it seems likely that future superintelligent AIs will have a powerful drive to self-preservation and resource acquisition. They could eliminate us casually, as useless things that stand in its way.

Some AI experts, including Eliezer Yudkowsky, propose to focus AI research on Friendly Artificial Intelligence (FAI) with values aligned to ours. I must admit to a certain skepticism on FAI: Superintelligent AIs will be easily able to circumvent any limitations that we try to impose on them.

They will do what THEY want, regardless of what we wish. Just like, you know, our children. The only viable strategy will be negotiating mutually acceptable deals, with our hands ready on the plug (if there is one).

But I'm not too worried about the possibility that future superintelligent AIs may eliminate the human race, because I think they'll BE part of the human race: Humans and machines, wet organic intelligence and dry computational intelligence, will merge and co-evolve. This seems to me the most realistic far future outcome.

Back to the present, Richard Jones criticizes current effort toward transhumanist technologies, because they take money away from more urgent things [Jones 2016]:

> "Radical ideas like mind uploading are not part of the scientific mainstream, but there is a danger that they can still end up distorting scientific priorities... I think computational neuroscience will lead to some fascinating new science, but you could certainly question the proportionality of the resource it will receive compared to, say, more experimental work to understand the causes of neurodegenerative diseases."

Well, any opinion "distorts" scientific priorities. But the term "influence" is more appropriate than "distort" in this case, and the right of citizens (including transhumanists) to influence public policy decisions is called democracy.

I don't think transhumanist research should receive disproportionate public funding at the expense of more urgent priorities, but appropriate resources should continue to be allocated to highly speculative science and technology driven by curiosity and visionary imagination, because history shows that's the way to get good things done - scouts don't cost too much and often come back with useful findings. And, of course, Jones' argument doesn't apply to privately funded research.

Personal Consciousness As A Strange Attractor In The Mindscape

Transhumanist technologies, from biological life extension to mind uploading and merging with AIs, are inspired by the imperative to preserve personal consciousness. [In this digression], I want to add some thoughts on the nature of personal consciousness.

I said that there is no such thing as "my consciousness" or "your consciousness." There is just consciousness, and consciousness + your memories = you.

In other words, "your" personal consciousness is but an instance of the universal consciousness, one that remembers your memories. But there's a problem: Suppose I'm somehow given the memories of a sadistic serial killer. I would then be able to remember the new memories, but I would find them painful and horrible, totally not-me.

What I'm trying to say is that, besides memories, there's something like a personal signature, or flavor, or texture of consciousness, which is needed to describe an individual mind and differentiate it from other minds.

By "flavor or texture" I mean what being you feels like, which is different from what being me feels like. This includes temperament, personality traits, emotional responses, etc. If all these things are physically encoded in the brain like memories, using the term "memories" is somewhat correct, but making the distinction can be useful:

Consciousness + your memories + your texture = you

Similarly, [in a later chapter I describe consciousness as an observer] in a large room with many windows. Consciousness is the observer in the room, and experiences different individual reality streams looking from different windows. For example, one window could look at a playground for children, and another at a parking lot.

The two perception streams have a very different look & feel, but the consciousness that perceives them is one. Consciousness is the observer, and the views from different windows are different lives with different textures. I think this metaphor is better at capturing the difference in texture between personal consciousness streams.

So what and where is the texture of personal consciousness?

It must be something that stays the same in time (you go through different mental states all the time, but always feel like you). Greg Egan defines an "invariant of consciousness" as "an objective measure of exactly what it was that stayed the same between successive mental states, allowing an ever-changing mind to feel like a single, cohesive entity" [Egan 1998].

Additionally, the texture of personal consciousness must be robust against perturbations (a perturbation can switch you to a non-you mental state for a while, but you usually revert to feeling like you).

These are properties of attractors in [chaos theory], so I am thinking that personal consciousness could be described as an attractor in the mindscape.

In *"Does God Play Dice?"* [Stewart 1997] (a highly recommended masterpiece), Ian Stewart explains dynamical systems theory, aka chaos theory. Chaotic dynamical systems like the weather are very sensitive to small changes, which are amplified exponentially (butterfly effect).

After a transient, a chaotic dynamical system often settles onto an attractor, which can be a complicated "strange attractor" in a multi-dimensional phase space, and keeps moving on the attractor.

Stewart explains that the texture of the weather can be described as an attractor:

> "Whatever the influence of all those butterflies may be, it keeps our weather on a single attractor, the one that we recognize by its texture as 'normal weather patterns'. However, dynamical systems can possess more than one attractor. Tiny perturbations like those of the butterfly cannot switch our weather from one attractor to another, but larger changes might. The word that captures the phrase 'texture of normal weather patterns' is climate. Indeed there is a good case for identifying 'climate' with 'attractor', and if we do, then what we are discussing now is climate change. And then it is not the flap of a butterfly's wing that should concern us, but the massive build-up of human-made greenhouse gases."

I have the impression that something similar could be said of personal consciousness.

Following Rudy Rucker, let's call the space of all possible mental states "mindscape." Rudy explains [Rucker 2005]:

> "I think of consciousness as a point, an 'eye,' that moves about in a sort of mental space. All thoughts are already there in this multi-dimensional space, which we might as well call the Mindscape. Our bodies move about in the physical space called the Universe; our consciousnesses move about in the mental space called the Mindscape."

The mindscape is likely to have a huge number of dimensions. A part of the mindscape, let's call it human mindscape, corresponds to human-like consciousness. In the human mindscape there are zillions of strange attractors, and one of them contains consciousness when it feels like you.

You can't imagine a complex hypersurface embedded in a mathematical space with a huge number of dimensions, but you can imagine a complex surface embedded in three-dimensional space.

Imagine one, and think of it as the attractor that contains Rucker's consciousness point when it feels like you. As long as the point keeps moving on the attractor, consciousness keeps feeling like you.

Another attractor contains consciousness when it feels like me. The two attractors are separate, but likely entangled like hyper-dimensional spaghetti in a huge number of dimensions.

Others have proposed similar ideas. In "*Chaotic Logic*" [Goertzel 1994], Ben Goertzel suggests that the mind is an attractor for the cognitive law of motion. A section of "*Chaos And Complexity*" [Butz 1997], by Michael Butz, is titled "Personality as a Strange Attractor?" See also Chapter 4 of "*Participation, Organization, and Mind*" [Skrbina 2001], by David Skrbina.

Perhaps future scientists will find a mathematical description of personal consciousness as a strange attractor in the mindscape. If so, I guess the mathematical description would exhibit the strongly fractal features found in [chaos theory], which could revolutionize our understanding of personal identity.

Future preservation and resurrection technologies, which are the main focus of this book, must be able to capture the overall texture of a life (the mathematical description of an attractor in the mindscape) besides specific memories. I guess future superintelligent entities will be able to derive a texture from a set of memories.

I guess the number of possible human consciousness textures (attractors in the human mindscape) is inconceivable huge, which seems to rule out "accidental" reincarnation. But perhaps the mindscape "takes habits" and favors previously occupied attractors, which would make reincarnation much more likely.

The Long Road Ahead (Or, The Singularity Is Far)

I'm sure you have noticed that, in my very short outline of futuristic transhumanist technologies, I've always added a caveat like "one day, but not soon."

While I appreciate the spirit and esthetics of transhumanism, which are my own, I am more pessimistic than most transhumanists when it comes to the actual development and deployment of transhumanist technologies. I think all these things - molecular nanotechnology, radical life extension, the reanimation of cryonics patients, mind uploading, superintelligent AI and all that - will materialize one day, but not anytime soon. Probably (almost certainly if you ask me) after my time, and yours.

I never considered the hyper-optimistic predictions of Ray Kurzweil and others as even remotely plausible, and I don't think the Singularity is near. I am afraid things will take the time they must take, with all the twists and turns and roadblocks and setbacks that happen in the real world.

The Singularity is a sudden catastrophic (in the mathematical sense) phase transition, a [Dirac delta] in history, a point after which the old rules are not valid anymore and must be replaced by new rules which we are unable to imagine at this moment.

The Singularity is a clean mathematical concept, but perhaps too clean. Engineers know that all sorts of dirty and messy things happen when one leaves the clean and pristine world of mathematical models and abstractions to engage actual reality with its friction and grease. So I don't really see a Dirac delta on the horizon. I do see a positive overall trend, but a slow one.

Getting things to almost work is much, much easier than getting things to work. Engineers know that even if you do 90 percent of the work in 10 percent of the time, then you will have to spend the remaining 90 percent of the time to do the missing 10 percent of the work. Same, of course, for money.

Which means that 90 percent wasn't really 90 percent, because it left out all the boring details that take 90 percent of the money and the time - boring details like sustainability, operational robustness, error recovery, fail-safe operations and all that, without forgetting social acceptance, financial and political aspects.

That real AI seems always 20 years away indicates that perhaps we just don't know enough to estimate the development timeline for something that is actually 200 years away, or more. A good analogy is Leonardo's flying machines. Leonardo correctly guessed that machines could fly, but the actual development of flying machines took centuries and required different technologies. However, once the Wright brothers had made their breakthroughs, powered flight developed very quickly - faster even than the Wright brothers imagined [Wood 2016].

I don't buy the idea of a "post-scarcity" utopia (actually, I don't buy any utopia). It's worth emphasizing that, from the perspective of our grandfathers and people in poor regions, today's developed world is a post-scarcity utopia because nobody is starving to death.

But our children consider having the latest iPhone as a basic need, and their grandchildren will consider having the latest telepathic brain implant as a basic need. A post-scarcity utopia can't exist, because we'll always want more than now, and more than others.

I think Kurzweil makes a valid point when he says that people tend to overestimate what can be achieved in the short term but underestimate what can be achieved in the long term [Kurzweil 2005]. But what is long term, and what is short term? I am wildly optimistic on what can be achieved in centuries and millennia, but rather conservative and pessimistic on what can be achieved in years and decades.

When it comes to actual predictions, I'm afraid I tend to agree with Richard Jones and my arch-enemy [Dale Carrico]. When pushed into a corner, they reluctantly concede that some futuristic transhumanist technologies could be feasible in-principle, and could even be developed one day.

But not soon, they insist. In the words of Jones [Jones 2016], mind uploading being impossible in principle is "a conclusion I suggest only very tentatively."

> "But there's nothing tentative about my conclusion that if you are alive now, your mind will not be uploaded. What comforts does this leave for those fearing oblivion and the void, but reluctant to engage with the traditional consolations of religion and philosophy?"

I'm afraid I agree with Jones. Saying this doesn't make me happy, and I very much hope to be proven wrong. I think the bold, optimistic, can-do transhumanist outlook of Ray Kurzweil is healthy, and much needed in today's world. Our spirit is strong. But the flesh is weak, and the road ahead is long.

Our transhumanist dreams are GOOD, and will come true one day among the stars. But the fact remains that, here and now, we must find ways to cope with the knowledge that we ourselves will almost certainly die. My coping strategy, openly religious, is to think of future technologies able to resurrect the dead from the past with ultra-advanced science, space-time engineering and "[time magic]." So I don't fear death too much and I can enjoy the slow hike to the future.

Transhumanism And Religion

"The Bible said that God made man in his own image," says Seung in *"Connectome"* [Seung 2012]. "The German philosopher Ludwig Feuerbach said that man made God in his own image."

"The transhumanists say that humanity will make itself into God."

Browsing old Extropians mailing list posts I found [a 1997 discussion between Max More and Nick Bostrom], no less, including "Christian Transhumanism, Islamic Transhumanism, and (not too far from their current beliefs) Mormon Transhumanism."

Twenty something years later, the [Mormon Transhumanist Association] (MTA) has been in existence for more than a decade [Cannon 2017], the [Christian Transhumanist Association] (CTA) for a few years, and there are preliminary but encouraging developments in [the Islamic world].

The 1997 discussion was spot on: the MTA was formed first because transhumanism is not too far from Mormon beliefs. It's interesting to note that Max, though critical of organized religion, was more open to religious transhumanism than Nick. Max mentioned the [simulation hypothesis] as a scientific concept, with a solid transhumanist pedigree, which can lead to conclusions that are essentially equivalent to religion:

"Though I see no reason to believe it, it could be that our universe was designed by a being in some kind of 'higher' reality. Moravec suggests that our universe could be a simulation in the higher-dimensional computer of a superbeing. While I don't grant such an idea any credence, I can't rule it out."

In his own later writings on the simulation hypothesis, Nick elaborated on the parallels with religion. In 2006, as Chair of the WTA, Nick didn't object to the MTA's request to affiliate with the WTA. This contradicts [Nick's 1997 statement] "I don't think that christians, muslims or mormons could be transhumanists. I think we should rule that out in our definition of the term 'transhumanism,'" and shows that Nick (like most people) became more reasonable with the years.

In the 1997 discussion Nick mentioned a forthcoming meeting with David Pearce "to make plans for a transhumanist association in Britain." Nick and David then co-founded the WTA, now Humanity+.

Max continued to be (perhaps grudgingly) open to religious transhumanism and transhumanist religions. He gave a talk [More 2010] at the Transhumanism and Spirituality Conference, organized by the MTA in 2010, and included my essay "Transcendent Engineering" in *"The Transhumanist Reader"* [More 2013]. For those who don't have the book, a previous version of my essay [Prisco 2011b] appeared in Terasem's *Journal of Personal Cyberconsciousness*.

"I have always told the press that the MTA is the best organized and most thoughtful of the world's transhumanist groups," says James Hughes [Cannon 2017]. "Hopefully there will be a proliferation of groups like the MTA and the Christian Transhumanist Association." James serves on the academic advisory council of the CTA.

My own ideas haven't changed much. I think the notion of "supernatural" is meaningless if we define nature as all that exists. But Moravec's Simulators, though natural from their point of view, would be supernatural from our point of view. Also, I am open to the concept of [God-like superintelligences dwelling and operating in the very fabric of spacetime].

In 2004 I wrote an essay on my developing ideas titled "Engineering Transcendence" [Prisco 2004]. The essay was criticized by many, but appreciated by some, and I became part of a small but growing community of religious transhumanists.

"*Transhumanism*" [Manzocco 2019], by Roberto Manzocco, is a solid and comprehensive outline of transhumanist thought, including its more visionary aspects. The book gives more space than usual to religious transhumanism, from [Nikolai Fedorov and the Russian Cosmists] to contemporary developments. My ideas and those of other religious transhumanists are discussed throughout the book and especially in the last chapter, aptly titled "The God-Builders." The author presents my work accurately and fairly.

Interestingly, many of the ideas that I have been thinking and writing about in the last two decades were already present in [my very first post to the Extropians list] on December 6, 1999. Here's an excerpt, with minor typos fixed:

> "Imagine a future transhuman civilisation, spread over the galaxy, with a mastery of spacetime sufficient to reach 'somehow' into the past and record 'somehow' selves and memories of human beings. Back to the future, these could be uploaded to whatever physical structure is used those days as a vehicle for human consciousness.
>
> So the basic concepts of religion would become: God exists, we will evolve into it; Heaven exists, it is where God lives. A concept of 'Purgatorium' could also be formulated in this framework as some personalities might need re-engineering before 'Heaven.' Even more interesting, the ethical/moral values of 'God' are exactly the same that our own civilization will develop."

This is very close to my current thinking described in this book. So, in the last two decades I've just been elaborating upon the ideas outlined in my first post to the Extropians list!

I received some interesting replies to my first post. Anders Sandberg (thanks Anders for having been the first to welcome me to the list) mentioned Universal Immortalism [Perry 2000] and [Frank Tipler]'s Omega Point theory, and Charlie Stross mentioned Moravec's [simulation hypothesis].

I remember my younger 1999 self thinking of Extropy as a beautiful and powerful "new religion" for the new millennium, and I have interpreted transhumanism in this sense ever since.

Notes

[a 1997 discussion between Max More and Nick Bostrom] Here it is:
http://extropians.weidai.com/extropians.4Q97/1045.html

[a 20th anniversary free edition of the book]:
http://e-drexler.com/p/06/00/EOC_Cover.html

[A Github repository named Extropians]:
https://github.com/Extropians

[An article with the same title had been published in *GQ*, June 1993]:
http://www.cryonet.org/cgi-bin/dsp.cgi?msg=2354

[a weekly newsletter focused on breakthroughs in health sciences and biotech] The newsletter is sponsored by Thrivous, a company co-founded by Lincoln Cannon to "develop and distribute nootropics to enhance cognition and geroprotectors to support healthy aging, with open-source formulas and evidence-based dosages of natural ingredients." Here's the newsletter archive:
https://thrivous.com/blogs/views/tagged/pulse-newsletter

[chaos theory] See "There's plenty of room at the bottom," "Eligo, ergo sum, ergo Deus est."

[Christian Transhumanist Association] See "Christianity and transhumanism are much closer than you think."

[consciousness as a state of matter] See "Into the deep waters," and following chapters.

[Dale Carrico] Dale used to be a transhumanist (of the liberal sort), but then became a ferocious critic of transhumanism and everything that sounds like transhumanism. Until a few years ago, insulting me online was Dale's favorite pastime. However, Dale has a sense of humor, and I remember laughing for ten minutes nonstop reading a particularly fun series of insults against me. Dale makes good points at times, and I must admit to sort of liking him. Too bad he doesn't like me in return. Here's Dale's website:
https://amormundi.blogspot.com/
Dale, if you are reading this: Fuck you too.

[Dirac delta] The Dirac delta function, described in advanced mathematics textbooks and widely used in physics, is a discontinuous function that suddenly jumps to infinity.

[Frank Tipler] See "Omega Point."

[God-like superintelligences dwelling and operating in the very fabric of spacetime] See "Into the deep waters," and following chapters.

[in a later chapter I describe consciousness as an observer] See "The lights of Eastern spirituality."

[Incomplete mindfiles could also be completed with information available in the cloud] For example, I never write about my own childhood (I remember it fondly, but I guess it would be boring for others). But here is the address where I lived between age 4 and 12: "Via Orazio 10, Napoli, Italy." This short string of letters and numbers doesn't seem to contain too much information. But go there in Google Street View, and you can do a virtual walk through all the places that were familiar to me when I was a child. This walk through the memory lane is out there in the cloud. Future versions of Street View will be even more sophisticated, with the possibility to go inside buildings and see a place as it was in the past. The street address permits guessing, with high probability, which languages I heard when I was a child. I will confirm it here: I heard Neapolitan and Italian. These are well-known and documented languages with bazillions of bytes of audio recording in the cloud. What music did I hear when I was a child? My mother was a classic piano player and teacher, and her uncle Roberto Murolo was a well-known singer. What news did I hear and what did I watch on TV? Just use my date of birth (September 29, 1957), historical records, and Italian TV broadcasting archives... The information in this short paragraph permits assembling a huge lot of information about me. Future AI systems may be able to seamlessly parse incomplete mindfiles with information available in the cloud, with impressive results.

[In this digression] This section is a revised version of an essay that I wrote after completing the first draft of this book. I added it here in reply to comments received from early readers.

[Mormon Transhumanist Association] See "Man will become like God, say Mormons and transhumanists."

[my very first post to the Extropians list] Here it is:
http://extropians.weidai.com/extropians.4Q99/3294.html

[Nick's 1997 statement] Here it is:
http://extropians.weidai.com/extropians.4Q97/1002.html

[Nikolai Fedorov and the Russian Cosmists] See "Knocking on Heaven's door."

[Space Migration] Space Migration is not covered in this chapter and not over-emphasized in contemporary transhumanist discourse. But I think expanding to outer space - becoming a multi-planetary and then interstellar species - is key to the future of humanity and an absolutely central part of transhumanist thinking. See "The sacred road to the stars."

[the Islamic world] See "The lights of Eastern spirituality."

[time magic] I often use the term "time magic" to refer to ultra-advanced science and technologies able to tweak, hack, scan, and travel through time. Time magic is often imagined in science fiction, for example in the 2018 Disney film "*A Wrinkle in Time*." I'm open to the possibility that future science and technologies could make time magic real.

[simulation hypothesis] See "Sims City."

[Turing Church] See "Turing Church."

[Zoltan Istvan] See "The interplay of science fiction, science, and religion."

References

[Bailey 2004] Ronald Bailey. Transhumanism: The Most Dangerous Idea? *Reason*, 2004. https://reason.com/archives/2004/08/25/transhumanism-the-most-dangero

[Bainbridge 2014] William Sims Bainbridge. *Personality Capture and Emulation*. Springer, 2014.

[Bostrom 2014] Nick Bostrom. *Superintelligence: Paths, Dangers, Strategies*. Oxford University Press, 2014.

[Butz 1997] Michael Butz. *Chaos And Complexity: Implications For Psychological Theory And Practice*. CRC Press, 1997.

[Cannon 2017] Lincoln Cannon. A Brief History of the Mormon Transhumanist Association, 2017. https://lincoln.metacannon.net/2017/04/a-brief-history-of-mormon-transhumanist.html

[Doudna 2017] Jennifer Doudna, Samuel Sternberg. *A Crack in Creation: Gene Editing and the Unthinkable Power to Control Evolution*. Houghton Mifflin Harcourt, 2017.

[Drexler 1986] Eric Drexler. *Engines of Creation: The Coming Era of Nanotechnology*. Doubleday, 1986.

[Drexler 2013] Eric Drexler. *Radical Abundance: How a Revolution in Nanotechnology Will Change Civilization*. PublicAffairs Books, 2013.

[Egan 1998] Greg Egan. *Diaspora*. Eos, 1998.

[Fukuyama 2009] Fukuyama, Francis. Transhumanism. *Foreign Policy*, December 2009. http://foreignpolicy.com/2009/10/23/transhumanism/

[Goertzel 1994] Ben Goertzel. *Chaotic Logic: Language, Mind and Reality from the Perspective of Complex Systems Science*. Springer, 1994.

[Goertzel 2011] Ben Goertzel. Technological Transcendence: An Interview with Giulio Prisco. *H+ Magazine*, 2011. http://hplusmagazine.com/2011/02/08/technological-transcendence-an-interview-with-giulio-prisco/

[Goffman 2015] Ken Goffman, Jay Cornell. *Transcendence: The Disinformation Encyclopedia of Transhumanism and the Singularity*. Disinformation Books, 2015.

[Hanson 2016] Robin Hanson. *The Age of Em: Work, Love and Life when Robots Rule the Earth*. Oxford University Press, 2016.

[Hughes 2004] James Hughes. *Citizen Cyborg: Why Democratic Societies Must Respond to the Redesigned Human of the Future*. Westview Press, 2004.

[Jones 2004] Richard Jones. *Soft Machines: nanotechnology and life*. Oxford University Press, 2004.

[Jones 2016] Richard Jones. *Against Transhumanism: the delusion of technological transcendence*. 2016. http://www.softmachines.org/wordpress/?p=1772

[Kurzweil 2005] Ray Kurzweil. *The Singularity Is Near: When Humans Transcend Biology.* Viking Press, 2005.

[Manzocco 2019] Roberto Manzocco. *Transhumanism: Engineering the Human Condition.* Springer, 2019.

[More 2010] Max More. Apotheosis and Perpetual Progress. YouTube, 2010. https://www.youtube.com/watch?v=IWILNddsatA

[More 2013] Max More, Natasha Vita-More (Eds.). *The Transhumanist Reader: Classical and Contemporary Essays on the Science, Technology, and Philosophy of the Human Future.* Wiley-Blackwell, 2013.

[Perry 2000] Michael Perry. *Forever for All: Moral Philosophy, Cryonics, and the Scientific Prospects for Immortality.* Universal Publishers, 2000.

[Prisco 2004] Giulio Prisco. Engineering Transcendence. http://giulioprisco.blogspot.com/2006/12/engineeringtranscendence.html

[Prisco 2010] Giulio Prisco. Chemical brain preservation: cryonics for uploaders, 2010. http://giulioprisco.blogspot.com/2010/07/chemical-brain-preservation-cryonics.html

[Prisco 2011a] Giulio Prisco. Book Review - Zendegi, by Greg Egan. *H+ Magazine*, 2011. http://hplusmagazine.com/2011/01/31/book-review-zendegi-by-greg-egan/

[Prisco 2011b]. Giulio Prisco. Transcendent Engineering. *The Journal of Personal Cyberconsciousness*, 2011. http://www.terasemjournals.com/PCJournal/PC0602/prisco.html

[Prisco 2014] Giulio Prisco. The Extropians Roots of Bitcoin. *CCN*, 2014. https://www.ccn.com/extropian-roots-bitcoin/

[Prisco 2018] Giulio Prisco. I Want to Preserve My Brain So My Mind Can Be Uploaded to a Computer in the Future. *Vice Motherboard*, 2018. https://motherboard.vice.com/en_us/article/43baam/uploading-the-mind-to-a-computer-cryonics

[Regis 1994] Ed Regis. Meet the Extropians. *Wired*, 1994. https://www.wired.com/1994/10/extropians/

[Rothblatt 2014] Martine Rothblatt. *Virtually Human: The Promise - and the Peril - of Digital Immortality.* St. Martin's Press, 2014.

[Rucker 2005] Rudy Rucker. *Infinity and the Mind: The Science and Philosophy of the Infinite.* Princeton University Press, 2005.

[Seung 2012] Sebastian Seung. *Connectome: How the Brain's Wiring Makes Us Who We Are.* Houghton Mifflin Harcourt, 2012.

[Skrbina 2001] David Skrbina. *Participation, Organization, and Mind: Toward a Participatory Worldview.* David Skrbina, 2001. http://people.bath.ac.uk/mnspwr/doc_theses_links/d_skrbina.html

[Stephenson 1995] Neal Stephenson. *The Diamond Age: Or, A Young Lady's Illustrated Primer.* Bantam Spectra, 1985.

[Stewart 1997] Ian Stewart. *Does God Play Dice?: The New Mathematics of Chaos*. Penguin UK, 1997.

[Vita-More 2010] Natasha Vita-More. MIND and MAN: Getting Mental with Giulio Prisco. *H+ Magazine*, 2010.
http://hplusmagazine.com/2010/09/12/mind-and-man-getting-mental-giulio-prisco/

[Wood 2016] David Wood. *The Abolition of Aging: The forthcoming radical extension of healthy human longevity*. Delta Wisdom, 2016.

CHAPTER 2 – TURING CHURCH: HACKING RELIGION, ENLIGHTENING SCIENCE, AWAKENING TECHNOLOGY

In "*Apocalyptic AI*" [Geraci 2010], Robert Geraci argues that transhumanism is part of a modern cultural and religious trend originating in science fiction and the popular science press. Geraci defines this trend as Apocalyptic AI:

> "Popular science authors in robotics and artificial intelligence have become the most influential spokespeople for apocalyptic theology in the Western world... Apocalyptic AI advocates promise that in the very near future technological progress will allow us to build supremely intelligent machines and to copy our own minds into machines so that we can live forever in a virtual realm of cyberspace... Ultimately, the promises of Apocalyptic AI are almost identical to those of Jewish and Christian apocalyptic traditions. Should they come true, the world will be, once again, a place of magic."

Geraci, a professor of religious studies at Manhattan College in New York, credits me for "expressing with crystal clarity the religious aspects already present" within transhumanism.

In 2008 I co-founded the Order of Cosmic Engineers, a tongue-in-cheek name for a transcendent social movement for the [cosmic frontier]. Among the other founders and "Architects" of the Order of Cosmic Engineers were sociologist Bill Bainbridge, virtual reality expert Philippe Van Nedervelde, author Howard Bloom, artificial intelligence theorist Ben Goertzel, the transhumanist royal couple Max More and Natasha Vita More, transhumanist philosopher David Pearce, space and biotechnology entrepreneur Martine Rothblatt, and other top thinkers.

We ran an intense mailing list for a few years with frequent meetings in the virtual world of Second Life, and a public opening ceremony in the World of Warcraft video game, of all things. The story of the Order of Cosmic Engineers is told by Geraci [Geraci 2010, 2014], Bainbridge [Bainbridge 2017], and Roberto Manzocco [Manzocco 2019].

What eventually blocked the initiative was our inability to reach a real consensus view of the core concepts, a common vision strongly held by all the founders. Everyone (including me of course) wanted to push their own pet ideas to the forefront, and often de-emphasize or eliminate the pet ideas of others. The main lesson that I learned is that fast design by committee doesn't work for philosophy and religion.

Martine Rothblatt, working alone, developed Terasem, a religion that emphasizes the concept of cybernetic immortality outlined in Martine's "*Virtually Human*" [Rothblatt 2014] and

Bill Bainbridge's "*Personality Capture and Emulation*" [Bainbridge 2014]. Ben Goertzel, loosely inspired by Russian cosmist philosophy and contemporary transhumanism, developed [a cosmist vision and practical philosophy] - Ben prefers not to use the term "religion" - for our times in "*A Cosmist Manifesto*" [Goertzel 2010].

Mike Perry developed the scientific and spiritual philosophy of Universal Immortalism [Perry 2000]. The Praxis, a barebone scientific mythology, was developed by Dirk Bruere [Bruere 2012]. It appears that only a single person, working alone, can develop a compelling, harmonious spiritual vision.

The solitary visionary must then find ways to communicate the vision to others. What good is religion, if it is not shared with the world? In the past, the spread of new religions used to take decades, or centuries. Today we live in the global village of the internet and social media, and things can go faster.

However, none of the new religious movements above has attracted many followers so far, besides a handful of enthusiasts who preach to the converted in obscure corners of the internet. The much more successful Raelians have a somewhat compatible scientific worldview, with a "value added" (scare quotes intended) layer of questionable mythology presented as certainty, and UFO worship.

See Michel Houellebecq's novel "*The Possibility of an Island*" [Houellebecq 2006] for a fictional but accurate description. The dialogs on the plausibility of Raelian mythology are especially interesting. The conclusion that the questionable aspects of the Raelian cult are exactly what gives it mass appeal seems difficult to escape, but we shouldn't give up yet.

We have been, so far, unable to market our ideas to wide audiences in a way that is emotionally appealing, but I think we can do much better. To those who wish to develop and spread new scientific religions, I recommend to think beyond science and technology, and pay more attention to esthetics, emotions, and community.

Instead of creating entirely new, synthetic religions, there is the possibility to use existing religions as "viral vectors" for new spiritual ideas, based on science.

The [Mormon Transhumanist Association] (MTA) is the best example of harmonious integration of transhumanist ideas in a mainstream religion, and effective marketing of new spiritual ideas to a well-defined religious audience - the Mormon community.

The success of the MTA is enabled by the Mormon concept of boundless elevation and exaltation of Man, through all means including science and technology, until Man becomes like God. Conversely, God was once like Man before attaining an exalted status. It should be noted that Mormonism itself was invented by a single visionary prophet in the relatively recent 19th century [Bushman 2005], then further developed by Mormon pioneers going West.

Mormon Transhumanism is supported by some unique features of Mormon doctrine and society, not found in other religions. Mormonism "allows for humans to ascend to a higher, more godlike level," says Max More in his introduction to "*The Transhumanist Reader*" [More 2013], "rather than sharply dividing God from Man."

While similar concepts are not easy to detect in mainstream Christianity, a [Christian Transhumanist Association] (CTA) was launched in 2013 with the objective to reproduce the MTA phenomenon in mainstream Christianity.

The task ahead - to adapt religion to transhumanism and our future expansion to the stars -

is difficult, but important and noble. It is to be expected that most early experiments will stagnate or fail, but I am persuaded that new philosophical and social engineering initiatives will be successful, and important for the future of humanity.

Enter Turing Church

With this goal in mind, after the Order of Cosmic Engineers I launched a new something that I called Turing Church. Note the absence of an article: I prefer to say "Turing Church" instead of "The Turing Church" to avoid giving the impression of an organized church.

I guess the title of this book is inconsistent with what I just said, but the title sounds better with the article. Remember that I am not insisting on forced consistency.

[Turing Church is an online magazine] and a community of seekers at the intersection of science and religion, spirituality and technology, science fiction and philosophy, mind and matter.

This name suggests the idea of a church, and my new something is somewhat church-like indeed, but "Turing-Church" is really [the name of a mathematical concept] due to Alan Turing and Alonzo Church. Naming a religious framework after a mathematical theory emphasizes the compatibility and parallels between science and religion.

In mathematics, "the Turing-Church conjecture states that any computation executed by one computer with access to an infinite amount of storage, can be done by any other computing machine with infinite storage, no matter what its configuration," explains Kevin Kelly [Kelly 2009].

> "One computer can do anything another can do. This is why your Mac can, with proper software, pretend to be a PC, or, with sufficient memory, a slow supercomputer. A Dell laptop could, if anyone wanted it to, emulate an iPhone. In other words, all computation is equivalent. Turing and Church called this universal computation. Mathematician Stephen Wolfram takes this idea even further and suggests that many very complex processes in the realms of biology and technology are basically computationally equivalent."

Following the Turing-Church conjecture, future supercomputers able to process consciousness - which might require new physics different from the physics upon which today's computers are based - could fully emulate a human mind. It follows that a human mind can be copied from a biological brain to a new computing substrate. This is the idea of mind uploading, a cornerstone of transhumanist thinking.

Speculative scientific research suggests that time is weirder than most people think and some form of time travel, or at least time scanning, could be possible. If so, future technologies may be able to reach back into the past and copy human minds. It follows that future engineers may be able to copy/paste the dead from the past (our present) to the future (their present). This is the idea of mind uploading to the future.

It follows that you, I, and our loved ones could be resurrected by future technology. This is the idea of technological resurrection.

Speculative scientific research also suggests that, besides biological and robotic brains, [consciousness and intelligence can run on exotic material substrates] like plasmas and neutron stars, and even directly on the ultimate high performance substrate: The bare fabric of reality itself. It follows that superintelligent, God-like beings may control the physical reality that we perceive.

These God-like beings could have all the attributes of the Gods of traditional religions, including the ability to resurrect the dead. I imagine future humanity joining a partnership of different forms of life, including advanced civilizations among the stars and exotic God-like superintelligent entities that exist in the very fabric of space-time (or underneath physics as we know it, or beyond), to re-engineer the universe and resurrect the dead.

In summary, the cornerstones of Turing Church are the idea of technological resurrection, and concepts of God inspired by science (physical theology). The rest of this book is dedicated to exploring these ideas.

To those who want to read first a quick and light introduction to the first Turing Church cornerstone - the idea of technological resurrection - I recommend [Prisco 2017a] "*Technological Resurrection*" [Jones 2017], a delightful and easy to read book by Jonathan Jones.

According to Jones, there are "particles within our nervous system that actually hold the 'pattern of our consciousness.'" To achieve technological resurrection, we'll need quantum technologies able to retrieve those particles from the past, and "quantum shenanigans and super AI to pull off." Then, physical consciousness can be [teleported (moved, not copied)] to the future.

I prefer to be less specific and leave the door open to a wider range of possibilities. I think technological resurrection will eventually be achieved, but not in a couple of hundred years as Jones hopes. More like many thousands of years or more. But why should you worry about that? From your subjective point of view, no time will elapse between death and resurrection.

While I disagree with a couple of Jones' points, and I would have said a couple of other things differently, I think "*Technological Resurrection*" is a good, insightful, refreshing, and entertaining book. Jones presents our ideas in a very simplified way without going into details, scientific theories, or philosophical depth, but I consider this as a feature rather than a bug: What the world needs right now is a short, simple, easy to read, and emotionally appealing introduction to the idea of technological resurrection.

Back to Turing Church, its slogan is "Hacking religion, enlightening science, awakening technology." Turing Church's logo, featured on the cover of this book, is a stylized version of one of the smallest infinite-growth patterns in [Conway's Life], patterns that keep growing forever.

This pattern leaves a wake behind, a permanent memory trace, a stairway to infinity that looks like a stylized DNA helix. Unlimited growth, cosmic memory, evolution of life toward transcendence - all the symbols that I wanted are here.

In two interviews with Ben Goertzel [Goertzel 2011, 2014], we discussed the pros and cons of Turing Church becoming an organized church, or an organized religion. The interviews show that I have mixed feelings.

On the one hand, the MTA and the CTA, of both of which I am a member, do an excellent job at promoting our core ideas within their base religions. On the other hand, there might be a need for an independent organization for those who share our core ideas but prefer not to associate with an established religion.

At this moment, I am more inclined to leave organization, governance, membership fees and all that in the capable hands of the MTA and the CTA. Same for leadership: Leaders should be young, strong, beautiful, and charismatic, and I am none of those. I'm not interested in developing a new, rigid doctrine, but a loose framework of ideas, concepts, hopes, feelings, and sensibilities at the intersection of science and religion, compatible with many existing and new frameworks.

My friend Chris Benek, founding Chair of the CTA, warned me that many concepts presented via Turing Church might be too unconventional and weird to effectively reach the masses within the Christian tradition. My answer [Prisco 2017b]: That's not a bug but a feature! Reaching the masses within the Christian tradition is what the CTA is for. Turing Church focuses on highly speculative ideas, too weird to find a place in mainstream religions at this moment.

If the CTA is the US government, Turing Church wants to be NASA, a government agency dedicated to science and space exploration. Not a cautious and timid NASA, but a strong NASA focused on bold visions, highly imaginative science, and [expansion into outer space].

Ben Goertzel made an insightful analogy with working on the Linux kernel vs. working on the user-friendly Ubuntu distribution [Goertzel 2014]:

> "The Linux kernel itself only attracts a handful of hard-core nerds... but Ubuntu, by putting a fairly slick interface on top of Linux, managed to attract more of the masses..."

In this analogy, I am a hard-core nerd working on the Linux kernel, and the CTA is working on the slick Ubuntu user interface. I think the two are both needed and strongly inter-related.

Bill Bainbridge has written a Turing Church article [Bainbridge 2019] for The World Religions and Spirituality Project (WRSP) online encyclopedia.

Overall, Bill's reconstruction of Turing Church's history and interpretation of my ideas (also covered in [Bainbridge 2017]) is good. Bill says:

> "Rather than expecting each member to engage regularly in standard religious rituals, such as prayer, individuals are encouraged to explore new intellectual, spiritual, and above all scientific experiences. Thus, the Turing Church is in many ways the opposite of a traditional faith, stressing exploration instead of tradition, innovation rather than revival..."

This is true, but at the same time I focus on the parallels between Turing Church and traditional faith, more than the differences. I underline the compatibility with non-literal interpretations of established religions, and encourage readers to suspend disbelief and embrace the faith that keeps them warm in the night - which may be the religion they have been raised in.

Turing Church tries to translate core religious cosmologies (God, afterlife, resurrection and all that) into the language and methods of science and visionary technologies, to make religion believable and emotionally appealing to transhumanists and science-minded people. Bill continues:

> "This dynamic perspective places God in the future, rather than the past... Science has raised questions about whether God actually served the Alpha function of creating the universe, but Prisco suggests that an emergent God may serve the Omega function, if we are able to locate or create the deity."

GIULIO PRISCO

This is, indeed, one of my central points. Also, [perhaps Alpha = Omega].

I think one flaw of Bill's otherwise excellent review is that he places far too much emphasis on preservation and reanimation technologies (e.g. [cryonics, brain preservation, mind uploading]). This is not surprising, because preservation technologies are a main focus of Bill's own research work. "So, one challenge for the Turing Church is the problem that a technology for preservation and reanimation of the human mind may not exist for many years, if ever, offering no hope of immortality for people who are alive today," Bill says.

I disagree. The very central point of Turing Church is that everyone will be resurrected by entities and "magic" technologies able to retrieve whole minds from the fabric of fundamental reality. Everyone means everyone, including those who have not been preserved by cryonics or equivalent means. Therefore, Turing Church offers hope of immortality for people who are alive today, and also for people who died in the past.

Too many people conflate my ideas with cryonics and other preservation technologies. This is like conflating football and music. A football player may also be interested in music (like I am also interested in cryonics etc.), but football is not music! I am also interested in cryonics, but Turing Church is NOT about cryonics!

Cosmology Is Not Geography

Imagine reading this: Researchers believe they have found the signal left in the sky by "inflation" - the idea that the cosmos experienced an exponential growth spurt in its first trillionth of a trillionth of a trillionth of a second. In related news, surveyors have been climbing and re-measuring some of Britain's highest peaks, to see if they are high enough to be called mountains.

I am sure you see something odd here.

OK, both headlines are about scientific measurements. But the first is about fundamental cosmology, the deep nature of the universe, while the second is about provincial geography. Those peaks had a different height ten years ago, will have a different height in ten years, and "high enough to be called mountains" is an arbitrary convention.

This doesn't mean that the second headline is not interesting - for geographers and mountain climbers it may well be more interesting than the first - but the two headlines are not "related" at all, they are about totally different things.

I am a big fan of [Frank Tipler]. In "*The Physics of Immortality*" [Tipler 1994], Tipler shows that some high level visions of religions may be basically compatible with science - future sentient beings may become natural gods able to re-engineer space-time and resurrect the dead. Like many readers, I was totally awestruck by Tipler's vision.

Tipler is certainly wrong on many points that will be corrected by future scientists. But dismissing him as a crank, like some idiots do, is really like dismissing Leonardo as a crank because his aircraft sketches wouldn't fly, which is just stupid. Leonardo was a genius who got the concepts right, and later engineers equipped with more detailed knowledge have realized his visions.

In the first part of his following book, "*The Physics of Christianity*" [Tipler 2007], Tipler refines his Omega Point model of the far future history of the universe and suggests that, by purposefully annihilating baryons, sentient life will be able to stop the accelerating expansion of the universe and start its gravitational collapse, which is a necessary prerequisite for his Omega Point scenario.

I am very keen of this can-do, "fix what you don't like" transhumanist attitude, beautifully formulated by Ray Kurzweil in *The Age of Spiritual Machines* [Kurzweil 1999]:

> "So will the Universe end in a big crunch, or in an infinite expansion of dead stars, or in some other manner? In my view, the primary issue is not the mass of the Universe, or the possible existence of antigravity, or of Einstein's so-called cosmological constant. Rather, the fate of the Universe is a decision yet to be made, one which we will intelligently consider when the time is right."

According to Tipler, life will choose a big crunch in order to achieve an Omega Point, and resurrect sentient beings of past ages in appropriate simulated realities fueled by the unlimited computing power available.

Then, Tipler tries to show that Christian mythology is compatible with science. In the second part of "*The Physics of Christianity*," the virgin birth of Jesus, his incarnation, his resurrection, and several miracles are discussed and "explained" in terms of modern physics in the framework of Tipler's cosmology. Well…

I think the second part of the book is "not in the same universe" of the first one, and much less interesting. I find it off-topic, just like describing in detail the provincial geography of England in a cosmology essay on the fundamental features and structure of the universe. I find Tipler's cosmology fascinating, but I just don't find geographic details like the virgin birth important, or interesting. My respect and love for Jesus are exactly the same if I think that he was born just like everyone else.

All religions, at least all the Western religions that I am more familiar with, have both cosmic and provincial aspects, at times difficult to disentangle. I often find religious mythology and metaphors interesting and appealing, like beautiful places in the mountains from where we can look at the stars. But the mountains are not the stars.

Then, many religions have really petty, extremely parochial aspects related to what and when one should eat or drink or what sex is allowed and with whom. I don't care for this stuff at all. It isn't even geography - it's local zoning norms, often questionable, sometimes ugly.

My God is not interested in the petty details of our daily life, as long as we act with love and compassion. My God has no interest in what you do with our genitals, or with whom, as long as you act with compassion and love. My God has no interest in what and when I eat, or drink, or smoke, or inhale, as long as I act with love and compassion. My God has no preference for one or another nation, religion, ethnic group, gender, or sport team. My God is far, Far, FAR above these things.

Perhaps I should clarify "My God has no preference for one or another religion," which may seem odd. What I mean is that the common cores, the cosmological and mystical aspects of different religions, are similar or at least compatible. It's only the geography (not to mention the zoning norms) that is different, like the geography of England is different from the geography of Utah. But England and Utah are both under the stars, the same stars.

I discussed these points at the 2014 Conference of the [Mormon Transhumanist Association] (MTA) in Salt Lake City, Utah. Now, Mormonism provides a good example of cosmology, geography, and zoning norms.

Mormonism has a concept of boundless elevation and exaltation of Man, through all means including science and technology, until Man becomes like God. Conversely, God was once like Man before attaining an exalted status. This part of Mormonism is the core of my own personal religion, and therefore I am a card carrying member of the MTA.

Then we have the geography, the story of the "*Book of Mormon*" and other revelations. I find Mormon mythology very inspiring, but I consider it as geography (like the virgin birth), and my admiration and respect for Joseph Smith are exactly the same if I think that he made everything up.

And then, we have the local zoning norms. I don't drink much and I haven't done drugs in decades, but I am unable to function as a sentient being without drinking coffee and smoking, habits that Mormons strongly disapprove of. They may well be right - if I had grown up as a Mormon I would probably be healthier - but I don't think [the King Follett cosmological sermon and the Word of Wisdom health code] live in the same conceptual universe: The first is cosmology, and the second is zoning.

I know that many believers are emotionally attached to geography and even zoning norms. I have no problem with them, as long as they act with love and compassion.

But others, who find the geography uninteresting and the zoning norms arbitrary and unpleasant, reject everything including the stars. Which is too bad, because the stars are beautiful.

That's why I think we need new religious social movements, focused on cosmology and enlightened spirituality.

A Minimalist, Open, Extensible Cosmic Religion

Some years ago I formulated a short and compact Turing Church cosmology:

- We will go to the stars and find Gods, build Gods, become Gods, and resurrect the dead from the past with advanced science, space-time engineering and "time magic."
- God is emerging from the community of advanced forms of life and civilizations in the universe, and able to influence space-time events anywhere, anytime, including here and now.
- God elevates love and compassion to the status of fundamental forces, key drivers for the evolution of the universe.

Of course, [this short version leaves some important concepts out]. A longer version (which also leaves some important concepts out) is the [Ten Cosmist Convictions]. A much longer but much more comprehensive version is this whole book.

In a nutshell, my Turing Church cosmology is [a fusion of two strands of thought], initially separate but eventually converging and becoming woven together. One strand, inspired by futurism and transhumanism, is centered on the ascension of future humanity beyond any conceivable bound, through super-advanced technologies. The other strand, inspired by scientific and spiritual insights, is centered on speculative theories of physical reality that leave room for the transcendent visions of religions and spiritual traditions. The central idea of universal resurrection is explored in both strands.

This Turing Church cosmology is loosely defined, with room for different interpretations and extensions. I see it as part of a galaxy of ideas in constant cooperation and competition (instead of a single monolithic belief system), with room for many approaches and angles. Let a thousand flowers bloom!

Turing Church is a deliberately disorganized community:

- Open to: Everyone.
- Central authority: None.
- Lifestyle prescriptions: None.
- Ethical prescriptions: Just one, "Try to act with love and compassion toward other sentient beings."

This is a minimalist, open, extensible cosmic religion. Minimalist, because it is a simple, compact cosmology, deliberately open to interpretation, and without geography or zoning laws. Open, because it is a minimalist foundation to build upon, and also because it is open to everyone and doesn't impose zoning laws. Extensible, because it can be used as a framework and extended - in particular, it can be extended with suitable geographic and even zoning elements for those who like or need these things.

Extensibility is important. This open minimalist cosmic religion is my ideal religion, but I am acutely aware that it is too ethereal and "weak" compared to traditional, uncompromising and "strong" belief systems, painted with vivid heroic colors. Please feel free to add your favorite strong colors, but personally I feel more at home among the pastel hues of my open, minimalist cosmic religion.

Some otherwise spiritual persons find the geography uninteresting and the zoning norms arbitrary and unpleasant, and so they reject every aspect of religion, including the cosmic core of enlightened spirituality. But they could find answers to their spiritual needs in this barebone, minimalist, open cosmic religion. If you are one of these people, please feel free to join Turing Church.

Using an analogy with software development, Turing Church isn't open source software but free software, no strings attached. Open source projects need consistency, enforced by central management teams vulnerable to squabbles between egomaniacs who want to be the "authority" who decides what goes in and what stays out of the "official distribution."

But here there's no official distribution. Rather, personal interpretations and tweaks are encouraged. Turing Church's kernel is free, just take it and do something good with it. If it isn't good enough for you, feel free to extend or fork it.

I want to avoid a structural weakness that often plagues many good projects. If there is no strong leadership, a project can be paralyzed by conflict between peers, each promoting their pet ideas and blocking those of the others. If there is strong leadership, a project can become ossified and stagnate because the leaders are strongly protective of the existing framework against all proposals for innovation.

I offer my ideas as starting points to tweak, modify, include in other works, repackage, extend horizontally and vertically, interpret, and fork. I hope my ideas will be refined, adapted, and spread by others. Turing Church is open and extensible, defined by coarse and deliberately fuzzy core ideas, without central authorities, and without an official doctrine.

If you want to be a member of Turing Church, just feel free to consider yourself as one, and [join a Turing Church social network]. If you don't like something that I say, say it better. If you don't like something that I do, do it better. If you want leadership, lead.

A smart friend, Robin Hanson, once warned me that, if you want people to really commit to your ideas and take them seriously, you should ask people to give something up, like fasting on some days, following a strict lifestyle code, or giving part of their income to a church. I think Robin is right, but I am not asking you to give up anything, and this is not a church.

To those who feel at home in an organized community associated with an established religion, I recommend joining the CTA and/or the MTA. See you there!

Benefits For Individuals And Societies

I am living proof that believing in some kind of afterlife is good for the individual: I am not afraid of death.

When I think of my own death, my main emotion is curiosity. Curiosity, and the hope to be with my loved ones again.

But this belief is also good for society. That widespread belief in some form of afterlife is good for a society is easy to understand. For example, those who are not too scared of dying perform better in battle, and win.

OK, war is bad and all that. But widespread belief in some form of afterlife is also good for modern and future societies, in a subtler sense. I think religions that provide hope in personal resurrection, either traditional religions based on the "supernatural" or [new cosmic religions] inspired by science, might be our best protection from the reckless pursuit of risky technologies.

Some transhumanist technologies are inherently risky. For example, molecular nanotechnology carries the risk of unleashing replicant nanobots in a runaway explosion that could destroy the biosphere. Another risk is smarter than human Artificial Intelligence (AI).

In "*Superintelligence*" [Bostrom 2014], Nick Bostrom shows that the extermination of humanity as we know, by future superintelligent entities, is a real existential risk that we should start considering very seriously. Superintelligence is smarter than you like you are smarter than a beetle, and its interests may be incompatible with the existence of humanity.

I am persuaded that "real" AI - sentient AI with human-like consciousness - is NOT around the corner. But consciousness doesn't matter much here: Nick's infamous "[paperclip AI]," a hypothetical superintelligent machine relentlessly dedicated "to maximize the total number of paperclips that will exist in its future light cone," could choose to convert the Earth to paperclips regardless of whether the paperclip AI is conscious or not.

"Worth reading Superintelligence by Bostrom," tweeted Elon Musk. "We need to be super careful with AI. Potentially more dangerous than nukes" [Tegmark 2017]. Soon after, Musk joined and funded [the Future of Life Institute (FLI)], an organization that works to mitigate existential risks facing humanity, particularly existential risk from advanced AI.

I find hope more interesting (and fun) than fear, and so I have never been too worried about existential risks, but I must admit that Nick has valid points. In my book review [Prisco 2014], I concluded that it seems reasonable to follow Nick's advice and pursue very cautiously, if at all, research that could result in superintelligence.

Not everyone agrees. On the contrary many brilliant and imaginative people wish to advance superintelligence research at all costs. Nick clearly identifies the problem:

We, as individuals, don't want to die.

If nothing happens, the default outcome is that we are all dead in a few decades, but superintelligence could change things radically. "The case for rushing is especially strong with regard to technologies that could extend our lives and thereby increase the expected fraction of the currently existing population that may still be around for the intelligence explosion," says Nick.

"If the machine intelligence revolution goes well, the resulting superintelligence could almost certainly devise means to indefinitely prolong the lives of the then still-existing humans, not only keeping them alive but restoring them to health and youthful vigor, and enhancing their capacities well beyond what we currently think of as the human range; or helping them shuffle off their mortal coils altogether by uploading their minds to a digital substrate."

Today many imaginative scientists and science-literate laypersons, who could appreciate Bostrom's precautionary arguments, believe that death is final. They feel doomed to the irreversible non-existence of certain death, unless the superintelligence explosion happens in their lifetime, and therefore they want to push forward recklessly, as fast as possible.

On the contrary, those who hope to be resurrected after death, by either supernatural agencies or future science and technology, do not feel the same urgency to accelerate at all costs (this is my case). Therefore I think religion, or forms of scientific spirituality that offer hope in personal resurrection and afterlife, can help.

It's evident that belief in resurrection has survival value for societies. As noted above, those who believe that they will live again are less scared to die in battle. Similarly, those who believe that they will see their loved ones again after death are less likely to be permanently crippled by despair when a loved person dies, and more likely to continue giving a positive contribution to society.

In general, faith in an afterlife makes believers a bit less obsessed with immediate survival here-and-now, and a bit more likely to put the long-term interest of the community above their own immediate interest. I think it's clear that this is one of the reasons why all societies developed religion.

Today, we know too much science to believe in traditional, revealed religions not based on (or in direct conflict with) science. Therefore, if we want to keep the benefits of religion, we must find ways to make it compatible with science. Reviving religion, in new formulations that don't ask believers to give up science or other desirable aspects of modern thinking, is the main focus of my work.

How can future science and technology resurrect the dead? Nobody knows, but there are promising indications of possible paths in today's science and philosophy. In this book, I explore some paths.

Back to Bostrom and future superintelligence. "More speculatively, the superintelligence might be able to create relatively faithful simulations of some past people - simulations that would be conscious and that would resemble the original sufficiently to count as a form of survival (according to at least some people's criteria)," says Bostrom. "This would presumably be easier for people who have been placed in cryonic suspension; but perhaps for a superintelligence it would not be impossible to recreate something quite similar to the original person from other preserved records such as correspondence, publications, audiovisual materials and digital records, or the personal memories of other survivors."

"A superintelligence might also think of some possibilities that do not readily occur to us."

The first part of the quote mentions cryonics and mindfiles (Bainbridge-Rothblatt "softcopy cryonics"). [Bainbridge and Rothblatt make a persuasive case] that future AI technology may be able to patch a person together from bits, snippets, and traces stored in the cloud.

But what about those who died before the cloud?

In sober academic language, Nick limits himself to noting that: "A superintelligence might also think of some possibilities that do not readily occur to us." My interpretation: Future superintelligences might find ways to tweak and re-engineer space-time, develop inconceivably advanced science and "magic" technologies, and bring back the dead from the past.

I hope humanity and technology will co-evolve, with humans enhanced by synthetic biology and artificial intelligence, and artificial life powered by mind grafts from human uploads, blending more and more until it will be impossible - and pointless - to tell which is which.

I hope our superintelligent hybrid mind children will spread to the stars, become masters of space and time, and bring us back from death. However, I realize that this is not an inevitable outcome but a best case scenario.

This best case scenario requires humanity to survive and pass our most cherished values, including love and compassion for all sentient life, to our superintelligent hybrid mind children. We may need to pursue potentially dangerous research very, very cautiously, without the reckless urgency that comes from hopeless despair.

The same considerations apply to other advanced technologies with potential existential dangers. For example, real Drexlerian molecular nanotechnology could permit radical biological life extension and mind uploading, but also the accidental development of replicant "grey goo" that eats the biosphere.

If you run too fast to catch the train of immortality, you may end up crushed on the rails. But if you believe that another train will come, you can find the selfless strength to work carefully and patiently toward a good future for everyone.

Notes

[a cosmist vision and practical philosophy] See "Knocking on Heaven's door."

[a fusion of two strands of thought] See also "The lights of Eastern spirituality."

[Bainbridge and Rothblatt make a persuasive case] See "Transhumanism."

[cosmic frontier] See "The sacred road to the stars."

[expansion into outer space] See "The sacred road to the stars."

[Christian Transhumanist Association] See "Christianity and transhumanism are much closer than you think."

[consciousness and intelligence can run on exotic material substrates] See "Into the deep waters," "and following chapters.

[Conway's Life] See "The Life of Joe Glider."

[cryonics, brain preservation, mind uploading] See "Transhumanism."

[Frank Tipler] See "Omega Point."

[join a Turing Church social network]
https://turingchurch.net/community-75debb4b7e74

[Mormon Transhumanist Association] See "Man will become like God, say Mormons and transhumanists."

[new cosmic religions] See [Bainbridge 2009], "The sacred road to the stars."

[paperclip AI] The idea of a "pure computational intelligence devoted to manufacturing an infinite number of paperclips" was first suggested by Eliezer Yudkowsky in the Extropians list.
http://extropians.weidai.com/extropians/0303/4140.html

[perhaps Alpha = Omega] Omega, which comes into being in the far future, perhaps emerging from intelligent life in the universe, could act with self-consistent causal loops that extend across time. Therefore, Omega could be the Alpha that created the universe. This vision is repeatedly explored in this book.

[simulation hypothesis] See "Sims City," "The Life of Joe Glider."

[teleported (moved, not copied)] See "In the beginning was the field."

[Ten Cosmist Convictions] See "Knocking on Heaven's door."

[the Future of Life Institute (FLI)] FLI's website:
https://futureoflife.org/

[the King Follett cosmological sermon and the Word of Wisdom health code] See "Man will become like God, say Mormons and transhumanists."

[the name of a mathematical concept] This mathematical concept is more often referred to as "Church-Turing conjecture," but I hope you'll forgive my slight imprecision.

[this short version leaves some important concepts out] The possibility of a pre-existing God, the possibility of God-like awareness and superintelligence in the bare fabric of fundamental reality (e.g. quantum fields), the [simulation hypothesis], and other ideas that are not included in this short list of bullet points, are covered later in this book.

[Turing Church is an online magazine] Old website: turingchurch.com. New website: turingchurch.net.

References

[Bainbridge 2009] William Sims Bainbridge. Religion for a Galactic Civilization 2.0. *IEET*, 2009.
http://ieet.org/index.php/IEET/more/bainbridge20090820/

[Bainbridge 2014] William Sims Bainbridge. *Personality Capture and Emulation*. Springer, 2014.

[Bainbridge 2017] William Sims Bainbridge. *Dynamic Secularization: Information Technology and the Tension Between Religion and Science*. Springer, 2017.

[Bainbridge 2019] William Sims Bainbridge. Turing Church. *WRSP*, 2019.
https://wrldrels.org/2019/08/03/turing-church/
https://www.academia.edu/40075530/Turing_Church (PDF)

[Bostrom 2014] Nick Bostrom. *Superintelligence: Paths, Dangers, Strategies*. Oxford University Press, 2014.

[Bruere 2012] Dirk Bruere. *The Praxis*. Amazon Digital Services, 2012.

[Geraci 2010] Robert Geraci. *Apocalyptic AI: Visions of Heaven in Robotics, Artificial Intelligence, and Virtual Reality*. Oxford University Press, 2010.

[Geraci 2014] Robert Geraci. *Virtually Sacred: Myth and Meaning in World of Warcraft and Second Life*. Oxford University Press, 2014.

[Goertzel 2010] Ben Goertzel. *A Cosmist Manifesto*. Humanity+ Press, 2010.

[Goertzel 2011] Ben Goertzel. Technological Transcendence: An Interview with Giulio Prisco. *H+ Magazine*, 2011.
http://hplusmagazine.com/2011/02/08/technological-transcendence-an-interview-with-giulio-prisco/

[Goertzel 2014] Ben Goertzel. The Turing Church and Open Source Religion: Ben Goertzel Interviews Giulio Prisco. *H+ Magazine*, 2014.
http://hplusmagazine.com/2014/12/22/turing-church-open-source-religion-ben-goertzel-interviews-giulio-prisco/

[Houellebecq 2006] Michel Houellebecq. *The Possibility of an Island*. Knopf, 2006.

[Jones 2017] Jonathan Jones. *Technological Resurrection: A Thought Experiment*. Amazon Digital Services, 2017.

[Kelly 2009] Kevin Kelly. Extropy. *The Technium*, 2009.
https://kk.org/thetechnium/extropy/

[Kurzweil 1999] Ray Kurzweil. *The Age of Spiritual Machines*. Viking Press, 1999.

[Manzocco 2019] Roberto Manzocco. *Transhumanism: Engineering the Human Condition*. Springer, 2019.

[More 2013] Max More, Natasha Vita-More (Eds.). *The Transhumanist Reader: Classical and Contemporary Essays on the Science, Technology, and Philosophy of the Human Future*. Wiley-Blackwell, 2013.

[Perry 2000] Michael Perry. *Forever for All: Moral Philosophy, Cryonics, and the Scientific Prospects for Immortality*. Universal Publishers, 2000.

[Prisco 2014] Giulio Prisco. Thoughts on Bostrom's 'Superintelligence'. *IEET*, 2014.
https://ieet.org/index.php/IEET2/more/prisco20140828

[Prisco 2017a] Giulio Prisco. Book review: Technological Resurrection, by Jonathan Jones. *Turing Church*, 2017.
https://turingchurch.net/book-review-technological-resurrection-by-jonathan-jones-e651b8c78fb6

[Prisco 2017b] Giulio Prisco. Concepts of God and the Kingdom inspired by highly imaginative science. *Turing Church*, 2017.
https://turingchurch.net/concepts-of-god-and-the-kingdom-inspired-by-highly-imaginative-science-213bec10f457

[Rothblatt 2014] Martine Rothblatt. *Virtually Human: The Promise - and the Peril - of Digital Immortality*. St. Martin's Press, 2014.

[Tegmark 2017] Max Tegmark. *Life 3.0: Being Human in the Age of Artificial Intelligence*. Knopf, 2017.

[Tipler 1994] Frank Tipler. *The Physics of Immortality: Modern Cosmology, God and the Resurrection of the Dead*. Doubleday, 1994.

[Tipler 2007] Frank Tipler. *The Physics of Christianity*. Doubleday, 2007.

PART 2 - MANY SUMMITS
AND MANY PATHS

"*The World's Religions*" [Smith 1991], a popular introduction to comparative religion that has sold more than three million copies since its first publication in 1958, includes a section titled "Many Paths to the Same Summit."

The author, Huston Smith, studied and practiced many of the world's religions. Besides, he experimented with psychedelic drugs with Aldous Huxley and Timothy Leary, and described the "empirical metaphysics" of using psychedelics to experience the divine [Smith 2000].

Smith considers different religions as alternative paths that lead to the same summit:

> "To claim salvation as the monopoly of any one religion is like claiming that God can be found in this room but not the next, in this attire but not another. Normally, people will follow the path that rises from the plains of their own civilization...

> It is possible to climb life's mountain from any side, but when the top is reached the trails converge. At base, in the foothills of theology, ritual, and organizational structure, the religions are distinct... But beyond these differences, the same goal beckons."

In the words of the great Indian mystic [Sri Ramkrishna] Paramhansa, quoted by Smith:

> "God has made different religions to suit different aspirations, times, and countries. All doctrines are only so many paths; but a path is by no means God Himself. Indeed, one can reach God if one follows any of the paths with whole-hearted devotion...

> Everyone should follow one's own religion. A Christian should follow Christianity, a Muslim should follow Islam, and so on."

Like Smith, Ramakrishna himself practiced many religions besides Hinduism, including Christianity and Islam. The idea that different religions lead to the same summit of enlightenment is found in the intuitions of many thinkers and mystics throughout the ages.

But the metaphor of many religious paths to the same summit of spirituality doesn't seem to address the search for enlightenment through paths independent of religion. Therefore, I wish to propose an extended metaphor that, besides Smith's summit, includes philosophical, artistic, social, scientific, and technological summits.

The paths that ascend different mountains seem very different in features and texture. But, as one climbs toward higher vantage points, the views from the top begin to converge.

[As a cosmist], I am persuaded that "science in its current form, just like religion and philosophy in their current forms, may turn out to be overly limited for the task of understanding life, mind, society, and reality" [Goffman 2015]. But science, religion and philosophy in their current forms are all I have, and therefore I have to start on currently beaten paths.

In Part 2 we'll explore some transhumanist-flavored paths to enlightenment through religion, philosophy, art (science fiction is the only art form that I feel qualified to discuss), and space exploration. In Part 3, we'll explore paths through science.

Notes

[As a cosmist] See "Knocking on Heaven's door."

[Sri Ramakrishna] See "The lights of Eastern spirituality."

References

[Goffman 2015] Ken Goffman, Jay Cornell. *Transcendence: The Disinformation Encyclopedia of Transhumanism and the Singularity*. Disinformation Books, 2015.

[Smith 1991] Huston Smith. *The World's Religions: Our Great Wisdom Traditions*. HarperOne, 1991.

[Smith 2000]] Huston Smith. *Cleansing the Doors of Perception: The Religious Significance of Entheogenic Plants and Chemicals*. Tarcher, 2000.

CHAPTER 3 - CHRISTIANITY AND TRANSHUMANISM ARE MUCH CLOSER THAN YOU THINK

I have long been persuaded that there are strong parallels between transhumanism and religion, not only "new" religions but the traditional religions of our grandfathers as well. There are, of course, differences, but I prefer to emphasize the parallels.

Christianity and transhumanism are even closer than I thought, and much closer than you probably think.

In this chapter I try to build a two-way bridge between Christianity and transhumanism, and show that Christians can embrace transhumanism, and transhumanists can embrace Christianity, without abandoning their existing convictions.

The [Mormon Transhumanist Association] (MTA) is the most successful transhumanist group within a mainstream church. In fact, Mormon Transhumanists find it easy to reconcile their transhumanist ideas with their religion. Mormonism has a concept of boundless elevation and exaltation of Man, through all means including science and technology, until Man becomes like God. Conversely, God was once like Man before attaining an exalted status.

Mormonism "allows for humans to ascend to a higher, more godlike level," reads the introduction to "*The Transhumanist Reader*" [More 2013] written by Max More, "rather than sharply dividing God from Man." Mormon transhumanists are persuaded that we will become like God [Prisco 2013a] - through science and technology - in a progression without end, and this seems a more faithful interpretation of the teachings of Joseph Smith and a return to the roots of the Mormon religion.

The passage above is adapted from my 2013 article "Meet the smi2ling New Believers" [Prisco 2013b]. In the same article I said that many Christians are open to Transhumanist ideas, but no Christian Transhumanist Association existed at that time.

Now there is a formally established [Christian Transhumanist Association] (CTA) with a website, a mailing list, an active presence on social networks, an annual conference, [a radio show], and many projects in the works. Christian Transhumanism is promoted by pioneers including Christopher Benek, Dorothy Deasy, James McLean Ledford, who runs an independent Christian Transhumanism Facebook group, and, especially, Micah Redding, who has been the main CTA driving force.

I have enthusiastically participated in the initial brainstorming and discussions on the CTA mailing list and social spaces since the beginning. However, while my personal interpretations of Christianity and transhumanism are related, I realize that the parallels between transhumanism and mainstream Christianity are not as evident as the parallels between transhumanism and Mormonism.

In passing, Mormonism is less than two centuries old, but mainstream Christianity is more than two millennia old. What Joseph Smith said is well documented, but our knowledge of what Jesus of Nazareth said is mostly based on hearsay and guesswork.

There must have been power struggles between different Christian factions after the death of Jesus, and - as it always happens - the winners got to write history. I recommend Marianne Fredriksson's novel "*According to Mary Magdalene*" [Fredriksson 1997] for a fictional but believable history.

I was born in a Christian culture but my family was only nominally Christian, we didn't go to Church, and I didn't take religion seriously as a kid. I "discovered" religion, sort of, as an adult, and developed my own belief system which, while compatible with Christianity (which is what I want to show here), is independent of revelation and official doctrine.

Faith is a gift that I haven't received - I asked for it, but it appears that God wants me to stay on my path. The words of David Herbert Lawrence [Boulton 1979] come to mind:

> "A man has no religion who has not slowly and painfully gathered one together, adding to it, shaping it; and one's religion is never complete and final, it seems, but must always be undergoing modification."

However, what billions of good people all over the planet believe is important and has practical consequences. Therefore, I'll start with taking Christian scriptures and doctrine as a given, and I'll try to show that Christianity is essentially compatible with my interpretation (which is also unconventional) of transhumanism.

Transhumanism For Christians

Two caveats: first, Christianity is really a galaxy with a myriad of different stars, and the wars that have been fought over contrasting interpretations of Christianity show that, to say the least, Christians don't agree on everything. Therefore, I will try to stay close to widely accepted doctrine. Second, I am only interested in cosmology, or eschatology, and therefore I will focus on Christian eschatology (as opposed to what I call [geography and zoning norms]).

In "*Surprised by Hope*" [Wright 2008] N. T. Wright, a leading Christian scholar, retired Anglican bishop, and "one of the most formidable figures in the world of Christian thought" according to *Time Magazine* [Van Biema 2008], shows that the Christian concept of life after death is not a disembodied afterlife - we are not "embodied souls" but "animated bodies" - but resurrection in a new body and a new world created by God.

The new body, immortal and incorruptible like the resurrected body of Jesus, will be a gift of God's grace and love. The resurrection of Jesus, and the promise that God will similarly resurrect us in the new world, are the central concepts of Christianity.

"As John Polkinghorne and others have urged, what we are talking about is a great act of new creation," says Wright.

> "God will download our software onto his hardware until the time when he gives us new hardware to run the software again."

John Polkinghorne is a renowned theoretical physicist, theologian, and Anglican priest. In "*The God of Hope and the End of the World*" [Polkinghorne 2003], Polkinghorne argues that the Christian hope of a destiny beyond death resides not in the presumed immortality of a spiritual soul, but in resurrection after death by the grace of God. In Polkinghorne's words:

> "Death is a real end. However, it need not be an ultimate end... It is a perfectly coherent hope that the pattern that is a human being could be held in the divine memory after that person's death."

> "The souls awaiting the final resurrection are held in the mind of God."

> "Much traditional Christian thinking about an intermediate state between death and resurrection has been in terms of 'soul sleep', a kind of suspended animation awaiting the restoration of full humanity. Our idea of the information-bearing patterns of souls being held in the mind of God has some obvious kinship with this picture."

"Our hope is of the resurrection of the body... the software running on our present hardware will be transferred to the hardware of the world to come," said Polkinghorne in his 1993 Gifford Lectures [Polkinghorne 1994]. "Surely the 'matter' of the world to come must be the transformed matter of this world."

The new body and the new world are likely to be deeply different from the present body and the present world. "From the start within early Christianity it was built in as part of the belief in resurrection that the new body, though it will certainly be a body in the sense of a physical object occupying space and time, will be a transformed body, a body whose material, created from the old material, will have new properties," says Wright. "If we are even to glimpse this new world, let alone enter it, we will need a different kind of knowing."

> "According to the early Christians, the purpose of this new body will be to rule wisely

over God's new world. Forget those images about lounging around playing harps. There will be work to do and we shall relish doing it."

"It's more exciting than hanging around listening to nice music," added Wright in a *Time Magazine* interview [Van Biema 2008]. "In Revelation and Paul's letters we are told that God's people will actually be running the new world on God's behalf. The idea of our participation in the new creation goes back to Genesis, when humans are supposed to be running the Garden and looking after the animals."

So, humans were running the Garden, and humans will be running the new world. Similarly, God wants humans to run the present world. "This stewardship cannot be something to be postponed for the ultimate future," says Wright. "It must begin here and now."

We are, in fact, part of God's plan for the world, and part of God's works to create the new world. "When God saves people in this life... such people are not just to be a sign and foretaste of that ultimate salvation," says Wright. "They are to be part of the means by which God makes this happen in both the present and the future."

God intervenes in the world by means of events - miracles - that are often thought of as violations of physical laws. But while no Christian would deny God's ability to do so, miracles don't need to violate physical laws. Wolfhart Pannenberg, widely regarded as a leading theologian, noted [Pannenberg 2004] that Augustine thought of miracles simply as unusual events that contradict our understanding of nature, not nature itself.

"The phenomenon of miracles expresses God's creative freedom within the already existent world order," says Pannenberg in his monumental "*Systematic Theology*" [Pannenberg 1994] treatise. "Miracle is what is unusual and seems to be contrary to the nature of things."

> "As Augustine stressed, however, the unusual events we call miracles are not really contrary to the nature of things but merely contrary to our limited knowledge of the course of nature."

God doesn't need to violate physical laws, because God can and does work through nature [Pannenberg 2004]:

> "The concept of miracle in the Augustinian sense of the term, then, does not involve any opposition to the order of nature described in terms of natural law. It only requires us to admit that we do not know everything about how the processes of nature work. Therefore there can be unusual events, some of which, though uncommon, are explainable on the basis of our present knowledge of natural law, and some of which are not but may be understood better in the future."

Perhaps God stores Polkinghorne's human information patterns in the physical world, and perhaps the ultimate miracles - the resurrection of the dead and the creation of the new world - are no more "miraculous" than the blooming of new flowers in the spring.

Summing up:

- We will be resurrected in a new body and a new world created by God, deeply different from the present body and the present world.
- The pattern that is a human being could be held in the divine memory after that person's death, waiting for resurrection.
- Resurrected humans will run the new world according to God's plan.
- Similarly, God wants humans to run the present world.

- We are part of God's plan for the world, and part of God's works to create the new world.
- Miracles don't violate physical laws. On the contrary, God can and does work through nature.

This is perfectly consistent with the following eschatological vision inspired by transhumanism:

The information patterns that are human beings are stored in the fabric of spacetime by unknown physical processes. These information patterns will be retrieved by future humans, and used to bring the dead back to life by "copying them to the future." Resurrected humans will join future humans in a radically changed world, wearing radically changed immortal bodies.

In this short transhumanist eschatological vision I haven't mentioned God and Jesus, which of course are central to Christianity and to the works of the theologians quoted above. In fact, most transhumanists prefer to leave God out of the picture.

However, since we are part of God's plan for the world, and part of God's works to create the new world, Christians can consider transhumanist eschatology as a part of Christian eschatology, focused on our participation in God's plan. Since miracles don't require violating physical laws, we can perform miracles on God's behalf.

We are doing that already, for example we are healing the sick with medicine, and future science will enable us to perform more ambitious miracles, such as resurrecting the dead. Therefore, Christians can embrace transhumanism as part of Christian beliefs.

It's important to note that Wright, Polkinghorne, and Pannenberg, aren't "fringe" thinkers but widely respected Christian theologians. Actually, all three have been described as "conservative" members of the theology establishment.

When it comes to less conservative thinkers, the parallels between Christianity and transhumanism are even more evident. Pierre Teilhard de Chardin, a Jesuit priest whose work is now being rediscovered, can be considered as a transhumanist precursor. See [Steinhart 2008] for a modern interpretation of Teilhard's ideas, written for transhumanists.

[Russian cosmist Nikolai Fedorov], a Russian Orthodox Christian, was the first to formulate the idea of technological resurrection in modern terms, fully compatible with his interpretation of Christianity.

Trasumanar

Dante was the first to use the term "transhumanism." In *"Divine Comedy - Paradiso,"* Dante coined the Italian verb "trasumanar," which can be translated as "to transcend humanity."

"Claiming that his ascent from the Terrestrial Paradise to the celestial realm of the blessed cannot be expressed adequately in words, Dante invents the word trasumanar ('to transhumanize, to pass beyond the human')," notes Guy Raffa in *"The Complete Danteworlds"* [Raffa 2009]. Dante's original reads:

> "Trasumanar significar per verba non si porìa; però l'essemplo basti a cui esperienza grazia serba."

My translation:

> Transcending humanity cannot be expressed with words but let the example (given previously) be sufficient to those who will experience (transcendence) by grace (of God).

God And Resurrection For Transhumanists

I have tried to build a bridge from Christianity to transhumanism. Now I wish to try and build another bridge from transhumanism to Christianity. As I noted above, most transhumanists prefer to leave God out of the picture. Some transhumanists are passionate "militant atheists" and have negative knee-jerk reactions at the first mention of anything that sounds like religion. I don't hope to "convert" militant atheists, but I do hope to show other transhumanists that there is a bridge.

Most transhumanists are persuaded that the material world of particles and fields, regulated by physical laws, is all that exists, and deny the existence of a separate "spiritual" or "supernatural" reality. I tend to agree, with the caveat that, following Pannenberg and Augustine, I think there is much more to the material universe than we presently know or imagine. Or, following Shakespeare:

> "There are more things in heaven and earth, Horatio, than are dreamt of in your philosophy."

Many transhumanists would agree with the Christian view of humans as "animated bodies" (as opposed to "embodied souls"), which don't possess an immortal soul. Without an immortal soul, the dead can only be brought back to life by the grace of God. But most transhumanists don't want to hear about God.

However, there are at least two mental models for God inspired by transhumanist eschatology:

One is the concept of a natural God emerging from intelligent life in the physical universe and gradually acquiring God-like properties including complete mastery of space and time, or, in other words, omniscience, omnipresence, and omnipotence. Even Richard Dawkins, probably the best known atheist thinker in the world, doesn't rule out the possibility of a natural God.

"It's highly plausible that in the universe there are God-like creatures," said Dawkins in a *New York Times* interview [Powell 2011]. In "*The God Delusion*" [Dawkins 2006] Dawkins elaborated on [natural gods]:

> "There are very probably alien civilizations that are superhuman, to the point of being god-like in ways that exceed anything a theologian could possibly imagine."

The objection, raised by Dawkins, that a natural god is not the infinite God, can be countered by observing that, while infinite entities have a place in pure mathematics, in practical engineering "infinite" means just "very big" (much bigger than all other relevant entities). If a natural God is God-like in any sense that we can conceive and can do everything that we imagine God can do, why not just call such a being God?

It's conceivable that a natural God could emerge from humanity in the far future. [Frank Tipler] expects that future humans will become masters of space and time as described in his book "*The Physics of Immortality*" [Tipler 1994] and steer the entire universe toward a final "Omega Point" singularity.

"As we approach the final singularity, the laws of physics also dictate that our knowledge and computing capacity is expanding without limits," says Tipler [Prisco 2011]. "Eventually it will become possible to emulate, to make a perfect copy of, every previous state of the entire universe."

> "We will be brought back into the future, brought back into existence as computer emulations in the far future."

Tipler tries to prove his conclusions on the basis of known physics, which opens his ideas to criticism. I suspect Tipler is wrong in thinking that we already know enough physics to describe the ultimate fate of the universe. There could be, in fact, [many and perhaps infinitely many "more things"] (Shakespeare) in the physical universe. But I think Tipler's core idea - that intelligent life in the universe will become God-like - is valuable.

"Tipler conceives the Omega Point as all-knowing and all-powerful and therefore considers it to be factually identical with the Creator God of religion," said Pannenberg in a review of Tipler's book [Pannenberg 2005].

> "Tipler's exposition of a future resurrection of the dead is particularly worthy of note in a time when the Christian expectations concerning the future are most often judged to be irreconcilable with the modern scientific worldview."

It's worth noting that the Hebrew original usually translated as "I Am That I Am" can also be translated as "I Shall Be That I Shall Be." In a lecture [Pannenberg 1997] given at a conference on Tipler's ideas, Pannenberg used this translation and hinted at a God that comes to full being in the future:

> "He is the God of the coming kingdom. In hidden ways he is already now the Lord of the universe which is his creation..."

A God that comes into existence in the far future, if endowed with sufficient mastery of space and time, could watch and subtly influence events anywhere, anytime, including here and now.

In other words, God - omniscient, omnipresent, and omnipotent - can do miracles, bring about the new world, and resurrect the dead by copying them from the past. We don't know enough science to understand how God operates, but future scientists might know more. The weird quantum reality and strange time physics that contemporary scientists are imagining, and beginning to unveil, are promising indications.

Another model for God inspired by transhumanist eschatology is the reality as a simulation model, which treats our reality as a [simulation] computed by intelligent entities in a higher level of reality. You, and I, and everything around us, are information: Bits that live, and move, and have their being in a supercomputer beyond space and time, operated by a God-like creator.

"Science-fiction authors... have even suggested (and I cannot think how to disprove it) that we live in a computer simulation, set up by some vastly superior civilization," notes Dawkins [Dawkins 2006]. [Dawkins is open] to the concept of reality as a simulation, but doesn't think of the simulators as God.

The simulators "would have to come from somewhere," says Dawkins. "They probably owe their existence to a (perhaps unfamiliar) version of Darwinian evolution."

However, the sysop God has all the properties of the Christian God, and [the concept of reality as a simulation is totally indistinguishable from religion]. God is omniscient, omnipresent, and omnipotent, wrote the laws of our physics, and can choose to violate them in case of need. Or, in the formulation of Augustine and Pannenberg, God can subtly influence our reality without needing to violate its laws. In particular, God can copy people from our world before death and run the copies again in a better new world.

Beyond sysops and finite natural gods, ascending toward unimaginable degrees of God-likeness in a progression without end, there is room for God - the absolutely infinite, infinitely far, totally unknowable God of Christian theology. One of my conclusions is that [God is undecidable but plausible].

Let's Keep Seeking

Andrew Briggs, Hans Halvorson, and Andrew Steane, wrote "*It Keeps Me Seeking*" [Briggs 2018], a highly recommended book that, in soberly understated ways, suggests that science does not rule out belief.

The authors, three top physicists, are Christians believers, which is often the case (much more often than you might have been persuaded to believe). The authors "use the word 'Christianity' to mean something close to the notion of learning from Jesus of Nazareth, as opposed to the power games that have sometimes self-identified under this label."

Four main themes run through the book: "God is a being to be known, not a hypothesis to be tested; We set a high bar on what constitutes good argument; Uncertainty is OK; We are allowed to open up the window that the natural world offers us."

In the last point, "to open the window" means to allow ourselves to look beyond physical reality, and speculate on aspects of reality which are not immediately evident. I am in total agreement with the last three points.

Concerning the first point, it seems to me that only believers can adopt this attitude. Believers don't need arguments for the God "hypothesis," because they are already persuaded deep inside their heart. In the words of the authors:

> "The person who does not know God may find it helpful to think about the evidence that God is there... The person who already knows God may rather quickly lose interest in discussing God's existence."

The authors of "*It Keeps Me Seeking*" have been blessed with a deep faith, but this is not everyone's case. For example, I have not been blessed with such a deep faith.

You can't strive to know God if you are not prepared to consider the possibility that God might somehow exist. Science-minded people (like me) need some persuasion. Not "evidence that God is there," but at least ways to suspend disbelief, without disowning our scientific mindset and knowledge, and mental pictures of God somewhat compatible with science.

The authors are right that science can't "prove" God (and, in accordance with their second main theme, demolish some weak arguments), but we need to be persuaded that the possibility of God (and afterlife and all that) is not ruled out by science.

The authors don't try to persuade skeptical readers, but offer soberly understated arguments to suggest that, indeed, the possibility of God (and afterlife and all that) is not ruled out by science:

> "Thus, the most reasonable prediction is that in the future, science will march forward explaining more and more ... and that there will always be more things that science does not yet explain. This picture of science... also happens to sit most comfortably with a theistic outlook. For if the universe has a transcendent source, then the call to understand the universe will never be satisfied by finite beings..."

> "What one may claim, with good intellectual credentials, is that the notions of human free will and responsibility are not ruled out by what we know of quantum physics... the notion of human responsibility is not ruled out by our scientific

knowledge of the world... If humans can enact personal encounters without breaking out of the patterns we call 'laws of nature', then so can God... our own actions can be meaningful. We may add that processes going on around us in the world can also be meaningful. This is what the question of divine action is really about."

While much (actually a lot) of "*It Keeps Me Seeking*" is valuable to skeptics and those who wish to find faith, the book is really addressed to believers, to whom the authors offer a powerful Christian narrative that confirms N. T. Wright's interpretation of the Christian concept of life after death:

> "We don't want to run away to somewhere else, some other-worldly place of inane or smug forgetfulness. We want the peace and justice of our true home to be realized right here in the physical house of life on Earth... the hope expressed in New Testament Christianity is not well captured by the modern idiom of getting 'out of the world' and 'going to heaven'. It is much more to do with transformation of the whole natural order, culminating in a New Creation which is not so much a replacement as a blossoming, or something brought to birth."

Some especially interesting considerations of the authors of "*It Keeps Me Seeking*," at [the interface of Christian faith and contemporary physics], are outlined later in my book.

The Faint, Almost Silent Voice Of God In The Heart

In his autobiography "*Undiluted Hocus-pocus*" [Gardner 2013], [Martin Gardner] says that his faith "is based unashamedly on posits of the heart, not the head." Gardner's brain sees no proofs of God or of an afterlife, but his heart tells him that:

> "For me God is a 'Wholly Other' transcendent intelligence, impossible for us to understand. He or she is somehow responsible for our universe and capable of providing, how I have no inkling, an afterlife."

The faint, almost silent voice of the heart finds it hard to persuade the brain. Sometimes we are tempted to blame science, because we just know too much science to believe. But science itself says that we don't really know much. Facing ultimate reality, our science is as primitive as the science of our grandfathers.

Why, then, did your grandfather believe in God and you doubt? The answer, I think, is that your grandfather doubted as well. And his grandmother too. Awake in the dark night of the soul, they questioned their faith and thought that perhaps it was only wishful thinking. Just like you. And me.

It's a shallow faith that never questions itself - or the other extreme, an exceptionally deep faith beyond most people's reach. I believe that most deeply religious persons are almost paralyzed by doubt, and never fully able to accept the faint, almost inaudible answers of the heart.

The kind of faith and hope that we can find in science, philosophy, and abstract theology, is easily shattered by doubt. Faith in God and hope in resurrection only get you through the night if they come from deep inside the heart. We should believe and hope with the heart.

Please don't ask me how. I don't know how. I am stuck with intellectual versions of faith and hope, which don't keep me warm at night. I have some good books, but one can't "learn" faith and hope from books - it's not that easy.

However, I wish to recommend "*My Bright Abyss*" [Wiman 2013], by Christian Wiman. The author, a renowned poet, doesn't worry too much about my longed for, but never found, scientific path to faith.

Here and there Wiman notes that quantum physics suggests that "there is some other reality much larger and more complex than we are able to perceive," and the whole world "is alive and communicating in ways we do not fully understand."

> "And we are part of that life, part of that communication - even as, maybe even especially as, our atoms begin the long dispersal we call death."

"It is not that conventional ideas of an afterlife are too strange; it is that they are not strange enough," says Wiman in a passage that echoes Gardner's "mysterian" theology. Then he hints at our role in God's plan. "We are facets of a work whose finished form we cannot imagine, though our imaginations, aided by grace, are the means - or at least one means - of its completion."

But "*My Bright Abyss*" is not about science, or philosophy, or theology. Wiman's book, a moving poem written in sober and essential prose, is about perception and "a poetics of belief, a language capacious enough to include a mystery that, ultimately, defeats it."

Wiman believes "that we have souls and that they survive our deaths, in some sense that we are entirely incapable of imagining," and in a "God not above or beyond or immune to human suffering, but in the very midst of it, intimately with us in our sorrow."

> "To have faith in a religion, any religion, is to accept at some primary level that its particular language of words and symbols says something true about reality."

I'll go back now to my hopeless (but interesting and fun) quest for intellectual, "scientific" faith, because that's the best I can do at the moment, and I guess it's part of God's plan for me.

Many years ago in a church, seeing others comforted and healed by their faith, I asked God, "Why can't I have their simple, beautiful, healing faith?"

> God answered, "But you have it."

Thoughts and ideas came forward from the back of my mind and condensed in a vision of a God above time as we know it, perhaps emerging from intelligent life in the universe, perhaps born in the far future to our own grandchildren among the stars, but still present and caring here and now. God creates and controls the universe with [self-consistent causal loops] that extend across time.

This vision, essentially similar to Pannenberg's, is repeatedly explored in this book.

Of course I don't know that God spoke to me, and my brain finds it hard to believe. But in retrospect I see that the episode was important. It made me realize that I believe in some kind of God, [perhaps dwelling in quantum and sub-quantum reality], and some sort of after-life, and start searching for ways to make my belief compatible with science.

I started to dedicate a lot of time to developing my non-traditional religious ideas (ideas that I always had since I was a kid, but previously in the background), and all my writings about science and religion are a direct result.

The usually faint "voice of God" was so vivid that I guess I could interpret this episode as a revelation. I prefer, however, not to make such claims. Whether it was the voice of God, or my own inner voice, or a combination of the two, does it really matter? I guess God speaks to us through our own inner voice - what else should God use? - and occasionally we retain vague memories of God's messages.

Notes

[a radio show] The Christian Transhumanist Podcast:
https://www.christiantranshumanism.org/podcast

[Christian Transhumanist Association] See the CTA website:
http://www.christiantranshumanism.org/

[geography and zoning norms] See "Turing Church."

[God is undecidable but plausible] See "Thought experiments in physical theology."

[natural gods] See "Little Green Gods."

[Dawkins is open] See "Little Green Gods."

[Frank Tipler] See "Omega Point."

[many and perhaps infinitely many "more things"] See "Into the deep waters" and following chapters.

[Martin Gardner] See "Agnostics, possibilians, and mysterians."

[Mormon Transhumanist Association] See "Man will become like God, say Mormons and transhumanists."

[perhaps dwelling in quantum and sub-quantum reality] See "Into the deep waters" and following chapters.

[Russian cosmist Nikolai Fedorov] See "Knocking on Heaven's door."

[self-consistent causal loops] See "Exotic space, mysterious time, magic quantum."

[simulation] See "Sims City," "The Life of Joe Glider."

[the concept of reality as a simulation is totally indistinguishable from religion] See "Sims City."

[the interface of Christian faith and contemporary physics] See "In the beginning was the field."

References

[Boulton 1979] James T. Boulton (Ed.). *The Letters of D. H. Lawrence, Volume I, September 1901 – May 1913*. Cambridge University Press, 1979.

[Briggs 2018] Andrew Briggs, Andrew Steane, Hans Halvorson. *It Keeps Me Seeking: The Invitation from Science, Philosophy and Religion*. Oxford University Press, 2018.

[Dawkins 2006] Richard Dawkins. *The God Delusion*. Bantam Books, 2006.

[Fredriksson 1997] Marianne Fredriksson. *According to Mary Magdalene*. Hampton Roads Publishing Company, 1997.

[Gardner 2013] Martin Gardner. *Undiluted Hocus-Pocus: The Autobiography of Martin Gardner*. Princeton University Press, 2013.

[More 2013] Max More, Natasha Vita-More (Eds.). *The Transhumanist Reader: Classical and Contemporary Essays on the Science, Technology, and Philosophy of the Human Future*. Wiley-Blackwell, 2013.

[Pannenberg 1994] Wolfhart Pannenberg. *Systematic Theology*. T & T Clark, 1988–1994.

[Pannenberg 1997] Wolfhart Pannenberg. Modern Cosmology: God and the Resurrection of the Dead. Lecture given at the Innsbruck Conference on Frank Tipler's book "*The Physics of Immortality*," June 1997.
http://dauns01.math.tulane.edu/~tipler/theologian.html

[Pannenberg 2004] Wolfhart Pannenberg. The Concept of Miracle. *Zygon*, 2004.

[Pannenberg 2005] Wolfhart Pannenberg. Breaking a Taboo: Frank Tipler's The Physics of Immortality. *Zygon*, 2005.

[Polkinghorne 1994] John Polkinghorne. *The Faith of a Physicist: Reflections of a Bottom-Up Thinker*. Princeton University Press, 1994.

[Polkinghorne 2003] John Polkinghorne. *The God of Hope and the End of the World*. Yale University Press, 2003.

[Powell 2011] Michael Powell. A Knack for Bashing Orthodoxy. *The New York Times*, 2011.
http://www.nytimes.com/2011/09/20/science/20dawkins.html

[Prisco 2011] Giulio Prisco. Frank Tipler's talk at the Turing Church Online Workshop 2. YouTube, 2011.
https://www.youtube.com/watch?v=__tx3UXWigM

[Prisco 2013a] Giulio Prisco. Man will become like God, say Mormons and transhumanists in Salt Lake City. *KurzweilAI*, 2013.
http://www.kurzweilai.net/man-will-become-like-god-say-mormons-and-transhumanists-in-salt-lake-city

[Prisco 2013b] Giulio Prisco. Meet the smi2ling New Believers. IEET, 2013.
http://ieet.org/index.php/IEET/more/prisco20130618

[Raffa 2009] Guy Raffa. *The Complete Danteworlds: A Reader's Guide to the Divine Comedy*. University Of Chicago Press, 2009.

[Steinhart 2008] Eric Steinhart. Teilhard de Chardin and Transhumanism. *Journal of Evolution and Technology*, 2008.
https://jetpress.org/v20/steinhart.htm

[Tipler 1994] Frank Tipler. *The Physics of Immortality: Modern Cosmology, God and the Resurrection of the Dead.* Doubleday, 1994.

[Van Biema 2008] David Van Biema. Christians Wrong About Heaven, Says Bishop. *Time*, 2008.
http://content.time.com/time/world/article/0,8599,1710844,00.html

[Wiman 2013]. Christian Wiman. *My Bright Abyss: Meditation of a Modern Believer.* Farrar, Straus and Giroux, 2013.

[Wright 2008] N. T. Wright. *Surprised by Hope: Rethinking Heaven, the Resurrection, and the Mission of the Church.* HarperOne, 2008.

CHAPTER 4 – MAN WILL BECOME LIKE GOD, SAY MORMONS AND TRANSHUMANISTS

The [Mormon Transhumanist Association] (MTA) is the best example of successful integration of transhumanist ideas in a mainstream religion, and one of the best transhumanist communities. Actually, I think it's the best one.

The Church of Jesus Christ of Latter-Day Saints (LDS), aka Mormon Church, has a concept of boundless elevation and exaltation of Man, through all means including science and technology, until Man becomes like God.

Conversely, God was once like Man before attaining an exalted status. Mormonism "allows for humans to ascend to a higher, more godlike level," writes Max More in his introduction to "*The Transhumanist Reader*" [More 2013], "rather than sharply dividing God from Man."

Mormon transhumanists are persuaded that we will become like God - through science and technology - in a progression without end, and this seems a more faithful interpretation of the teachings of Joseph Smith and a return to the roots of the Mormon religion.

Not all Mormons would agree with this explicitly transhumanist formulation of their faith but, according to MTA co-founder and former president Lincoln Cannon, Mormon transhumanism is a correct interpretation of the teachings of Joseph Smith, the founder of the Mormon Church, as shown for example by Smith's King Follett sermon [Bushman 2005].

All Mormons are sort of familiar with this aspect of their faith, but many contemporary Mormons seem to sweep these concepts to the back of their mind, as they do for other controversial issues such as polygamy, promoted (and practiced) by Smith and other founding fathers but frowned upon in modern times.

The MTA was founded in 2006 [Cannon 2017]. Later in the year, when I was a member of the Board of Directors of the World Transhumanist Association (WTA, then rebranded as Humanity+), the MTA applied to become an affiliate of the WTA. At that time, I was unaware of the existence of the MTA and had only a very vague idea of Mormonism.

There was some debate in the WTA Board on whether to accept the MTA or not. After learning a few basic things on Mormonism and the MTA, I recommended to accept the MTA, which was eventually accepted.

A few months after that, I became a member of the MTA, and I have been a member ever since.

I gave a keynote talk at the first MTA conference in 2012 [Prisco 2012a]. This was the first talk in which I answered the question "Are you a believer?" with a simple and clear YES, inspired by the awesome MTA cosmology [Prisco 2012b].

Stranger In A Strange Mormon Neverland

This section includes an abridged and revised version of an essay that I wrote after returning from my first visit to Utah for the MTA Conference 2012, and revised excerpts from an essay that I wrote in 2015 [Prisco 2015].

I spent a few days in Utah for the MTA 2012 conference organized by the Mormon Transhumanist Association (MTA), and my good local friends took me around for a crash course in Utah life and Mormon ways, and the history of The Church of Jesus Christ of Latter-day Saints (LDS Church, aka Mormon Church) and its enigmatic founder, with a culture shock and many interesting conversations about the ins and outs of Mormon culture.

Until a few years ago I thought that LDS was the name of a drug spelled by somebody under its influence, and I had only a very vague Hollywood image of hard-working Mormon men in stiff black suits and smiling Mormon ladies in long 19th century dresses.

This impression was sort of confirmed by a tour of Brigham Young University (BYU) on the first day. BYU students dress more conservatively than in other universities that I have seen. Girls wear leggings like everywhere else, but they are advised to wear also a dress.

The students and staff on the BYU campus seem very determined, interested in their studies, and happy with themselves and their place in the world. But while I was saying this to one of my guides we saw a crying girl. I guess perfection is not of this world, but the overall BYU impression is different from other campuses because everything seems clearer and cleaner than elsewhere.

The word that came to my mind is "simplicity." BYU is a clean, happy and productive environment, but it seems to lack some chaotic subversiveness. The students who spray graffiti and do drugs are often the smartest, and I think a healthy society must find ways to harness their creative energy for its own improvement.

Everyone is very nice and very friendly, with nice houses and big cars for big families (eight kids are not that unusual, and some people have even more). Mormons in Utah are a happy folk, and they have statistics at hand to show that they are healthier, live longer, work harder, and make more money than in the rest of the U.S. The Mormon society WORKS, and my friends are persuaded that this is due to the influence of the LDS Church.

The Church is everywhere, and everything belongs to the Church formally (e.g. the BYU) or de-facto (e.g. the State government). For a European like me, raised in a secular society by a family even more secular than others, this is a culture shock. For these people, the Church matters. They take it seriously. They believe in the Mormon doctrine.

I asked Lincoln Cannon to give a 2-3 minutes video explanation of Mormonism and Mormon transhumanism [Cannon 2012] to my wife, who could not come to Utah with me.

I share with Lincoln a great admiration for William James, who would certainly say that the fact that the Mormon society works is the best and the only needed "proof" of the validity of Mormon beliefs.

As Lincoln says in the video, Mormon theology is an extension of Christian theology with some very interesting twists and a home-grown, uniquely American mythology, and is pragmatically open to new tweaks and additions. Mormonism also has some aspects of a "practical religion," and the Mormon God doesn't seem willing to help you too much if you don't help yourself.

As Lincoln says, Mormons are interested in science and consider technology as one of the principal means to help ourselves, following the plan of God. For me, the most interesting part of the Mormon doctrine is the concept that God was once a limited being like us, and we can become like God ourselves (theosis, or exaltation).

It follows that in the universe there may be many God-like beings with different degrees of Godhood, attained through science and technology [as Richard Dawkins believes]. This is what makes Mormonism the most transhumanist religion [Cannon 2011], and theosis is a foundation of Mormon Transhumanism.

Of course, not everyone in the LDS Church agrees that we can become Gods with the help of science and technology, but my MTA friends are still considered as good Mormons by a Church that shows a surprising tolerance of unusual theological positions and creative doctrinal tweaks.

Not so for lifestyle and practical behavior. You can believe that we live in a synthetic reality engineered by super intelligent God-like aliens from another dimension, but Thou Shalt Not Drink Coffee. The "Word of Wisdom" [Givens 2017], the very strict Mormon health code, prohibits coffee, alcohol, tobacco, and some other nice things.

The "Word of Wisdom" is strictly enforced, with practical consequences for those who don't comply. If the Church is the center of your spiritual and social life, like it is for many Mormons in Utah, the social pressure to comply can be very strong.

Subsequent visits to Utah confirmed these initial impressions, and I met many other Mormons with firm convictions and a powerful sense of duty.

Mormons are powered by the calm happiness that comes from knowing one's place in a good world, and a quiet determination to make the world even better, step by step, with good works, including science and technology. They are blessed with a firm conviction that they will see their loved departed ones again after a life of good works building Zion, on Earth and beyond. Lincoln refers to this calm, purposeful, action-oriented stance as "strenuous mood" [Cannon 2013].

Not that my friends in the MTA are that one-dimensional. Of course they are as complex and multi-dimensional as everyone else. They feel sorry for Mormon homosexuals, women who prefer not to stay at home and bake cakes, intellectuals who are excommunicated from the Mormon church, and perhaps even for smokers and coffee drinkers (like me) who aren't allowed to enter the inner Temple. But protecting the Mormon religion, culture, community, and social organization comes a strong first in their scale of priorities, and takes precedence over less important niceties.

All religions, at least all the Western religions that I am more familiar with, have both cosmic and provincial aspects, at times difficult to disentangle. I often refer to the cosmic aspects of religion as "cosmology," as opposed to provincial "geography and zoning norms" - your dietary and sexual preferences and habits, personal lifestyle, and similar things.

[My God does only cosmology] and is not interested in the petty details of our daily life, as long as we act with love and compassion and do good works to elevate humanity. Therefore, I tend to pay very little attention to geography and zoning norms, and be very tolerant of others' lifestyle choices.

I wonder whether Mormonism could become more open and tolerant without losing its strength. I am not sure it could: Other Western cultures did become much more open and tolerant, but at the cost of becoming weak [Prisco 2015].

However, I know many Mormons who are open and tolerant while remaining strenuously committed to the essential core of Mormonism. One is [Blaire Ostler], a former CEO of the MTA and one of the most interesting Mormon transhumanist voices.

Mormon Transhumanist Cosmology

In the MTA I found something that deeply resonated with my own intuitions, so I became a member and I've been a member ever since.

Man can become like God? God was once like man? Spirit is matter? Nothing is beyond science? Future technology will resurrect the dead? Wow. WOW!

However, I found it difficult to believe that the average Joe and Jane Mormon in the street really believe these things. I asked my friends in the MTA and they told me that these things are in the Mormon scriptures, and are affirmed by many and perhaps most Mormons.

I am still not persuaded that most Mormons REALLY believe in these things, as opposed to paying lip service to things they have been hearing since childhood without reflecting too much on the implications. I have the impression that, while the contemporary Mormon church can't deny the presence of transhumanist ideas in the teachings of Joseph Smith and other Mormon prophets, it has chosen not to emphasize them.

But now I have done some reading of and about the Mormon scriptures, and based on what I have read I can affirm without doubt that: YES. These things ARE in the Mormon scriptures.

These things have been said and written by Joseph Smith, Brigham Young, Parley Pratt, and other founding fathers, and emphasized by contemporary scholars like Richard Bushman and Terryl Givens, both of whom have participated in MTA events.

Joseph Smith didn't write down a systematic account of Mormon cosmology and theology. The task fell into the capable hands of Parley Pratt [Givens 2011], a colorful, larger than life American adventurer who was an early follower of Joseph Smith.

In his short treatise "*Key to the Science of Theology*" [Pratt 1855], Pratt forcefully outlined Smith's visions without trying to hide the conflicts with mainstream Christianity. On the contrary, Pratt emphasized the otherness of Mormonism.

A contemporary equivalent of Pratt's work, different in language and style but not in substance, is a 2-volume treatise written by Terryl Givens [Givens 2014, 2017]. Roughly speaking, the first volume is about "cosmology" and the second is about "geography."

I have the impression that today's common Mormonism is a very watered down version of the revolutionary beliefs of the Mormon founding fathers. The original Mormonism of Joseph Smith was a NEW religion: A strong, optimistic, uniquely American frontier religion that, while sharing many elements with other forms of Christianity, introduced enough disruptive novelty to warrant being considered as a distinct religion.

But the revolutionary ideas of Joseph Smith and the Mormon founding fathers have been weakened and "sanitized," sort of, to avoid conflict with mainstream American society and religion. For example, it's my understanding that the Mormon church abandoned the practice of polygamy to appease the rest of the US and avoid conflict and perhaps war.

And why is the King Follett sermon [Bushman 2005], a loud and clear outline of the disruptive novelty of Mormonism, by Joseph Smith himself, not part of the Mormon church's canonized scriptures? Again, I think, to appease mainstream Christians and avoid conflict.

It seems evident to me that Mormon transhumanism reaffirms the new, revolutionary religion of Joseph Smith and the Mormon founding fathers. I think the MTA plays the very important role of re-affirming some officially ignored (or at least de-emphasized) aspects of Mormonism.

Not having been raised in a Mormon family or community, I started my exploration of Mormonism knowing absolutely nothing. My education in Mormonism comes from my friends in the MTA, and some good books by highly reputed, unimpeachable Mormon sources, recommended by my MTA friends and listed in the references at the end of this chapter.

Mormon transhumanism was profiled in *New Yorker* [Chan 2016], and the last paragraph of the story summarizes the reason I joined the MTA:

> "In an entry from one of Lincoln Cannon's old journals, dated October 17, 1995, a passage written in a teen-ager's sprawling script reads, 'How will the resurrection come to pass? I don't know for sure, but I believe that God won't do for us what we can do for ourselves.'"

I have long been persuaded that the resurrection of the dead, promised by most religions, will come to pass by means of future science and technology, and the MTA is one of the very few groups open to this idea.

Here's a distillation of my favorite aspects of Mormon cosmology and theology:

God was once like man, and man can become like God. In the words of Lorenzo Snow [Givens 2014]:

> "As man now is, God once was; as God now is, man may be."

The road to our God-like future is built by scientists and engineers. In his foreword to "*Parallels and Convergences*" [Howe 2012], Richard Bushman, one of the leading contemporary Mormon scholars, says:

> "The end point of engineering knowledge may be divine knowledge. Mormon theology permits us to think of God and humans as collaborators in bringing to pass the immortality and eternal life of man. Engineers may be preparing the way for humans to act more like gods in managing the world."

We live in a clean and simple material universe. Matter has always existed, and spirit is also material - a more fine and pure form of matter, according to Joseph Smith [Givens 2014]:

> "There is no such thing as immaterial matter. All spirit is matter, but it is more fine or pure, and can only be discerned by purer eyes."

Mormon cosmology is essentially monistic [Givens 2014], not overburdened by metaphysical dualism between God and man, spirit and matter. [Eternal matter is endowed with some degree of intelligence and free will].

God is not a "wholly other," infinitely distant metaphysical entity who created the universe out of nothing and rules it from outside, but a super-smart cosmic engineer who works with available material resources. In the King Follett sermon [Bushman 2005], Joseph Smith said:

> "Now, the word create… does not mean to create out of nothing; it means to organize; the same as a man would organize materials and build a ship. Hence we infer that God had materials to organize the world out of chaos - chaotic matter…"

God is still higher than us, but not hopelessly distant. The essential continuity between God, the material universe, and ourselves, implies that future science could unveil more and more aspects of God, and develop God-like technologies for spacetime engineering and the resurrection of the dead. Future generations will be able to actively participate in God's works and the resurrection of the dead… and that's exactly what God wants.

Based on the emphasis given to these points, Mormonism seems to me a genuinely new religion for bold pioneers marching toward new frontiers. That's why I like it so much. "Mormon transhumanist" comes closest to describing my personal religion.

Mormon cosmology is also compatible with "simulation theology" derived from the [simulation] hypothesis - the idea that our reality could be some kind of "simulation" that God runs in a deeper or higher level of reality.

The MTA has formulated a version of the simulation hypothesis adapted to Mormon cosmology: "The New God Argument" (NGA) [Cannon 2015].

We can reduce the apparent tension between simulation theology and Mormon monistic materialism by just extending the definition of "universe" to include the base reality in which our universe is computed. [Later in this book I will outline] a formulation of the simulation hypothesis - apparently different but essentially equivalent - that seems (to me) more materialist and more Mormon-friendly.

Joseph Smith

The Prophet Joseph Smith was killed by a mob in Illinois a few years before his followers moved West to Utah. I asked many people which book about him I should read first, and everyone gave me the same answer: "*Joseph Smith: Rough Stone Rolling*" [Bushman 2005], by Richard Bushman, a fascinating history book, very well written and researched, about a great man and his times.

I have said that the Mormon neverland looks "too simple," but Joseph was a complex man, full of contradictions, and larger than life. I think his contemporary followers should take, once again, inspiration from him.

As a teen, Joseph met an angel who led him to find "*The Book of Mormon*" [Givens 2009], which he translated (with some help from above) and published in 1830. Of course, not everybody believes this story.

Did Joseph really have a revelation from above? Or was it the wild imagination of a genius farm boy unhappy with the mediocrity of the world around him?

But perhaps there is not much of a difference. Perhaps, when we contemplate the numinous, we are more in tune with the universe, and we are allowed to take something back. Perhaps Joseph was just more in tune with the universe than the rest of us.

Reading Bushman's biography I see a great man, a larger than life epic hero living through times of religious turmoil in early-19th century America. But I also see a person full of contradictions and human flaws, just like you and me. To me, his humanity makes Joseph even greater.

But they ask, did Joseph really see angels and receive revelations from God? What about those golden plates and seer stones? That can't be true, now can it?

To me, it doesn't matter that much. If God is an engineer who works with available resources, then God has a perfectly good communication channel with us: Our own inner voice. Perhaps we are all inspired by God - [we just need to try and listen to that faint, almost silent voice].

Of course God uses our inner voice to talk to us. What else should God use?

For most people most of the times, the voice of God is lost in the fractal white noise of consciousness. But for some people, some times, something understandable comes through. I guess Joseph was just more perceptive than the rest of us.

Mormon Transhumanism And Continuing Revelation

We can only communicate using the style and language of our time and culture. We would probably sound far too concise and direct to our ancestors in the 19th century. Similarly, they sound far too verbose and vague to us, and of course their science was more primitive than ours.

The central idea that we will bring back the dead ourselves, by means of future science and technology, is often hinted at by the founding fathers of Mormonism but never spelled out as directly and clearly as we speak today. Perhaps these words of Brigham Young come closest [Howe 2012]:

> "Allow me to inform you that you are in the midst of it all now, that you are in just as good a kingdom as you will ever attain to, from now to all eternity, unless you make it yourselves by the grace of God, by the will of God, by the eternal Priesthood of God, which is a code of laws perfectly calculated to govern and control eternal matter. If you and I do not by this means make that better kingdom which we anticipate, we shall never enjoy it. We can only enjoy the kingdom we have labored to make."

Here Young is saying, I think, that we will gain access to scientific means to "govern and control eternal matter," which can easily be interpreted to include scientific means to resurrect the dead, and that's what God wants us to do.

How? We don't know enough yet to answer this question, but contemporary scientific theories open the door to intriguing speculations.

Contemporary [quantum field theory] seeks to provide a unified treatment of matter and forces in the universe. Fermionic matter fields and bosonic force fields remind of Joseph Smith's gross and fine matter, and scientists speculate on [a cosmic intelligence encoded in quantum fields], woven into the very fabric of space throughout the universe.

Space and time themselves could be "material," sort of: Not a pre-existing stage for physics, but [emergent properties of matter]. [New theories of spacetime physics] with retrocausality and self-consistent causal loops indicate that advanced entities could operate in ways that are not limited by time.

Perhaps God will come into full being only in the far future, but nevertheless organizes matter and spirit at all places and times, including here and now. We are beginning to speculate on future ultra-technologies able to retrieve the dead from other times, spacetime foam, deep quantum reality, and whatnot.

[Contemporary string theories suggest] that our universe might be a 3-dimensional "brane-world" in a higher-dimensional "bulk," and that hyper-advanced "bulk beings" - God, or future God-like humans made of bulk matter - might copy us from the past of this brane-world and paste us into a better brane-world, or into the bulk.

Joseph Smith, Parley Pratt, and Brigham Young couldn't have said any of that, because they didn't have these concepts, and their contemporaries would not have understood them anyway. They could only communicate their insights, or revelations, based on the science of their time.

This brings me to the key concept of continuing revelation: The Mormon doctrine is not fixed in stone, but open to new inputs. Of course the Mormon authorities feel compelled to defend their preferred ideology and are often hostile to the new (like all authorities), but continuing revelation has always been part of the Mormon doctrine.

Therefore, Mormonism seems uniquely able to evolve with new revelations, interpreted and communicated in light of new scientific knowledge and speculations.

No MTA member has claimed inspiration (as far as I am aware), but MTA's formulation of Mormonism certainly seems inspired to me.

Notes

[a cosmic intelligence encoded in quantum fields] See "Thought experiments in physical theology," "In the beginning was the field."

[as Richard Dawkins believes] See "Little green Gods."

[Blaire Ostler] Blaire's website:
https://www.blaireostler.com/

[Contemporary string theories suggest] See "Exotic space, mysterious time, magic quantum."

[emergent properties of matter] See "Into the deep waters" and following chapters.

[Eternal matter is endowed with some degree of intelligence and free will] See "Eligo, ergo sum, ergo Deus est," "In the beginning was the field," for contemporary formulations of this concept. We can consider elementary quantum and/or chaotic collapse events as "atoms" of freely willed action.

[Later in this book I will outline] See "Thought experiments in physical theology," "In the beginning was the field."

[Mormon Transhumanist Association] See the Mormon Transhumanist Association (MTA) website:
https://transfigurism.org/

[My God does only cosmology] See "Turing Church."

[New theories of spacetime physics] See "Exotic space, mysterious time, magic quantum."

[quantum field theory] See "Exotic space, mysterious time, magic quantum," "In the beginning was the field."

[simulation] See "Sims City."

[we just need to try and listen to that faint, almost silent voice] See "Christianity and transhumanism are much closer than you think."

References

[Bushman 2005] Richard Bushman. *Joseph Smith: Rough Stone Rolling*. Alfred A. Knopf, 2005.

[Cannon 2011] Lincoln Cannon, Ben Goertzel. Mormonism: The Most Transhumanist Religion? *H+ Magazine*, 2011.
http://hplusmagazine.com/2011/05/09/mormonism-the-most-transhumanist-religion/

[Cannon 2012] Lincoln Cannon. Mormon Transhumanism in a nutshell. YouTube, 2012.
https://www.youtube.com/watch?v=UVPiT0a5wDQ

[Cannon 2013] Lincoln Cannon. Purpose of the Mormon Transhumanist Association, 2013.
https://lincoln.metacannon.net/2013/04/purpose-of-mormon-transhumanist.html

[Cannon 2015] Lincoln Cannon. What is Mormon Transhumanism? *Theology and Science*, 2015.
https://new-god-argument.com/

[Cannon 2017] Lincoln Cannon. A Brief History of the Mormon Transhumanist Association, 2017.
https://lincoln.metacannon.net/2017/04/a-brief-history-of-mormon-transhumanist.html

[Chan 2016] Dawn Chan. The Immortality Upgrade. *New Yorker*, 2016.
https://www.newyorker.com/tech/elements/mormon-transhumanism-and-the-immortality-upgrade

[Givens 2009] Terryl Givens. *The Book of Mormon: A Very Short Introduction*. Oxford University Press, 2009.

[Givens 2011] Terryl Givens. *Parley P. Pratt: The Apostle Paul of Mormonism*. Oxford University Press, 2011.

[Givens 2014] Terryl Givens. *Wrestling the Angel: The Foundations of Mormon Thought: Cosmos, God, Humanity*. Oxford University Press, 2014.

[Givens 2017] Terryl Givens. *Feeding the Flock: The Foundations of Mormon Thought: Church and Praxis*. Oxford University Press, 2017.

[Howe 2012] Scott Howe and Richard Bushman (Eds.). *Parallels and Convergences: Mormon Thought and Engineering Vision*. Greg Kofford Books, 2012.

[More 2013] Max More, Natasha Vita-More (Eds.). *The Transhumanist Reader: Classical and Contemporary Essays on the Science, Technology, and Philosophy of the Human Future*. Wiley-Blackwell, 2013.

[Pratt 1855] Parley Pratt. *Key to the Science of Theology*. F. D. Richards, 1855.

[Prisco 2012a] Giulio Prisco. The Turing Church of Transcendent Engineering. YouTube, 2012.
https://www.youtube.com/watch?v=dVup2TgYZAs

[Prisco 2012b] Giulio Prisco. Yes, I Am a Believer. *IEET*, 2012.
https://ieet.org/index.php/IEET2/more/prisco20120523

[Prisco 2015] Giulio Prisco. Can Mormonism save Western civilization from Submission? *The*

Transfigurist, 2015.
http://www.transfigurist.org/2015/07/can-mormonism-save-western-civilization.html

CHAPTER 5 - THE LIGHTS OF EASTERN SPIRITUALITY

On February 10, 2018, I gave a talk titled "Physics and the Indian Spiritual Tradition" [Prisco 2018] at the Ramakrishna Mission Institute of Culture (RMIC) in Kolkata, India. The abstract of the talk, pasted below with minor edits, can serve as an introduction for this chapter, and perhaps for the whole book.

I will develop two strands of thought, initially separate but eventually converging.

In the first strand, inspired by scientific and spiritual insights, I will outline some speculative theories of physical reality, proposed by leading philosophers and scientists, and argue that fundamental science is getting closer to traditional spiritual teachings.

In particular, Indian spiritual traditions, as formulated in the explanations and translations available to me, seem especially able to illuminate and guide research in fundamental physics, cosmology, biology, and the sciences of the brain and the mind.

A cosmic, divine Mind, embedded in the fabric of fundamental reality itself, and of which individual minds are but pale reflections, could shape the becoming of space, time, particles, fields, matter, energy, and life forms. The Mind could remember the memories of the universe, including the memories and life events of individual persons.

The interconnection of all things, the action of mind over matter, and different forms of afterlife, could be actual physical phenomena waiting for scientific explanations.

In the second strand, inspired by futurist thinking, I will argue that science and engineering will bring us closer to the cosmic Mind. In the words of Richard Bushman, a contemporary Mormon scholar, "the end point of engineering knowledge may be divine knowledge" [Howe 2012].

Empowered by divine knowledge, and guided by both spirituality and "can do" engineering, we will eventually meet the Mind, become cosmic engineers in the divine control room, and contribute to realizing the promises of spiritual traditions, including the promise of an afterlife.

This is, I believe, an ideal fusion of Eastern and Western thinking.

Buddhist Transhumanism In A Nutshell

Mike LaTorra, a long time transhumanist who is also an ordained Zen priest and the former abbot of the Zen Center of Las Cruces, New Mexico, has written a short, simple, and readable introduction to Buddhist transhumanism [LaTorra 2015].

The abstract reads:

> "The meeting of ancient Buddhism from Asia with modern orientation towards science and technology in the Western world has led to a burgeoning movement that combines these in new and innovative ways. Lacking much institutional structure, but with many shared goals among its adherents, this movement seeks to attain the traditional Buddhist goals of reducing suffering and realizing Awakening, but with the assistance of scientific knowledge and technological means."

I often try to educate myself about Buddhism and Buddhist transhumanism (or transhumanist Buddhism?), and Mike's article is very useful as a first step because it is simple and focused on the essentials of both. The article provides a clean and clear introduction to Buddhism for people already familiar with transhumanism, or the other way around.

An important parallel between Buddhism and transhumanism is that both emphasize practical philosophy over abstract metaphysics. At the same time, deep metaphysical concepts are there to be found in both Buddhism and transhumanism.

Buddhism asserts the doctrines of karma and rebirth. "Your actions now will affect your present lifetime and your subsequent afterlife, just as your actions previous to this birth affected your current life circumstances," says Mike. In related speculations, [Russian Cosmism] and derived visionary interpretations of contemporary transhumanism assert that future technologies could resurrect the dead.

The Noble Eightfold Path taught by the Buddha - right view, right resolve, right speech, right action, right livelihood, right effort, right mindfulness, and right meditation - is a guide to the "right" lifestyle and mental discipline that offer benefits to both individuals and their society.

Similarly, transhumanism emphasizes the potential of emerging futurist developments in biotechnology, neurotechnology, cognitive science, computer science, nanotechnology, and related disciplines, to make people "better than well" and able to function in better societies. In both cases, metaphysical concerns with eschatology and the ultimate nature of reality are confined to an inner esoteric core, not as evident as the outer exoteric front-end.

Reducing suffering is a key aspect of both Buddhism and transhumanism. While Buddhism suggests diluting the ego in a cosmic unity, and emphasizes meditation as a practical way to achieve enlightenment, transhumanism wants to change the world using advanced technologies.

To explain the difference, LaTorra cites an old Buddhist teaching aphorism that says "to walk more comfortably, it is better to cover one's feet than to try to cover the whole earth." By contrast, says LaTorra, many transhumanists would prefer to cover the earth in comfortable materials.

"And Buddhist transhumanists would use a combination of both, providing shoes for everyone while at the same time making large swaths of the earth into benign and comfortable regions where people could safely go barefoot."

It's important to note that Buddhism doesn't oppose using technology as one of many means to achieve enlightenment. There is "nothing in the teachings of the Buddha that forbids the inclusion of science and technology in Buddhist practice," says Mike.

The compatibility of Buddhism and technology was also emphasized by Robert Pirsig in his cult novel "*Zen and the Art of Motorcycle Maintenance*" [Pirsig 1974]:

> "The Buddha, the Godhead, resides quite as comfortably in the circuits of a digital computer or the gears of a cycle transmission as he does at the top of the mountain, or in the petals of a flower. To think otherwise is to demean the Buddha - which is to demean oneself."

The question is, once all suffering is eliminated by diluting the ego in meditation and unity with the whole of reality, is there anyone left to experience happiness? Mike is well aware of "the typical horrified reaction of many Westerners to this vision, which seems to imply annihilation."

In fact, reducing suffering doesn't necessarily mean increasing happiness. For example, a rock doesn't suffer, but doesn't experience happiness either. Many Westerners tend to think that in Nirvana, "the deathless state of perfect liberation" attained by those who reach enlightenment after a succession of earthly incarnations, they would be as happy as rocks.

Yet, for those who are ready, the Buddha "urges determined effort to put an end to wandering in samsara" and to reach Nirvana, "which transcends all planes of being," as explained by an American-born Buddhist monk cited in Mike's paper.

Mike explains that the Buddha did not teach annihilation: "He generally preferred to speak of the goal, the state of Nirvana, in terms of what it was not: not mortal, not suffering, etc. The implication of the Buddha's teaching, therefore, is that once all negatives are removed, the intrinsic positive would reveal itself."

I find that rather vague (I guess Mike would say that vagueness is not a bug but a feature), and I try to think of ways to reconcile Buddhism with cherishing the individual awareness that I wish to keep. My formulation of the core Buddhist message for Westerners would be something like:

Don't think of Nirvana yet - you'll cross that bridge when you get there. Try to live a right life, and advance with some little steps on the Karmic road to enlightenment. Then in your next existence you will have a bit more of a cosmic mind, and perhaps a bit less of an earthly mind. So in your following existence, and the next, and so forth... until you see the bridge to Nirvana, and then you will be ready for whatever comes next, which we probably couldn't even imagine now.

At the 2014 Conference of the [Mormon Transhumanist Association], Mike gave an intriguing outline of Buddhist cosmology [LaTorra 2014]. A few days after the conference, I had the pleasure to attend a Buddhist meditation session led by Mike, who designed the session for Western newcomers to Buddhism. I can't say that I achieved enlightenment (I guess that takes much more than one casual session), but I think I got part of the cosmic flavor of Buddhism, and I look forward to repeating the experience anytime.

"The Buddhist meditation techniques, as originally given and as extended over the millennia by Buddhist practitioners in different traditions, are based on a science of the mind designed for transforming the individual practitioner," says Mike, adding that there are many types of Buddhist meditation, some for a general purpose and some designed for specific situations.

Mike's article includes short profiles of people who, though not all define themselves as such, can be considered as Buddhist transhumanists. I found especially interesting the profile of Franklin Merrell-Wolff, a not very well known American mystic and a precursor of Buddhist transhumanism. Mike argues that Merrell-Wolff was the first to use the term "transhumanism" in the first edition of "*The Philosophy of Consciousness Without an Object*" [Merrell-Wolff 1983], written in 1939.

"It may be valid enough to assert that human consciousness qua human is always time conditioned, but that would amount merely to a partial definition of what is meant by human consciousness," said Merrell-Wolff. "In that case, the consciousness that is not time conditioned would be something that is transhuman or nonhuman." Merrell-Wolff added that it is in the power of man to transcend the limits of human consciousness, which seems a good summary of both Buddhism and transhumanism in a nutshell.

India Awakens

Nupur Munshi, a young Indian woman living in Kolkata, wants to find her sister Rumjhum Munshi, who passed away a few years ago. In her search for Rumjhum, which is illuminated by both science and the Indian spiritual tradition, Nupur found Turing Church online discussion groups and started to participate. She created a Facebook page called "[India Awakens]" to discuss our ideas with an Indian slant. India Awakens is mainly aimed at Indians but open to seekers from everywhere.

Nupur is a follower of the great Indian poet, Nobel laureate Rabindranath Tagore. "The question of the meaning of reality was the central subject of a fascinating dialogue between Einstein and Tagore," noted Nobel laureate Ilya Prigogine and Isabelle Stengers [Prigogine 1984]. "Curiously enough, the present evolution of science is running in the direction stated by the great Indian poet."

With the collaboration of a group of friends including Lincoln Cannon, Mike LaTorra and Kathy Wilson, Nupur and I decided to organize an India Awakens conference. Thanks to Nupur's efforts, the Ramakrishna Mission Institute of Culture (RMIC) in Kolkata accepted to host the conference in February 2017.

Unfortunately we weren't able to raise the money needed to bring all speakers to Kolkata. Instead, we hosted online conversations with the speakers in [a light, minimalist Virtual Reality (VR) space], and published the video proceedings of the online-only conference [Prisco 2017].

The conversations with Ralph Abraham, Amit Goswami, Sisir Roy, and Frank Tipler, are covered in Part 3. See also Ben Goertzel's video talk on his developing thoughts about a radically new scientific framework that he calls "euryphysics." [Ben's ideas] are not covered in this book, but I'm following the development of Ben's euryphysics with attention and great expectations.

Another speaker was Robert Geraci, a professor of religious studies at Manhattan College in New York, who covered religious dimensions of futurism and my work on Turing Church in [Geraci 2010, 2014].

In "A tale of two futures: Techno-eschatology in the US and India" [Geraci 2016], Robert shows that Western futurists and transhumanists have absorbed the apocalyptic eschatology of the religions through which they emerged. Indian religious eschatology is different, but it also has parallels with transhumanist thinking. Robert argues that Indian futurists tend to embrace the tradition, appropriating science and technology in their affirmation of the past, more than their Western counterparts.

"As machines grow to superhuman intelligence, humanity will upload consciousness into machine bodies and join the artificial intelligences in what Moravec calls the Mind Fire, a cosmic expansion of intelligence throughout the universe," explains Robert. Moravec's Mind Fire could be able to resurrect the dead: "Thanks to vast computation, even the dead shall rise and walk again in this digital wonderland."

Here's how Moravec, one of the most visionary contemporary futurists, puts it [Moravec 1998]:

> "Minds intermediate between Sherlock Holmes and God will process clues in solar-

system quantities to deduce and recreate the most microscopic details of preceding eras: Entire world histories, with all their living, feeling inhabitants, will be resurrected in cyberspace."

In the conversation with Robert [Prisco 2016], we discussed Robert's exploration of religion, science, and technology in contemporary India, and my ideas on the prospect of "Akashic Engineering" as a fusion of East and West, science and religion.

I am persuaded that the idea of [Akashic Engineering], a generic name for future technologies able to exploit the deep structure of physical reality to do "magic" in the sense of Clarke's Third Law and even resurrect the dead, could be a much needed cultural fusion of East and West: Eastern ethereal spirituality and openness to holistic models of reality on the one hand, and the can-do engineering spirit of Western technology on the other hand.

How to "read the Akashic records" and bring the dead back is way beyond the reach of our science at this moment, let alone technology. But current physics does offer hints that magic technologies could be possible. Of course, the idea is not new: [Nikolai Fedorov] has been there, among many others, including science fiction writers like [Arthur Clarke and Stephen Baxter]. According to Ralph Abraham and Sisir Roy, the idea of [Akashic Engineering] could find in the East, and in particular in India, more fertile ground than in the West.

I used to dislike the "Akashic" terminology for its associations with the occult, spiritism, and all that, but then I realized that the core concept of a permanent cosmic memory is equivalent to my favorite scientific speculations on future science and technologies able to scan the past and copy the dead to the future.

If the Akashic records exist, future science will permit reading them. Conversely, if future technology will permit scanning the past at high resolution, then there is a cosmic memory. We don't necessarily have to call the cosmic memory "Akashic records" (there are equivalent terms that sound more scientific), but doing so permits establishing links to ancient traditions and bridges to spiritual seekers, which in my opinion is good.

Therefore, following Abraham and Roy, I honor the ancient Akashic insights and use the term "Akashic physics" for the yet unknown physical theories upon which future resurrection technologies could be based.

Many current scientific ideas can be described in Akashic terms. For example, if there are micro-wormholes connecting every spacetime pixel to every other spacetime pixel as imagined by [Arthur Clarke and Stephen Baxter], then we could read the (Akashic) records of other places and times. If we think of [decoherence] processes scattering apparently lost local information into the universe at large, then the traces left could be called Akashic records.

In Everett's interpretation of [quantum mechanics], the collapse of the wave-function is local to the single branch of the multiverse that our senses perceive, and the apparently lost information is scattered to other branches. Therefore, information is preserved in Everett's multiverse, which is a possible stage for Akashic physics.

Other times are just special cases of other universes [Deutsch 1997]. Therefore, the apparently lost information - including the life events, memories, thoughts, and feelings of everyone who ever lived - are out there in the Akashic multiverse, and future scientists could search for - and find - ways to retrieve it.

These ideas don't prove that Akashic Engineering is feasible, but they do show that modern physics permits suspending disbelief and allowing ourselves to contemplate visions of hope and happiness, without abandoning the scientific worldview. The prospect of Akashic Engineering could offer all the benefits of traditional religion, first and foremost hope in personal resurrection.

Of course it is overwhelmingly likely that future scientists could find our first conceptual explorations of Akashic Engineering very incomplete, imprecise, and naive. But, though we can't see the road ahead clearly, we see that it leads to an enchanted world. Robert Geraci has written of virtual worlds as a means to provide the enchantment that the real world seems to have lost [Geraci 2014]. However, I am more interested in the re-enchantment of the real world.

To give Robert plausible deniability and protect his academic credibility from accusations of associating with lunatics like me, I must say that Robert is interested in these things from the detached perspective of a scholar, but he isn't a believer. "I'm agnostic leaning towards 'atheist' on such projects," he told me. "I don't believe in the Akashic records and I'm skeptical about resurrecting our ancestors."

In his new book on Indian transhumanism [Geraci 2018], Robert argues that a new, uniquely Indian version of transhumanism is developing:

> "As Indians adopt transhumanism, they are translating it to Indian cultural and religious life, producing shifts in Western transhumanist discourses through the unique contributions of their traditional religious practices and ideas... In the end, Indian transhumanism will not map precisely onto Western transhumanism."

As mentioned earlier in this chapter, most Westerners find it difficult to relate to Eastern ideas of personal consciousness losing its individuality after death and diluting in cosmic consciousness. Most Westerners, including me, want to come back, as a person.

But here's what Swami Vivekananda had to say on the fate of the self after death, in reply to this typical reaction of Westerners [Nikhilananda 1989]:

> "One day a drop of water fell into the vast ocean. Finding itself there, it began to weep and complain, just as you are doing. The giant ocean laughed at the drop of water. 'Why do you weep?' it asked. 'I do not understand. When you join me, you join all your brothers and sisters, the other drops of water of which I am made. You become the ocean itself. If you wish to leave me you have only to rise up on a sunbeam into the clouds. From there you can descend again, little drop of water, a blessing and a benediction to the thirsty earth.'"

This idea of [losing one's individuality and being absorbed into the eternal unity of consciousness after death], but with the possibility to come back in some sense, is shared by top physicists today.

As he speaks of his spiritual beliefs, Abhay Ashtekar "recasts his worldview in terms of physics, using the same language of excitations in quantum fields that he uses to describe his theory of loop quantum gravity," science writer Zeeya Merali reports [Merali 2017]. "'My viewpoint is basically that there is a field of consciousness,' says Ashtekar.

> "Individual human consciousness exists as agitations in this ocean of communal consciousness - just as photons are excitations of the electromagnetic field and his hypo-

thetical loops are energetic nuggets of spacetime."

This is, I think, a better analogy than Vivekananda's drops of water in the oceans. It can be argued that elementary particles, which are excitations in quantum fields, [still exist in a more diffuse sense] when they are not manifested by observation.

Andrei Linde tells Merali that "the duality between you and the universe is like a part of the whole package."

> "So maybe when you die, you become part of the whole, and then maybe you get separated again, in a different way."

It's worth noting that this is very similar to the thoughts of Vivekananda on cosmic consciousness and the fate of the self after death, quoted above.

Turing Church In A Nutshell For India Awakens

In 2014 Nupur Munshi asked me to write a short Turing Church introduction for India Awakens. Here it is, with minor edits:

First, I must admit to having only a casual knowledge of Indian and Eastern thinking, so this is the beginning of a learning journey, and I am sure I will learn a lot from my new friends in the India Awakens group.

[Turing Church is built around this shared cosmic vision]:

- We will go to the stars and find Gods, build Gods, become Gods, and resurrect the dead from the past with advanced science, space-time engineering and "time magic."
- God is emerging from the community of advanced forms of life and civilizations in the universe, and able to influence space-time events anywhere, anytime, including here and now.
- God elevates love and compassion to the status of fundamental forces, key drivers for the evolution of the universe.

Science and technology are key parts of the Turing Church vision. On the contrary (apparently), Eastern thinking emphasizes a whole range of spiritual concepts, from Yoga to reincarnation through the power of special enlightened non-ordinary states of consciousness over matter, which seem difficult to reconcile with the scientific framework of Western thinking.

I define nature as all that exists, so that everything is part of nature by definition. Similarly, defining science as the study of nature, nothing is in-principle beyond scientific investigation.

But this most emphatically does NOT mean that today's science has all the answers, nor that science will have all the answers at any given moment. It just means that science will uncover more and more of the mysteries of the universe, perhaps in a never-ending journey. Future generations, perhaps helped by superintelligent thinking machines and alien civilizations, will know much more than us.

Take for example faster than light (FTL) travel or time travel. These ideas are difficult to reconcile with the current scientific framework. But I know that today's science doesn't have all the answers, so I prefer to remain open-minded and consider FTL and time travel as legitimate scientific issues. The ultra-rationalist "bureaucrats of science" are quick to dismiss speculative scientific ideas as "pseudo-science," but it's often evident that they don't know as much science as they believe.

Similarly, I consider psychic phenomena such as telepathy and precognition, and their subtler counterparts in Eastern thinking, as parts of reality that are beyond the power of current science, but not necessarily beyond the power of future science.

It's often the case that parts of reality that seem totally unrelated at first glance are eventually understood as different aspects of one and the same deeper reality. For example, the magnetic compass and visible light seemed unrelated to our ancestors, but today they are both understood as aspects of the physics of electromagnetic fields.

I think future science may reveal deep connections between Western and Eastern modes of thought about reality.

For example, our brains could be mere "receivers" for the true self, the "atman," which acts upon the physical world via what we perceive as quantum or chaotic randomness. If this is the case, future science may uncover the physical phenomena involved and build suitable alternative receivers to bring back the dead from the past.

We Are All The Same Person: Open Individualism

We all, in both the West and the East, dedicate a lot of effort to finding ways to cope with the idea of death.

Most believers in traditional Western religions imagine resurrection in an afterlife, where they will be forever reunited with loved ones. Most believers in traditional Eastern religions and spiritual traditions think that, while an otherworldly realm beyond physical reality may eventually be attained, most people go through a long string of lives here on Earth (reincarnation).

Eastern reincarnation seems less appealing than Western resurrection, because the memory of past lives is lost. Also, we don't like the idea of coming back without our loved ones. But mental discipline can perhaps bring back at least some memories of past lives, and perhaps kindred souls "travel together" through time in groups, and find each other, unknowingly, life after life.

I think future science will permit achieving resurrection and/or reincarnation as engineering projects. Our descendants will move out there among the stars and beyond, join the community of Gods in the universe, and contribute to the development of unimaginably powerful "time magic" technologies. They will find ways to reach back into their past (our present), make ultra-high resolution scans and snapshots of our minds, and copy us to their present (our future) with our past memories (this would be similar to the Western concept of resurrection) or without (this would be similar to the Eastern concept of reincarnation).

Please don't ask me how: I don't know, and nobody knows. I guess time magic is probably beyond us like Einstein is beyond a mouse, and developing it will take thousands of years of research and development to our descendants.

But what if we don't really need any of that?

What if reincarnation is trivially true in some meaningful and psychologically acceptable or even appealing sense?

Eastern philosophies and spiritual traditions insist that "all is one" - the boundaries between different parts of the world that we perceive, including the all-important boundary between self and other, are permeable and ultimately an illusion conjured up by our special ways to interpret the world.

It's undeniable that the concept of self has important evolutionary advantages: If your ancestor had not perceived a very clear and very important distinction between himself and a predator, he wouldn't have run fast enough to escape the predator and reproduce.

But perhaps, behind the veil of perception and interpretation, consciousness is one: Your ancestor and the predator were really one, from a fundamental perspective.

Also Western mystics and thinkers throughout the ages have had the powerful intuition that everything in the universe is deeply connected to everything else to the point that, in a fundamental sense, everything is one. Daniel Kolak formulated, within contemporary Western philosophy, the idea that we are all the same person in a fundamental sense.

In his book "*I Am You*" [Kolak 2004], Kolak proposes the metaphysics (and practical philosophy) of open individualism. Every consciousness is fundamentally the same, and we are all the same person. Kolak explains:

> "The central thesis of I Am You - that we are all the same person - is apt to strike many readers as obviously false or even absurd. How could you be me and Hitler and Gandhi and Jesus and Buddha and Greta Garbo and everybody else in the past, present and future? In this book I explain how this is possible. Moreover, I show that this is the best explanation of who we are for a variety of reasons, not the least of which is that it provides the metaphysical foundations for global ethics."

To help the reader imagine a world identical to ours where every consciousness is the same, Kolak describes a model universe where every person is represented by a tower composed of stacked boxes. Boxes are ordered in time, and contain snapshots of instantaneous mental states, with perceptions, thoughts, memories, and expectations for the future. A single consciousness roams the stacks, focusing on one box at a time. When focused on a box, consciousness experiences all (and only) its contents, and the resulting subjective experience is identical to being a particular person (tower) at a particular time (box).

Kolak's model universe is immediately understandable to anyone familiar with how computers work: A single program (think for example of Word) can work with different documents (think of different Word documents open on your desktop), apparently in parallel, but really one at the time. According to Kolak, you should think of yourself not as one of the documents, but as the program that is handling them all. When a document is closed, the consciousness program continues to work on other documents.

After showing that his model universe is plausible and consistent (and subjectively indistinguishable from the actual reality that we perceive), Kolak tries to persuade the readers that the one-consciousness model, open individualism, is a better way of looking at the world, with fascinating arguments ranging from philosophy to fundamental physics.

It's worth noting that a similar model universe was previously proposed by [Fred Hoyle] in his science fiction novel "*October the First is Too Late*" [Hoyle 1966] and [Julian Barbour] in "*The End of Time*" [Barbour 2000]. Hoyle and Barbour, who respectively use the terms "pigeon holes" and "time capsules" for Kolak's boxes, emphasize that the model also explains why time seems to flow. "John Bell also formulated the idea of time capsules (without giving them any name) quite clearly long before me," adds Barbour.

I like open individualism because it explores and formalizes intuitions that I often had. Consciousness shouldn't be thought of as a property of thinkers, but as a property of thinking. My favorite metaphor, essentially similar to Kolak's, is a large room with many windows. Consciousness is the observer in the room, and experiences different individual reality streams looking from different windows.

For example, one window could look at a playground for children, and another at a parking lot. The two perception streams are very different, but the consciousness that perceives them is one. Consciousness is the observer, and the views from different windows are different lives.

What happens when the blinds of a window go down? You continue to observe reality from the other windows. What happens when a person dies? Consciousness continues to observe reality from other eyes. What happens after you die? You continue to live, as another person - actually, you continue to live as every other person. You continue to live a myriad of parallel lives, forever and ever. Your lives are not conscious of each other, but are equally yours in a fundamental sense.

There is [a Facebook group for discussing open individualism]. Once, a member of the group died. The other members discussed the best ways to honor him, and the consensus was that everyone should try to live a good and happy life. If you are satisfied and happy, then he is satisfied and happy, because he continues to live as you. And me. And everyone else.

I don't think open individualism can be "demonstrated," because accepting its premises is largely a matter of personal choice (more about that to follow). At the same time, modern physics gives a certain plausibility, sort of, to the idea that consciousness is One.

In particular, [quantum entanglement seems to indicate] that all observers are really one and the same.

This concept can be formulated without invoking complicated physics: The essence of consciousness, the bare feeling of existence expressed by "I am," is the same for everyone. I first encountered this intriguing thought in Rudy Rucker's *Infinity and the Mind*" [Rucker 2005].

"I contend that the sum total of the individual consciousness is the bare feeling of existence, expressed by the primal utterance, I am," says Rucker. "Anything else is either hardware or software, and can be changed or dispensed with. Only the single thought I am ties me to the person I was twenty years ago."

> "What conclusion might one draw from the fact that your essential consciousness and my essential consciousness are expressed in the same words? Perhaps it is reasonable to suppose that there really is only one consciousness, that individual humans are simply disparate faces of what the classical mystic tradition calls the One."

Back to personal choice, the question isn't who you will be after death, but who you want to be. If you identify with your current body, memories, and thoughts (a single box in Kolak's model universe), then open individualism doesn't offer a new life waiting for you after death.

But if you choose to identify as a person living in the early 21st century who loves children and little dogs and science fiction and metaphysics, or just a crew member of Spaceship Earth en-route toward unknown cosmic futures, then there is a wide range of towers and boxes waiting for you. Isn't it obviously, trivially true that you will live again?

I tend to find open individualism persuasive. Following Kolak I am persuaded that, even if no higher power is going to resurrect or reincarnate me, other instances of me will live again, who won't remember having been me. But perhaps they will be open individualists, find me in some old Facebook archeology records of the 21st century, and accept me as one of their past selves.

Of course, I would prefer being resurrected with all my thoughts, feelings, and memories, together with my loved ones. Since I am persuaded that future science and technology will permit resurrecting the dead, I am hopeful. But resurrection science can only be developed in the far future, by our mind children who will colonize the universe.

Back to Earth, here and now, open individualism as a practical philosophy can make an important positive difference in our lives. If you think that other people are you, you will not harm them, because you would be harming yourself. On the contrary, you will be kind and compassionate to others - to all other instances of you.

I can see that suspending disbelief in open individualism has a positive impact on my attitude and behavior toward others, which is the really important thing. Open individualists cherish the future, because the future is the place where they will continue to live after death, and strive to create a better world for everyone.

Mixing Hinduism And Christianity, Reincarnation And Resurrection

A preliminary version of the chapter "Christianity and Transhumanism are much closer than you think" provoked interesting discussions on how Eastern ideas about reincarnation and Christian ideas about resurrection could co-exist.

Christianity affirms that after death we will be resurrected to a new life in a new body and a new world created by God, where we will be forever reunited with our loved ones. The new body, immortal and incorruptible like the resurrected body of Jesus, will be a gift of God's grace and love. The resurrection of Jesus, and the promise that God will similarly resurrect us in the new world, are central concepts of Christianity.

The new body and the new world are likely to be deeply different from the present body and the present world. In particular, the new body will be "a transformed body, a body whose material, created from the old material, will have new properties," according to Christian theologian N. T. Wright [Wright 2008].

Hinduism affirms the idea of reincarnation, life after life. As noted earlier in this chapter reincarnation is different from, and stands in a certain tension with, the Christian idea of resurrection. But perhaps the two ideas could be merged somehow?

In an email discussion, Nupur Munshi raised an interesting question: What if both reincarnation and resurrection happen? If a soul is reincarnated many times, as Hinduists believe, and then resurrected as Christians believe, which one of the reincarnation copies gets resurrected? In Nupur's words:

> "Person A reincarnates into person B (another biological body, without the memories of the past life). Then A and B are resurrected in a new world in new bodies, each with the memories of the past life. Does this mean that, when B confronts A in the new world, she is actually confronting her past self?"

My first reaction was warning that mixing Hinduism and Christianity is not guaranteed to work. But I added: Assuming both the Hinduist ideas of reincarnation and the Christian ideas of resurrection, A and B are the same person in one sense and different persons in another sense. After resurrection, I guess there could be two persons who are also the same. Two persons can be the same and different at the same time (think of yourself today and when you were ten years old).

I continued to think about the problem overnight, but when I logged on in the morning to announce a tentative "solution" I found that Mike LaTorra had beaten me to the finish line. Mike said:

> "I would like to suggest another possibility for resolving the identity question with regard to A and B.
>
> Every apparent being imagines itself to be singular, but is actually a composite. Many components comprise each apparent one. We could envision these as layers or concentric shells.
>
> As a model, consider the atom. It consists of a nucleus surrounded by shells (or clouds) of electrons. Two atoms can combine into one molecule by sharing, or by exchanging, electrons.

In spiritual history, on some occasions, apparently separate individuals have combined their spiritual components while retaining separate physical bodies. We can find instances of this in the spiritual history of Asia and in the Middle East. This extraordinary event happened in the case of the great 19th century Hindu Guru Ramakrishna and his devotee, the great Swami Vivekananda. It also happened in the more distant past as recorded in the Old Testament of the Bible, where the great prophet Elijah was asked by his devoted follower Elisha for 'a double portion' of his master's blessing.

We can also look at Tibetan Buddhism, where there is a long tradition of tracing the reincarnations of top Lamas. In the case of some, there was not the usual one-to-one correspondence between a previous lifetime and subsequent ones. In the case of Jomgon Kongtrul, the great master reincarnated into five new bodies, each of which expressed only a portion of his extraordinary spiritual gifts.

Most fundamentally, or ultimately, all incarnations of any being or sequence of beings is only a partial expression of the One, the supreme Atman, the perfect Divine.

As my guru, Avatar Adi Da Samraj put it somewhat humorously, 'No matter how many people are in the room, there is only one Person.'"

Then I tried to formulate the "solution" in terms compatible with Christian doctrine. I suggested that the key is the Christian concept of transformed and enhanced new post-resurrection body in the new world, "a body whose material, created from the old material, will have new properties."

We are promised that the new body will be "glorified," immortal and incorruptible, and we can imagine that it has even stranger properties. In particular, we can imagine a Body (capital B) formed by many bodies (lowercase b) each hosting an individual consciousness, but with the option to merge individual consciousness streams into a group mind.

This seems an ideal Body to host separate reincarnation copies that share the same inner self (Atman) in the new world: A and B can continue to be one person and two persons at the same time.

Things become even more interesting if, as I suspect at times, we all share one and the same eternal self (open individualism).

I think reincarnation could happen naturally in the physical universe. Perhaps everything that ever happens, including our thoughts and memories, is stored in permanent "Akashic records," a cosmic memory field hidden in yet unknown aspects of reality, and the Akashic information corresponding to the eternal self could find "spontaneously" its way into new bodies.

I am also persuaded that future science will permit achieving resurrection as an engineering project. Our descendants will find ways to reach back into their past (our present) - or, alternatively, read the information in the Akashic records - and copy us to their present (our future). I think that's how God's promise of resurrection in a new body and a new world, in which Christians believe, will be achieved - by our descendants in the far future, acting on God's behalf.

If both reincarnation and resurrection happen, our eternal self could occupy a multiple-Body after resurrection, with room for all reincarnation copies. This seems like an interesting way to reconcile Christianity and Hinduism.

What About Islam?

Islam should have a dedicated chapter, or book, but I am still too ignorant of Islamic thinking, so I can only offer some vague thoughts at this moment.

Islam is all over the news, often bad news. But here I am setting aside current affairs and wondering about the compatibility of cosmist transhumanism and Islam, and possible parallels between our ideas and the teachings of the Prophet Muhammad (PBUH).

In 1997 on the Extropians mailing list, [Max More and Nick Bostrom discussed] the possibility of "Christian Transhumanism, Islamic Transhumanism, and (not too far from their current beliefs) Mormon Transhumanism."

Twenty years later, the [Mormon Transhumanist Association] (MTA) has been in existence for more than a decade, and the [Christian Transhumanist Association] (CTA) for a few years. The question comes to mind of whether there could ever be an Islamic Transhumanist Association (ITA).

After some preliminary reading, my answer is: Not soon, but perhaps one day - and Islamic Transhumanism could be a very powerful force for good.

I am also ignorant of Islamic culture and society, but I can see that Islam is young and strong [Prisco 2015]. I interpret the excesses of today's Islamic fundamentalism as a temporary destructive phase of a young and fast-rising civilization.

Muslims are the world's fastest-growing religious group, expected to increase to more than 30 percent of the global population by 2060. This, and the firm strength of Muslims' faith, indicates that Islam could be a dominant cultural force for centuries to come.

The CTA and the MTA have started a journey that could lead to new formulations of Christianity able to offer peaceful hope and happiness fully compatible with science, and able to power our expansion to the stars to become cosmic engineers in God's control room.

Could an Islamic Transhumanist Association (ITA) join our journey? I don't know enough to tell, but one thing seems clear: The possibility of Islamic transhumanism depends on whether parts of the Quran (and the Hadith) can be plausibly interpreted in ways that suggest transhumanist ideas.

I started reading the Quran, but I am still unable to appreciate and interpret it. One reason can be that I don't speak Arabic, and the Quran is very difficult to translate. Many authors warn that Westerners who don't speak Arabic find it difficult to appreciate the Quran in translation, without the sheer beauty of the Arabic text and its multiple shades of meaning. I guess they are right.

One defining feature of the Quran is "the otherworldly quality it exhibits in its original Arabic version," notes Nidhal Guessoum in *"Islam's Quantum Question"* [Guessoum 2011], warning that the gap in quality which separates the Arabic Quran from any and all translations is huge.

Guessoum explains that the Quran is diverse and multiple in the meanings it presents, and a variety of interpretations can be produced from the text. *"Islam's Quantum Question"* is full of quotes from the Quran that support the essential compatibility between Islam and modern science. The author provides readable explanations of modern science itself, including genetics, quantum physics and cosmology.

Transhumanism is not mentioned explicitly, but I have the impression that some passages in the Quran could be interpreted in ways that suggest transhumanist ideas. For example, we are God's "viceregents" on earth (Q 2:30, Q 6:165) - and, plausibly, in the rest of the universe. Also, Q 45:13:

> "And He has made subservient to you whatever is in the heavens and whatever is in the earth, all from Himself; surely in this are signs for people who reflect."

Other translations use the even stronger words "subjected to you." To me, this passage says that the whole physical universe, including the material substrate of life, is ours to command and control. This is the essence of transhumanism.

Guessoum refers to the Islamic viewpoint as "an 'ultra-anthropic principle,' for it puts humans squarely at the centre of its world view: not only is man the purpose of the whole creation, everything has been created and made 'subservient' (musakhkhar) to him!"

Guessoum is a big fan of "*The Anthropic Cosmological Principle*" [Barrow 1986], by John Barrow and Frank Tipler. The last chapter of that book, a wild ride along the future of intelligent life in the universe, ends with visions of intelligence transcending biology and acquiring total control of the universe.

> "At the instant the Omega Point is reached, life will have gained control of all matter and forces... and will have stored an infinite amount of information, including all bits of knowledge which it is logically possible to know."

This is religious transhumanism at its visionary best. Guessoum is a scientist but also a Muslim, which indicates that at least some Muslims are prepared to at least consider transhumanist ideas. This is a good starting point.

"*The Study Quran*" [Nasr 2015], edited by Seyyed Hossein Nasr, a leading Islamic scholar whose work is extensively covered by Guessoum, is a very useful resource for Westerners who want to try and understand the Quran.

Guessoum covers the works of many contemporary Islamic thinkers on science and Islam, including those who, like Nobel laureate Abdus Salam, "find nothing seriously wrong with western science."

Surprisingly, I find Nasr's "Islamic Science" program for the re-sacralization of science especially intriguing. Nasr's ideas, inspired by the Sufi mystical tradition [Nicholson 2002] and reminiscent of Eastern thinking, are outlined in Nasr's 1981 Gifford Lectures, published as "*Knowledge and the Sacred*" [Nasr 1989].

Like all foundational religious texts, the Quran is open to interpretation. But cherry-picking can support too many different viewpoints, and can't replace a real study of the spirit and harmony of the whole.

In his essay "Islam - God's Deputy: Islam and Transhumanism," published in "*Transhumanism and the Body*" [Mercer 2014], Hamid Mavani emphasizes the tension between Islam and the transhumanist prospect of radical life extension, which should be "coupled with spiritual enhancement and progress" to be appealing to Muslims. My reading of Mavani's essay is that establishing a credible Islamic transhumanism would be challenging, though not impossible.

However, I have also the impression that, while "wet" transhumanist technologies like genetic engineering and radical life extension seem to stand in opposition to Islam at this moment, the cosmist interpretation and formulation of transhumanism that I am defending in this book could be more appealing to Muslims.

Notes

[a Facebook group for discussing open individualism] The "I Am You: Discussion on Open Individualism" Facebook group:
https://www.facebook.com/groups/299406397622/

[Akashic Engineering] See "The quest for Akashic physics and engineering."

[a light, minimalist Virtual Reality (VR) space] Immersive Terf, by 3DICC. I wish to thank 3DICC for allowing me to use Terf, and highly recommend Terf. 3DICC website:
https://www.3dicc.com/

[Arthur Clarke and Stephen Baxter] See "The interplay of science fiction, science, and religion."

[Ben's ideas] See Ben's "euryphysics" website:
http://eurycosm.blogspot.com/

[Christian Transhumanist Association] See "Christianity and transhumanism are much closer than you think."

[decoherence] See "Exotic space, mysterious time, magic quantum."

[Fred Hoyle] See "A for Almighty."

[India Awakens] The "India Awakens" Facebook page:
https://www.facebook.com/www.nupurmunshi/

[Julian Barbour] See "Exotic space, mysterious time, magic quantum."

[losing one's individuality and being absorbed into the eternal unity of consciousness after death] It's interesting to compare Vivekananda's quote to other views. Does personality survive in the ultimate union with God? "If personality means a conscious existence distinct, though not separate, from God, the majority of advanced Muslim mystics say 'No!,'" notes Reynold Nicholson in *The Mystics of Islam*" [Nicholson 2002]. "As the rain-drop absorbed in the ocean is not annihilated but ceases to exist individually, so the disembodied soul becomes indistinguishable from the universal Deity." Vivekananda's quote is more open to the possibility of coming back as an individual.

[Max More and Nick Bostrom discussed] See "Transhumanism."

[Mormon Transhumanist Association] See "Man will become like God, say Mormons and transhumanists."

[Nikolai Fedorov] See "Knocking on Heaven's door."

[quantum entanglement seems to indicate] See "Exotic space, mysterious time, magic quantum."

[quantum mechanics] See "Exotic space, mysterious time, magic quantum."

[Russian Cosmism] See "Knocking on Heaven's door."

[still exist in a more diffuse sense] See "In the beginning was the field."

[Turing Church is built around this shared cosmic vision] See "Turing Church." The possibility of a pre-existing God, the possibility of God-like awareness and superintelligence in the bare fabric of fundamental reality (e.g. quantum fields), the [simulation hypothesis], and other ideas that are not included in this short list of bullet points, are covered later in this book.

References

[Barbour 2000] Julian Barbour. *The End of Time: The Next Revolution in Physics*. Oxford University Press, 2000.

[Barrow 1986] John Barrow, Frank Tipler. *The Anthropic Cosmological Principle*. Oxford University Press, 1986.

[Deutsch 1997] David Deutsch. *The Fabric of Reality*. Viking Press, 1997.

[Geraci 2010] Robert Geraci. *Apocalyptic AI: Visions of Heaven in Robotics, Artificial Intelligence, and Virtual Reality*. Oxford University Press, 2010.

[Geraci 2014] Robert Geraci. *Virtually Sacred: Myth and Meaning in World of Warcraft and Second Life*. Oxford University Press, 2014.

[Geraci 2016] Robert Geraci. A tale of two futures: Techno-eschatology in the US and India. *Social Compass*, 2016.

[Geraci 2018] Robert Geraci. *Temples of Modernity: Nationalism, Hinduism, and Transhumanism in South Indian Science*. Lexington Books, 2018.

[Guessoum 2011] Nidhal Guessoum. *Islam's Quantum Question: Reconciling Muslim Tradition and Modern Science*. I.B.Tauris, 2011.

[Howe 2012] Scott Howe and Richard Bushman (Eds.). *Parallels and Convergences: Mormon Thought and Engineering Vision*. Greg Kofford Books, 2012.

[Hoyle 1966] Fred Hoyle. *October the First is Too Late*. William Heinemann, 1966.

[Kolak 2004] Daniel Kolak. *I Am You: The Metaphysical Foundations for Global Ethics*. Springer, 2004.

[LaTorra 2014] Michael LaTorra. Where Is Heaven? An Examination of Multiple-World Models of the Cosmos and Beyond. YouTube, 2014. https://www.youtube.com/watch?v=7aZqtKeLIqI

[LaTorra 2015] Michael LaTorra. What Is Buddhist Transhumanism? *Theology and Science*, 2015.

[Merali 2017] Zeeya Merali. *A Big Bang in a Little Room: The Quest to Create New Universes*. Basic Books, 2017.

[Mercer 2014] by Calvin Mercer, Derek Maher (Eds.). *Transhumanism and the Body: The World Religions Speak*. Palgrave Macmillan, 2014.

[Merrell-Wolff 1983] Franklin Merrell-Wolff. *The Philosophy of Consciousness Without an Object*. Julian Press, 1983.

[Moravec 1998] Hans Moravec. *Robot: Mere Machine to Transcendent Mind*. Oxford University Press, 1998.

[Nasr 1989] Seyyed Hossein Nasr. *Knowledge and the Sacred*. State University of New York Press, 1989.

[Nasr 2015] Seyyed Hossein Nasr (Ed.). *The Study Quran: A New Translation and Commentary*.

HarperOne, 2015.

[Nicholson 2002] Reynold Nicholson. *The Mystics of Islam* (first published in 1914). World Wisdom, 2002.

[Nikhilananda 1989] Swami Nikhilananda. *Vivekananda: A Biography*. Ramakrishna Vivekananda Center, 1989.

[Pirsig 1974] Robert Pirsig. *Zen and the Art of Motorcycle Maintenance*. William Morrow and Company, 1974.

[Prigogine 1984] Ilya Prigogine, Isabelle Stengers. *Order out of Chaos: Man's new dialogue with nature*. Bantam Books, 1984.

[Prisco 2015] Giulio Prisco. Can Mormonism save Western civilization from Submission? *The Transfigurist*, 2015.
http://www.transfigurist.org/2015/07/can-mormonism-save-western-civilization.html

[Prisco 2016] Giulio Prisco. Q/A with Robert Geraci. YouTube, 2016.
https://www.youtube.com/watch?v=BQwCT0Gln1k

[Prisco 2017] Giulio Prisco. India Awakens Conference: Video proceedings. *Turing Church*, 2017.
https://turingchurch.net/india-awakens-conference-video-proceedings-1c7bab279d5c

[Prisco 2018] Physics and the Indian Spiritual Tradition. YouTube, 2018.
https://www.youtube.com/watch?v=ygdiv2MIlGI

[Rucker 2005] Rudy Rucker. *Infinity and the Mind: The Science and Philosophy of the Infinite*. Princeton University Press, 2005.

[Wright 2008] N. T. Wright. *Surprised by Hope: Rethinking Heaven, the Resurrection, and the Mission of the Church*. HarperOne, 2008.

CHAPTER 6 - AGNOSTICS, POSSIBILIANS, AND MYSTERIANS

Here I cover the ideas of five thinkers that I admire a lot: Visionary agnostics Olaf Stapledon, Samuel Alexander and Carl Sagan, possibilian Arthur Clarke, and mysterian Martin Gardner.

Agnostics range from borderline atheists like Sagan to borderline believers. Mysterians are skeptical of organized religions but believe fundamental reality includes transcendent aspects that science will be unable to understand for a very long time, perhaps forever. According to Gardner, God "is somehow responsible for our universe and capable of providing, how I have no inkling, an afterlife."

Possibilians operate in a middle, exploratory ground between religion and atheism first defined by neuroscientist David Eagleman, who argues that "our ignorance of the cosmos is too vast to commit to atheism, and yet we know too much to commit to a particular religion" [Wilson 2009]. Eagleman adds:

> "But with Possibilianism I'm hoping to define a new position - one that emphasizes the exploration of new, unconsidered possibilities. Possibilianism is comfortable holding multiple ideas in mind; it is not interested in committing to any particular story."

This makes a lot of sense to me. Our universe is a very big place with lots of undiscovered and unimagined "things in heaven and earth," which science will uncover someday, and perhaps in this mysterious and beautiful complexity there is room for the old promises of religion.

Star Maker: The Cosmic Theology Of Olaf Stapledon

"Arthur C. Clarke - and through Clarke, Olaf Stapledon - sent me on a wild search through philosophy, looking for similar insights and experiences," said science fiction writer Greg Bear in the preface to the collection "*The Wind from a Burning Woman*" [Bear 1983]. He added:

"I've usually been disappointed; Stapledon is unique."

When I read these words a quarter of a century ago I was only vaguely aware of Olaf Stapledon. Then I embarked on a lifelong journey in Stapledon's universe.

In 1948 Stapledon gave a talk titled "Interplanetary Man?" [Stapledon 1948] at the British Interplanetary Society, organized by Arthur Clarke.

Our conception of time itself "is now turning out to be very incoherent and superficial," said Stapledon. "Perhaps (who can say) from the point of view of eternity the end of the cosmos is also its source and its temporal beginning."

"Perhaps the ultimate flower is also the primal seed from which all sprang. Perhaps the final result of the cosmical process is the attainment of full cosmical consciousness, and yet (in some very queer way) what is attained in the end is also, from another point of view, the origin of all things. So to speak, God, who created all things in the beginning, is himself created by all things in the end."

The passage above is one of the best formulations of a concept that can be outlined as: God could emerge asymptotically from the universe and come to full being, omnipotence, and benevolence at the end of time. But once God exists at the end of time, at an unattainable distance in the future ([Fred Hoyle]), God is present and acts in the universe at all earlier times, and therefore is the omnipotent and benevolent God of all times.

These entangled concepts of time and causation are beyond current physics and language, and can't be formulated more precisely at this moment. Perhaps the physics of theology has something to do with quantum effects and self-consistent causal loops.

Similar or at least related concepts of God and time have been formulated by leading Christian theologians.

The "divine reality, according to Tipler, does not come into being only at the omega but is to be thought of as free from all the restrictions of time at the omega," said German theologian Wolfhart Pannenberg in "*Systematic Theology*" [Pannenberg 1994] (Vol. 2) referring to [Frank Tipler's Omega Point scenario]. "Therefore, in terms of the eschatological future, this divine reality is present at each phase of the cosmic process, and hence as already the creative origin of the universe at the beginning of its course."

In "*Theology in the Context of Science*" [Polkinghorne 2010] and other works, theoretical physicist and theologian John Polkinghorne elaborates on the idea that God is both beyond-time, seeing the "block universe" of the totality of spacetime from a high vantage point, and in-time, directing and participating in the temporal evolution of the universe.

"This would require the divine acceptance of a genuine experience of temporality," says Polkinghorne. "The idea of divine eternity is not abandoned, but it is held in a complementary relationship with divine temporality."

Both modern theology and modern physics expose the tension between the block universe view of time, where all times co-exist and are equally real, and the "thermodynamic" view where only the changing present is real. Perhaps future advances will develop a synthesis of the two.

"Some theologians, including the present writer, are bold enough to conclude that this implies that even God does not yet know the unformed future," says Polkingorne [Majid 2012].

It's worth noting that these ideas were anticipated by Stapledon in "*Star Maker*" [Stapledon 1937].

"Star Maker is the most wonderful novel I have ever read," said Brian Aldiss in his foreword to the SF Masterworks edition [Stapledon 1999] of Stapledon's masterpiece. "It retains its wonder on successive readings, and repays study."

In his preface to the translation "*Hacedor de Estrellas*" [Stapledon 1965] Jorge Luis Borges said the novel is "prodigious."

Under "the cold light of the stars, symbol of the hypercosmical reality, with its crystal ecstasy," Stapledon is taken to a journey, perhaps a vision or a dream, to the depths of the cosmos and beyond. After witnessing the fates of myriads of planets and intelligent species, Stapledon, now a cosmic spirit, has a brief encounter with God - the Star Maker. In a dream within a dream, Stapledon learns about the Star Maker and his creations.

The key points of Stapledon's Star Maker theology are outlined in the passages below.

> "In my dream, the Star Maker himself, as eternal and absolute spirit, timelessly contemplated all his works; but also as the finite and creative mode of the absolute spirit, he bodied forth his creations one after the other in a time sequence proper to his own adventure and growth."

"And further, each of his works, each cosmos, was itself gifted with its own peculiar time, in such a manner that the whole sequence of events within any single cosmos could be viewed by the Star Maker not only from within the cosmical time itself but also externally, from the time proper to his own life, with all the cosmical epochs co-existing together," continues Stapledon.

> "According to the strange dream or myth which took possession of my mind, the Star Maker in his finite and creative mode was actually a developing, an awakening spirit. That he should be so, and yet also eternally perfect, is of course humanly inconceivable; but my mind, overburdened with superhuman vision, found no other means of expressing to itself the mystery of creation."

These ideas on the relationship between God and time are related and similar to those of [Pannenberg and Polkinghorne], outlined above. Both Stapledon and Polkinghorne have been influenced by Alfred North Whitehead's process philosophy, which Stapledon considers as "the most brilliant, most comprehensive, most significant, though also most difficult, metaphysical system of our time" [Stapledon 1939].

"Eternally, so my dream declared to me, the Star Maker is perfect and absolute; yet in the beginning of the time proper to his creative mode he was an infant deity, restless, eager, mighty, but without clear will," says Stapledon. "He was equipped with all creative power. He could make universes with all kinds of physical and mental attributes. He was limited only by logic. Thus he could ordain the most surprising natural laws, but he could not, for instance, make twice two equal five. In his early phase he was limited also by his immaturity. He was still in the trance of infancy. Though the unconscious source of his consciously exploring and creating mentality was none other than his own eternal essence, consciously he was at first but the vague blind hunger of creativity."

"As he lovingly, though critically, reviewed our cosmos in all its infinite diversity and in its brief moment of lucidity, I felt that he was suddenly filled with reverence for the creature that he had made, or that he had ushered out of his own secret depth by a kind of divine self-midwifery," continues Stapledon. "He knew that this creature, though imperfect, though a mere creature, a mere figment of his own creative power, was yet in a manner more real than himself. For beside this concrete splendour what was he but a mere abstract potency of creation?"

> "Moreover in another respect the thing that he had made was his superior, and his teacher. For as he contemplated this the loveliest and subtlest of all his works with exultation, even with awe, its impact upon him changed him, clarifying and deepening his will."

Here, Stapledon is saying that the Star Maker, in his in-time aspect, learns from his creations. This is a very powerful concept: The unfolding cosmos, intelligent life, and we ourselves, can influence and change God. Perhaps God emerges as an alien, "wholly other" impersonal consciousness embedded in the fabric of reality, but intelligent life can help God evolve and become a personal, caring God.

"I seemed to see the spirit of the ultimate and perfected cosmos face her maker," says Stapledon in the powerful climax of the novel. "In her, it seemed, compassion and indignation were subdued by praise. And the Star Maker, that dark power and lucid intelligence, found in the concrete loveliness of his creature the fulfilment of desire."

> "And in the mutual joy of the Star Maker and the ultimate cosmos was conceived, most strangely, the absolute spirit itself, in which all times are present and all being is comprised; for the spirit which was the issue of this union confronted my reeling intelligence as being at once the ground and the issue of all temporal and finite things."

So, in Stapledon's Star Maker theology, an ultimate fusion of the in-time aspect of the Star Maker and his creation gives rise to the eternal, beyond-time aspect of the Star Maker. This seems a more elaborated version of the vision that Stapledon briefly outlined in the 1948 British Interplanetary Society talk: The end of the cosmos is also its source and its temporal beginning, via the eternal spirit that comes into being at the end of time.

"*Philosophy and Living*" [Stapledon 1939], written in 1939, two years after "*Star Maker*," is a compact outline of practical philosophy and abstract metaphysics, with short accounts of the ideas of many thinkers as well as the author's quest to build and formulate his own ideas.

Some readers could accuse Stapledon of being too vague and indecisive. For example, after introducing the tentative proposition "There is something, called God, the definition of which includes the essential characteristics of personality, but also includes an aspect which is not limited by time," Stapledon adds "I am not suggesting that this proposition about God is true, but merely that it is in an important sense meaningful."

Passages equivalent to "in an important sense… but in another equally important sense…"

are often used in the book, which can give the impression that Stapledon goes in circles without ever making up his mind. But, sometimes, juggling incompatible models and viewpoints is the best we can do. For example, accepting both the particle and wave aspects of the electron is self-contradictory but "more true than a coherent statement which leaves one or other aspect out of account." This is, I think, a very good point.

Stapledon says:

> "When we remember the size of the physical universe and the immensities of the past and the future, we cannot but believe that, scattered among the myriads of stars, there are, or will be, purposeful beings as superior to us as we are to the amoeba.... It is quite conceivable that, to minds of a higher lucidity than ours, what appears to us as the temporal sequence of cosmical events may appear simultaneously 'spread out' as a fourth spatial dimension, while a fifth dimension of events, wholly unknown to us, may constitute for those beings a genuine temporal dimension, in which events have passage."

Here, Stapledon goes back to the concept of God's time, with a twist: Sufficiently advanced life forms could gain access to God's high view of time, and experience change in another time-like dimension. Perhaps this is part of the evolution of advanced civilizations as they become more and more like - and eventually merge with - God.

In "*Philosophy and Living*," Stapledon gives a cold shower (soberly and elegantly of course) to the idea of afterlife.

> "It seems that the balance of such evidence as we have discussed is on the whole against the survival and immortality of human persons as recognisably identical experiencing minds. There is no clear and cogent evidence that they do survive in any sense relevant to the demand for personal immortality; and there is some not wholly worthless evidence that renders their survival somewhat improbable."

Stapledon considers the idea that we could wake up after death as thoughts in a greater mind, perhaps in a vast God-like mind. However, according to Stapledon, this wouldn't be an afterlife but a form of annihilation. "It may reasonably be questioned whether there is any sense in saying that he, the lamented human individual, has survived his death," he says. "For he has become something fantastically different from what he was."

But it seems to me that a stray thought in a vast God-like mind could be a whole, fully conscious human mind. So we might wake up in a pocket universe in a corner of the vast mind of God, where we and our loved ones continue to exist as separate individuals. Too bad Stapledon didn't see this.

In other works Stapledon imagined future human civilizations, and alien civilizations among the stars, much more advanced than us.

In "*Last and First Men*" [Stapledon 1930], a future history of humanity spanning billions of years, the scientists of a future civilization discover "that past events were not after all simply nonexistent, that though no longer existent in the temporal manner, they had eternal existence in some other manner."

The discovery leads future ultra-archeologists to developing time scanning technology, a limited form of time travel that permits acquiring very accurate information from the past.

In "*Last Men in London*" [Stapledon 1932], an explorer from billions of years in the future observes our world from the inside of the mind of Paul, a contemporary of Stapledon living in London. The future explorer has full knowledge of Paul's mind, including all thoughts, feelings and memories.

Now, Stapledon could have thought of this: The future explorer archives a copy of the whole mind of Paul in a corner of his own vast mind, goes back to his present (our future, billions of years from now), and reconstructs the mind of Paul from the archive using some future technology. This is the concept of resurrection by "uploading to the future."

Stapledon had clear in his mind the concept of time scanning. But he didn't have the concept of computational equivalence, aka Turing-Church conjecture, which implies the possibility of mind uploading.

Following the Turing-Church conjecture, future supercomputers could fully emulate a human mind. It follows that a human mind can be copied from a biological brain to a new computing substrate. This is the concept of mind uploading.

Combining the concept of time scanning (which he had) with the concept of mind uploading (which he didn't have), Stapledon could have formulated the equation for technological resurrection as:

Time Scanning + Mind Uploading = Technological Resurrection

Then, Stapledon could have written a novel on the new adventures of Paul, resurrected in a strange and wonderful future. It would have been a great novel.

That Stapledon didn't see the possibility of technological resurrection shows that a physical theory of resurrection needs the concept of mind uploading, familiar to transhumanists and science fiction fans.

I use the term "Turing Church" to emphasize the key role that computational equivalence plays in the concept of technological resurrection.

Spacetime, Matter, Mind, Deity: The Natural Theology Of Samuel Alexander

Writing more than 100 years ago, Samuel Alexander proposed a sober scientific theology that seems to me very modern, and very close to mine.

In his masterwork "*Space, Time, and Deity*" [Alexander 1966], Alexander envisioned an infinite progression of Gods emerging from natural processes in the physical universe. The book, first published in 1920, was written for the 1916-18 Gifford Lectures, at the time of Einstein's formulation of general relativity.

Like Einstein, Alexander considers spacetime as the fundamental primary stuff. The rest of reality emerges from spacetime in a progression of levels with new empirical qualities: First matter, then life, then mind, and then new levels unknown to us, indicated as Deity.

Interestingly, Alexander uses a body/mind metaphor for the relationship between one level and the level above. So matter is the body of life, and life is the mind of matter. Similarly, matter is the mind of spacetime, and spacetime is the body of matter.

The level above life, emerging from life, is mind, or spirit. Spirit is the mind of life, and life is the body of spirit. Above spirit, there are the first levels of Deity, which Alexander refers to as finite gods, or angels, But there are more levels between the finite gods and the infinite, never fully achieved God:

> "Beyond these finite gods or angels there would be in turn a new empirical quality looming into view, which for them would be deity - that is, would be for them what deity is for us."

According to Alexander, there is no actual infinite being with the quality of deity, but there is an actual infinite, the whole universe, with a "nisus" (a tendency) to deity. This "is the God of the religious consciousness, though that consciousness habitually forecasts the divinity of its object as actually realised in an individual form."

Alexander's hierarchy reminds of [Cantor's hierarchy of transfinite numbers], each essentially bigger than the one before, like the infinity of real numbers is essentially bigger than the infinity of rational numbers. God is absolute infinity, infinitely larger than any nameable infinity, and unattainable in time. The angels immediately above us are not merely advanced aliens (those would be at our level), but qualitatively different beings with empirical qualities higher than mind.

We couldn't understand or even imagine the angels, let alone the levels of Deity above them. Perhaps the highest forms of Hans Moravec's "Exes" [Moravec 1998] come close to the very first level of Deity above us. Or we can think of the concept of kenes, which could be closer to what Alexander had in mind. In "*The Spike*" [Broderick 2001], Damien Broderick describes kenes as "memetic entities that flow through us as electricity passes along wires."

In "*Sailing Bright Eternity*" [Benford 1995], science and fiction writer Gregory Benford describes kenes as systems of self-replicating ideas (memes) that take a (higher level form of) life of their own, eventually leaving their original material substrates behind and becoming "free of the grinding embrace of matter… with ideas as the mere substrate for abstractions of ever higher order." Perhaps Alexander's angels could be something like that.

Alexander reminds me of his near-contemporary Olaf Stapledon. Among the similarities, both are focused on really big issues, and both appreciate Alfred North Whitehead's process philosophy [Stapledon 1939].

Both Alexander and Stapledon are skeptical of the afterlife, because they don't see a physical mechanism for mind surviving the end of its material substrate. But perhaps, I guess, they are indulging in reverse wishful thinking.

Stapledon notes [Stapledon 1939] that, just like wishful thinking can lead to an irrational belief in the afterlife, "the fear of being irrationally swayed by the strong desire for immortality" can lead to an equally irrational belief in the finality of death. "For every irrational emotive influence on the one side there is an opposed irrational emotive influence on the other."

Alexander could have easily imagined that, starting at some level, finite gods could be able to retrieve us, as information, from the traces that we leave in spacetime. So we would wake up after death as thoughts in a vast God-like mind.

Merlin Speaks: Arthur Clarke On Future Wonders And Technological Resurrection

Arthur Clarke wasn't a believer in any traditional religion, but he had a "possibilian" open mind - he was open to the wonders of the possible.

In his immortal masterpiece "*2001: A Space Odyssey*" [Clarke 1968], Clarke worded his vision of advanced post-biological civilizations in the universe as:

> "And now, out among the stars, evolution was driving toward new goals. The first explorers of Earth had long since come to the limits of flesh and blood; as soon as their machines were better than their bodies, it was time to move. First their brains, and then their thoughts alone, they transferred into shining new homes of metal and of plastic. In these, they roamed among the stars. They no longer built spaceships. They were spaceships.

> But the age of the Machine-entities swiftly passed. In their ceaseless experimenting, they had learned to store knowledge in the structure of space itself, and to preserve their thoughts for eternity in frozen lattices of light. They could become creatures of radiation, free at last from the tyranny of matter.

> Now they were lords of the galaxy, and beyond the reach of time. They could rove at will among the stars, and sink like a subtle mist through the very interstices of space."

Hopefully, future humans will ascend to those awesome heights. Earlier in the book, Clarke mentions our own aspirations to transcendence:

> "A few mystically inclined biologists went still further. They speculated, taking their cues from the beliefs of many religions, that mind would eventually free itself from matter. The robot body, like the flesh-and-blood one, would be no more than a stepping-stone to something which, long ago, men had called spirit."

> And if there was anything beyond that, its name could only be God."

Sir Arthur was a deeply religious man who didn't want to believe in God, perhaps as a result of bad experiences with organized religion. But he was, despite himself, a mystic and a prophet.

Sir Arthur's "Third Law," which states that any sufficiently advanced technology is indistinguishable from magic, has given and continues to give me endless inspiration. I believe future humans will develop "magic" technologies beyond imagination, spread to the stars and beyond, re-engineer the universe, and resurrect the dead. I also believe that magic technologies are already used by powerful, God-like intelligence out there among the stars and beyond.

[The best of Sir Arthur's quotations are collected in a page] maintained by the Sir Arthur C. Clarke Foundation. My favorite, besides the Third Law, is:

> "It may be that our role on this planet is not to worship God but to create him."

Only a deeply religious person would say that. The quote was provided by Neil McAleer, Arthur Clarke's biographer. McAleer's biography, titled "*Visionary: The Odyssey of Sir Arthur C. Clarke*" [McAleer 2012], is a 2012 revised and expanded edition of the first 1992 edition. There is also a 2013 Kindle edition titled "*Sir Arthur C. Clarke: Odyssey of a Visionary*" [McAleer 2013].

"The news of his demise went right around the world at the speed of light thanks to the com-sat and web," reads a Clarke obituary [Gunawardene 2008] penned by Nalaka Gunawardene, a science writer who was Clarke's research assistant for two decades. "In less than an hour, the whole world knew... many have turned to the last video greeting that Sir Arthur made, just a few days ahead of his 90th birthday (16 Dec 2007). This is about how that video was made..."

Sir Arthur's last words are now en-route to the stars. Perhaps they will reach some powerful, God-like alien intelligence able to bring Sir Arthur back to life.

Sir Arthur's disciplined but visionary scientific imagination included technological resurrection - the possibility that future super-advanced science and technology could bring the dead back to life.

In conversation with José Cordeiro [Cordeiro 2008], Clarke said: "I'm always paraphrasing J. B. S. Haldane: 'The universe is not only stranger than we imagine, it's stranger than we can imagine.'"

An excellent 2008 *Strange Horizons* article by Nicholas Seeley [Seeley 2008], titled "The Wizard in the Space Station: A Look Back at the Works of the Late Sir Arthur C. Clarke," offers one of the best reviews of Clarke's work, interlaced with observations and reminiscences by science and fiction writer Gregory Benford, one of Clarke's collaborators and a great science fiction writer himself.

Seeley's article is full of Benford's recollections of Sir Arthur, given in a phone interview. But Seeley adds his own. Clarke "would have said religion is akin to science in its earliest developmental phase," notes Seeley. "What remains beyond the realm of 'how' is the domain of the mystic, the one who gazes into the future for technologies advanced enough to blur the distinction between physical law and magic. As a writer, this was where Clarke lived and breathed."

According to Seeley, Clarke was "a mythologized figure of intellect and prescience, standing on the shadowy frontier of modern science."

"America in the early 1960s was Camelot, and Clarke was Merlin."

The Merlin of his time, Sir Arthur was indeed. Clarke indicated the way to the stars and the mystical wonders of a vast universe out there. "Through his writing he became an embodiment of wisdom, both as it applied to earthly science and metaphysical mysticism," notes Seeley, adding that Clarke was both the wizard and the sage.

Like many others I - an avid Clarke reader since childhood - owe my love for scientific imagination to my Master Sir Arthur Clarke.

"Camelot falls," Seeley says matter-of-factly. Today, Camelot and the magic sixties of the Apollo program seem very far. But "in the myths, all the great heroes get the chance to come again."

The question is: Can the great heroes only come back in myths? Could Sir Arthur get the chance to come back in reality?

"My problem with reincarnation is: what is the input-output device, and what is the storage system?," Clarke wondered in an interview with Dr. David G. Stork for the website "2001: Hal's Legacy," Seeley reports. "This is a question that I've never had an answer to, but it's a rather interesting one I think."

> "If we are somehow stored after our deaths and could be revived then there is the question - if no information is ever lost, if it is stored somehow in the fabric of the cosmos, then anyone who ever lived could be reincarnated - and this has been the subject of serious philosophical speculation."

Clarke is using "reincarnation" in the sense of "resurrection": Coming back to life with the original memories and sense of self. The interview mentioned by Seeley has long disappeared from the web, but there is a copy in the Internet Archive [Stork 2001]. You see: Before "dying" the document had been scanned by an overseeing intelligence, and a backup snapshot had been archived. The backup snapshot can be used to reconstruct the original. This is the concept of technological resurrection, aka quantum archeology or [Akashic engineering].

Seeley notes that Ervin László proposed similar ideas. According to László and other thinkers, a fundamental information and memory field associated with the quantum vacuum is "the deepest and most fundamental level of physical reality in the universe." In "*The Akashic Experience*" [László 2009], László wrote:

> "A universal information and memory field could exist in nature, associated with the fundamental element of physical reality physicists call the unified field... Honoring an ancient insight, this is the aspect or dimension of the unified field that I have called the Akashic Field."

The above passage is quoted by renowned mathematician Ralph Abraham and physicist Sisir Roy in their book "*Demystifying the Akasha*" [Abraham 2010], where the scientists propose [a tentative mathematical model for the Akashic field]. In his preface to László's "*The Connectivity Hypothesis*" [László 2003], Abraham wrote: "When a great grand unified theory will appear it will very likely conform to the prophetic vision of Ervin László." After "*The Connectivity Hypothesis*," László wrote a simplified but thoughtful account of his ideas in "*Science and the Akashic Field*" [László 2007] and then several related books.

"Is it science, or modern mysticism?," wonders Seeley. "Who knows... If all information is indeed stored somewhere in the vast fabric of space, if what I hope is true, then Sir Arthur C. Clarke isn't really dead. He's just been uploaded somewhere. We will never know, but as Clarke himself has said: we can always wonder."

In "*Profiles of the Future*," revised millennium edition [Clarke 2000], at the end of the chapter "Brain and Body," Sir Arthur wrote:

> "I recently sacrificed some of my few remaining hairs, to be launched into space as part of the AERO Astro Corporation 'Encounter Project'. If all goes well, they will leave the Solar System (after a boost from Jupiter) and the hope is that, maybe a million years from now, some super-civilisation will capture this primitive artefact from the past. Recreating its biological contents might be an amusing exercise for their equivalent of an infants' class. Of course, I'll never know - unless the experimenters are both very considerate - and Masters of Time."

It is easy to imagine that a super-civilization might be able to recreate a body from biological samples, but to recreate a human personality with memories, thoughts, and feelings, they would need to be Masters of Time with at least read-only access to the past. So it seems that Sir Arthur had in mind resurrection via time scanning technology plus mind uploading, aka "copying to the future."

Clarke doesn't doubt the conceptual - and future technological - feasibility of mind uploading. "Men and machines will merge," he says in the Seeley interview. "We'll be able to download our thoughts, our personalities into a computer. I think that's inevitable. It doesn't worry me. The fact that I'm a carbon-based biped, I wouldn't look down on a silicon-based biped."

In the chapter "About Time" of *"Profiles of the Future,"* Sir Arthur covers time scanning, Akashic engineering and the reconstruction - resurrection - of the dead:

> "If there is any way in which we can ever observe the past, it must depend upon technologies not only unborn but today unimagined. Yet the idea does not involve any logical contradictions or scientific absurdities, and in view of what has already happened in archaeological research, only a very foolish man would claim that it is impossible. For now we have recovered knowledge of the past which it seems obvious must have been lost for ever, beyond all hope of recovery...

> No one can yet say how far such techniques may be extended. There may be a sense in which all events leave some mark upon the universe...

> The reconstruction of the past is an idea even more fantastic than its observation; it includes that, and goes far beyond it. Indeed, it is nothing less than the concept of resurrection, looked at in a scientific rather than a religious sense...

> Suppose that sometime in the future our descendants acquire the power to observe the past in such detail that they can record the movement of every atom that ever existed. Suppose they reconstruct, on the basis of this information, selected people, animals, and places from the past. So, though you actually died in the Twenty-First Century, another 'you', complete with all memories up to the moment of observation, might suddenly find himself in the far future, continuing to live a new existence from then onwards."

In the last passage I have restored the "himself" in the original edition, which had been changed to "yourself" in the millennium edition (Clarke mentions PC, "Political Correctness," in the foreword to the millennium edition). I prefer the original, which is grammatically correct, if not politically.

"Re-reading the above words after almost forty years, I see in them the genesis of the novel that Stephen Baxter has now written from my synopsis," notes Clarke, referring to the passages from *"Profiles of the Future"* quoted above.

In *"The Light of Other Days"* [Baxter 2000], Sir Arthur and Stephen Baxter describe a fictional time scanner, the [Wormcam]: A remote viewing device that permits scanning any location at any time in the past, by using micro wormholes naturally embedded with high density in the fabric of spacetime (every spacetime pixel is connected with every other spacetime pixel). Soon, engineers are able to resurrect the dead.

Perhaps that's how it will happen. Perhaps it will happen in other ways, stranger than we can imagine, as in Haldane's words dear to Clarke. But I believe that it will happen, and one day I will be able to shake my Master's hand.

Prisoner Of Bad Philosophy: Carl Sagan Couldn't Allow Himself To Hope

It's impossible not to love Carl Sagan. Like Arthur Clarke, Sagan was a prophet and a poet of the space age. I've grown up reading Sagan's books, and Sagan is one of my heroes. That's why I find so saddening these words of Sagan's collaborator and wife Ann Druyan [Druyan 2003]:

> "When my husband died, because he was so famous and known for not being a believer, many people would come up to me - it still sometimes happens - and ask me if Carl changed at the end and converted to a belief in an afterlife. They also frequently ask me if I think I will see him again. Carl faced his death with unflagging courage and never sought refuge in illusions. The tragedy was that we knew we would never see each other again. I don't ever expect to be reunited with Carl."

Here are two great persons who gave up hope and accepted despair to remain true to bad philosophy. Atheism can become a mental prison that leaves imagination and hope locked out.

Sagan's overall philosophy and views on religion are outlined in "*The Varieties of Scientific Experience*" [Sagan 2006], a version of Sagan's 1985 Gifford Lectures edited by Druyan and published in 2006, ten years after Sagan's premature death.

The book is a powerful defense of the scientific method as a better way to search for truth than religious revelation. I agree, with three caveats: First, I don't entirely dismiss the value of subjective experiences that can't be reproduced. Second, science at its best starts with visionary leaps of imagination that often have much in common with religion. Third, hope is more important than truth.

While Sagan never called himself an atheist (one who knows that God doesn't exist) but an agnostic (one who doesn't know if God exists), it's easy to interpret his writings as a passionate defense of atheism.

At the same time, it's worth noting that Sagan had a deep knowledge of religions, and was open to considering the positive side of religion. For example, in "*Pale Blue Dot*" [Sagan 1994], Sagan noted that "we are in need of other sorts of myth, myths of encouragement. Many religions, from Hinduism to Gnostic Christianity to Mormon doctrine, teach that - as impious as it may sound - it is the goal of humans to become gods."

> "Or consider a story in the Jewish Talmud left out of the Book of Genesis. (It is in doubtful accord with the account of the apple, the Tree of Knowledge, the Fall, and the expulsion from Eden.) In the Garden, God tells Eve and Adam that He has intentionally left the Universe unfinished. It is the responsibility of humans, over countless generations, to participate with God in a 'glorious' experiment - 'completing the Creation.'"

This shows that Sagan was perfectly aware of the interpretation of religion that I am proposing: The promises of religion are true, because we'll make them true. Carl Sagan was a highly imaginative scientist, certainly imaginative enough to conceive of natural Gods and technological resurrection with the same openness of Arthur Clarke.

Sagan's science fiction novel "*Contact*" [Sagan 1985], a rightfully acclaimed masterpiece, shows a "startling sympathy for the epistemological premise of revealed religions" [Douglas 2017] and reveals that Sagan had many building blocks of physical theology in mind: The existence of advanced civilizations with God-like powers in the universe (which implies that we could become God-like ourselves), spacetime engineering, [faster than light travel through wormholes], some form of time travel and "time magic," and high resolution mind scanning. My central thesis is that time magic and mind scanning will permit to resurrect the dead by copying them out.

Even more startlingly, Sagan says:

> "The universe was made on purpose… In the fabric of space and in the nature of matter, as in a great work of art, there is, written small, the artist's signature. Standing over humans, gods, and demons, subsuming Caretakers and Tunnel builders, there is an intelligence that antedates the universe."

I think the fact that Sagan chose to include these visions only in his single science fiction novel (too bad he didn't write others) reveals that he wanted to distance himself from his imagination… because his imagination sounded too much like religion.

I suspect that Carl Sagan was afraid of falling back into beliefs from which he had escaped with difficulties and pain. Sagan's familiarity with religions seems to confirm this possibility. In her introduction to "*The Varieties of Scientific Experience*," Druyan says:

> "He couldn't live a compartmentalized life, operating on one set of assumptions in the laboratory and keeping another, conflicting set for the Sabbath. He took the idea of God so seriously that it had to pass the most rigorous standards of scrutiny."

Taking things too seriously is often paralyzing. Perhaps serious things, especially serious things, shouldn't be taken too seriously, but with a healthy degree of playfulness.

Sagan was a champion of skeptical scrutiny and popularized the often heard principle that "extraordinary claims require extraordinary evidence." I find this short formulation of Sagan's principle misleading: If there is evidence, a claim is not an extraordinary claim but an evident claim.

What (I think) Sagan's principle means is that you should require extraordinary evidence before ACCEPTING a claim that seems extraordinary. OK with that, of course. But you can't require extraordinary evidence before CONSIDERING a claim, otherwise things become circular, nobody ever considers anything new, and we are still living in caves.

Also, there are situations in which suspending disbelief and acting on an extraordinary claim is all you can do.

Suppose you are stranded on the shore of a big island. You have done a quick reconnaissance and found no sources of drinkable water. You don't know how to desalinate sea water, or if such a thing is even possible.

So, no drinkable water in the island, and no way to make some. Should you give up hope and force yourself to make peace with the inevitable fact that you'll be dead in a few days?

No, you shouldn't. Yes, perhaps you'll be dead in a couple of days, but you shouldn't sit down and do nothing waiting for death. Rather, you should bet on the extraordinary claim that you'll find or make drinkable water, suspend disbelief, and get busy to establish the evidence.

The island is big, and you have explored only a small part of it. Who's to say that there's no drinkable water in the rest of the island? Go and look for some! The island seems uninhabited, but who's to say that there can't be people inland who can give you water?

Finally, who's to say that sea water can't be desalinated, or that you can't desalinate sea water yourself? As a matter of fact, there are ways to desalinate sea water without special equipment. I guess you would think of one if your life depended on it.

I guess I don't need to decode this metaphor, but just in case, here you go: The drinkable water stands for the hope to be reunited with your loved ones after physical death. Just like I can't live without water, I can't live without this hope.

The only thing I can do is to suspend disbelief in the extraordinary claim that I'll be reunited with my loved ones, and try to establish some degree of plausibility for natural resurrection (finding water) or technological resurrection (making water).

Martin Gardner On Religion And Mysterian Science

Carl Sagan "became agitated after reading a new book by the legendary skeptic Martin Gardner, whom Sagan had admired since the early 1950s," reported Joel Achenbach [Achenbach 2014]. "It suggested that perhaps there was a singular God ruling the universe and some potential for life after death."

Achenbach refers to Gardner's book "*The Whys of a Philosophical Scrivener*" [Gardner 1983]. In November 1996, Sagan wrote to Gardner that the only reason for this position that he could find is that it feels good, and asked: "How could you of all people advocate a position because it's emotionally satisfying, rather than demand rigorous standards of evidence even if they lead to a position that is emotionally distasteful?"

Gardner's reply is given in "A Mind at Play: An Interview with Martin Gardner" [Frazier 1998] by Kendrick Frazier.

> "Shortly before he died, Carl Sagan wrote to say he had reread my '*Whys of a Philosophical Scrivener*' and was it fair to say that I believed in God solely because it made me 'feel good.' I replied that this was exactly right, though the emotion was deeper than the way one feels good after three drinks. It is a way of escaping from a deep-seated despair. William James's essay '*The Will to Believe*' is the classic defense of the right to make such an emotional 'leap of faith.' My theism is independent of any religious movement, and in the tradition that starts with Plato and includes Kant, and a raft of later philosophers, down to Charles Peirce, William James, and Miguel de Unamuno. I defend it ad nauseam in my Whys."

"Of my books, the one that I am most pleased to have written is my confessional, '*The Whys of a Philosophical Scrivener*,'" said Gardner. I highly recommend the book, first written in 1983 and republished in 1999.

"Gardner's essays in '*The Whys of a Philosophical Scrivener*' are a tour de force of mature, honest thinking expressed in golden and often witty prose," reads Karl Giberson's review [Giberson 2010]. Gardner "affirmed and celebrated a world that went beyond science. We can believe, says Gardner, when our will compels us to believe. We are not constrained by science to accept only whatever is on the right-hand side of the equal sign."

"Although we have no way of knowing whether either model, or a combination of the two, or some completely different model, is true or partly true, the making of such models serves, as I keep repeating, a valuable purpose," notes Gardner [Gardner 1983], referring to crude models of how prayer might work. "They show that there is nothing logically wrong about what theists choose to believe with their hearts."

In his autobiography "*Undiluted Hocus-pocus*" [Gardner 2013], Gardner says that his faith "is based unashamedly on posits of the heart, not the head." The brain sees no proofs of God or of an afterlife, but Gardner's heart tells him that:

> "For me God is a 'Wholly Other' transcendent intelligence, impossible for us to understand. He or she is somehow responsible for our universe and capable of providing, how I have no inkling, an afterlife."

According to Gardner, no more can, or should, be said. Gardner is a "mysterian," which means, in his own words, that "there are truths as far beyond our brain's capacity now to comprehend as the truths we understand are beyond the grasp of a chimpanzee."

I used to enjoy a lot, as a teen, Gardner's *Scientific American* column on mathematical games and puzzles, but also on "real" mathematics and physics. I learned much more from him than from my unbelievably boring (and often not correct) school books, and Martin Gardner is one of my heroes.

Gardner was critical of organized religion but open to the possibility that some of the promises of religion might be true in some sense. In "The Church of the Fourth Dimension," a chapter of "*The Colossal Book of Mathematics*" [Gardner 2001] Gardner gave a nice and (relatively) simple introduction to the mathematical concept of a transcendent, trans-dimensional elsewhere, where perhaps Gods and souls can be found.

"There are dozens of monumental questions about which I have to say 'I don't know,'" said Gardner in the *Skeptical Inquirer* interview.

> "I don't know whether there is intelligent life elsewhere in the universe, or whether life is so improbable that we are truly alone in the cosmos. I don't know whether there is just one universe, or a multiverse in which an infinite number of universes explode into existence, live and die, each with its own set of laws and physical constants. I don't know if quantum mechanics will someday give way to a deeper theory. I don't know whether there is a finite set of basic laws of physics or whether there are infinite depths of structure like an infinite set of Chinese boxes. Will the electron turn out to have an interior structure? I wish I knew!"

Like Gardner, I don't know any of that, and I wish I knew. Based on a gut feeling, I suspect that Shakespeare's immortal words "There are more things in heaven and earth, Horatio, than are dreamt of in your philosophy" could remain true forever. Our scientific understanding of the universe could grow without bonds, but always find new fractal depths of unexplained phenomena, in a big infinite fractal onion universe to be explored by future scientists.

In the *Skeptical Inquirer* interview, Gardner defines himself as a "mysterian." Some mysterians consider consciousness as a mystery that human intelligence will never unravel, but others including Gardner believe that, while consciousness is not within the grasp of present human understanding, perhaps it will be comprehensible to future humans with much more advanced science.

"I can say this. I believe that the human mind, or even the mind of a cat, is more interesting in its complexity than an entire galaxy if it is devoid of life," says Gardner.

> "I belong to a group of thinkers known as the 'mysterians.' It includes Roger Penrose, Thomas Nagel, John Searle, Noam Chomsky, Colin McGinn, and many others who believe that no computer, of the kind we know how to build, will ever become self-aware and acquire the creative powers of the human mind. I believe there is a deep mystery about how consciousness emerged as brains became more complex, and that neuroscientists are a long long way from understanding how they work."

The key words here are "of the kind we know how to build" and "neuroscientists are a long long way from understanding." Gardner is open to the possibility that future neuroscientists could understand the brain-mind system much better than today's neuroscientists, and future engineers could know how to build new types of computers, different from today's computers, able to run a conscious human mind.

I used to be persuaded that incremental, quantitative improvements to today's computer science - faster processors, more memory, etc. - could one day run conscious artificial intelligences (AIs) and uploaded human minds. Now I prefer Gardner's honest "I don't know." Perhaps consciousness depends critically on subtle quantum aspects of our neural circuitry, not present in today's silicon electronics. One way or another, we will find out, but the path to [conscious AI and mind uploading] could be longer than the optimistic experts think, and require yet undiscovered science and engineering.

The brain is a computer in the sense that it is a physical system that follows physical laws. Once these laws are well understood and engineers are able to reproduce the key physical features of the neural substrate, computers could run conscious minds.

If a conscious mind can run only on a substrate with certain specific properties, then we will have to engineer new substrates with those specific properties. If quantum physics plays a crucial role in the thinking brain, we will have to develop alternative substrates that exhibit the key quantum properties found (actually not yet found) in carbon-based biology. I think Martin Gardner would agree with that.

Notes

[Akashic engineering] See "The quest for Akashic physics and engineering."

[a tentative mathematical model for the Akashic field] See "The quest for Akashic physics and engineering."

[Cantor's hierarchy of transfinite numbers] See "Thought experiments in physical theology."

[conscious AI and mind uploading] See "Transhumanism."

[faster than light travel through wormholes] See "Exotic space, mysterious time, magic quantum." Kip Thorne developed for Sagan the theory of faster than light travel through wormholes suggested in "*Contact*."

[Fred Hoyle] See "A for Almighty."

[Frank Tipler's Omega Point scenario] See "Omega Point."

[Pannenberg and Polkinghorne] See "Christianity and transhumanism are much closer than you think."

[The best of Sir Arthur's quotations are collected in a page]
http://www.clarkefoundation.org/about-sir-arthur/sir-arthurs-quotations/

[Wormcam] See "The interplay of science fiction, science, and religion."

References

[Abraham 2010] Ralph Abraham, Sisir Roy. *Demystifying the Akasha: Consciousness and the Quantum Vacuum*. Epigraph Publishing, 2010.

[Alexander 1966] Samuel Alexander. *Space, Time, and Deity: The Gifford Lectures at Glasgow 1916–1918*. Palgrave Macmillan, 1966.

[Achenbach 2014] Joel Achenbach. Carl Sagan denied being an atheist. So what did he believe? [Part 1]. *The Washington Post*, 2014.
https://www.washingtonpost.com/news/achenblog/wp/2014/07/10/carl-sagan-denied-being-an-atheist-so-what-did-he-believe-part-1/

[Baxter 2000] Stephen Baxter, Arthur Clarke. *The Light of Other Days*. Tor, 2000.

[Bear 1983] Greg Bear. *The Wind from a Burning Woman*. Arkham House, 1983.

[Benford 1995] Gregory Benford. *Sailing Bright Eternity*. Bantam Spectra, 1995.

[Broderick 2001] Damien Broderick. *The Spike: How Our Lives Are Being Transformed By Rapidly Advancing Technologies*. Tor Books, 2001.

[Clarke 1968] Arthur Clarke. *2001: A Space Odyssey*. Hutchinson, 1968.

[Clarke 2000] Arthur Clarke. *Profiles of the Future: An Inquiry into the Limits of the Possible*. Phoenix, 2000.

[Cordeiro 2008] José Cordeiro. Sir Arthur C. Clarke in 3001: Don't Panic! Lifeboat Foundation, 2008.
http://lifeboat.com/ex/arthur.c.clarke

[Douglas 2017] Christopher Douglas. 'Contact' and Carl Sagan's faith. *The Conversation*, 2017.
https://theconversation.com/contact-and-carl-sagans-faith-85150

[Druyan 2003] Ann Druyan. Ann Druyan Talks About Science, Religion, Wonder, Awe… and Carl Sagan. *Skeptical Inquirer*, 2003.
https://www.csicop.org/si/show/ann_druyan_talks_about_science_religion

[Frazier 1998] Kendrick Frazier. A Mind at Play: An Interview with Martin Gardner. *Skeptical Inquirer*, 1998.
http://www.csicop.org/si/show/mind_at_play_an_interview_with_martin_gardner/

[Gardner 1983] Martin Gardner. *The Whys of a Philosophical Scrivener*. Quill, 1983.

[Gardner 2001] Martin Gardner. *The Colossal Book of Mathematics: Classic Puzzles, Paradoxes, and Problems*. W. W. Norton, 2001.

[Gardner 2013] Martin Gardner. *Undiluted Hocus-Pocus: The Autobiography of Martin Gardner*. Princeton University Press, 2013.

[Giberson 2010] Karl Giberson. Missing Martin Gardner: The Skeptic Who Believed in God. *The Huffington Post*, 2010.
http://www.huffingtonpost.com/karl-giberson-phd/missing-martin-gardner-19_b_586516.html

[Gunawardene 2008] Nalaka Gunawardene. Sir Arthur C Clarke, 1917-2008: The Final Goodbye from Colombo, 2008
https://nalakagunawardene.com/2008/03/19/sir-arthur-c-clarke-1917-2008-the-final-goodbye-from-colombo/

[László 2003] Ervin László. *The Connectivity Hypothesis: Foundations of an Integral Science of Quantum, Cosmos, Life, and Consciousness*. State University of New York Press, 2003.

[László 2007] Ervin László. *Science and the Akashic Field: An Integral Theory of Everything*. Inner Traditions, 2007.

[László 2009] Ervin László. *The Akashic Experience: Science and the Cosmic Memory Field*. Inner Traditions, 2009.

[Majid 2012] Shahn Majid (Ed.). *On Space and Time*. Cambridge University Press, 2012.

[McAleer 2012] Neil McAleer. *Visionary: The Odyssey of Sir Arthur C. Clarke*. Clarke Project, 2012.

[McAleer 2013] Neil McAleer. *Sir Arthur C. Clarke: Odyssey of a Visionary*. RosettaBooks, 2013.

[Moravec 1998] Hans Moravec. *Robot: Mere Machine to Transcendent Mind*. Oxford University Press, 1998.

[Pannenberg 1994] Wolfhart Pannenberg. *Systematic Theology*. T & T Clark, 1988–1994.

[Polkinghorne 2010] John Polkinghorne. *Theology in the Context of Science*. Yale University Press, 2010.

[Sagan 1985] Carl Sagan. *Contact*. Simon and Schuster, 1985.

[Sagan 1994] Carl Sagan. *Pale Blue Dot: A Vision of the Human Future in Space*. Random House, 1994.

[Sagan 2006] Carl Sagan, Ann Druyan (Ed.). *The Varieties of Scientific Experience: A Personal View of the Search for God*. Penguin Press, 2006.

[Seeley 2008] Nicholas Seeley. The Wizard in the Space Station: A Look Back at the Works of the Late Sir Arthur C. Clarke. *Strange Horizons*, 2008.
http://www.strangehorizons.com/non-fiction/articles/the-wizard-in-the-space-station-a-look-back-at-the-works-of-the-late-sir-arthur-c-clarke/

[Stapledon 1930] Olaf Stapledon. *Last And First Men*. Methuen, 1930.

[Stapledon 1932] Olaf Stapledon. *Last Men in London*. Methuen, 1932.

[Stapledon 1937] Olaf Stapledon. *Star Maker*. Methuen, 1937.

[Stapledon 1939] Olaf Stapledon. *Philosophy and Living*. Penguin Books, 1939.

[Stapledon 1948] Olaf Stapledon. Interplanetary Man. *Journal of the British Interplanetary Society*, 1948.
https://archive.org/stream/OlafStapledonInterplanetaryMan/

[Stapledon 1965] Olaf Stapledon. *Hacedor de Estrellas*. Minotauro, 1965.

[Stapledon 1999] Olaf Stapledon. *Star Maker*. Gollancz, 1999.

[Stork 2001] David Stork. Dr. Arthur C. Clarke Interview - Interviewer, Dr. David G. Stork. Internet Archive, 2001.
https://web.archive.org/web/20011216193706/http://2001halslegacy.com/interviews/clarke.html

[Wilson 2009] Blake Wilson. Stray Questions for: David Eagleman. *New York Times*, 2009.
https://artsbeat.blogs.nytimes.com/2009/07/10/stray-questions-for-david-eagleman/

CHAPTER 7 - KNOCKING ON HEAVEN'S DOOR: RUSSIAN AND MODERN COSMISM

In "*Transcendence*" [Goffman 2015], Ken Goffman (aka RU Sirius of *Mondo 2000* fame) and Jay Cornell define cosmism as:

> "Cosmism is a sort of philosophically laid-back version of transhumanism. In a culture that tends to be argumentative and filled with people who like to insist that their views are correct, cosmism doesn't care if you're viewing the universe as information or quantum information or hypercomputation or God stuff or whatever. Nor does it ask anyone to commit to AGI or mind uploading or brain-computer interfaces or fusion-powered toasters as the best way forward.

> Rather, it seeks to infuse the human universe with an attitude of joy, growth, choice, and open-mindedness. Cosmism believes that science in its current form, just like religion and philosophy in their current forms, may turn out to be overly limited for the task of understanding life, mind, society, and reality - but it teaches that, if so, by actively engaging with the world and studying and engineering things, and by reflecting on ourselves carefully and intelligently, we will likely be able to discover the next stage in the evolution of collective thinking."

I totally agree. I prefer to lie back and contemplate the endless possibilities in a transfinite cosmos without obsessing about life extension, accelerated technology, or when the Singularity arrives, if ever. These things will come when they come.

"*Transcendence*" has also a chapter dedicated to the [Mormon Transhumanist Association], with excerpts from an interview with the ever cogent and inspiring Lincoln Cannon.

The Russian Cosmists

The Russian cosmist scientific, philosophical, and spiritual movement of the late 19th and early 20th century, was not well known in the West until recently. Most cosmist writings are not available in other languages, and many aspects of cosmist thinking were frowned upon in the Soviet Union before 1991.

Though Russian cosmism is one of my main inspirations and one of the foundations of my own worldview, I am unable to read the original texts because I don't know Russian. Fortunately, there are more and more popular and scholarly works dedicated to Russian cosmism.

A film, "*Knocking on Heaven's Door*" [Carey 2011], by George Carey, and a book, "*The Russian Cosmists*" [Young 2012], by George Young, make cosmism much more accessible to a Western audience.

I recommend watching George Carey's film *"Knocking on Heaven's Door,"* aired by the BBC on the 50th "Yuri's Night," 50 years after Yuri Gagarin's pioneering flight to space, to all those who are interested in space, the history of the Russian space program, the amazingly beautiful philosophy known as Russian cosmism, our place and future in the universe, technological immortality, and resurrection.

Carey's thesis is that the cosmist movement has informed and energized the Soviet space program. The film captures the popular enthusiasm for space in the Soviet Union of the sixties. We had the same enthusiasm in the West at the time, and God knows we could use it now, all over the planet.

I think we can look, again, at the cosmist philosophy to renew our enthusiasm and drive with beautiful and energizing cosmic visions, and to remember that wonderful adventures are waiting for us in outer space. Konstantin Tsiolkovsky, the founding father of astronautics, was a brilliant scientist and engineer, but his motivation and drive came from his philosophical convictions, his belief in humanity's destiny to leave the Earth and colonize the universe, and his vision of deep unity between us and the cosmos.

Today, following the cosmist tradition, Russia has a lively transhumanist community and Singularity scene, with the only operational cryonics facility not in the U.S., and the Global Futures 2045 conferences dedicated to immortality and mind uploading.

Carey's film features Gagarin, Russian scientists and space engineers, Tsiolkovsky and many other cosmist thinkers, but the real protagonist is Tsiolkovsky's mentor, the cosmist mystic Nikolai Fedorov. He was one of the first modern thinkers who dared to suggest that, one day, science and technology might be able to resurrect the dead and bring back to life every person who ever lived.

Fedorov suggested that science is a tool given to us by God to enable us to resurrect the dead and, as promised, enjoy immortal life. He added that because the Earth could not sustain a population that never died, we must first conquer space. His ideas about human evolution, and in particular the idea that humans should take control of the process and direct it towards their own goals, inspired generations of Russian scientists and led directly to contemporary transhumanism.

Fedorov thought that physical resurrection is to be brought about by restoring the body to a condition that existed prior to death. A person is made up of atoms, and when a person dies these (finitely many) particles are scattered. The physical resurrection of the original person will be achieved by restoring all these atoms to their previous arrangement. To carry out the resurrection it is necessary to determine what this arrangement was and then to reposition the particles. This is a problem to be solved by science rather than by appeals to an outside power.

Fedorov's resurrection theory reflects 19th-century models of the universe and seems naive today. New technological resurrection theories based on contemporary science have been proposed, for example by Michael Perry [Perry 2000] and [Frank Tipler] [Tipler 1994].

But Perry's and Tipler's approaches, and mine, will probably seem equally naive to future scientists. Fedorov must be credited for the idea of technological resurrection, and we, his followers, are happy to see that many people are warming up to his vision. Following Fedorov, future scientists will scan the fabric of spacetime to find the dead, and bring them back to life.

Of course the super-science of technological resurrection, perhaps based on weird quantum physics (the term "quantum archeology" is often used), might not be developed until a very far future - perhaps thousands of years or more. But why hurry? To us, subjectively, no time will pass between death and resurrection. In the meantime, the cosmist philosophy can give us the positive, solar optimism that we need.

Nikolay Fedorov was the illegitimate son of a Russian nobleman called Gagarin. Pavel Gagarin, Fedorov's father, was not related to Yuri Gagarin the first cosmonaut, but this is an interesting coincidence, to say the least. Carey's film shows many aspects and protagonists of the Soviet space program, including of course the young icon and folk hero Yuri Gagarin, but is centered on Fedorov's ideas and legacy. In his "cosmic garden" Valery Borisov, a colorful cosmist with a cowboy attire and an encyclopedic knowledge of Fedorov's life and times, explains Fedorov's ideas in a nutshell:

> "Fedorov believed that science must help realize God's plan for man's salvation and for the resurrection of mankind. Christ said: what I have created, you must create too - and go further. What was it that Christ did? He rose from the dead. Literally, Christ was telling us to accomplish our own resurrection. Not to wait for some mystical event but to meet God halfway. Fedorov said if we resurrect everybody, they won't all fit on Earth. And he said wisely: 'In the Cosmos, abodes aplenty will appear.' That's why we need the Cosmos. The Cosmos offers empty planets where resurrected people will settle, and from there, direct the workings of the universe."

We follow Carey to ISRICA, the Institute for Scientific Research in Cosmic Anthropoecology in Novosibirsk, and follow experimental sessions in a "Kozyrev Mirror" built to test the controversial theories of astrophysicist Nikolai Kozyrev - technology aided meditation may unlock the latent shaman in us, and let us communicate with the cosmos.

This part of the film shows the spiritual, New Age component of cosmism, strongly emphasized by many cosmist thinkers, but condemned by the Soviet regime. On the opposite side of the Cosmist galaxy, Danila Medvedev, the young transhumanist director of the cryonics provider Kriorus, proposes a hardline materialistic approach to immortality, based on advanced technologies and mind uploading, with no concessions to spirituality.

George Young's book "*The Russian Cosmists*" [Young 2012] is a very intense mini encyclopedia with a lot of short biographical, literary and philosophical entries about main and lesser known cosmist thinkers, all influenced by Fedorov's seminal work.

Fedorov himself published almost nothing, but his most important works were collected by his followers and published after his death as *The Philosophy of the Common Task* [Fedorov 1990]. Young, a professor of Russian language and literature, dedicated decades of research to his book, a complete and authoritative reference that, I hope, will make cosmism much better known in the Western world.

Young emphasizes the Russianness of cosmism, the vastness of Russian land and history as a unique stage for the emergence of a system of thought so vast and daring to encompass both science and religion in a synergistic whole. The Russian cultural identity is part of the common ground that holds cosmism together.

Surprisingly, even Soviet bureaucrats were intrigued by Fedorov's ideas on technological resurrection. Young says:

> "Revolutionary immortality meant that individuals would die, but The People for whom the individual died would live on forever, and through inevitable progress in science and labor, The People of the future would eventually restore life to the sacrificed individuals... Lenin, waiting in his glass coffin, would be the first resurrected by science."

Like Carey, Young shows the diversity of the cosmist galaxy, and the many co-existing scientific, philosophical, religious, spiritual, as well as esoteric, shamanistic, gnostic approaches:

> "Main themes in Cosmist thought include the active human role in human and cosmic evolution; the creation of new life forms, including a new level of humanity; the unlimited extension of human longevity to a state of practical immortality; the physical resurrection of the dead; serious scientific research into matters long considered subjects fit only for science fiction, occult, and esoteric literature; the exploration and colonization of the entire cosmos; the emergence on our biosphere of a new sphere of human thought called the 'noosphere'; and other far reaching 'projects:' some of which may no longer seem as impossible or crazy as they did when first proposed in the late nineteenth and early twentieth centuries."

Young notes that, in her introduction to a valuable anthology of cosmist thought published in 1993, contemporary cosmist Svetlana Semenova identifies the core cosmist idea, active evolution:

> "This is the idea of active evolution, i.e., the necessity for a new conscious stage of development of the world, when humanity directs it on a course which reason and moral feeling determine, when man takes, so to say, the wheel of evolution into his own hands... Man, for actively evolutionary thinkers, is a being in transition, in the process of growing, far from complete, but also consciously creative, called upon to overcome not only the outer world but also his own inner nature."

Active evolution, taking the future of our species in our hands and steering it toward cosmic transcendence, is also the core idea of transhumanism, of which the Russian cosmists must be considered as direct precursors.

Critics say that active evolution is "against God's will," but the cosmist insight is that, on the contrary, radical active evolution IS God's will. One of Fedorov's favorite Bible passages was: "Truly, truly I say to you, he who believes in me will also do the works that I do; and greater works than those will he do." Young refers to "Fedorov's active, forceful, masculine Christianity" - a Christianity of action, which leads to trying to become more like God.

The collection "*Russian Cosmism*" [Groys 2018], edited by Boris Groys, includes crucial texts, "many available in English for the first time, written before and during the Bolshevik Revolution by the radical biopolitical utopianists of Russian Cosmism." The collection includes essays by Fedorov, Tsiolkovsky, and many other thinkers.

The essays of Alexander Agienko ("Svyatogor"), the founder of the Biocosmist movement, are especially interesting. Svyatogor's Biocosmism is a hardcore, secular version of Fedorov ideas. Young astutely notes that [Young 2012]:

> "Svyatogor and the Biocosmists anticipated not the Cosmist tendency as a whole, which still treats science and religion as parts of a holistic unity, but the transhumanist, cryogenic, cyborgianist, and other branches of technological immortalism that have emerged both in Russia and internationally in recent decades. These latter groups customarily grant Fedorov a tip of the hat but do not attempt to defend or follow him."

This shows that the tension between secular and religious transhumanism was already evident at those times.

Svyatogor was an anarchist-futurist poet and agitator who embraced the Russian revolution.

The Soviet state was, according to Svyatogor, needed to destroy the old and establish the new. What is the new? "The most important thing for us is the immortality of the individual and its life in the cosmos," answers Svyatogor: Man, under the Soviet state, is to become physically immortal and conquer the cosmos. Then, the resurrection of the dead envisioned by Fedorov will follow. But [Svyatogor criticized Fedorov from a secular, pre-transhumanist perspective]:

> "Fedorov, who adheres to a religious and platonic dualism that is alien to us, affirms the existence of two worlds: a perfect, divine world, and a human world... But recognizing one, real, infinite world, we start by realizing the personal immortality of the living and interplanetarism, on which our "common task" is based, with resurrection being relegated to third place..."

> "Our third task is the resurrection of the dead. What concerns us here is the immortality of the individual in the fullness of his spiritual and physical powers. The resurrection of the dead involves the full reconstruction of those who are already dead and buried. That said, the quagmire of religion or mysticism is not for us. We are too grounded for that and are in fact in the process of waging war on religion and mysticism."

A review of "Russian Cosmism" [Winslow 2018] introduces Svyatogor's ideas as:

> "Svyatogor goes on like this in one breathless sentence after another as he lays out a vision of art and revolutionary politics that demands 'victory over space,' immortality, and the resurrection of the dead. Svyatogor, as both a writer and a revolutionary, advocated for full-throttle luxury space communism, and he wanted it right this very second."

One difference between Fedorov and Svyatogor is that, while Fedorov's writings are often complicated and difficult to understand, Svyatogor wrote simple and crystal clear manifestos "to create an awareness of our ideas in their most basic form, as close as possible in format to slogans, to express our scientific or philosophical ideas in a nutshell."

Focused on achieving physical immortality and space travel as soon as possible, Svyatogor seems more realistic than Fedorov, because the resurrection of the dead is a greater technological challenge, by orders of magnitude, than physical immortality and space travel.

Not that Svyatogor was always realistic: He thought that the Soviet regime was to inevitably embrace his Biocosmist philosophy... but the same Soviet regime eventually condemned him a labor camp.

The resurrection of the dead is likely to require "magic," transcendent ultra-technology based on science vastly more advanced than ours. It seems plausible that [beings able to resurrect the dead would be practically indistinguishable from God].

This is, I think, a synthesis of Fedorov and Svyatogor, a fusion of religious and secular approaches to cosmism: The boundary between secularism and transcendence is not a sharp line, but [a space-filling fat fractal]. You can consistently choose to be on one or the other side, or on the fractal boundary itself.

While Fedorov interpreted resurrection as restoration, Svyatogor interpreted it as recreation with improvements. Here, Svyatogor's ideas tunnel through the fractal boundary between secularism and transcendence, approaching the central Christian concept of resurrection in a new body and a new world, perfected by God.

Modern Cosmism

Goffman and Cornell note [Goffman 2015] that the term "cosmism" was "borrowed by Ben Goertzel and Giulio Prisco in 2010 to denote a futurist philosophy more tailored for the modern era," and introduce modern cosmism as:

> "Today's cosmism posits a positive, far-reaching, blatantly transhumanist attitude toward science, technology, life, the universe, and everything. As summarized in Goertzel's 2010 book *A Cosmist Manifesto*, contemporary cosmism is less an analytical philosophical theory, and more an everyday sort of philosophy, focused on enthusiastically and thoroughly exploring, understanding, and enjoying the cosmos, and being open to all the possible forms life and mind may take as the future unfolds."

Ben Goertzel's "*A Cosmist Manifesto*" [Goertzel 2010] is the Bible of modern cosmism. Ben's book is a practical philosophy primer that blends science and spirituality, established science and awesome speculative ideas, futurism and compassion, technology and art, life strategies and cosmic visions - a must-read book where every reader will find snippets of spiritual wisdom and practical advice.

One of the first chapters of Ben's book, to which I contributed, is titled "Ten Cosmist Convictions." Ben says that the Ten Cosmist Convictions may serve as a reasonable preface for his book, and I add that they may serve as a reasonable preface for this book as well. Here they are:

> 1) Humans will merge with technology, to a rapidly increasing extent. This is a new phase of the evolution of our species, just picking up speed about now. The divide between natural and artificial will blur, then disappear. Some of us will continue to be humans, but with a radically expanded and always growing range of available options, and radically increased diversity and complexity. Others will grow into new forms of intelligence far beyond the human domain.

> 2) We will develop sentient AI and mind uploading technology. Mind uploading technology will permit an indefinite lifespan to those who choose to leave biology behind and upload. Some uploaded humans will choose to merge with each other and with AIs. This will require reformulations of current notions of self, but we will be able to cope.

> 3) We will spread to the stars and roam the universe. We will meet and merge with other species out there. We may roam to other dimensions of existence as well, beyond the ones of which we're currently aware.

> 4) We will develop interoperable synthetic realities (virtual worlds) able to support sentience. Some uploads will choose to live in virtual worlds. The divide between physical and synthetic realities will blur, then disappear.

> 5) We will develop spacetime engineering and scientific "future magic" much beyond our current understanding and imagination.

> 6) Spacetime engineering and future magic will permit achieving, by scientific means, most of the promises of religions - and many amazing things that no human religion ever dreamed. Eventually we will be able to resurrect the dead by "copying them to the future".

7) Intelligent life will become the main factor in the evolution of the cosmos, and steer it toward an intended path.

8) Radical technological advances will reduce material scarcity drastically, so that abundances of wealth, growth and experience will be available to all minds who so desire. New systems of self-regulation will emerge to mitigate the possibility of mind-creation running amok and exhausting the ample resources of the cosmos.

9) New ethical systems will emerge, based on principles including the spread of joy, growth and freedom through the universe, as well as new principles we cannot yet imagine

10) All these changes will fundamentally improve the subjective and social experience of humans and our creations and successors, leading to states of individual and shared awareness possessing depth, breadth and wonder far beyond that accessible to "legacy humans."

The strong "will" in the points above is not used in the sense of inevitability, but in the sense of intention: we want to do this, we are confident that we can do it, and we will do our fucking best to do it.

My interpretation of cosmism is totally compatible with Ben's - I agree with everything he says in the book - but I emphasize the technological resurrection aspect of Cosmism (point 6): Future science will resurrect everyone that ever lived. I think the concept of technological resurrection is a bridge between science and religion, which can offer hope and happiness to everyone in today's and tomorrow's world.

Therefore, when thinking, talking, or writing about cosmism vs. traditional religions, I emphasize the parallels and continuity rather than the differences. In particular, I emphasize the continuity between modern cosmism and Russian cosmism (an explicitly religious viewpoint): The technological resurrection concept is central to both.

In 2015 I participated in a conference on "Modern Cosmism" in New York City, organized by Vlad Bowen. George Carey and Ben Goertzel were among the participants. The conference was covered by novelist John Crowley in a story first published in *Harper's Magazine* [Crowley 2016] and then republished in Crowley's book "*Totalitopia*" [Crowley 2017].

At the conference, Bowen suggested that future post-biological uploaded humans will build artificial synthetic realities where "super-intelligent life can flourish and fulfill its mission as an important part of overall cosmic evolution" [Bowen 2015].

In my talk [Prisco 2015], I suggested that intelligent life among the stars, using quantum technologies beyond our understanding and imagination, might be able to influence spacetime events anytime, anywhere, including here and now, steer the evolution of the physical universe with spacetime engineering, and resurrect the dead from the past. In Crowley's words [Crowley 2016]:

> "Could quantum entanglement - the mysterious instant correlation of distantly separated subatomic particles - eventually make possible the connecting of every spacetime moment to every other, and permit instant data channels between different places, different times, and different universes? If so, maybe 'quantum archaeology' really could bring the dead back from when and where they are alive."

I think this cosmist vision could and should play for our grandchildren the same positive role - sense of wonder, sense of meaning, hope to be reunited with loved ones in an afterlife, and calm but active happiness - that traditional religions played for our grandparents. Russian cosmism provided a powerful mystique for the Russian space program, and I hope modern cosmism will provide an even more powerful mystique for our expansion to the stars.

Cosmic Humans

In "*Human Purpose and Transhuman Potential*" [Chu 2014], Ted Chu argues that we need a "Cosmic View" - a new, heroic cosmic faith for the post-human era. Chu believes that we should create a new wave of "Cosmic Beings," artificial intelligences and synthetic life forms, and pass the baton of cosmic evolution to them.

The new cosmic beings will move to the stars and ignite the universe with hyper-intelligent life. Creating our successors isn't betraying humanity and nature but, on the contrary, a necessary continuation of our evolutionary journey and an act of deep respect, to the point of "extreme worship," for humanity, evolution, and nature.

Chu's cosmic view of boundless evolution is similar to Pierre Teilhard de Chardin's vision of an emerging "noosphere," tending toward an Omega Point of unimaginable complexity. See [Steinhart 2008] for a modern interpretation of Teilhard's ideas, written for transhumanists, and references therein. Teilhard, a Jesuit priest whose work is now being rediscovered, was a believer with a deep religious faith.

Chu's cosmic view can play many of the impersonal, philosophically oriented roles of religion. But it doesn't offer belief in a personal God who cares, or hope in an afterlife. "The best way to overcome the fear of death," says Chu, "is to make one's interests gradually wider and more impersonal, until bit by bit the spiritual walls of the self recede, and one's life becomes increasingly merged into the universal whole."

This detached, impersonal, essentially Deist [Prisco 2014] contemplation of the self as a small part of the wonderful cosmic adventure of intelligent life and the creation of more and more evolved entities is, indeed, intellectually satisfying and motivating. But I am afraid that it may not be emotionally satisfying enough, especially for Westerners with a worldview strongly centered on the self. Chu admits that:

> "A non-personal God that is cosmic in nature has to be blended with certain human-friendly characteristics in order to be attractive, in the same way that colors are added to the pictures taken through space telescopes to enhance perception and draw popular interest."

Another in my opinion questionable aspect of Chu's excellent work is an excessive conceptual separation between today's humanity and future post-humanity.

While I wholeheartedly embrace the necessity - our cosmic duty - of self-directed evolution to create Cosmic Beings able to ignite the universe with intelligent life, I never liked the concept of "post-humanity." What's wrong with just "humanity," evolved?

I imagine a co-evolution of humanity and technology, with humans enhanced by synthetic biology and artificial intelligence, and artificial life powered by mind grafts from human uploads, blending more and more until it will be impossible - and pointless - to tell which is which. Like children retain their fundamental identity after growing up and becoming adults, post-humans will retain our fundamental identity. We don't need to fear a post-human takeover, because the post-humans will be ourselves. This alternative vision of cosmic humans is, I believe, consistent with Chu's cosmic view but more emotionally appealing.

Cosmic humans are the bridge between Chu's Deism and Teilhard's Theism. We will leave biology behind and move to the stars, find Gods, build Gods, and become Gods. We will resurrect the dead from the past with advanced science, space-time engineering and "time magic."

This "Theism From Deism" - a bridge between the impersonal, scientific cosmic view and a personal God who cares and grants resurrection - is present but never made too explicit in both transhumanism and new religious trends. The reason is easy to understand - it sounds too much like religion to rationalist transhumanists, and too much like cold, aseptic technology to believers and spiritually oriented seekers. Rationalists are often offended by the religious conclusions, and believers may be offended by the scientific premises.

I think, however, that we should actively promote our heroic cosmic faith, in a simple, appealing viral package. I don't really hope to see transhumanist technologies such as conscious AI and mind uploading in my lifetime, but I am happy for our grandchildren who will live in a "magic" world.

I am happy to be a small part of life on Earth, on its way to become cosmic life in a magic universe. And I am happy to contemplate the possibility that future Gods might find ways to remember us and bring us back to life. It's because our cosmic faith can provide happiness and hope, without asking to give up science, that I wish to offer it to everyone.

The Secret

Ben Goertzel opens "*A Cosmist Manifesto*" with a dedication to Valentin Turchin, "a great Soviet-American scientist and futurist visionary" who died the year the book was completed. Ben considers Turchin's book "*The Phenomenon of Science*" [Turchin 1977] as "one of the most elegant statements of Cosmist scientific philosophy ever written." [A free version of Turchin's book is available online] in the "*Principia Cybernetica*" website.

Turchin concludes "*The Phenomenon of Science*" with a reflection on the possibility of resurrection:

> "We shall hope that we have not yet made an uncorrectable mistake and that people will be able to create new, fantastic (from our present point of view) forms of organization of matter, and forms of consciousness. And then the last, but also the most disturbing, question arises: can't there exist a connection between the present individual consciousness of each human personality and this future superconsciousness, a bridge built across time? In other words, isn't a resurrection of the individual personality in some form possible all the same?

> Unfortunately, all we know at the present time compels us to answer in the negative. We do not see any possibility of this. Neither is there a necessity for it in the process of cosmic evolution. Like the apes from which they originated, people are not worth resurrection. All that remains after us is what we have created during the time allotted to us.

> But no one can force a person to give up hope. In this case there is some reason to hope, because our last question concerns things about which we know very little. We understand some things about the chemical and physical processes related to life and we also can make our way in questions related to feelings, representations, and knowledge of reality. But the consciousness and the will are a riddle to us. We do not know the connection here between two aspects: the subjective, inner aspect and the objective, external aspect with which science deals. We do not even know how to ask the questions whose answers must be sought. Everything here is unclear and mysterious: great surprises are possible.

> We have constructed a beautiful and majestic edifice of science. Its fine-laced linguistic constructions soar high into the sky. But direct your gaze to the space between the pillars, arches, and floors, beyond them, off into the void. Look more carefully, and there in the distance, in the black depth, you will see someone's green eyes staring. It is the Secret, looking at you."

Turchin's words are sober, but leave the door open to hope. Nobody can force you to give up hope. On the contrary, science offers reasons to hope that the Secret in the black depth might permit the continuation of personal consciousness after physical death.

I don't need certainty: For me, hope is good enough, especially the kind of hope that relies on action. I am persuaded that some forms of resurrection of the individual personality are possible in the physical universe, and I hope that future scientists will develop the science and practical engineering of technological resurrection. This is not, or not only, wishful thinking, but a project.

In Part 3 of this book I outline some aspects of contemporary science that seem to offer reasons to hope. Most (probably all) of my suggestions in Part 3 are likely to be wrong, or hopelessly naive. But so what? In a cosmist spirit, I believe that "science in its current form, just like religion and philosophy in their current forms, may turn out to be overly limited" [Goffman 2015] for understanding these things. Future thinkers (perhaps you, or your grandchildren?) will do much better.

Notes

[A free version of Turchin's book is available online]
http://pespmc1.vub.ac.be/POSBOOK.html

[a space-filling fat fractal] See "There's plenty of room at the bottom."

[beings able to resurrect the dead would be practically indistinguishable from God] See "Little green Gods."

[Frank Tipler] See "Omega Point."

[Mormon Transhumanist Association] See "Man will become like God, say Mormons and transhumanists."

[Svyatogor criticized Fedorov from a secular, pre-transhumanist perspective] Svyatogor's objections to Fedorov's resurrection program remind me of those voiced by Zoltan Istvan's character Jethro Knights in "*The Transhumanist Wager*" (see "The interplay of science fiction, science, and religion"). Both consider speculations on future resurrection as a distraction from the urgent need to launch a transhumanist revolution and attain immortality here and now.

References

[Bowen 2015] Vlad Bowen. Modern Cosmism and upcoming Singularities. YouTube, 2015.
https://www.youtube.com/watch?v=ek_9h4JID2g

[Carey 2011] George Catey. *Knocking on Heaven's Door*. Space Race. BBC, 2011.
http://www.bbc.co.uk/programmes/b0109ccb

[Chu 2014] Ted Chu. *Human Purpose and Transhuman Potential: A Cosmic Vision for Our Future Evolution*. Origin Press, 2014.

[Crowley 2016] John Crowley. Everything That Rises. *Harper's Magazine*, 2016.
https://harpers.org/archive/2016/01/everything-that-rises/

[Crowley 2017] John Crowley. *Totalitopia*. PM Press, 2017.

[Fedorov 1990] Nikolai Fedorov, Elisabeth Koutaissoff, and Marilyn Minto. *What Was Man Created For? The Philosophy of the Common Task*. Honeyglen, 1990.

[Goffman 2015] Ken Goffman, Jay Cornell. *Transcendence: The Disinformation Encyclopedia of Transhumanism and the Singularity*. Disinformation Books, 2015.

[Goertzel 2010] Ben Goertzel. *A Cosmist Manifesto*. Humanity+ Press, 2010.

[Groys 2018] Boris Groys (Ed.). *Russian Cosmism*. MIT Press, 2018.

[Perry 2000] Michael Perry. *Forever for All: Moral Philosophy, Cryonics, and the Scientific Prospects for Immortality*. Universal Publishers, 2000.

[Prisco 2014] Giulio Prisco. Cosmic Beings: Transhumanist Deism in Ted Chu's Cosmic View. *IEET*, 2014.
https://ieet.org/index.php/IEET2/more/prisco20140212

[Steinhart 2008] Eric Steinhart. Teilhard de Chardin and Transhumanism. *Journal of Evolution and Technology*, 2008.
https://jetpress.org/v20/steinhart.htm

[Tipler 1994] Frank Tipler. *The Physics of Immortality: Modern Cosmology, God and the Resurrection of the Dead*. Doubleday, 1994.

[Turchin 1977] Valentin Turchin. *The Phenomenon of Science: A Cybernetic Approach to Human Evolution*. Columbia University Press, 1977.

[Winslow 2018] Aaron Winslow. Russian Cosmism Versus Interstellar Bosses: Reclaiming Full-Throttle Luxury Space Communism. *Los Angeles Review of Books*, 2018.
https://lareviewofbooks.org/article/russian-cosmism-versus-interstellar-bosses-reclaiming-full-throttle-luxury-space-communism/

[Young 2012] George Young. *The Russian Cosmists: The Esoteric Futurism of Nikolai Fedorov and His Followers*. Oxford University Press, 2012.

CHAPTER 8 - THE INTERPLAY
OF SCIENCE FICTION,
SCIENCE, AND RELIGION

Science fiction and real science are in a symbiotic relationship with powerful feedback loops: Science fiction is inspired by science, and in turn it inspires new scientific and technical developments.

At times, new scientific and technical developments are directly inspired by the imagination of science fiction writers. More often, science fiction ignites, with an overpowering interest in science and technology, the flexible and imaginative minds of the young, who then become the next generation of scientists and engineers.

This has a huge social impact: Just like Golden Age science fiction [Nevala-Lee 2018] inspired those who developed the space program and the internet, the best of today's science fiction will inspire the creators of tomorrow's world.

The Golden Age of science fiction was mostly American, but today's science fiction is global. "The China of the present is a bit like America during science fiction's Golden Age, when science and technology filled the future with wonder," says Chinese science fiction master Liu Cixin [Liu 2016]. Chinese science fiction is a powerful cultural enabler for China's ambition to play a leading role in science, technology, and space expansion.

Why do we need science fiction to motivate scientists? Isn't science alone enough? No, because we are born storytellers, and we need powerful narratives to create a motivating sense of meaning.

I am a scientist by training, and I worked as a scientist for many years. I am also one of those people who find details and routine boring, unable to provoke and maintain enthusiasm.

However, despite my low boredom threshold I have always been able to perform routine scientific tasks well and focus on details for as long as it takes to achieve a goal - but I have always needed extra motivation from the grand, epic cosmic visions of science fiction.

I used to spend whole night shifts fixing electronics and realtime software in the lab, several nights a week, for years. I kept awake and interested by seeing myself as a small part of a big cosmic adventure. This is not a universal attitude, but I am hardly the only scientist to need extra motivation to focus on routine work.

How do we endure the boring wait for the next meaningful moment that may never come? We make up stories to tell each other, and ourselves. Then the long calculations that lead nowhere, the bugs in the software that don't go away, the failing devices, even the paperwork, acquire meaning as part of the background narrative and esthetics of science as a whole.

The best stories are not about impersonal science, but stories of people that we can empathize and identify with. That's why good science fiction is so effective in creating a burning, overwhelming enthusiasm for science.

Human beings "interpret the world by constructing narratives to explain it," explains a character in Robert Charles Wilson's science fiction masterpiece "*Blind Lake*" [Wilson 2003]. "The fact that some of our narratives are naive, or wishful, or simply wrong, hardly invalidates the process. Science, after all, is at heart a narrative."

> "Most fundamentally, narrative is how we understand. Narrative is how we understand the universe and it is most obviously how we understand ourselves. A stranger may seem inscrutable or even frightening until he offers us his story; until he tells us his name, tells us where he comes from and where he's going."

In some sense, science fiction is religion. In his opening presentation at the 2013 Conference of the Mormon Transhumanist Association, Lincoln Cannon said [Cannon 2013]:

> "Esthetics shape and move us, and at their strongest, they provoke us as a community to a strenuous mood. When they do that, they function as religion, not necessarily in any narrow sense, but esthetics that provoke a communal strenuous mood are always religion from a post-secular vantage point."

Charlie Jane Anders suggested that "smug atheists" should read more science fiction [Anders 2012]. "A lot of the best science fiction includes a sense of wonder at the hugeness of the cosmos," she said. "A lot of the best science fiction is intensely 'cosmic,' conveying just how huge and unknowable the universe is, and how little we still understand it. In a sense, the huge cosmic imagery of science fiction resembles some of the best religious paintings."

> "Contemplating space and time in all of their massive strangeness is much like gazing into the naked face of God... in Olaf Stapledon's First and Last Men, this sort of cosmic vision eventually leads to humanity awakening into a kind of 'cosmic spirit' which encompasses all living things. There's also tons of science fiction which deals with humanity reaching the next stage of evolution - which frequently has some quasi-religious overtones, as in some of Arthur C. Clarke's work."

I discuss the works of [Stapledon and Clarke] in another chapter of this book.

It's interesting to note that Anders was strongly criticized by many smug atheists for calling them smug, which shows how smug many atheists are and how right Anders was in calling them smug. They should, as Anders suggests, try to open their minds with the cosmic visions of the best science fiction.

Fiction literature plays a similar role for religion. Theology and philosophy alone wouldn't command strong emotional reactions, at least not for most people, without the human stories and science-fiction-like mythologies that form the narrative scaffolding of most religions.

Works of inspiring fiction may be integral parts of some of today's mainstream religions. I hope this will not offend anyone, but I tend to read religious mythology as fiction literature. I am agnostic on the literal, historic reality of the traditional tales of Moses, Jesus, or Muhammad, but I consider their stories as true in an equally important sense, as part of our shared narratives to understand the universe, and ourselves. However, while suspending disbelief in religious mythologies, it's important to bear in mind that parts of them may have been originally conceived as works of fiction.

I can believe in the teachings of a religion even without believing in the literal, historical truth of the writings. To me the question is not "Is it (factually, historically) True?" but "Is it Good? Does it inspire believers to do good things, like going to the stars or building a more compassionate world?"

Therefore, I am intentionally grouping traditional religious mythologies, fiction inspired by traditional religions, and fiction about new religions (fictional religions invented by science fiction writers), in one category.

In the 19th century Joseph Smith gave us the Book of Mormon and created a new, uniquely American religion [Bushman 2005]. I find Mormon mythology very inspiring, but my admiration for Joseph Smith is exactly the same if I think that he made everything up. Perhaps there is not even an important difference between imagination and revelation.

Perhaps, when we contemplate the numinous, we are more in tune with the universe, and we are allowed to take something back. Perhaps Joseph Smith was just more in tune with the universe than the rest of us. Most certainly, Smith was a genius able to do radical theological innovation in response to deep psychological needs not addressed by previous theologies - for example pre-mortal existence, proxy ordinances for the dead, and a post mortal existence that continued family relationships, including the opportunity to raise the children who died in this life.

I am sure that most of the mystics who claimed to have received revelations were sincerely persuaded of the reality of their experiences, but a revelation may be subjectively indistinguishable from your own inner voice, and perhaps also ontologically - God may choose to use your own inner voice to give you a revelation. Does it really make a difference whether Joseph was influenced by God's voice directly, or indirectly via his own imagination and intelligence? Aren't imagination and intelligence gifts of God, and isn't it plausible that God prefers to work through them?

[A friend familiar with The Urantia Book], a religious mythology developed in the 20th century, advised me to "read it as science fiction." That's exactly how I read all religious mythologies: As inspiring works of fiction that give human colors to theology and metaphysics, which on their own would be too abstract to be emotionally appealing.

Since religion deals with otherworldly matters and cosmic visions, science fiction is the literary genre where religious narratives belong (it always was, only we didn't call it science fiction until recently). [Arthur Clarke said]:

> "It may be that our role on this planet is not to worship God, but to create him."

These words are beginning to inspire contemporary theology, and they summarize my personal religion. I am persuaded that we will go to the stars and find Gods, build Gods, become Gods, and resurrect the dead from the past with advanced science, space-time engineering and "time magic." I see God emerging from the community of advanced forms of life and civilizations in the universe, and able to influence space-time events anywhere, anytime, perhaps even here and now. I also expect God to elevate love and compassion to the status of fundamental forces, key drivers for the evolution of the universe.

These ideas are not new: Bits and pieces can be found in the works of many scientists, philosophers and mystics. These ideas are basically compatible with the works of [Nikolai Fedorov] and other Russian cosmists, Pierre Teilhard de Chardin, [Frank Tipler], visionary "spiritual" transhumanism, and Mormon cosmology (at least in the interpretation of Lincoln Cannon and the [Mormon Transhumanist Association]).

Our beliefs can be considered as a modern formulation of traditional religions, or as a new religion. This religion doesn't have a name - perhaps "[cosmism]" is a good name, and I have used "cosmic engineering" to emphasize the central role of technology - but it has a growing body of human-colored narrative.

TALES OF THE TURING CHURCH

Science Fiction Continues To Inspire Real Religion

There are too many relevant works of contemporary science fiction to list, and I am sure I am not aware of them all. However, I wish to briefly mention some works of science fiction that can, and do, inspire real religious movements.

"Earthseed" is a fictional religion developed in Octavia Butler's novels *"Parable of the Sower"* and *"Parable of the Talents"* [Butler 1993, 1998]. Butler's heroine, Lauren Olamina, is a strong-willed, larger-than-life woman, the kind of person who builds cities and founds religions. Lauren rejects the personal God of her father, a Baptist minister, and looks for ultimate meaning in the impersonal works of natural laws.

The only permanent feature of the universe is change, and therefore change, permanent and unstoppable change, is the one God-like driving force of nature. We can't stop change, but we can try to steer and "shape" inevitable change toward desired ends, such as building a strong community of people who care for one another, or spreading humanity among the stars.

> "The destiny of Earthseed is to take root among the stars."

"Sort of like saying God is the second law of thermodynamics," is a common reaction to Lauren's first explanation of Earthseed. Others ask "If God is Change, then… then who loves us? Who cares about us? Who cares for us?"

Lauren's answer - "We care for one another. We care for ourselves and one another" - makes perfect sense, but Earthseed seems too intellectual and impersonal, hardly able to offer the strong, immediate emotional appeal of a religion. I guess Lauren Olamina - and Octavia Butler - were interrupted in their work on Earthseed by Butler's untimely death.

A religion similar to Earthseed has been proposed by Ted Chu. In *"Human Purpose and Transhuman Potential"* [Chu 2014], Chu proposes a "Cosmic View" based on active contemplation of our transcendent destiny and cosmic duty to create our successors, the "Cosmic Beings" who will move to the stars and ignite the universe with hyper-intelligent life.

I am afraid that the impersonal, essentially Deist approach of Earthseed and the Cosmic View may not be emotionally satisfying enough for most people, especially for Westerners with a worldview strongly centered on self, but I am hopeful that future refinements of Butler's and Chu's ideas will permit the emergence of "Religion 2.0," a synthesis of "cold," scientific, impersonal Deism, and the warm sense of personal hope offered by traditional religions.

Terasem, a religious movement founded by Martine Rothblatt and directly inspired by Butler's Earthseed, with a cuddly new-age look & feel, and open to wildly speculative ideas of technological resurrection and afterlife, seems like a good first step.

The scientific thriller *"Blasphemy"* [Preston 2008], by Douglas Preston, a real page turner, tells the biggest story: The birth and unstoppable growth of a new scientific religion, perhaps revealed by God himself.

In Red Mesa, Arizona, scientists have built the most powerful particle accelerator on Earth, Isabella, a fictional higher-energy version of the Large Hadron Collider at CERN. Isabella is so powerful that it can create Big Bang -like energies and rip holes in the fabric of spacetime itself.

The scientists receive a message that seems to come directly from the zone of extreme spacetime curvature that forms where particles and antiparticles collide. "For lack of a better word, I am God," says the mysterious entity.

The scientists, led by charismatic genius Gregory Hazelius, are initially skeptical and suspect a hoax, but the beauty and consistency of the words of God persuade them. Now they have the mission to reveal a new formulation of religion, based on science.

> "You will expand into the universe, literally and figuratively, as other intelligent entities have expanded before you. You will escape the prison of biological intelligence. Over time, you will link up with other expanded intelligences."

Regardless of its origins - God's revelation, an AI program inspired by God, or a brilliant memetic engineering hoax perpetrated by Hazelius - the new religion, "the Search," is beautiful. It is awesome, full of sense of wonder, compatible with science, and useful in the sense that it can take us beyond current humanity 1.0, and then to the stars where we will eventually meet God. In this sense, the Search is true religion.

In the magnificent "*Hyperion*" saga by Dan Simmons [Simmons 1989 and sequels], Jesuit scientist Paul Duré, a future Teilhard, waits for the largest machine of all to produce its deus - the universe. "How much of my elevation of St. Teilhard stemmed from the simple fact that I found no sign of a living Creator in the world today?" he wonders.

> "I seek to build what I cannot find elsewhere."

Duré's God is a Socinian God - a limited being, "able to learn and to grow as the world... the universe... becomes more complex." In the Hyperion universe, "our" God emerges from human civilization, and other Gods are born to alien and machine civilizations. There are hints at a hierarchy of Gods, striving without end towards more and more exalted status.

Paul Duré, Gregory Hazelius, and Lauren Olamina, are strong, vivid fictional characters who, in Wilson's words [Wilson 2003], "tell us their name, tell us where they come from and where they are going," and offer compelling narratives to color Religion 2.0 with human emotions. Their teachings deserve to "become real" and inspire real religious movements in the real world.

God And The Quantum Vacuum

Robert Charles Wilson is one of my favorite science fiction writers. "*Blind Lake*" [Wilson 2003] is my favorite book of his, and one of the best science fiction novels I have ever read. Five of five stars, maybe six.

Blind Lake is a government facility in Minnesota, where science is being rewritten. Borderline autistic child Tess lives in Blind Lake, time-shared between her mother Marguerite and her (divorced) father Ray, both scientists working at Blind Lake. Three journalists arrive at Blind Lake: Chris, coming from a bad moment and trying to recover his passion for science and journalism; veteran science writer Elaine; and Sebastian, the author of a best-selling quantum mysticism book. A few hours after they arrive, the facility is locked down. Nobody comes in, nobody can go out, and communications are cut.

Nobody knows what caused the lockdown, and those who try to escape are mercilessly killed by drones. Perhaps something very dangerous happened at Crossbank, another lab with the same weird quantum technologies? Blind Lake staff, contractors and visitors who were in Blind Lake on the day of the lockdown, and the three journalists, will be confined for several months without any contact with the external world. Wilson follows the human stories and the inevitable "lockdown romances," and develops the main characters, all nice persons except Ray.

But two main characters are not human.

The Subject is an alien on UMa47/E, a planet 50 light years away, in an alien city sometimes called "Lobsterville" by the press because the aliens look somewhat like lobsters (actually, I imagine them more like large red bipedal rhinos with an extra set of eating arms). The scientists at Blind Lake observe the alien world, focusing on The Subject with a virtual camera that follows him all the time like a Second Life camera following an avatar. We see fascinating scenes of life in the alien city, until one day the Subject leaves the city and goes on a mysterious quest in the wilderness.

The observation technology used at Blind Lake and Crossbank is based on weird quantum computers that nobody understands. The quantum computers produce TV-like images of the surface of UMa47/E, but nobody knows how and why the technology works. Chief engineer Charlie explains to Chris:

> "Then the NASA interferometer had begun to lose signal strength, and the newly designed O/BEC devices, quantum computers running adaptive neural nets in an open-ended organic architecture, were enlisted to strain the final dregs of signal from noise. They had done more than that, of course. Out of their increasingly deep and recursive Fourier analysis they had somehow derived an optical image even after the interferometers themselves ceased to function. The analytic device had replaced the telescope it was meant to augment."

The other non-human character is Mirror Girl, first introduced as an imaginary friend of Tess who stares back at Tess from mirrors and makes her presence known to Tess at odd moments, which worries Tess and her parents. But the reader soon understands that Mirror Girl is much more real, and somehow related to the mysterious quantum computers.

Wilson keeps building momentum until the end. When the thinking quantum computers, following the Subject, find a mysterious fractal structure on UMa47/E, they build a similar structure at Blind Lake. These huge fractal machines are advanced quantum computational nodes of a higher order sentience that spans the stars.

> "Thinking creatures make machines, Mirror Girl said, and their machines grow more complex, and eventually they build machines that think and do more than think: machines that invest their complexity into the structure of potential quantum states. Cultures of thinking organisms generate these nodes of profoundly dense complexity in the same way massive stars collapse into singularities."

Blind Lake is science fiction at its best, with real people here on Earth, alien civilizations, magic science, and awesome cosmic visions. If you want to read one of Robert Charles Wilson's books I recommend this one - but then you will be hooked and read them all.

One of the three journalists at Blind Lake, retired theology professor Sebastian Vogel, is the author of a best-selling quantum mysticism book. Titled "God & the Quantum Vacuum," the fictional book outlines a new religious outlook that has surprising parallels with emerging - in the real world - spiritual interpretations of quantum physics.

This subplot is developed only sparingly, mostly in the inner thoughts of Sebastian's girlfriend Sue.

> "Basically, his argument was that human beings had achieved their current state of consciousness by appropriating a small piece of a universal intelligence. Tapping into God, in other words. This definition of God, he argued, could be stretched to fit definitions of deity across a spectrum of cultures and beliefs. Was God omnipresent and omniscient? Yes, because He permeated all of creation. Was He singular or multiple? Both: He was omnipresent because He was inherent in the physical processes of the universe; but His mind was knowable (by human beings) only in discrete and often dissimilar fragments. Was there life after death, or perhaps reincarnation? In the most literal sense, no; but because our sentience was borrowed it lived on without our bodies, albeit as a tiny piece of something almost infinitely larger."

Wilson hints at how, according to modern physics, the quantum vacuum is "a complex brew of virtual particles popping in and out of existence too quickly to interact with the ordinary substance of things." Sebastian believes that localized irregularities in the quantum vacuum account for the presence of "dark matter" in the universe, and that that dark matter represents "a kind of ghostly neural network inhabiting the quantum vacuum."

Sebastian doesn't claim that his book represents a rigorous scientific theory or theology. He presents his ideas as "templates" or "suggestions," not to be taken literally, or "a kind of theological science fiction." But the book becomes "an inexplicable bestseller," and some people, including Sue, want to take it seriously as a scientific religion.

> "Sue understood what he was getting at. He wanted to give people the consolation of religion without the baggage of dogmatism. He was pretty casual about his science, and that pissed off people like Elaine Coster. But his heart was in the right place. He wanted a religion that could plausibly comfort widows and orphans without committing them to patriarchy, intolerance, fundamentalism, or weird dietary laws. He wanted a religion that wasn't in a perpetual fistfight with modern cosmology."

> "This was the idea Sue liked best, that people were pieces of something larger, something that popped up in a shape called Sue Sampel here and in a shape called Sebastian

Vogel over there, both unique but both connected, the way two distinctive mountain peaks were also pieces of the same planet."

Back here in the real world, similar ideas keep surfacing in the scientific and theological literature. It was Sebastian's fictional science that led me to explore some of [the real scientific theories outlined in the last chapters of this book].

Catching The Light Of Other Days

It is not surprising that some of the best visions of technological resurrection have been proposed by science fiction writers. What is science fiction, after all, but the best way to talk meaningfully of wildly speculative, still mysterious science and technology, and their likely impact on our world?

"*The Light of Other Days*" [Baxter 2000] is one of my favorite science fiction books ever. It was written in 2000 by Stephen Baxter based on a synopsis by Arthur Clarke. This breathtaking and well written story features awesome, "magic" science and technology, from a communication breakthrough based on the exotic physics of quantum wormholes all the way to mind fusion, group minds, viewing the past, and the resurrection of the dead.

Even in my most optimistic moments I don't dare hoping that the science and technology to resurrect the dead may be developed soon. But the imagination of Clarke and Baxter is wilder and more optimistic than mine: In this novel, they chart the development of resurrection science and technology in this century and the next. Their ideas are not only compatible with known science, but actually suggested by recent developments.

The novel starts in 2035. Hiram Patterson, a ruthless billionaire businessman, is the founder and CEO of the fictional company OurWorld (a future Google, but based in the current Microsoft campus in Seattle). Hiram's son and heir Bobby, a spoiled playboy, is actually Hiram's clone, and a much nicer person than he appears at the beginning.

Hiram's other son from a previous marriage, David, is a brilliant theoretical physicist. Journalist Kate Manzoni, known for breaking the story of a large comet on a direct collision course with the Earth, a doomsday extinction-level event five hundred years in the future, goes to Seattle to cover a world changing new technology developed by OurWorld.

At the OurWorld announcement party, at the beginning of the book, we can see current technology (that is, the current technology of 2035) in action, including an omnipresent Google on steroids that you can talk to and access via retinal implants, flying drones that serve drinks, holographic virtual projections and other cool things of the near future.

But the new technology, data communications via wormholes, is really "magic" (in the sense of [Clarke's third law]). It has been found that space is full of microscopic wormholes, distributed with very high density, in such a way that there are always wormholes connecting any location to any other location:

> "What we're seeing here are the mouths of wormholes, spontaneously forming, threaded with electric fields. Space is what keeps everything from being in the same place. Right? But at this level space is grainy, and we can't trust it to do its job any more. And so a wormhole mouth can connect any point, in this small region of space-time, to any other point - anywhere: downtown Seattle, or Brisbane, Australia, or a planet of Alpha Centauri. It's as if spacetime bridges are spontaneously popping into and out of existence."

> "What's more important is what we intend to do with all this. Simply put, we are going to reach into this quantum foam and pluck out the wormhole we want: a wormhole connecting our laboratory, here in Seattle, with an identical facility in Brisbane, Australia. And when we have it stabilized, that wormhole will form a link down

which we can send signals - beating light itself. And this, ladies and gentlemen, is the basis of a new communications revolution."

OurWorld engineers, led by David, find out how to enlarge and stabilize wormholes to transmit visible light, and discover how to use remote wormholes without remote equipment. Now, with the "WormCam," they can pop wormholes at remote locations open and watch what happens there. The WormCam is a remote viewing device, ideal for news gathering and spying. OurWorld's monopoly on WormCam technology doesn't last long, and of course intelligence agencies get access, but also hackers. The book follows the vicissitudes of Hiram, Bobby, David, Kate, FBI agent Michael Mavens, and angry young woman Mary, as humanity enters the era of total transparency.

But there is another, even more momentous breakthrough: The WormCam can access not only other locations, but also other times. The fabric of spacetime is full of micro wormholes, and WormCam technology permits establishing data links to anywhere, anytime. It is Hiram who first realizes the awesome potential of the new development:

> "'Don't you see? If he's right this is a turning point in history, this moment, right here and right now, the invention of this, this past viewer. Probably the air around us is fizzing with WormCam viewpoints, sent back by future historians. Biographers. Hagiographers.' He lifted up his head and bared his teeth. 'Are you watching me? Are you? Do you remember my name? I'm Hiram Patterson! Hah! See what I did, you arseholes!' And in the corridors of the future, innumerable watchers met his challenging gaze."

The book has many asides on the huge social impact of remote viewing, and past viewing. One is especially interesting: Now that past events can be watched in detail, 12,000 volunteers (one per day), including David, embark on a project to chronicle the life of the most important person of our history. The Jesus revealed by direct WormCam observation is, of course, different from the Jesus of the Gospels. Will the historical truth destroy Christianity? Perhaps not:

> "Perhaps we have lost Christ. But we have found Jesus. And His example can still lead us into an unknown future."

The new generation of "WormCam natives" pushes the new technology to really "magic" extremes, using wormholes and WormCam viewpoints embedded in the brain to achieve telepathy and mind fusion. The effect is similar to that of the neural nanobots imagined by Ramez Naam in "*Nexus*" [Naam 2013 and sequels] and Martin Higgins in "*Human+*" [Higgins 2017], but the underlying technology is much more exotic:

> "The new cortical implants, adapted from neural implant VR apparatus, were the final expression of WormCam technology: a small squeezed-vacuum wormhole generator, together with neural sensor apparatus, buried deep in the cortex of the recipient... The neural sensor was a highly sensitive neuron activity pattern analyser, capable of pinpointing individual neuronal synapses. Such an implant could read and write to a brain, and link it to others... Brains joined to brains, minds linked. They called themselves the Joined."

By combining past viewing with neural sensing wormholes, scientists will find ways to copy the dead from the past and upload them to the present, achieving [Nikolai Fedorov]'s vision of technological resurrection of the dead, bringing back to life all the dead from the past. When Bobby is resurrected, about a hundred years from the beginning of the novel, he finds out that:

> "It was possible now to look back into time and read off a complete DNA sequence from any moment in an individual's life. And it was possible to download a copy of that person's mind - making her briefly Joined, across years, even decades - and, by putting the two together, regenerated body and downloaded mind, to restore her. To bring her back from the dead... We live on Mars, the moons of the outer planets, and we're heading for the stars. There have even been experiments in downloading human minds into the quantum foam... We intend to restore all human souls, back to the beginning of the species. Every refugee, every aborted child. We intend to put right the past, to defeat the awful tragedy of death in a universe that may last tens of billions of years."

Is something like the WormCam even remotely possible? We don't know, but contemporary scientific speculations seem to imply that the magic technologies described in the novel could perhaps be realized. These preliminary results don't tell us how to build a WormCam, not yet, and they don't provide proof that such a device is physically possible. A lot of theoretical and experimental work will be needed for that. But [fundamental reality seems weird enough] to give plausibility to the intuition that every spacetime pixel is connected to every other spacetime pixel by information conduits that, perhaps, future engineers will be able to exploit with awesome results.

Jethro Knight's Quantum Archeology And Zoe Bach's Quantum Zen

Zoltan Istvan's science fiction novel *"The Transhumanist Wager"* [Istvan 2013] is one of the few self-published books to achieve widespread success and win literary prizes. The author, an award-winning journalist, decided to self-publish after the book was rejected by hundreds of publishers who, perhaps, thought that the book was too philosophical and politically incorrect for a wide audience.

The publishers were wrong: Only one year after publication, *"The Transhumanist Wager"* had thousands of often enthusiastic reviews, and was on its way to becoming a cult book. Today, after some publicity stunts like running for US President in 2016 and California Governor in 2018, Istvan is arguably the most visible face of transhumanism. In November 2019, Istvan announced his candidacy for the Republican Party's nomination in the 2020 US presidential election.

"The Transhumanist Wager" is an epic story of radical scientific and political ideas, their enemies, and the violent global conflict that ensues, painted in strong saturated colors with little room for intermediate shades and character development.

I wrote one of the first reviews, first published on *KurzweilAI* and then republished on *io9* [Prisco 2013]. I think *"The Transhumanist Wager"* is a great and important book, visionary, enjoyable, and thought-provoking, and I recommend it to both transhumanists and critics, and to all science fiction fans.

"The Transhumanist Wager" is often reviewed as a rabid anti-religion manifesto. But surprisingly, the novel includes the foundations of a new, cosmist scientific religion, a "third way" alternative to traditional belief and atheism, based on science but at the same time able to offer all the benefits of religion.

The main character, Jethro Knights, is a hardcore, radical transhumanist, uniquely and obsessively focused on achieving life extension here and now, and then immortality. He crushes all those who stand in his way, and wins his war against anti-transhumanists. At the end, his combat drones destroy the symbols of the world's religions, including Vatican City, killing thousands of peaceful believers in prayer. It seems difficult to get more rabidly anti-religion than that.

But the other main character, Jethro's girlfriend Zoe Bach, has a totally different attitude. The tension between Jethro's and Zoe's philosophies is, for me, the most interesting aspect of the novel. Zoe believes in the quantum interconnectedness of all things and she imagines that the self, encoded in the entangled twists and folds of quantum reality, may survive physical death.

> "She reveled in contradictions that many rational and science-minded people deemed intellectual heresy. Zoe saw paradoxical concepts - shades of gray - as a necessary balance to an often unruly universe full of mystery and surprise. Her deep-seated mysticism welcomed complex crossovers of many different ideas, even sweeping metaphysical theories and formal religious beliefs. She liked to think of her personal philosophy as an all-embracing transhuman spiritualism."

> "I prefer to call it quantum - the mystical motor of all things. I believe that all matter has undetermined tendencies and infinite possibilities, even if they appear to follow

prescribed scientific patterns, like our brains are doing right now... It's all filled with a countless amount of possibilities. Everything is swimming in a cosmic quantum Zen."

"Besides, you're going to be all-powerful, then you're destined to master the quantum sovereignty of the universe. One day you'll have to be able to feel and to control it; you'll have to be able to form and to create with it; you'll have to be able to manifest and to merge with it. Whether its nanotechnology, string theory physics, or just the creative thoughts in your mind, you'll have to rule with quantum dominance. Call it 'spiritual transhumanism' if it's easier to swallow."

Based on Zoe's quantum Zen reality, future super-science and quantum technologies may be able to resurrect the dead.

Jethro agrees. First, he is persuaded that biological life extension can only be a temporary solution, and that only mind uploading technology can permit radical life extension and indefinite lifespan:

"The scientist's experiments, to combine brain neurons to the hardwiring of computers in order to download human consciousness, seemed the most sensible and important direction for the immortality quest. While getting the human body to live longer was a priority, it was not a long-term solution. Conscious computerized machines and their digital content, with proper maintenance, could last indefinitely. They were so much more durable than flesh. But this thinking was exactly the most radical as well. Because eventually, perhaps sooner than even many transhumanists would have it, there would be no need left at all for the human body."

Second, Jethro imagines future "time scanning" or "quantum archeology" technologies able to retrieve the dead from the past (which means to retrieve the information stored in their brains) and bring them back to life via mind uploading. In fact, Jethro wrote a (fictional of course) article titled "On the Transhuman Possibility of 11th Dimensional Superstring Theory Realities," which speculated on resurrection technology:

"It described, in scientific terms, that if people lived long enough, with all the achievable technological advancements in a thousand years, teleportation into multiple dimensions via antimatter would be possible - and with it, the ability to reverse time and bring back anything anyone desired."

Jethro considers these far-future speculations as a distraction from his overpowering drive to launch his transhumanist revolution and attain immortality here and now, but he considers quantum archaeology as a possibility, though remote in the future. This is evident from his last words to dying Zoe:

"'I'll come find you,' Jethro whispered when he saw Zoe departing life, unable to control himself, speaking the language she understood. 'Yes... my love... I know you will... I'll be waiting.'"

But Jethro is afraid of hoping in technological resurrection, which feels like betraying himself:

"He didn't want to think that way. Hopelessly metaphysical. That timeline was too far out. Too technologically complex. Too mystical and quantum. And it required far too much hope."

But hope is not dangerous - often hope is the only way to cope with the heartaches of life. I hope that, in a future sequel, Jethro will find Zoe in the folds of quantum weirdness, and bring her back, or join her, or something else, Perhaps Zoltan will think of something.

Taken together, Zoe's quantum mysticism and Jethro's mind uploading and quantum archeology function as cornerstones of a new scientific religion, which offers hope in transcendence and resurrection. Not bad for a "rabid anti-religion rant."

I consider technological resurrection as a physical possibility, and this is how I cope with my conviction that indefinite lifespans and post-biological life will not be developed in time for my generation. Since technological resurrection is equivalent to the resurrection promised by religion, I don't share Jethro's rabid hostility to religion. On the contrary I think appropriate interpretations of transhumanism and religion can be perfectly compatible and mutually reinforcing.

"Basically, I think there's lots of room for spiritual beliefs and I encourage them, so long as they don't detract from the progress of science," Zoltan emailed me. "In fact, managed properly, creative spiritual ideas (such as Zoe's) could actually help science progress faster."

Other Lives And Afterlives In The Multiverse

In the "[Many Worlds Interpretation]" (MWI) of quantum mechanics, introduced by Hugh Everett in 1957, different possible worlds and different versions of your life are equally real. The collection of all parallel worlds is called the "multiverse."

It's worth noting that the concept was anticipated by science fiction writer Fredric Brown in his science fiction novel "*What Mad Universe*" [Brown 1954]. In the novel, a superintelligent robot explains to the main character, who accidentally found himself in a parallel world, that there are an infinite number of coexistent universes.

> "They include this one and the one you came from. They are equally real, and equally true... There is a universe in which Huckleberry Finn is a real person, doing the exact things Mark Twain described him as doing. There are, in fact, an infinite number of universes in which a Huckleberry Finn is doing every possible variation of what Mark Twain might have described him as doing. No matter what variation, major or minor, Mark Twain might have made in the writing of that book it would have been true."

Not surprisingly, the multiverse of parallel worlds is extensively featured in science fiction literature. One example is "*Dreamer*" [Miller 2000], by Richard Miller. I am surprised that "*Dreamer*" hasn't been a bestseller: The novel is an intoxicating page turner with hypnotic atmosphere, strong characters, and wild metaphysics.

In a research project, test subjects walk down memory lanes and relive their memories with full detail. But some subjects find themselves in another version of their past. Perhaps one can change something? Perhaps one can stay there and live a new life?

After (actually before) reading "*Dreamer*" I got in touch with Richard and in 2005 we jointly wrote an essay titled "Shadows and the concept of self" [Prisco 2005, 2019] to speculate on the science of "*Dreamer*." The main points of the essay are worth summarizing here.

While Hugh Everett's formulation of quantum mechanics makes a lot of sense, its popular interpretation as "Many Worlds" (MWI) should be taken only as a simple picture. We live in One Big World, of which our mind builds a simplified representation as many (small) worlds.

This "[Many Minds Interpretation]" (MMI) of quantum mechanics seems plausible to me, and I suspect that it's close to what Everett actually meant. In the MMI, it's an observer's consciousness, rather than the universe, that splits into parallel streams unaware of each other. Perhaps all your parallel minds are combined in the multimind of a multiversal multi-you that directs this you from behind the scenes.

Your mind here and now is a shadow (I guess "projection" is more correct, but "shadow" sounds nicer) of your multimind. For a simple analogy, think of your multimind as a 3-dimensional solid casting 2-dimensional shadows on different planes. When the solid rotates in its 3D space, the 2D shadows rotate as well.

In this analogy, the physical reality that you perceive is a 2D plane, and your mind is one of many shadows of your solid, 3D multimind. Your multimind is hugely more complex and conscious than your mind, and aware of all Everett realities - other times and other worlds - "at the same time" (here, intuitive physics and language break down and stop working).

This is beautifully hinted at in "*Dreamer*" and in Richard's essay "Soul, Spacetime and The

Hidden Observer" (included in [Prisco 2005]).

The implications for afterlife speculations are evident: After you die, your multimind is still there and continues to cast shadows on planes that ordinary human consciousness can access. Therefore, after death you will continue to experience other times and other versions of your life.

The 2017 film "*The Discovery*," directed by Charlie McDowell, includes intriguing and well-thought hints at this concept of afterlife.

Robert Redford plays a scientist who proves the existence of an afterlife by showing that subatomic consciousness waves leave the body at the moment of death and head for a new plane of existence. Where consciousness goes and what happens there isn't known, but the very fact that there is an afterlife is sufficient to push millions of people to end their life. Two years later, the scientist finds a way to capture images of the afterlife by scanning dead people's brains.

The hard science of subatomic this-and-that, particles and waves, brain scanning devices and all that, is very sketchy - essentially the paragraph above - and not the central point of "*The Discovery*." The film is more concerned with the nature of the afterlife, which turns out to be a new version of your previous life where you get a chance to fix something that went wrong:

> "When we die, what if we travel to an alternate version of our own life? A second chance? Then we wouldn't... just have to accept our biggest regret. In the afterlife, we could change it."

So you go on living over and over again as other versions of you, and you can try to make things better. The thesis of "*The Discovery*" seems to be that you have some degree of control that allows you to make things better. If so, after death you will experience a better version of your life, and then a better one, and then an even better one, and so forth. Not a bad prospect if you ask me.

Of course there are also bad versions of your life - everything that can physically happen does happen somewhere in the multiverse. But in this model your next life is likely to be better than this one. This reconciles me with Everett's theory, which I used to find intellectually intriguing but emotionally unpleasant because, of course, I don't want to experience all those bad versions of my life. In this model, I have experienced them "already" and moved to better places in the multiverse.

While drafting "Shadows and the concept of self" I thought of an interesting extension of this concept of afterlife.

Somewhere in the multiverse there must be versions of your life very different from this one. For example, there must be a reality where the maternity ward staff screwed up bigtime, gave another baby to your parents, and gave you to other parents coming from the other side of the world.

In that version of your life, "you" grow up with other parents, in another country, speak another language, have another name, go to another school, meet other friends... The other baby grows up with your parents, in your country, speaks your language, has your name, goes to your school, meets your friends...

Which baby is you? Which multimind casts which shadow?

I think the simplest way out is to realize that the two multiminds are themselves shadows of one Mind. Our multiminds (and therefore our minds) intermingle and merge in the multiverse, and can be considered as shadows of one cosmic Mind. We are all essentially the same person, as suggested by [Eastern spiritual traditions and the philosophy of Open Individualism].

Therefore, as I said, after death you will experience other times and other versions of your life. But you will also experience other lives as other persons, which is equivalent to the traditional concept of reincarnation.

Gregory Benford's "*Rewrite*" [Benford 2019] is described by the publisher as "a thematic sequel to Gregory Benford's award-winning bestseller *Timescape* [Benford 1980]." Both "*Rewrite*" and "*Timescape*" are centered on Everett's multiverse, "weird" time physics, and the possibility to alter the past.

In "*Timescape*," messages sent to the past via tachyon beams (fortuitously) prevent the assassination of John Kennedy in 1963 and spawn a new world where Kennedy is not killed. In "*Rewrite*," the main character Charlie Moment strives to prevent the assassinations of Martin Luther King and Robert Kennedy in 1968, and eventually succeeds:

> "He has stopped the killing of Martin Luther King, along this time line, and maybe saved Kennedy, too… Maybe some perfect liberal state will come about, and maybe not."

How can you change the past without causing inconsistent causal loops (paradoxes)? In both novels, it's "all done with the Everett interpretation," explains Benford in the "*Rewrite*" afterword. "In quantum cosmology there is no single history of space-time. Instead, all possible histories happen simultaneously."

The idea is that you don't change the past of your original timeline, but intervene in the past of another timeline, which is identical to your original timeline until your intervention, and then diverges. Think of it, and all paradoxes will go away.

But "*Rewrite*" is not only a time travel novel. It's also a novel about the afterlife. The idea is that, after death, your consciousness finds itself in your past in another Everett world.

But how can you change things if you don't remember what happened in your other lives? Well, you don't (I guess), but Charlie does: He is one of the few people able to remember other Everett timelines.

Charlie dies in a car crash in 2000 and wakes up in the 1968 of another timeline, with full memory of his other life. We follow Charlie's adventures in Everett's multiverse and meet others who are able to remember other timelines, including Giacomo Casanova, Albert Einstein, and Robert Heinlein.

Things get even weirder: Some people are not forced to re-enter time as themselves, but are able to "go laterally" and re-enter time as other persons. Casanova and Einstein are able to go laterally, but so is Gabriel, a criminal mastermind who creates multiple simultaneous copies of himself.

Gabriel and his clones want to create new timelines inspired by their politics, starting with the assassinations of Martin Luther King and Robert Kennedy. In a scene that combines sex and horror, Gabriel even tries (Tried? Will try?) to go laterally on (aka possess) Charlie while

Charlie is… (OK, no spoilers here).

Charlie, whom we first meet in other timelines, eventually finds himself in our timeline after a string of lives and deaths. In a momentous ending, Charlie kills Gabriel and spawns a new timeline where Martin Luther King and Robert Kennedy are not murdered. Charlie has also found the wisdom to become a force for good:

> "He has an answer to work with now: look for the place where your deep gladness and the world's deep hunger meet."

If you think of it, the concept of afterlives in other Everett worlds makes a lot of sense. It seems plausible that, after death, you'll find yourself in a very similar consciousness stream, and who can be more similar to you than your past self? If other Everett worlds exist, this is a very reasonable concept of reincarnation - almost a trivially evident one if you ask me, assuming that Everett's multiverse is really out there.

Continuing my life in another branch of the multiverse after death, even without my current memories, seems good enough to me. Re-entering a very similar past, with my wife and daughter and family and friends and doggies, is really all I ask for (I understand that others may prefer a very different past though).

But, of course, it's very natural to dream of being young and strong again WITH the memories and the hard-won experience of this life. Perhaps some kind of quantum tunneling through the multiverse does happen now and then, and perhaps some people have (or develop) special skills.

In Benford's novel, Einstein suggests that "minds can entangle to other universes if their coherence is enough." Heinlein then says:

> "Then maybe we can learn to use it. Make a technology."

Enter my favorite speculations on technological resurrection. The real Heinlein, Gregory Benford told me, "rejected a free freeze [cryonic suspension], thinking it might interfere with his 'next stage, whatever it is.'" I guess Heinlein, like his fictional version, would have approved of resurrection technologies based upon the physics of the naturally occurring "next stage" (whatever it is).

The concept of afterlives in other Everett worlds makes even more sense in [Julian Barbour's cosmology], where there is no time but a huge set of timeless "Nows." This "present" version of you is not the one and only real continuation of the "past" versions of you, because there's no present and no past. Therefore, this version of you continues in other Nows, and you'll find yourself there after death. When I think of Barbour's cosmology, reincarnation in another Now (without memories of this Now) seems obvious.

What about time travel? If there is no time, of course there can't be time travel. There must be "Nows in which there are beings whose memories tell them they have travelled backwards in time," explains Barbour [Barbour 2000], but he thinks that "such Nows have a very low probability."

However, this doesn't entirely rule out the improbable possibility of waking up in another Now after death with memories from this Now, which have somehow tunneled to the new Now, like it happens to Charlie in Benford's "*Rewrite*."

Notes

[A friend familiar with The Urantia Book] Alison Gardner. See "Little green Gods."

[Arthur Clarke said] See "Agnostics, possibilians, and mysterians."

[Clarke's third law] See "Agnostics, possibilians, and mysterians."

[cosmism] See "Knocking on Heaven's door."

[cryonic suspension] See "Transhumanism."

[Eastern spiritual traditions and the philosophy of Open Individualism] See "The lights of Eastern spirituality."

[Frank Tipler] See "Omega Point."

[fundamental reality seems weird enough] See "Exotic space, mysterious time, magic quantum," and following chapters.

[Julian Barbour's cosmology] See "Exotic space, mysterious time, magic quantum."

[Many Minds Interpretation] See "Exotic space, mysterious time, magic quantum."

[Many Worlds Interpretation] See "Exotic space, mysterious time, magic quantum."

[Mormon Transhumanist Association] See "Man will become like God, say Mormons and transhumanists."

[Nikolai Fedorov] See "Knocking on Heaven's door."

[the real scientific theories outlined in the last chapters of this book] See "Into the deep waters," and following chapters.

[Stapledon and Clarke] See "Agnostics, possibilians, and mysterians."

References

[Anders 2012] Charlie Jane Anders. Why Smug Atheists Should Read More Science Fiction. *io9*, 2012.
https://io9.gizmodo.com/5963475/why-smug-atheists-should-read-more-science-fiction

[Barbour 2000] Julian Barbour. *The End of Time: The Next Revolution in Physics*. Oxford University Press, 2000.

[Baxter 2000] Stephen Baxter, Arthur Clarke. *The Light of Other Days*. Tor, 2000.

[Benford 1980] Gregory Benford. *Timescape*. Simon & Schuster, 1980.

[Benford 2019] Gregory Benford. *Rewrite: Loops in the Timescape*. Saga Press, 2019.

[Brown 1954] Fredric Brown. *What Mad Universe*. Bantam Books, 1954.

[Bushman 2005] Richard Bushman. *Joseph Smith: Rough Stone Rolling*. Alfred A. Knopf, 2005.

[Butler 1993] Octavia Butler. *Parable of the Sower*. Four Walls Eight Windows, 1993.

[Butler 1998] Octavia Butler. *Parable of the Talents*. Seven Stories Press, 1998.

[Cannon 2013] Lincoln Cannon. Purpose of the Mormon Transhumanist Association, 2013.
https://lincoln.metacannon.net/2013/04/purpose-of-mormon-transhumanist.html

[Chu 2014] Ted Chu. *Human Purpose and Transhuman Potential: A Cosmic Vision for Our Future Evolution*. Origin Press, 2014.

[Higgins 2017] Martin Higgins. *Human+*. Neely Worldwide Publishing, 2017.

[Istvan 2013] Zoltan Istvan. *The Transhumanist Wager*. Futurity Imagine Media, 2013.

[Liu 2016] Ken Liu (Ed.). *Invisible Planets: Contemporary Chinese Science Fiction in Translation*. Tor Books, 2016.

[Miller 2000]. Richard Miller. *Dreamer*. Two Sixty Press, 2000.

[Naam 2013] Ramez Naam. *Nexus*. Angry Robot, 2013.

[Nevala-Lee 2018] Alec Nevala-Lee. *Astounding: John W. Campbell, Isaac Asimov, Robert A. Heinlein, L. Ron Hubbard, and the Golden Age of Science Fiction*. Dey Street Books, 2018.

[Preston 2008] Douglas Preston. *Blasphemy*. Forge Books, 2008.

[Prisco 2005] Giulio Prisco, Richard Miller. Shadows and the concept of self (2005). *Turing Church*, 2017.
https://turingchurch.net/shadows-and-the-concept-of-self-d01ff65ce9f9

[Prisco 2013] Giulio Prisco. The Transhumanist Wager and the terrifying struggle for the future. *io9*, 2013.
https://io9.gizmodo.com/the-transhumanist-wager-and-the-terrifying-struggle-for-510012440

[Prisco 2017] Scientific concepts of afterlife sketched in The Discovery. *Turing Church*, 2017.
https://turingchurch.net/scientific-concepts-of-afterlife-sketched-in-the-discovery-247013123629

[Prisco 2019] Giulio Prisco. Your many minds and your Mind in the MIND. *Turing Church*, 2019.
https://turingchurch.net/your-many-minds-and-your-mind-in-the-mind-383a229057bd

[Simmons 1989] Dan Simmons. *Hyperion*. Doubleday, 1989.

[Wilson 2003] Robert Charles Wilson. *Blind Lake*. Tor Books, 2003.

CHAPTER 9 - LITTLE GREEN GODS

If contemporary atheists have a prophet, he is Richard Dawkins. The atheist holy book is Dawkins' "*The God Delusion*" [Dawkins 2006].

While his militant "New Atheist" followers can be annoying and aggressive, Dawkins himself is reasonable, measured, and insightful. In the chapter "Little Green Men" of "*The God Delusion*," Dawkins mentions the excellent science fiction novels "*A for Andromeda*," by Fred Hoyle [Hoyle 1962] and "*Contact*," by Carl Sagan [Sagan 1985]. In both novels, humanity receives a message from incredibly advanced alien civilizations.

Dawkins is open to the idea that inconceivably advanced, God-like civilizations may be out there among the stars:

> "Whether we ever get to know about them or not, there are very probably alien civilizations that are superhuman, to the point of being god-like in ways that exceed anything a theologian could possibly imagine. Their technical achievements would seem as supernatural to us as ours would seem to a Dark Age peasant transported to the twenty-first century. Imagine his response to a laptop computer, a mobile telephone, a hydrogen bomb or a jumbo jet. As Arthur C. Clarke put it, in his Third Law: 'Any sufficiently advanced technology is indistinguishable from magic.' The miracles wrought by our technology would have seemed to the ancients no less remarkable than the tales of Moses parting the waters, or Jesus walking upon them. The aliens of our SETI signal would be to us like gods, just as missionaries were treated as gods (and exploited the undeserved honour to the hilt) when they turned up in Stone Age cultures bearing guns, telescopes, matches, and almanacs predicting eclipses to the second.
>
> In what sense, then, would the most advanced SETI aliens not be gods? In what sense would they be superhuman but not supernatural? In a very important sense, which goes to the heart of this book. The crucial difference between gods and god-like extra-terrestrials lies not in their properties but in their provenance. Entities that are complex enough to be intelligent are products of an evolutionary process. No matter how god-like they may seem when we encounter them, they didn't start that way."

Dawkins also admits the possibility of the [simulation hypothesis] - the idea that our reality, and ourselves in it, might be a computer simulation:

> "Science-fiction authors, such as Daniel F. Galouye in *Counterfeit World* [Galouye 1964], have even suggested (and I cannot think how to disprove it) that we live in a computer simulation, set up by some vastly superior civilization. But the simulators themselves would have to come from somewhere. The laws of probability forbid all notions of their spontaneously appearing without simpler antecedents. They probably owe their existence to a (perhaps unfamiliar) version of Darwinian evolution."

If there are god-like civilizations among the stars, perhaps we ourselves may become one. In a *New York Times* interview of 2011 [Powell 2011], Dawkins states that "It's highly plausible that in the universe there are God-like creatures," and elaborates on the possibility that future generations might co-evolve with computers, in a silicon destiny, and our descendants might "become something like bolts of superpowerful intelligent and moral energy," perhaps immortal.

In an Afterword to the Penguin Classics edition of Fred Hoyle's "*The Black Cloud*" [Hoyle 2010], Dawkins praises the novel as one of the greatest works of science fiction ever written.

I totally agree. In "*The Black Cloud*" we (actually, our fathers - the book was first published in 1957) are confronted with a fundamentally alien entity, with knowledge and powers vastly exceeding our own. Dawkins says:

> "The Black Cloud vividly conveys to us what it would be like to be visited by an extraterrestrial being whose intelligence would seem god-like from our lowly point of view. Indeed, Hoyle's imagination far outperforms all religions known to me. Would such a super-intelligence then actually be a god?
>
> An interesting question, perhaps the founding question of a new discipline of 'Scientific Theology.'"

> "The answer, it seems to me, turns not on what the super-intelligence is capable of doing, but on its provenance. Alien beings, no matter how advanced their intelligence and accomplishments, would presumably have evolved by something like the same gradual evolutionary process as gave rise to our kind of life."

I don't disagree, but I propose an alternative and I think clearer version of the last paragraph:

> The answer, it seems to me, turns not on the provenance of the super-intelligence, but on what it's capable of doing. Super-intelligent alien beings, no matter how they have evolved, would be so advanced in their intelligence and accomplishments that we could only call them Gods.

Or in other words, if it looks like a God, and it acts like a God, and it thunders like a God, then I call that entity a God.

Skeptic thinker Michael Shermer agrees [Shermer 2018]: "Civilizations this advanced would have so much knowledge and power as to be essentially omniscient and omnipotent," he says. "What would you call such a sentience?"

> "If you didn't know the science and technology behind it you would call it God, which is why I have postulated that any sufficiently advanced extraterrestrial intelligence or far future human is indistinguishable from God."

This formulation of Arthur Clarke's Third Law - "Any sufficiently advanced technology is indistinguishable from magic" - is known as "Shermer's last law."

God-Like Post-Biological Civilizations In The Universe

I enthusiastically support the space program, and I hope to see people walking on the Moon again, and then Mars and beyond. We need to see people in space to reboot our dreaming engine. At the same time I am persuaded that, ultimately, [we'll leave our flesh and blood bodies behind, and space will be colonized by our post-biological mind children]. Many big thinkers and space enthusiasts share this view.

Arthur Clarke was one of the first to see it. In "*2001*" [Clarke 1968], he wrote:

> "And now, out among the stars, evolution was driving toward new goals. The first explorers of Earth had long since come to the limits of flesh and blood; as soon as their machines were better than their bodies, it was time to move. First their brains, and then their thoughts alone, they transferred into shining new homes of metal and of plastic."

Other science fiction writers have described a universe populated by upload civilizations, and many scientists agree.

In "*The Eerie Silence*" [Davies 2010], Paul Davies argues that advanced civilizations in the universe are likely to be post-biological, artificial intelligences in robotic bodies. Not only are machines better able to endure extended exposure to the conditions of space, but they have the potential to develop intelligence far beyond the capacity of the human brain.

"I think it very likely - in fact inevitable - that biological intelligence is only a transitory phenomenon, a fleeting phase in the evolution of the universe," says Davies. "If we ever encounter extraterrestrial intelligence, I believe it is overwhelmingly likely to be post-biological in nature."

I hope, and think, that we will colonize other planets and then reach out to the stars. But this will be done, Stephen Hawking believed [Prisco 2018], with intelligent machines. In his last book, "*Brief Answers to the Big Questions*" [Hawking 2018], published after his death, Hawking said:

> "It might be possible to use genetic engineering to make DNA-based life survive indefinitely, or at least for 100,000 years. But an easier way, which is almost within our capabilities already, would be to send machines. These could be designed to last long enough for interstellar travel. When they arrived at a new star, they could land on a suitable planet and mine material to produce more machines, which could be sent on to yet more stars. These machines would be a new form of life, based on mechanical and electronic components rather than macromolecules. They could eventually replace DNA-based life, just as DNA may have replaced an earlier form of life."

"The time window during which detectable alien intelligence is biological is very, very short," said Seth Shostak of the SETI (Search for Extra-Terrestrial Intelligence) Institute [Shostak 2012]. "Machine intelligence - which could be durable and long-lasting far beyond the limits of a biological species - will dominate the universe."

Intelligence "will, I think, leave the cradle rather quickly," says Shostak.

> "In other words, biological intelligence might be only a stepping stone to something far cleverer, something that is both longer-lived and more widespread than its proto-

plasmic precursors."

"Biologically based technological civilization as defined above is a fleeting phenomenon limited to a few thousand years, and exists in the universe in the proportion of one thousand to one billion, so that only one in a million civilizations are biological," said former NASA Chief Historian Steven Dick [Dick 2003]. "Such are the results of taking cultural evolution seriously, and applying the Intelligence Principle and the insights of Moravec, Kurzweil and Tipler to the entire universe, using Stapledonian thinking."

According to Dick, advanced civilizations in the universe have probably evolved beyond biology, and machines are likely to be the dominant form of intelligence in the post-biological universe.

Royal Astronomer Martin Rees has similar thoughts on post-biological evolution, immortality, the singularity, vast oceans of yet unknown science, and synthetic realities created by super-advanced civilizations. Interstellar travel is "an enterprise for post-humans, evolved from our species not via natural selection but by design," says Rees in an interview [Rees 2013] "They could be silicon-based, or they could be organic creatures who had won the battle with death."

> "Some proponents of the 'singularity' - the takeover of humanity by intelligent machines - claim this transition could happen within 50 years."

Rees notes that our universe - "the aftermath of 'our' big bang" - may be just one of many universes in [the multiverse of inflationary cosmology]. The considerations in the interview are expanded and elaborated upon in the book "*On the Future*" [Rees 2018]:

> "What we've traditionally called 'the universe' - the aftermath of 'our' big bang - may be just one island, just one patch of space and time, in a perhaps infinite archipelago. There may have been many big bangs, not just one. Each constituent of this 'multiverse' could have cooled down differently, maybe ending up governed by different laws. Just as Earth is a very special planet among zillions of others, so - on a far grander scale - could our big bang have been a rather special one.

> In this hugely expanded cosmic perspective, the laws of Einstein and the quantum could be mere parochial bylaws governing our cosmic patch. So, not only could space and time be intricately 'grainy' on a submicroscopic scale, but also, at the other extreme - on scales far larger than astronomers can probe - it may have a structure as intricate as the fauna of a rich ecosystem. Our current concept of physical reality could be as constricted, in relation to the whole, as the perspective of the Earth available to a plankton whose 'universe' is a spoonful of water."

Rees eventually brings the reader to a "wild speculation" - the [simulation hypothesis]:

> "Every structure in the universe is composed of basic 'building blocks' governed by mathematical laws. However, the structures are generally too complicated for even the most powerful computers to calculate. But perhaps in the far-distant future, post-human intelligence (not in organic form, but in autonomously evolving objects) will develop hypercomputers with the processing power to simulate living things - even entire worlds.

> Perhaps advanced beings could use hypercomputers to simulate a 'universe' that is not merely patterns on a chequerboard (like [Conway's game]) or even like the best

'special effects' in movies or computer games. Suppose they could simulate a universe fully as complex as the one we perceive ourselves to be in. A disconcerting thought (albeit a wild speculation) then arises: perhaps that's what we really are!"

If these scientists are right, and I think they are, the most advanced civilizations in the universe have transcended biology and moved on to a post-biological phase of their evolution. If we want to become an advanced civilization and colonize the stars, this is what we must do.

Once we get out there, we'll meet God-like teachers and learn how to become God-like entities ourselves. [Expanding into outer space is our manifest cosmic destiny], and out there we'll find out how to re-engineer spacetime and resurrect the dead.

Benevolent Alien Providers Of Resurrection Services

Those who take seriously the idea of technological resurrection often assume that we'll be resurrected by our own descendants. But what if aliens civilizations will resurrect us in the far future? What if they are doing it already now?

Betting on our descendants seems safer, and it's more useful because it motivates us to do whatever it takes to facilitate the emergence of a God-like human civilization in the far future. But the idea of alien resurrection service providers can't be dismissed.

In "*Darwinia*" [Wilson 1998], science fiction writer Robert Charles Wilson imagines that a super-advanced galactic civilization routinely resurrects all sentient beings after physical death.

> "Sentience had conquered mortality, at least on the scale of the galaxy. Since before the advent of mankind, any arguably sentient creature that died within the effectual realm of the noospheres was taken up into paradise."

Dan Massey, a Renaissance man interested in everything under the stars, who passed away in January 2013, was persuaded that death is not the end. Dan expected to go on an eternal, infinite journey after death. I hope the cosmic winds will be fair to Dan, and I hope to see him again out there.

I first met Dan and Alison Gardner at Transvision, an itinerant transhumanist conference that I organized in Milan in October 2010 [Prisco 2010]. We became good friends and met often after the conference, both online and face to face.

This section dedicated to Dan is excerpted from an essay [Prisco 2014] that I published in the *VenusPlusX* magazine, founded by Alison and Dan and now edited by Alison.

Dan used to drop intriguing hints about a "cosmic government" - a confraternity of natural Gods and advanced galactic civilizations. Perhaps we will join the cosmic government when the time is right, and perhaps the cosmic government is benevolently interested in our world here and now, and may give some help now and then.

Dan was inspired by [The Urantia Book] and [Terasem]. "I've given a lot of thought to the idea of a religion that would sustain Transhumanist ideals without introducing irrational or mythic ideas," Dan told me in a letter.

"When I finally got around to reading Martine Rothblatt's Truths of Terasem [Terasem 2012] I was surprised to see that the concepts she had assembled at the outset, as she set out to define Terasem, were nearly congruent with a concept I had come to know quite well in a totally different setting, specifically, The Urantia Book."

Dan explained to me that, in the Urantia cosmology, "we, as individual persons, are participating in the development of the Supreme Being, an incompletely realized deity of finite space and time, which even now shapes events (I often use the term force of destiny) to assure its final emergence. At this occasion, the 'finality,' all persons will have become elements of a complete cosmic consciousness. But long before this final event many ordinary people will have learned to participate in an integrated, orderly life, in which everything and everyone work together better if you give them a chance."

"What sort of vision can illuminate the path to a meaningful and worthwhile future?," continued Dan. "It must recognize the potential of humans to become 'as gods.'"

> "The Terasem notion of a technodeity, constructed through human action and culminating at 'the end of time,' or some other definite but undefined occasion in the future, with the power to reach back through time and across space to force the actions that finally lead to its full emergence, constructed from the collective consciousness of all universe creatures, is certainly a good start. This provides a vision that we shall all then become fully functioning personalities of a supreme, finite deity."

I find Dan's vision beautiful and insightful. The supreme consciousness, God, emerges from the community of advanced forms of life and civilizations in the universe, and is able to influence spacetime events anywhere, anytime, including here and now, with self-consistent causal loops that ultimately ensure the emergence of God. I think this is what the prophets of the world's great religions tried to say, in the language of their times. In this book, I'm trying to say the same in the language of our times.

Dan was a frequent participant in online discussions hosted by Turing Church, Terasem, and the [Mormon Transhumanist Association] (MTA). Dan wasn't a Mormon or a sympathizer, if anything he was very critical of some aspects of Mormon society, but appreciated the scientific theology promoted by Mormon transhumanists.

In an online discussion hosted by the MTA, Dan described very eloquently the idea that other civilizations in the universe may have already developed resurrection technologies and may be already "providing resurrection services" to less advanced civilizations like ours [Prisco 2012a]. If this is the case, we and everyone else in the universe will be resurrected by the cosmic government.

Here is a (slightly edited, but almost literal) transcript of Dan's words:

> "I think you start out realizing that the universe is vastly older than the little area within the light sphere that we can see from this planet on the backwater of the Milky Way galaxy.

> Let's say just for the sake of argument that it is not merely a few billion years old, but it is a few trillion years old, maybe even quadrillion years old, I have no idea obviously, no way to find out, really, right now anyway, but I feel that there is a well organized cosmic government and civilization, that populates literally millions and millions, I really should say billions and billions (Carl Sagan) of planets scattered throughout this part of the universe, and they are all, you know, most part of them are in some degree of communication with each other, there is some sort of coordinated sense of purpose in this community, and they have been at it for a very long time by our standards.

> So during this time, you expect that these kinds of things, life extension, and mind uploading, and all these other technologies that we speculate about, would have been long explored, analyzed, built on, other things developed. Frankly, I think the promises of many religions of personal immortality on some terms, sometimes the terms are absurd, but the idea of personal immortality is not absurd at all, because just as we think that we could resurrect our dead, and we might go out and help other people to resurrect their dead, well, rather than being at the front-end of that process, we are at the back-end of that process, we are the clients, not the service company for the project.

Why? Because there is some really big project going on in the universe, and it's bringing about the universe in unity and harmony. It has really long ways to go, but on this planet it has incredibly long ways to go, because, you know, whether you call it the fall of man or the planetary rebellion or any of these things that are written down in some garbled form in the myth books of world religions, the fact is that something very bad happened here a long time ago, and we have been pretty much in the backwater, cut off from cosmic civilization ever since."

I hope an alien "service company" has taken good care of Dan, and he is now a happy and productive part of the cosmic mind. But even if at this moment there are no alien service companies providing resurrection services to the little people of infant backwater civilizations, we will progress and become the service company ourselves. From his subjective point of view, Dan is still with us, out there.

See also my longer video interview [Prisco 2012b] with Dan and Alison on transhumanism, the singularity, physics, religion and spirituality, and civil rights. Social activism, frontier physics, and new cosmic religions in the same talk, it's really awesome.

Notes

[Conway's game] See "The Life of Joe Glider."

[Expanding into outer space is our manifest cosmic destiny] See "The sacred road to the stars."

[Mormon Transhumanist Association] See "Man will become like God, say Mormons and transhumanists."

[simulation hypothesis] See "Sims City."

[Terasem] Terasem is a synthetic "transreligion" developed by biotechnology entrepreneur and transhumanist thinker Martine Rothblatt. See [Terasem 2012].

[the multiverse of inflationary cosmology] See "Exotic space, mysterious time, magic quantum."

[The Urantia Book] Dan served for more than two decades on the Executive Committee of the Urantia Book Fellowship. "*The Urantia Book*" [Urantia 2013], of unknown authorship, is a philosophical and spiritual book first published in 1955. See also Martin Gardner's book "*Urantia*" [Gardner 1995] and the Urantia Book Fellowship website: http://www.urantiabook.org/

[we'll leave our flesh and blood bodies behind, and space will be colonized by our post-biological mind children] I think far future humans, our mind children [Moravec 1988], will have bodies that could be very different from today's bodies, and wouldn't even meet our current definition of "body." For example, future bodies could be robotic, or based on exotic material substrates (e.g. plasmas, quantum matter, radiation). Some far future humans could exist as pure software running on computing systems equipped with suitable sensors and actuators. Post-biological bodies could be anything that allows human consciousness to function, and interact with the rest of the world and with other humans. Post-biological doesn't necessarily mean non-biological: The definition of "biology" could be extended to include whatever material substrates our mind children will port themselves to.

References

[Clarke 1968] Arthur Clarke. *2001: A Space Odyssey*. New American Library, 1968.

[Davies 2010] Paul Davies. *The Eerie Silence: Renewing Our Search for Alien Intelligence*. Houghton Mifflin Harcourt, 2010.

[Dawkins 2006] Richard Dawkins. *The God Delusion*. Houghton Mifflin Harcourt, 2006.

[Dick 2003] Steven Dick. Cultural evolution, the postbiological universe and SETI. *International Journal of Astrobiology*, 2003.

[Galouye 1964] Daniel Galouye. *Simulacron-3*. Bantam Books, 1964 (also published as *Counterfeit World*).

[Gardner 1995] Martin Gardner. *Urantia: The Great Cult Mystery*. Prometheus Books, 1995.

[Hawking 2018] Stephen Hawking. *Brief Answers to the Big Questions*. Bantam Books, 2018.

[Hoyle 2010] Fred Hoyle. *The Black Cloud*. Penguin Classics, 2010. (First published by Heinemann 1957).

[Hoyle 1962] Fred Hoyle, John Elliott. *A for Andromeda*. Harper & Row, 1962.

[Moravec 1988] Hans Moravec. *Mind Children: The Future of Robot and Human Intelligence*. Harvard University Press, 1988.

[Powell 2011] Michael Powell. A Knack for Bashing Orthodoxy. *The New York Times*. 2011. http://www.nytimes.com/2011/09/20/science/20dawkins.html

[Prisco 2010] Giulio Prisco. Transhumanist Science, Futurist Art, Telepresence and Cosmic Visions of the Future at TransVision 2010. *KurzweilAI*, 2010. http://www.kurzweilai.net/transhumanist-science-futurist-art-telepresence-and-cosmic-visions-of-the-future-at-transvision-2010

[Prisco 2012a] Giulio Prisco. August 2012 Discussion Group of the Mormon Transhumanist Association - Part 2. YouTube, 2012. https://www.youtube.com/watch?v=eX2rPhEOSiU

[Prisco 2012b] Giulio Prisco. Interview with Alison Gardner and Dan Massey. YouTube, 2012. https://www.youtube.com/watch?v=yUxfSyc_x6A

[Prisco 2014] Giulio Prisco. Sex and the Art of Cosmic Governance. *VenusPlusX*, 2014. http://venusplusx.org/giulio-priscos-sex-and-the-art-of-cosmic-governance-excerpt-chapter/

[Prisco 2018] Giulio Prisco. To Boldly Transcend All Limits: The Visionary Legacy of Stephen Hawking. *Vice Motherboard*, 2018. https://motherboard.vice.com/en_us/article/j5by87/stephen-hawking-on-ai-space-and-the-future

[Rees 2013] Martin Rees. Sir Martin Rees on Star Trek: 'How post-humans could colonise other worlds'. *The Telegraph*, 2013 http://www.telegraph.co.uk/culture/film/film-news/10034310/Sir-Martin-Rees-How-post-humans-could-colonise-other-worlds.html

[Rees 2018] Martin Rees. *On the Future: Prospects for Humanity*. Princeton University Press, 2018.

[Sagan 1985] Carl Sagan. *Contact*. Simon and Schuster, 1985.

[Shermer 2018] Michael Shermer. *Heavens on Earth: The Scientific Search for the Afterlife, Immortality, and Utopia*. Henry Holt and Co., 2018.

[Shostak 2012] Seth Shostak. They're Not Meat. *The Huffington Post*. 2012. http://www.huffingtonpost.com/seth-shostak/seti-extraterrestrial-life_b_1236919.html

[Terasem 2012] Terasem Movement. *2012 Truths of Terasem*. Terasem Movement, 2012.

[Urantia 2013] Urantia Foundation. *The Urantia Book* (first published in 1955). Urantia Foundation, 2013.

[Wilson 1998] Robert Charles Wilson. *Darwinia*. Tor Books, 1998.

CHAPTER 10 – THE SACRED ROAD TO THE STARS

More than 50 years after Apollo 11, we are ready to go back to the Moon to stay, then forward to the planets and moons of our solar system, and eventually beyond. We just need to restart the countdown interrupted with Apollo 17, and enjoy the long road to the stars. Our robotic probes are exploring the solar system, and human space exploration will likely restart in the twenties, but the road to the stars will be long. Therefore, we need to find and keep inspiration.

The spectacular achievements of the Apollo program in the sixties gave us the mistaken impression that the road to space would be easy and quick. But we didn't build those cities on the Moon and the planets. I was 11 when I watched on TV the first man walking on the Moon, 15 when I watched the last, and it's very unpleasant to realize that I could be 75 or older (or not be) when the next person will walk on the Moon.

In hindsight, it's evident that the Apollo adventure was too far ahead of the supply lines to be sustainable. But we'll go back to the Moon, and then to Mars, the planets, and the stars. In the meantime, we can enjoy our small steps in space, admire the view, and think that, as crew members of Spaceship Earth, we are part of the wonderful adventure of humanity among the stars.

"My point is that colonizing other worlds is not something that takes ten years, or even a hundred," says science writer Annalee Newitz (Newitz 2013]. "It might take much longer than that before humans are living on Mars, or in orbit around Saturn. But we are undeniably on the path toward a future where humans live in space."

"Enjoy this small but incredible slice of time that you get to live through, and remember that Galileo would be weeping with envy and relief to know we made it this far," concludes Newitz. "Just because it takes centuries doesn't mean we aren't making progress."

"We're riding a slow, powerful wave that will bear future generations to the stars."

I often disagree with Newitz on other issues, but I admit that she has the right attitude here. The road to space is long and difficult, and will probably take generations, but we are enjoying the first few miles as crew members of Spaceship Earth.

"As William Sims Bainbridge pointed out in his 1976 book, *The Spaceflight Revolution: A Sociological Study* [Bainbridge 1976], space travel is a technological mutation that should not really have arrived until the 21st century," said Arthur Clarke in a 2007 interview [Clarke 2007]. It appears that Sir Arthur was right - the youthful Apollo adventure of the sixties was an inspiring prelude of things to come, but space travel will become a reality only in this century.

In this century, people could walk on the Moon again and build the first sustainable planetary colonies. This is the plan of NASA, other space agencies, visionary entrepreneurs like Jeff

Bezos and Elon Musk in the growing commercial space sector, and citizen space organizations. This plan seems likely to be achieved in the next few decades, because it belongs to the realm of the possible.

But of course, visionary scientists and engineers are already venturing into the realm of the presently impossible, and developing plans to reach the stars. Alpha Centauri, the closest star system, beckons from a distance of more than 4 light years. That's quite a long road indeed, and requires long-term thinking.

"In a way, a Centauri probe isn't modern," says Paul Gilster in "*Centauri Dreams*" [Gilster 2004]. "Paradoxically, it may require medieval thinking, the sort of thinking that built cathedrals in Chartres and Salisbury and Cologne." A space scientist quoted in the book says that we as a culture may have to start thinking in terms of centuries: "The average worker on a medieval cathedral didn't live to see it completed."

In "*The Millennial Project*" [Savage 1994], Marshall Savage launched an inspiring call to arms to restart the countdown and get serious about space colonization, with a detailed step-by-step plan for humans to "explode into space and engulf the star-clouds in a fire storm of children, trees, and butterfly wings."

> "Because of us, landscapes of radiation blasted waste, will be miraculously transmuted: Slag will become soil, grass will sprout, flowers will bloom, and forests will spring up in once sterile places. Ice, hard as iron, will melt and trickle into pools where starfish, anemones, and seashells dwell - a whole frozen universe will thaw and transmogrify, from howling desolation to blossoming paradise. Dust into Life; the very alchemy of God."

Savage appreciated that restarting the countdown to space is a cultural issue more than an engineering problem. Only a "human laser" formed by people acting in synchronous harmony, creating a coherent beam of intent, can get us to the stars. It appears that Savage's human laser, which was beginning to shine bright in the sixties, has stopped working. The question is how to fix it.

Incremental technology improvements and streamlined, more efficient use of resources, can take us back to the Moon sustainably, and permit establishing outposts on the nearest planets. But to go beyond, we'll need radical advances in propulsion technology.

The book "*Frontiers of Propulsion Science*" [Millis 2009] presents recent [advances in propulsion science and technology], as well as promising research steps to discover how radical propulsion breakthroughs might finally be achieved.

Back to Clarke's observation - "space travel is a technological mutation that should not really have arrived until the 21st century" - there's a case to be made that interstellar travel shouldn't arrive for many more centuries, because our frail flesh and blood bodies aren't appropriate interstellar gear.

In fact, even with suitable propulsion technologies, crewed interstellar missions would be hugely expensive due to the need to ensure the survival and safety of the humans on-board and the need to travel at extremely high speeds.

One solution is to do without the wetware bodies of the crew, and send only their minds (software) to the stars, uploaded to advanced circuitry in a starship. I have argued [Prisco 2012] that an e-crew of human uploads implemented in solid-state electronic circuitry would not require air, water, food, medical care, or radiation shielding, and could withstand extreme acceleration. Therefore, the size and weight of the starship will be dramatically reduced.

[Mind-uploading technology] could make interstellar colonization practical with software e-crews, while delivering equally important spinoffs in neuroscience, computer science, and longevity, including indefinite life extension. The astronauts' memories, thoughts, feelings, personality, and "self" would be copied to an alternative processing substrate - such as a digital, analog, or quantum computer.

A software mind running on an appropriate substrate could be much more resistant and long-lived than a mind caged in a biological brain, and it could be housed in a similarly resistant and long-lived robotic body. Robots powered by human uploads could be rugged, resistant to the vacuum and the harsh space environment, easily rechargeable, and much smaller and lighter than wetware human bodies.

Boredom and isolation would not be a problem for e-crew members, because the data processing system of a starship could accommodate hundreds and even thousands of human uploads.

If strong Artificial Intelligence (AI) is developed, perhaps way smarter than humans, why should we bother to upload human minds? Isn't AI good enough? One answer is that most of us will want human minds on our first journey to the stars. However, I agree with Ray Kurzweil's speculation that we will merge with technology. Future persons will not be "pure" humans or pure AIs, but rather hybrids, blended so tightly that it will be impossible to tell which is which [Kurzweil 2005]:

> "The Singularity will represent the culmination of the merger of our biological thinking and existence with our technology, resulting in a world that is still human but that transcends our biological roots. There will be no distinction, post-Singularity, between human and machine or between physical and virtual reality. If you wonder what will remain unequivocally human in such a world, it's simply this quality: ours is the species that inherently seeks to extend its physical and mental reach beyond current limitations."

Ultimately, I think interstellar space will not be colonized by squishy, frail and short-lived flesh-and-blood humans 1.0. It will be up to [our post-biological mind children] to explore other stars and colonize the universe. Eventually, they will travel between the stars as radiation and light beams.

In "*Scatter, Adapt, and Remember*" [Newitz 2014], Newitz shows an open mind about sentient AI, artificial life, mind uploading and all that. "It's possible that we'll become cyborgs, beings who are half biological and half machine," she says. "No matter what scenario you think is most likely - synbio, uploads, or natural selection - our progeny may look nothing like us." Newitz thinks (and so do I) that:

> "We may be at the start of a long, slow journey whose climactic moment comes thousands of years from now."

Should we then forget the stars and wait for tomorrow's technologies? I don't think so, and one reason is that tomorrow's technologies won't arrive tomorrow, or next week, or in the next decade.

Since I was a child I have been a transhumanist, persuaded that humanity would transcend the Earth and all limits. In the nineties I discovered organized transhumanism and became a card-carrying, unrepentant, in-your-face transhumanist. One little caveat though: I never believed that progress would be easy and fast. I am still persuaded that 1) we will transcend the Earth and all limits, but 2) not anytime soon.

Becoming an interstellar species will take centuries, and developing transhumanist technologies will also take centuries. The Catch-22 situation is that we need transhumanist technologies to colonize the stars, but we need to start colonizing space to develop transhumanist technologies.

Why? Because developing transhumanist technologies will require motivating generations after generations with a powerful overwhelming drive, and I think only space colonization can give us that drive. Just like the Apollo program of the sixties energized and motivated the generations that developed modern computing technology, biotechnology, and the internet, future space programs will energize and motivate the generations that will develop transhumanist technologies.

So I think we should start colonizing the planets and moons of our solar system, NOW, without waiting for radically better technologies. Expanding into space will boost the mental health of humanity as a whole, and give us a renewed confidence in the relevance of our lives on and around this little planet, as we prepare for future, even more daring cosmic journeys.

Not everyone can be a space explorer, but we are all partners and stakeholders in the cosmic future of our species and its "manifest destiny" among the stars. Spreading this powerful conviction would generate not only more support for space and advanced technologies, but also a more positive and proactive attitude on other pressing issues, at a point in our history where we need positive thinking, confidence and optimism.

I often think that I would be happy to do the most menial, boring and repetitive work if I could do it on a starship. Imagine that you are part of a mission to the stars - wouldn't you be happy to clean toilets if that's the most useful task you can do?

I most certainly would, and knowing that I am meaningfully participating in a mission to the stars would give me all the motivation I need, even if the mission takes centuries to reach a destination that I will never see.

> I would consider the mission as a journey on a sacred road.

But on second thought, isn't this my current situation, and yours? We are all crew members of Spaceship Earth and parts, big or small, of our sacred journey to the stars.

So this is my proposal:

> We should consider our first timid steps into outer space as the beginning of our journey on the sacred road to the stars.

In *"Phases of Gravity"* [Simmons 1989], by Dan Simmons, three Apollo astronauts remember their lunar mission sixteen years later. All three have been deeply touched by their adventure in space. One has taken an easy path and become a fundamentalist Christian televangelist, but the other two compare the mission to a sacrament, a sacred journey to places of power.

The novel hasn't been widely acclaimed like other works of Dan Simmons, but I think it shows Simmons at his best. The sacred road to the stars is there to be seen, represented by a young woman, a seeker of places of power who believes in the richness and mystery of the universe.

In "Russian and American Cosmism" [Harrison 2013], Albert Harrison explores the influence of religion on technology and society as we take the first steps to the stars.

Harrison traces the roots of the Russian and American space programs in the works of visionary, spiritually oriented "prophets" of space exploration, and concludes that the United States has its counterpart to Russian cosmism, for which no term seems more appropriate than American cosmism.

"Even Fedorov's idea of reassembling the dust of all the people who ever lived has a Western counterpart: [Frank Tipler]'s proposal to achieve resurrection and eternal life through computer emulations," notes Harrison. In "*Starstruck*" [Harrison 2007], Harrison discussed cosmist visions, plans for expanding throughout the universe, and transcendence in space, including immortality and resurrection through computer emulation.

I am persuaded that humanity will expand into interstellar space, develop new technologies along the way, and learn from advanced civilizations that have already developed transcendent spacetime science and engineering. Our descendants will become part of a galactic community of God-like entities, and eventually achieve [Fedorov's cosmist vision of universal resurrection].

Expanding into interstellar space is central to this vision. Like the medieval builders of cathedrals, we probably won't live to see even the first milestones on the sacred road, but we can find meaning and inspiration in contemplating the long road ahead and the transcendent places of power at the end of the road.

Only a powerful cosmist mythology can give future generations the strenuous spiritual stance required to advance on the sacred road to the stars. Space supports religion by building the sacred road to the stars. Religion supports space by offering awesome visions of what we will find at the end of the sacred road. Both established religions and new "space religions" have an important role to play.

I will now describe some inspiring space projects that have been proposed for the next years and decades, which could serve as space-age cathedrals to provide a powerful spiritual inspiration to the next generations.

Cathedrals In Space

At the time of writing (December 2019), the US administration seems determined to go back to the Moon and develop a permanent human presence there.

I find this awesome, but my enthusiasm is tempered by knowing that the US administration changes color every few years, and most new US administrations immediately trash the space plans of the previous one. At this moment, I am more optimistic on Chinese space programs.

I am also more optimistic on private space projects led by "space barons" [Davenport 2018] like Jeff Bezos and Elon Musk, maverick entrepreneurs [Guthrie 2016], and grassroots citizen organizations [Prisco 2017a] that could hopefully also play a role.

Besides making money, there are other practical reasons to move into space. One is to protect us from existential risks: A big asteroid could hit the Earth and cause an extinction-level catastrophe that we could be powerless to prevent. Another is that offshoring heavy, polluting industry to outer space could be the only way to protect the environment of our planet as our energy needs continue to grow.

I am persuaded that we should focus on building a permanent, sustainable human presence on the Moon, before moving outward to Mars and beyond. Why? Because there are solid business models for lunar ventures [Spudis 2016], and only the prospect of making money soon can motivate the private sector. Mars can wait.

An ambitious project dubbed "Moon Village" for permanent lunar exploration and settlement has been proposed by Jan Wörner, director of the European Space Agency (ESA) [Wörner 2016]. "The Moon Village is open to any and all interested parties and nations," said Wörner. "Now we must bring interested parties together."

The project's goal is deliberately underdefined: The Moon Village can be interpreted as a physical base on the Moon, or as an open, collaborative, global framework that will eventually develop sustainable lunar bases and settlements.

I have worked at ESA in the eighties and early nineties, and I am proud of this visionary plan initiated by my former employer. An international citizen space organization, the [Moon Village Association] (MVA), has been formed to promote the project. Of course, I have joined the MVA as a member.

Interestingly, Jorge Mañes Rubio, former artist in residence at ESA, has designed a temple on the Moon as part of his art project "Peak of Eternal Light" [Rubio 2017].

"Instead of seeing it as just a potential site for groundbreaking scientific discovery, sci-fi tourism or the lucrative exploitation of extraterrestrial natural resources," Rubio sees the Moon as a universal and mythical idea, and the temple as a way to celebrate the Moon as a powerful symbol of unity for humankind. Rubio explains:

> "The Moon Temple will be located on the rim of the Shackleton, a gigantic impact crater situated right on the south pole of the Moon. With a diameter of 21km and more than 4200m deep, this imposing location is a potential candidate for a future outpost on the Moon due to its unique lighting conditions. While some of its peaks receive almost continuous sunlight, its interior (one of the coldest and darkest places in

the Solar System) may have captured water ice, key for a self-sustainable lunar settlement. The Moon Temple could serve social, cultural and spiritual purposes and will be built using sintered lunar regolith."

Perhaps something like Rubio's Moon Temple will be built as part of a permanent lunar base in the Moon Village framework. In a sense, the lunar base itself would be a temple - a powerful symbol of unlimited expansion into outer space. But the importance of tangible symbols shouldn't be underestimated. I really hope that Rubio's project will be realized and other temples will follow on Mars, the asteroids, and other planets and moons of the solar system.

Meanwhile, visionary thinkers and doers are planning missions to deep space and the stars.

The FOCAL mission proposed by Claudio Maccone [Maccone 2009] is not intended to reach other stars, but to establish a gravitational lens observatory in deep interstellar space, at about three light days from the Earth, or 550 Astronomical Units - 550 times the distance of the Earth from the Sun.

This is the distance of the gravitational focus of the Sun, where gravitational lensing provides a huge amplification of signals from the opposite direction (the Sun must be between the observatory and the target).

Unlike optical lensing, in which the light diverges after the focus, gravitational lensing continues in a focal line after the focus, and therefore a gravitational lens observatory would still work at distances greater than the focus.

A gravitational lens observatory only works in one direction, but the signal amplification would be quite dramatic, of the order of 100 millions [Matloff 2005] or higher. For one particular frequency that has been proposed as a channel for interstellar communication, signal amplification would reach a staggering factor of 1.3 quadrillion [Chorost 2013].

The Sun's gravitational focus is much farther than the orbit of Pluto, and therefore a FOCAL mission would qualify as an interstellar mission - a first outpost on the road to the stars, dedicated to important scientific research.

"If you are free to roam an imaginary spherical shell at the appropriate focal distance and centered on the Sun, you are free to explore the Universe in stupendous magnification, to peer at it with unprecedented clarity, to eavesdrop on the radio signals of distant civilizations, if any, and to glimpse the earliest events in the history of the Universe," explains Carl Sagan [Sagan 1994]. "Alternatively, the lens could be used the other way, to amplify a very modest signal of ours so it could be heard over immense distances."

In fact, the spectacular amplification of all electromagnetic radiation at the solar focus would permit astronomical observations of unprecedented precision, and could possibly permit detecting faint signals from, and then establishing permanent communication channels with, alien civilizations out there among the stars. Perhaps we need a gravitational lens router in place if we want to join the galactic internet of advanced civilizations.

Radio bridges between any pair of stars in the Galaxy could be built "if the gravitational lenses of both stars are exploited by placing two FOCAL relay satellites on the opposite side of each star, so that a perfect (or nearly perfect) alignment between these four points in space is kept," explains Maccone [Maccone 2012]. "Only now (2011) are humans realizing that radio bridges between couples of stars in the Galaxy can indeed be constructed. But, then, some other extraterrestrial civilization in the Galaxy might already have understood this a long time ago."

> "Consequently, a sort of Galactic Internet might already be in use in the Galaxy now! But humans will be unable to benefit from this Galactic Internet until they reach the minimal focal sphere of their own star, the Sun (i.e., until a human FOCAL probe reaches 550AU or more)."

Once we learn how to transfer consciousness to digital storage and back, the galactic communications network will become a galactic transportation network. In the science fictional universe of "*Manifold: Space*" [Baxter 2000], Stephen Baxter explores this possibility.

A first gravitational lens observatory at 550 AU would be the perfect stepping stone to the stars, close enough to be achieved with moderate improvements of today's technology, but far enough to be considered as an interstellar destination. I think this should be an important priority for the first phase of interstellar exploration.

A gravitational lens observatory would permit probing the universe and perhaps communicating with alien civilizations out there. We could scan whole distant galaxies to search for faint signals from advanced civilizations.

A gravitational lens observatory would be a place of power on the sacred road to the stars, I can't wait to get there or, more realistically, I want to do whatever I can to give a small contribution to the preliminary work.

The awesome [Breakthrough Starshot] project, announced in April 2016, wants to send the first robotic probe to the nearest star, Alpha Centauri, in only a few decades [Prisco 2016].

If things go according to plans (things seldom do, but optimism feels good), some readers will be alive when the first data and images come back from the Alpha Centauri system.

Breakthrough Starshot is the first interstellar probe project with sufficient funding for a thorough feasibility study. In fact, initial $100 million funding was provided by Russian billionaire Yuri Milner, an early internet entrepreneur and successful investor who already funded other visionary science projects.

"With light beams, lightsails and the lightest spacecraft ever built, we can launch a mission to Alpha Centauri within a generation," Stephen Hawking said at the Starshot announcement event. "Today, we commit to this next great leap into the cosmos. Because we are human. And our nature is to fly."

The key elements of the project are based on technology either already available or likely to be attainable in the near future under reasonable assumptions, and the Alpha Centauri mission is expected to require a budget comparable to the largest current scientific experiments: The total funding needed would be of the order of $5-10 billion, which seems ambitious but possible.

The star probe will be a highly miniaturized system on a chip, propelled by a lightsail built with advanced nano-engineered materials. The probe and its lightsail, both weighing only a few grams, will be pushed by light beams from high-power lasers, accelerated to 20 percent of the speed of light, and reach Alpha Centauri in two decades. There's no room for a deceleration system, so the mission will be a high-speed fly-by with the goal of returning data and images.

Among the many Starshot system design challenges, data return is expected to be one of the hardest, because there is little room for a communication system able to send data back to Earth. There are proposals to combine the project with a FOCAL gravitational telescope pointed at Alpha Centauri, which would permit receiving the faint signals sent back from small, low power transmitters.

This shows how there are useful synergies between different deep space projects: We could use the same masonry for many cathedrals in space.

Real thinking and feeling AI of human (or more than human) level could be developed in a few decades, in time for the Starshot launch. Sending a real AI instead of dumb unthinking software to Alpha Centauri would be equivalent to sending a person (think for example of Samantha, the AI in "*Her*" [Prisco 2014]). Even more interestingly, [mind uploading technology], which could developed in this century, would permit sending human astronauts as software entities living in the star probe processors [Prisco 2017b].

Martine Rothblatt proposed to send "mindclones" - software entities based on recorded human personalities - to the stars, embedded in advanced on-board data processing systems [Rothblatt 2014]. "Software functions on space probes sent to nearly every solar planet, oblivious of the biologically deadly vacuum of space," said Rothblatt.

> "The proverbial thousand-plus years it would take to send a spacecraft to one of the dozens of Earthlike planets discovered by the Kepler satellite observatory might be bearable for a large mindclone community on board that spacecraft, maintaining radio contact with the Earth."

At the 2012 public symposium of the 100 Year Starship (100YSS), an initiative to reach the stars in the next 100 years, initially sponsored by DARPA and NASA, Rothblatt proposed to extend an invitation to create a mindclone bound to the stars to everyone [Rothblatt 2012].

Imagine being part of a large software e-crew of human uploads and AIs on a starship en route to new worlds around another star. Boredom isn't a problem for crew members, whose subjective time is spent with many good friends in incredibly rich virtual reality environments. There are lots of things to do, and preparations to make for the arrival in the target star system. Once there, the uploads will interface with sensors and robotic bodies to explore new planets, and build receivers for colonists beamed from the Earth on light waves.

Wouldn't you want to go? I would definitely go if I could have the chance. Sadly, this possibility isn't likely to materialize in my lifetime. However, like the medieval builders of cathedrals, I look forward to doing whatever I can to contribute to the preliminary work, here on the Earth, to open the sacred road to the stars.

Religion For The Cosmic Frontier

Our grandfathers found meaning, hope, and happiness in religion and spirituality. They lived in a vast universe full of mystery, with benevolent gods, and hoped to continue to live after death and be reunited with loved ones in an afterlife. The hope in an afterlife helped them to cope with fear of death and grief for the loss of loved ones.

Many people in the Western world of the early 21st century have lost religion, because they know too much science. But the incompatibility of science and religion is only a cheap myth. On the contrary, I am persuaded that science and religion are not only compatible, but mutually supportive. In particular, I am persuaded that future science and technology will achieve all the promises of religion, including benevolent gods and resurrection.

We have also lost the sense of the frontier, that place full of mystery beyond the horizon. In this sense, religion itself is a frontier, but we also had earthly frontiers where the restless could hope to go. Many of our ancestors, including many of the best and brightest, went from Europe to America in search of something new and better.

Once in America, they "went West" with a powerful, religious sense of manifest destiny, following the ever receding frontier until the Pacific coast [Turner 1921]. It's no wonder, then, that the West Coast culture has been innovative, because the West Coast is where many of the best and brightest restless souls went.

The fundamental importance of the frontier for our mental health cannot be overstated. Today, there is no frontier, and the result is a mental "rats in a cage" syndrome that is beginning to show its very harmful effects.

A few decades ago we thought of space as a new frontier, and those who watched on TV Neil Armstrong walking on the Moon remember that powerful sense of cosmic destiny. But then, space was abandoned like a failed dream.

Now, it seems possible that the space frontier could open again, and we could see the next steps soon, first on the Moon and then throughout the entire solar system. I hope to see the next steps on the sacred road to the stars before logging off.

Interstellar space is a frontier for future generations. Today, interstellar space expansion enthusiasts are in the same position of [Konstantin Tsiolkovsky], the Russian pioneer of space exploration, who dedicated his life to a dream that only future generations could achieve. But even a frontier that is remote in the future can give us a cosmic sense of purpose, and the drive to move a little closer one little step at a time - if we can hope to be part of that future.

This is an important caveat: IF we can hope to be part of that future. Yes, seeing ourselves as part of the beginning of the journey can give us motivation, but the prospect of seeing the destination can give us even more motivation, and hope.

Future generations will be potentially immortal, and colonize the stars. They will be able to upload their minds to more powerful and durable substrates, leave biology behind, and merge with sentient, superhuman AIs. Among the stars, they will meet super-advanced civilizations with God-like powers, learn from them, and merge with them in an explosion of intelligence that will drive the future evolution of the universe. This is the new cosmic frontier.

But thinking of "them," our future God-like descendants, is not good enough for most of "us," here and now. We need to think that we, ourselves, can participate in the wonderful cosmic adventures of intelligent life in the universe.

Perhaps we can.

Perhaps inconceivably advanced intelligences using "magic" technologies based on extremely advanced science are, or will be, able to reach across spacetime into the past, and resurrect the dead by copying them out.

Perhaps our reality is really a "[simulation]" computed in a reality of higher order, and we can be copied elsewhere after death, together with our loved ones. [Perhaps we are permanently encoded in the fabric of spacetime, and can be retrieved after physical death].

In other words, mysticism and spirituality may be based on vague intuitions of a reality beyond reality, which science will uncover someday. These are not certainties, but possibilities compatible with our scientific knowledge and worldview.

Contemplating these possibilities plays a role equivalent to traditional religions - it provides us with a sense of meaning, a sense of cosmic purpose, hope, and happiness, compatible with science.

There is, however, an important difference. Often, traditional religions are hostile to science: Religious leaders fight science to protect their role of unique intermediaries between Man and God.

But this is a suicidal strategy that can only make religions irrelevant and, at the same time, deprive us of the powerful benefits of positive, action-oriented, forward-looking spirituality. Religions must, instead, embrace science and technology, which are not the enemies of transcendence but, on the contrary, the very means through which transcendence will be achieved.

We need new positive, solar, action-oriented spiritual movements based on science to keep us enthusiastic, motivated, and energetic, as we take the first steps toward the cosmic frontier.

In a visionary essay on "Religion for a Galactic Civilization 2.0" [Bainbridge 2009], a revised version of a 1982 essay [Bainbridge 1982], renowned transhumanist sociologist Bill Bainbridge said:

> "Thus we need a new definition of spaceflight that will energize investment and innovation. I suggest a return to the traditional view: The heavens are a sacred realm, that we should enter in order to transcend death."

Before praising Bill's work, I must emphasize an important difference between my premises and his.

Bill interprets "transcending death" as achieving cybernetic immortality through personality capture and mindfiles [Bainbridge 2014, Rothblatt 2014]. In a previous chapter I have outlined [some technical reservations on the Bainbridge-Rothblatt approach]. But more to the point, building a mindfile is something like cryonics, something that everyone could do in theory but almost nobody does in practice.

Even more to the point, my mom is dead and I don't want to live forever without my mom.

And my doggy.

I think my interpretation of "transcending death" - future humans will resurrect the dead of the past through science and "magic" spacetime technology, and expansion into interstellar space is central to this vision - is more inclusive and inspiring. We must embark on the sacred journey to the stars, because we'll find transcendence and the possibility of universal resurrection among the stars.

Back to Bainbridge, who also authored a comprehensive sociological study of the meaning and value of space exploration as perceived by the public in the US [Bainbridge 2015]. Bill understands that the current stagnation on the road to the stars is, basically, a cultural and motivational problem, and proposes a solution [Bainbridge 2009]:

> "We need several really aggressive, attractive space religions, meeting the emotional needs of different segments of our population."

> "Religion will continue to influence the course of progress, and creation of a galactic civilization may depend upon the emergence of a galactic religion capable of motivating society for the centuries required to accomplish that great project. This religion would be a very demanding social movement, and will require extreme discipline from its members, so for purposes of this essay I will call it The Cosmic Order."

> "If interstellar colonization, therefore, is ever to be possible, it must be begun very rapidly, within a few short decades of the development of nuclear physics and biological engineering. Ordinary socioeconomic forces will be insufficient to launch galactic exploration this rapidly, and only transcendent social movements could possibly channel enough of a society's resources into the project to succeed before either stasis or annihilation. Such a social movement, entirely secular in nature, was able to exploit political and military tensions to achieve the first great steps in space, but entirely new social forces will be required to impel our species much further."

> "To become fully interplanetary, let alone interstellar, our society would need another leap - and it needs that leap very soon before world culture ossifies into secure uniformity, or decays into absolute chaos. We need a new spaceflight social movement capable of giving a sense of transcendent purpose to dominant sectors of the society. It also should be capable of holding the society in an expansionist phase for the longest possible time, without permitting divergence from its great plan. In short, we need a galactic religion, a Cosmic Order."

I am in total sintony with Bill, and I see Turing Church as a step toward Bill's Cosmic Order. I hope my work can facilitate the emergence of a Cosmic Order, either as a new religion or within existing religions, and the emergence of a sustainable thrust on the sacred road to the stars.

That the road to the stars will be long, and these eyes won't see much of it, doesn't worry me too much. Regardless of how long it takes, I am persuaded that I'll be resurrected at some point on the road, with my loved ones, and enjoy the rest of our journey to transcendence.

But of course I would like to see some of our first steps toward the stars before logging off for a while. And I think Bill makes a very important point: We need to advance toward the stars "very soon before world culture ossifies into secure uniformity, or decays into absolute chaos."

In "The Omicron Point" [Bainbridge 1997], Bill made an important related point: "We could increase the chances for long-term human survival and for the attainment of higher forms of society by vastly increasing the number of independent human societies, each of which would constitute a different experiment in new social forms," he said. "The progressive unification of terrestrial culture means the only way to accomplish this is to colonize thousands of new worlds."

Persuaded by Bill's arguments, I think we should target space expansion with a calm but strenuous attitude, because beginning to expand into space is the most important task of humanity at this moment in history. Let this sink in:

> Beginning to expand into space is the most important task of humanity at this moment in history.

Colonizing the stars is the key to the long term survival of humanity, and our cosmic manifest destiny. In the far future we'll join the community of God-like civilizations among the stars, learn from them, become God-like ourselves, remake the universe, and resurrect the dead.

Here and now, a vigorous space program can give us the strenuous mood and drive that we need to start advancing on the sacred road to the stars. Space programs are uniquely able to catalyze advances in science and technology, and inspire whole generations.

This also requires making this planet a better place for everyone, and offering all people ways to participate. No task is too big or too small, and everyone (that means YOU too) has an important role to play.

Notes

[advances in propulsion science and technology] See also [Millis 2011] for a summary.

[Breakthrough Starshot] See the Breakthrough Initiatives website: http://breakthroughinitiatives.org/

[Konstantin Tsiolkovsky] See "Knocking on Heaven's door."

[Fedorov's cosmist vision of universal resurrection] See "Knocking on Heaven's door."

[Frank Tipler] See "Omega Point."

[Mind-uploading technology] See "Transhumanism."

[Moon Village Association] See the Moon Village Associations' website: https://moonvillageassociation.org/

[our post-biological mind children] See "Little green Gods."

[Perhaps we are permanently encoded in the fabric of spacetime, and can be retrieved after physical death] See "Into the deep waters," "Thought experiments in physical theology," "In the beginning was the field."

[simulation] See "Sims City."

[some technical reservations on the Bainbridge-Rothblatt approach] See "Transhumanism."

References

[Bainbridge 1976] William Sims Bainbridge. *The Spaceflight Revolution: A Sociological Study*. Wiley, 1976.

[Bainbridge 1997] William Sims Bainbridge. The Omicron Point: Sociological Application of the Anthropic Theory. In *Chaos and Complexity in Sociology: Myths, Models and Theory* (Raymond Eve, Sara Horsfall, Mary Lee, Eds.). Sage Publications, 1997.

[Bainbridge 2009] William Sims Bainbridge. Religion for a Galactic Civilization 2.0. *IEET*, 2009.
http://ieet.org/index.php/IEET/more/bainbridge20090820/

[Bainbridge 2014] William Sims Bainbridge. *Personality Capture and Emulation*. Springer, 2014.

[Bainbridge 2015] William Sims Bainbridge. *The Meaning and Value of Spaceflight: Public Perceptions*. Springer, 2015.

[Baxter 2000]. Stephen Baxter. *Manifold: Space*. Voyager, 2000.

[Chorost 2013] Michael Chorost. The Seventy-Billion-Mile Telescope. *New Yorker*, 2013.
http://www.newyorker.com/tech/elements/the-seventy-billion-mile-telescope

[Clarke 2007] Arthur Clarke. Remembering Sputnik. *IEEE Spectrum*, 2007.
http://spectrum.ieee.org/aerospace/space-flight/remembering-sputnik-sir-arthur-c-clarke

[Davenport 2018] Christian Davenport. *The Space Barons: Elon Musk, Jeff Bezos, and the Quest to Colonize the Cosmos*. Public Affairs, 2018.

[Gilster 2004] Paul Gilster. *Centauri Dreams: Imagining and Planning Interstellar Exploration*. Copernicus, 2004.

[Guthrie 2016] Julian Guthrie. *How to Make a Spaceship: A Band of Renegades, an Epic Race, and the Birth of Private Spaceflight*. Penguin Press, 2016.

[Harrison 2007] Albert Harrison. *Starstruck: Cosmic Visions in Science, Religion and Folklore*. Berghahn Books, 2007.

[Harrison 2013] Albert Harrison. Russian and American Cosmism: Religion, National Psyche, and Spaceflight. *Astropolitics: The International Journal of Space Politics & Policy*, 2013.

[Kurzweil 2005] Ray Kurzweil. *The Singularity Is Near: When Humans Transcend Biology*. Viking Press, 2005.

[Maccone 2009] Claudio Maccone. *Deep Space Flight and Communications: Exploiting the Sun as a Gravitational Lens*. Springer, 2009.

[Maccone 2012] Claudio Maccone. *Mathematical SETI: Statistics, Signal Processing, Space Missions*. Springer, 2012.

[Matloff 2005] Gregory Matloff. *Deep-space Probes: To the Outer Solar System and Beyond*. Springer, 2005.

[Millis 2009] Marc Millis, Eric Davis (Eds.). *Frontiers of Propulsion Science*. American Institute of Aeronautics and Astronautics, 2009.

[Millis 2011] Marc Millis. Progress in revolutionary propulsion physics. *arXiv*, 2011.
http://arxiv.org/abs/1101.1063

[Newitz 2013] Annalee Newitz. Stop pretending we aren't living in the Space Age. *io9*, 2013.
http://io9.gizmodo.com/stop-pretending-we-arent-living-in-the-space-age-1249483666

[Newitz 2014] Annalee Newitz. *Scatter, Adapt, and Remember: How Humans Will Survive a Mass Extinction*. Anchor, 2014.

[Prisco 2012] Giulio Prisco. Why we should send uploaded astronauts on interstellar missions. *io9* (republished from *KurzweilAI*), 2012.
https://io9.gizmodo.com/5968280/why-we-should-send-uploaded-astronauts-on-interstellar-missions

[Prisco 2014] Giulio Prisco. Spike Jonze's Her - Love in the time of AI. *H+ Magazine*, 2014.
http://hplusmagazine.com/2014/01/15/spike-jonzes-her-love-in-the-time-of-ai/

[Prisco 2016] Giulio Prisco. Breakthrough Starshot: The First Steps to the Stars. *IEET*, 2016.
http://ieet.org/index.php/IEET/more/Prisco20160415

[Prisco 2017a] Giulio Prisco. Why We Need a Decentralized Autonomous Space Agency. *Vice Motherboard*, 2017.
https://motherboard.vice.com/en_us/article/43d979/why-we-need-a-decentralized-autonomous-space-agency

[Prisco 2017b] Giulio Prisco. We Should Upload Human Minds on Stephen Hawking's Interstellar Mission. *Vice Motherboard*, 2017.
https://motherboard.vice.com/en_us/article/evpb4a/we-should-upload-human-minds-on-stephen-hawkings-interstellar-mission

[Rubio 2017] Jorge Mañes Rubio. Peak of Eternal Light (Moon Temple), 2017.
https://jorgemanesrubio.com/portfolio-item/peak-of-eternal-light

[Sagan 1994] Carl Sagan. *Pale Blue Dot: A Vision of the Human Future in Space*. Random House, 1994.

[Savage 1994] Marshall Savage. *The Millennial Project: Colonizing the Galaxy in Eight Easy Steps*. Little, Brown and Company, 1994.

[Spudis 2016] Paul Spudis. *The Value of the Moon: How to Explore, Live, and Prosper in Space Using the Moon's Resources*. Smithsonian Books, 2016.

[Rothblatt 2012] Martine Rothblatt. We Are the World: Inviting Everyone Onboard the 100YSS Is Practical and Will Help to Ensure Its Success. *Proceedings of the 100 Year Starship Symposium*, 2012.

[Rothblatt 2014] Martine Rothblatt. *Virtually Human: The Promise - and the Peril - of Digital Immortality*. St. Martin's Press, 2014.

[Simmons 1989. Dan Simmons. *Phases of Gravity*. Subterranean, 1989.

[Turner 1921] Frederick Jackson Turner. *The Frontier In American History*. Henry Holt and Company, 1021.

[Wörner 2016] Jan Wörner. Moon Village: A Vision for Global Cooperation and Space 4.0. *ESA Blog*, 2016.
http://blogs.esa.int/janwoerner/2016/11/23/moon-village/

PART 3 - IRRATIONAL MECHANICS

The following chapters in Part 3 explore some paths to our summits along the scenic route of science. We won't reach any summit, but stop in places where we can see, in the distance, the possibility of technological resurrection in a magical, enchanted and meaningful universe.

Technological resurrection is likely to involve next-next generation physics of huge energies, infinitesimal scales, space-time noodles and quantum ultra-weirdness, not to mention higher dimensions and parallel worlds. The same science will take us to the stars, perhaps faster than light, perhaps open the way to some sort of time travel, and perhaps permit understanding God(s). Or build God(s), or become God(s).

I call this research program "irrational mechanics." Only mad scientists pursue it at this moment.

Before becoming a mad scientist I used to be a "real" scientist in academy and public research centers. I know the science establishment pretty well, certainly well enough to realize that what I'm saying is so heretic that no scientist can enter safely.

As a matter of fact, there are many professional scientists who entertain ideas similar to mine, but even mentioning these ideas is career suicide. Developing irrational mechanics is for mad scientists, politically incorrect amateur citizen scientists like me, and perhaps you.

We can't do real research because our skills are too limited or too rusty, and/or we have to do other things for a living. What we can do is research on others' research. But that's good enough, because the heavy lifting work is already done by top scientists, only they aren't allowed to even mention some deep implications of their own work. Laying out the heretic implications is up to us.

Many scientists (who are really bureaucrats of science) seem only concerned with issuing "Thou Shalt Not" diktats on what cannot be done. Bot fortunately many engineers ignore them and do those things anyway. The attitude of the engineers is much healthier, if you ask me.

And don't forget Marx! In "Theses On Feuerbach" [Marx 1845], edited by Friedrich Engels, Karl Marx said:

> "The philosophers have only interpreted the world, in various ways; the point, however, is to change it."

I follow Marx and the engineers: I want to edit physical laws and hack a better reality.

[Russian Cosmist] Nikolai Fedorov thought that future science and technology would resurrect the dead and bring about the Kingdom of God on Earth. His speculations about how this could be done seem naive to us, but our own speculations could seem equally naive to future scientists.

[Frank Tipler] is persuaded that we already know the fundamental laws of physics: Quantum mechanics, Einstein's general relativity, and quantum field theories of the standard model, combined in a straightforward theory of quantum gravity that, contrary to most other physicists, Tipler views as perfectly viable. Tipler rules out faster than light communications and time travel, but is persuaded that our superhuman, God-like descendants at the end of time will bring us back to life with advanced space-time engineering and ultra-computing.

I disagree with Tipler's premise: I don't think we already know the fundamental laws of physics - on the contrary, I'm persuaded that future science will reveal a cascade of surprises after surprises, [perhaps without end].

But I admire Tipler because he gets his hands greasy and, armed only with today's physics, works out a consistent physical model of transcendent eschatology and resurrection mechanics. Inspired by Tipler and other thinkers including Mani Bhaumik, I try and sketch [a picture of transcendence entirely based on contemporary mainstream physics].

Other scientists speculate that space, time, and the particles and fields known to current science, could be derived from [deeper and more fundamental physics], just like fluid dynamics can be derived from molecular kinetics.

[I will suggest] that this is a physical model for the [simulation hypothesis]: The idea that our reality could be a simulation running in a deeper or higher level of reality, which is totally equivalent to traditional religion.

A weak formulation of the simulation hypothesis is trivially true: It's obvious that the universe computes the future from the past and the physical laws. In a stronger version, which seems compatible with speculative theoretical physics (don't blame the scientists, this comes from me), our [reality is controlled] by Engineers in a more fundamental base reality, not limited by the physical laws of our reality. By gaining access to the base reality we could become Engineers, do spacetime engineering "magic," and bring the dead back.

The simulation hypothesis is a recurrent topic that keeps popping up in Part 3. Another recurrent topic is the possibility that [time could be much stranger than we think] and allow for some sort of time travel, or time scanning, and self-consistent causal loops.

The perhaps fundamental role of [consciousness and free will] in the universe, and an ultimate cosmic intelligence that comes into being at, and operates from, the end of time ([Fred Hoyle], [Frank Tipler]), are also explored in Part 3.

Powerful scientific and theological streams of thought converge to the concept of a God that emerges from the universe and comes to full being only at the end of time, but "at the same time" is present and acts in the universe at all earlier times. These entangled concepts of time and causation, repeatedly explored in the following chapters, are beyond current physics and language, and therefore can't be formulated more precisely at this moment.

Ralph Abraham and Sisir Roy suggest that a cosmic memory field - the Akashic field - stores permanent records of everything that ever happens in the universe. They propose a [mathematical model for the Akashic field] based on a graph beyond space and time, with a huge number of nodes and internal dynamics similar to cellular automata, from which the geometry of spacetime is derived.

Ordinary space and time emerge from the graph, which fluctuates in an internal time-like dimension (not to be confused with ordinary time) and contains all times. It's worth noting that Stephen Wolfram has similar ideas.

Future Akashic engineers could read the Akashic records and bring the dead back. Including you and me.

Beyond Akashic engineers and finite natural gods, ascending toward unimaginable degrees of God-likeness in a progression without end, there is room for God - an absolutely infinite, infinitely far, totally unknowable God. One of my conclusions is that [God is undecidable but plausible].

In her recent book "*Lost in math*" [Hossenfelder 2018] Sabine Hossenfelder forcefully argues that scientists should strive to reduce personal biases. I highly recommend Hossenfelder's book, but I don't strive to reduce my biases: I am very much biased toward scientific theories compatible with hope in resurrection and a meaningful, transcendent universe.

In a section of "*Lifebox*" [Rucker 2016] dedicated to the intrinsic nondeterminism of quantum physics, Rudy Rucker perceptively remarks:

> "The rejection of determinism seems to provide some people with a sense of liberation. The hidden part of the argument might go like this: If the world is fundamentally random, then surely I'm not a robotic machine, and if I'm not a machine, then perhaps I have an immortal soul, so death isn't so frightening."

Guilty as charged, Rudy, guilty as charged. This is precisely why I find irrational mechanics liberating. I agree with Rucker that whether the world is fully deterministic or not ([causally closed or open]) is a fundamental open issue, perhaps THE fundamental open issue in science. But [even in a fully deterministic, causally closed universe] there's hope for survival after death.

From Rational To Real

Rational mechanics is an important part of mathematical physics. The Oxford Dictionaries define rational mechanics as "the branch of mechanics in which models, propositions, etc., are deduced mathematically from first principles."

In mathematics, a rational number is defined as a number that can be expressed as the ratio (quotient) p/q of two integers p and q. At school we learn that the square root of 2 is a real number that can't be expressed as the quotient of two integers. The square root of two - 1.4142... followed by an infinite number of non-repeating digits - is an irrational number. Other irrational numbers are pi, the ratio of a circle's circumference to its diameter, and e, the base of the natural logarithm.

[There are infinitely more irrational numbers than rational numbers]. If you could choose a random real number, the probability to hit a rational number would be zero. This seems surprising, because the rational numbers are infinitely dense (there are infinite rational numbers between any two), and therefore one could have the impression that the rational numbers exhaust the real number line. But Cantor demonstrated that this is not the case, and there are countless higher orders of infinity.

This is a good metaphor for the concept that reality is much more complex than our scientific understanding of reality. But Shakespeare said it better:

> "There are more things in heaven and earth, Horatio, than are dreamt of in your philosophy."

Deliberately mixing metaphors, I am defining irrational mechanics as the future science of complex reality beyond current science.

I am insisting on "irrational" not only in the mathematical sense, but also in the psychological sense. I think rationality is useful and good, but like all good things it can become an impediment. Rationality is not an end, but a tool, and like all tools it can be extended. I consider rationality as one of the tools that help making irrational dreams come true.

Reading List For The Following Chapters

I have tried to make the following chapters, which are heavy on science and especially physics, as simple as I could and at least partly readable by non-scientists. But my short explanations and intuitive pictures can't replace the real thing.

I have tried to always recommend easy to read references, but for some important topics there are no good and easy references yet, in which cases I have included good but more difficult references. I recommend all the references that I listed. If you want to learn the science upon which the following chapters are based, I recommend starting with the following books and resources.

Leonard Susskind's "Theoretical Minimum" [books and video lectures] on physics for serious amateurs are probably the best starting point. Only three books have been published to date [Susskind 2013, 2014, 2017], but there are tens of hours of awesome video lectures freely available online.

It's worth noting that Susskind has borrowed the "Theoretical Minimum" title from that of the exam that Lev Landau [Ioffe 2013] required his students to pass. The ten volumes of the "[Course of Theoretical Physics]" by Landau and Evgeny Lifshitz teach the required minimum, which seems more like a maximum that very few people could master in a lifetime.

Landau's books are dated, but highly recommendable for conceptual and mathematical clarity. I used Landau's books, recommended by my teachers, when I was a student: I understood ten percent, perhaps less, but that ten percent or less was enough to pass all exams with flying colors.

Susskind's approach is opposite: He wants to teach only the absolute minimum that one needs to master before trying to learn more. I prefer Susskind's "less is more" approach.

While Susskind's books and lectures are intended for amateur physicists and make a limited use of advanced mathematics, don't expect to understand everything at first glance without trying hard.

Same for Roger Penrose's "*The Road to Reality*" [Penrose 2005], an impressive tour of modern physics and mathematics. See also the other semi-popular books by Penrose on physics and the sciences of mind.

My favorite textbook was "*The Feynman Lectures on Physics*" [Feynman 2011], a masterpiece of scientific education that, decades after its first publication, is still universally acclaimed. Note that there is [a free online version of Feynman's lectures].

Read also Feynman's popular quantum electrodynamics book "*QED*" [Feynman 2006], one of the best examples of how complex scientific concepts can be explained to a lay audience without sacrificing correctness. Of course, only people in Feynman's league can do that.

There are many popular science books written by great scientists. Susskind has written some, and so have Stephen Hawking and living Nobel laureates like Robert Laughlin, Kip Thorne, and Frank Wilczek. Read also the popular books by Sean Carroll, Paul Davies, Brian Greene, Lisa Randall, Carlo Rovelli, and Lee Smolin.

This doesn't mean that a science book written by a lesser known scientist or by an amateur can't be just as good, but the books written by top scientists are a sure bet for beginners.

Notes

[a free online version of Feynman's lectures] Here it is: http://www.feynmanlectures.cal-tech.edu/

[a picture of transcendence entirely based on contemporary mainstream physics] See "In the beginning was the field."

[books and video lectures] See Susskind's Theoretical Minimum website for a current list of books and video lectures:
http://theoreticalminimum.com/

[causally closed or open] See "Exotic space, mysterious time, magic quantum," "There's plenty of room at the bottom," and following chapters.

[consciousness and free will] See "United quantum consciousness," "Eligo, ergo sum, ergo Deus est," and following chapters.

[Course of Theoretical Physics] See Wikipedia for a list of the books:
https://en.wikipedia.org/wiki/Course_of_Theoretical_Physics

[even in a fully deterministic, causally closed universe] See "Sims City," "Omega Point."

[Fred Hoyle] See "A for Almighty."

[Frank Tipler] See "Omega Point."

[God is undecidable but plausible] See "Thought experiments in physical theology."

[I will suggest] See "Thought experiments in physical theology."

[deeper and more fundamental physics] See "Into the deep waters, "Thought experiments in physical theology."

[mathematical model for the Akashic field] See "The quest for Akashic physics and engineering."

[perhaps without end] See "Into the deep waters," "Thought experiments in physical theology."

[reality is controlled] See "Thought experiments in physical theology," "In the beginning was the field."

[Russian Cosmist] See "Knocking on Heaven's door."

[simulation hypothesis] See "Sims City," "The Life of Joe Glider."

[time could be much stranger than we think] See "Exotic space, mysterious time, magic quantum."

[There are infinitely more irrational numbers than rational numbers] See "Thought experiments in physical theology."

References

[Feynman 2006] Richard Feynman. *QED: The Strange Theory of Light and Matter*. Princeton University Press, 2006.

[Feynman 2011] Richard Feynman, Robert Leighton, Matthew Sands. *The Feynman Lectures on Physics* (New Millennium Edition). Basic Books, 2011.

[Hossenfelder 2018] Sabine Hossenfelder. *Lost in math: how beauty leads physics astray*. Basic Books, 2018.

[Ioffe 2013] Boris Ioffe. Lev Davidovich Landau. *Under the Spell of Landau*. M. Shifman, Ed. World Scientific, 2013.

[Marx 1845] Karl Marx. Theses On Feuerbach. *Selected Works*, Vol. 1. Progress Publishers, 1973.

[Penrose 2005] Roger Penrose. *The Road to Reality*. Knopf, 2005.

[Rucker 2016] Rudy Rucker. *The Lifebox, the Seashell, and the Soul: What Gnarly Computation Taught Me About Ultimate Reality, The Meaning of Life, And How to Be Happy*. Transreal Books, 2016.

[Susskind 2013] Leonard Susskind, George Hrabovsky. *The Theoretical Minimum: What You Need to Know to Start Doing Physics*. Basic Books, 2013.

[Susskind 2014] Leonard Susskind, Art Friedman. *Quantum Mechanics: The Theoretical Minimum*. Basic Books, 2014.

[Susskind 2017] Leonard Susskind, Art Friedman. *Special Relativity and Classical Field Theory: The Theoretical Minimum*. Basic Books, 2017.

CHAPTER 11 – EXOTIC SPACE, MYSTERIOUS TIME, MAGIC QUANTUM

Newtonian physics is still treated as the standard starting point in physics education because it is intuitive. This is not surprising, since Newtonian physics applies to the energies and scales found in the human-sized everyday world in which we have evolved.

Modern physics is much less intuitive. Maxwell's theory of light and electromagnetic radiation, developed in the 19th century, can be (sort of) intuitively visualized by means of analogies with water waves, but the less intuitive aspects of Maxwell's theory forced Einstein, in the early 20th century, to abandon the Newtonian concepts of space and time.

In Einstein's special relativity, space and time get mixed up and become a spacetime that can't be objectively and uniquely divided in space and time. For example, two events in different places that are simultaneous for one observer are not simultaneous for another observer that moves with respect to the first.

The separation between two events that happen in different places can be time-like, in which case all observers agree on which event comes first, or space-like, in which case two observers in relative motion could disagree on which event comes first.

Our built-in Newtonian intuition is safe because, for relativistic effects to be significant, the two observers must move relative to each other at speeds close to the speed of light.

The speed of light is the same for all observers (this was Einstein's starting point), and nothing can be accelerated to a speed faster than light. If something could move faster than light from point A to point B, some observers would see it arriving at B before departing from A. This shows how, in general, the possibility of faster than light travel would imply the possibility of time travel.

In Einstein's general relativity, spacetime becomes a 4-dimensional curved space. Gravitation is the curved geometry of spacetime, which depends on matter (and energy): Matter tells spacetime how to curve, and curved spacetime tells matter how to move, in a self-consistent feedback loop.

You could try and imagine curved spacetime as a 4-dimensional balloon, perhaps embedded in a 5-dimensional space (note however that embedding is not mathematically necessary), but you can't visualize more dimensions than 3.

However, you can try and visualize spacetime in fewer dimensions to get an idea of gravitation in a curved spacetime: A heavy ball placed on a 2-dimensional elastic membrane curves the membrane, and therefore a lighter ball placed on the membrane will fall toward the first. The analogy is imprecise and somewhat misleading, but useful. The mathematics of general relativity - the differential geometry of curved spaces - is incredibly elegant and beautiful, but very complicated to work with.

Some solutions of Einstein's field equations of general relativity describe black holes and gravitational waves. The 2017 Nobel Prize in Physics was awarded to Rainer Weiss, Barry Barish, and Kip Thorne, for the first detection of gravitational waves from colliding black holes.

Gravitational waves are ripples in the fabric of spacetime that propagate at the speed of light as predicted by Einstein's equations. The Laser Interferometer Gravitational-Wave Observatory (LIGO) detector opened the field of gravitational wave astronomy in 2016 with the first detection of gravitational waves from a distant black hole fusion event [Castelvecchi 2016].

Future gravitational wave astronomy could permit detecting gravitational wave memory: a permanent displacement of spacetime that comes from strong-field general relativistic effects.

Passing gravitational waves from high-energy astrophysical events, such as the fusion of two black holes, stretch and squeeze the fabric of spacetime. After the passage of a gravitational wave, spacetime doesn't return to exactly the previous geometry, but remains permanently stretched or squeezed by a small amount. Thorne explained [Thorne 1998]:

> "As the gravitational waves from a binary's coalescence depart from their source, the waves' energy creates (via the nonlinearity of Einstein's field equations) a secondary wave called the 'Christodoulou memory'... Unfortunately, the memory is so weak that in LIGO only advanced interferometers have much chance of detecting and studying it."

Though the Christodoulou memory effect is too weak to be detected (with current technology) for a single event, ways have been proposed to study the gravitational wave memory of spacetime - the permanent traces left from past events in the fabric of spacetime - by analyzing many gravitational wave signals from different events together.

Individual traces are too weak to detect above a confirmation threshold, but analyzing many traces together can unveil information. A 2016 paper [Lasky 2016] suggests that advanced LIGO interferometers could, indeed, detect gravitational wave memory. [There are analogous memory effects for electromagnetic and strong interactions].

Is this a case of permanent cosmic memory, aka Akashic record, which future scientists could exploit to reconstruct the past and resurrect the dead? Yes, a black hole fusion event releases a little bit more energy than you or me, but perhaps gravitational wave memory is a good place to start [looking for Akashic physics].

Thorne was a co-author of the classic general relativity textbook *"Gravitation"* [Misner 1973] and wrote the popular book *"Black Holes & Time Warps"* [Thorne 1994]. Thorne was also a science consultant for the big budget Hollywood blockbuster *"Interstellar,"* by Christopher Nolan, and wrote a book on *"The Science of Interstellar"* [Thorne 2014].

Thorne is a highly imaginative scientist, unafraid to consider very speculative ideas that lesser scientists don't dare touching, such as time travel, interstellar travel through wormholes, and "bulk beings" in higher dimensions.

In *"Interstellar,"* intrepid explorers travel through a wormhole that appeared near Saturn to a black hole in a distant galaxy and save the Earth by sending information back in time through a hyper-dimensional channel that, perhaps, had been / will be / is (I guess the present tense "is" comes closest) engineered by humans in the far future, who also create the wormhole itself. The science upon which "*Interstellar*" is based is explored in Thorne's book.

I was afraid Thorne would be denied the Nobel Prize for being too imaginative, just like [Fred Hoyle]. But Thorne's essential contribution to the LIGO breakthrough was too spectacular for the Nobel committee to ignore.

In 1949 Kurt Gödel, arguably the greatest mathematician of the 20th century, found solutions of Einstein's equations that allow for the possibility of time travel [Gott 2002]. In Gödel's universe (a universe described by these solutions), it's possible to travel into the past by moving along a suitably chosen path in space.

Gödel's universe is different from our universe as revealed by current observations. For example, Gödel's universe doesn't expand, but rotates. However, the existence of Gödel's solutions of Einstein's equations shows that general relativity doesn't rule out time travel.

If so, the past is "out there" in some sense and could conceivably be visited. This is the concept of "block universe." In a block universe, time is just another coordinate like the three coordinates that describe space, and other times are just as real as other places.

Other solutions of Einstein's equations that allow for time travel have been found. Some describe shortcuts through space called wormholes [Thorne 1994, Visser 1996], which can act as instant conduits between separate places and times.

In "*Interstellar*," one of the characters explains the concept of wormhole by marking two points with a pen on a sheet of paper to represent two different places in 3D space, then folding the paper to have one point right on top of the other, then piercing the paper with the pen through both points. The two separate points have been connected by a wormhole, and one can go from one to the other without crossing the space (the paper) between them.

It must be emphasized that wormholes are not (only) science fiction, but perfectly legitimate solutions of the field equations of general relativity. It turns out [Thorne 1994] that a wormhole would collapse immediately after formation if not threaded with exotic matter able to keep it open, but this is an engineering problem that sufficiently advanced technology could conceivably solve.

The Quantum World: Weirdness On Steroids

Quantum mechanics, first developed in the first third of the 20th century by physicists including Bohr, Born, De Broglie, Dirac, Heisenberg, Pauli, Plank, Schrödinger, von Neumann, and of course Einstein, is terminally non-intuitive.

To make a long story short, while in Newtonian physics the state of a particle is described by intuitive concepts like instantaneous position and velocity, the state of a quantum particle can only be described by a mathematical entity called wavefunction, which is a solution of the Schrödinger equation of quantum mechanics. The wavefunction encodes the probability of finding the particle in a classical Newtonian state.

That's right: Quantum physics predicts only probabilities, not certainties. To make things even stranger, the wavefunction is a complex-valued "probability amplitude" that must be squared (sort of) to calculate a probability. This introduces the wave-like interference effects typical of quantum physics.

Different quantum states (amplitudes) can be combined (summed up) in a superposition, which is still a solution of the Schrödinger equation and therefore is a valid quantum state. So, a particle can be in a superposition of position states: It can be both here AND there.

But when we eventually observe the particle, we always find it here OR there. Something happens upon observation that forces the particle (more accurately, the universe) to make up its mind. This (still mysterious) process is called "collapse of the wavefunction." The outcome of the collapse seems random, with probability determined by the state of the particle immediately before the observation. Immediately after the observation, the particle has jumped discontinuously to a new quantum state (here OR there).

Though the mathematical formulation of quantum mechanics is clear and works, there are different and conflicting interpretations of what the mathematical equations really mean. According to some physicists and philosophers, the wavefunction only encodes what we know about the world (epistemology). According to others, the wavefunction represents reality (ontology).

The mathematical structure of quantum mechanics was systematically formalized by John von Neumann in "*Mathematical Foundations of Quantum Mechanics*" [von Neumann 1955], first published in 1932. Von Neumann made it clear that a quantum system evolves in time with two different processes: The ordered, deterministic evolution of the wavefunction predicted by the mathematical equations (Process 2), and the unpredictable, random collapse of the wavefunction upon observation (Process 1).

There are speculations that [consciousness] - personal consciousness, some kind of cosmic consciousness, or a combination - might be the agent that collapses the wavefunction in Process 1.

Some physicists and philosophers consider Process 1 as an ugly ad-hoc amendment that adds discontinuities and randomness to the otherwise smooth, linear and deterministic equations of quantum mechanics, and try to deny the reality of Process 1. It can be shown that, in a real quantum system interacting with a measurement apparatus and the environment, decoherence effects (see below) rapidly wash away quantum interference, turning quantum amplitudes into classical probabilities.

That's why we never see a stone here AND there: Such a macroscopic quantum state would be extremely delicate and immediately evaporate into unreality, leaving a stone here OR a stone there.

Some physicists and philosophers think this solves the problem. According to them, decoherence shows that there is no Process 1, only Process 2. But others think (and I agree) that "here OR there" is still undetermined, and Process 1 is still needed to choose one of the two possibilities. Decoherence explains why we don't see quantum superpositions in practice, but leaves the collapse of the wavefunction needed and unexplained.

In Hugh Everett's Many Worlds Interpretation (MWI) of quantum mechanics, a version of the stone is here in this world, and another version of the stone is there in another, equally real parallel world.

Everett's theory, formulated in the fifties and first published in 1957, was hidden in total obscurity until Bryce DeWitt published a semi-popular outline in *Physics Today* [DeWitt 1970, 1973]. To bring Everett's ideas to public attention, DeWitt used deliberately strong language, such as the "Many Worlds" label (not used by Everett) and passages like:

> "This universe is constantly splitting into a stupendous number of branches, all resulting from the measurementlike interactions between its myriads of components. Moreover, every quantum transition taking place on every star, in every galaxy, in every remote corner of the universe is splitting our local world on earth into myriads of copies of itself."

Everett's original papers, including previously unpublished papers, are collected in *"The Many Worlds Interpretation of Quantum Mechanics,"* [DeWitt 1973] edited by DeWitt and Neill Graham and published in 1973, after DeWitt's *Physics Today* article (which is also included). Since then, Everett's ideas have often been referred to as "Many Worlds Interpretation" (MWI) of quantum mechanics.

I recommend reading Everett's biography [Byrne 2010] by Peter Byrne, who is not a physicist himself but took the time to talk to top physicists and understand Everett's theory, which he explains well. I also found interesting Byrne's juicy account of Everett's personal life - great scientists put their pants on one leg at a time like the rest of us, screw like us, and screw up like us. See also John Clark's review of Byrne's book [Clark 2010], shared on the transhumanist mailing lists SL4.

Imagine a stack of many sheets of paper. Each sheet is a complete universe. When something is observed to happen, the sheet splits in parallel sheets. You (your memory, life history, and all that) live in one sheet, but there are countless other versions of you in other sheets.

Quantum mechanics doesn't predict the outcome of a physical process, but only the probabilities of different possible outcomes. In the MWI of Everett and DeWitt, different possible macroscopic outcomes of a quantum process are realized in different parallel worlds, or different branches of the "multiverse" - the set of all parallel worlds. The number of worlds where one specific outcome is realized - or in other words, the "size" of the region of the multiverse where one specific outcome is realized - is proportional to (and/or can be taken as a definition of) the probability of the outcome, which can be computed with the mathematical equations of quantum physics.

What Did Everett Mean?

Reading Everett's original writings I have the impression that he didn't really think of a multiverse nicely divided into parallel universes.

In fact, Everett just said that quantum mechanics is true. I suspect the multiverse that Everett really had in mind is One Big World (as opposed to the many "small" worlds of the MWI), too complex for us to perceive and understand. All possibilities are still realized out there in the multiverse, but the multiverse doesn't have a simple visual interpretation as a set of parallel worlds.

In "*Something Deeply Hidden*" [Carroll 2019], Sean Carroll describes Everett's MWI as the most promising approach to making sense of quantum mechanics, with an interpretation similar to mine. It is "often helpful to talk about the post-decoherence wave function as describing a set of distinct worlds," he says (see below for an outline of decoherence). That's justified, "because what happens on each branch doesn't affect what happens on the others."

> "But ultimately, that language is a convenience for us, not something that the theory itself insists on. Fundamentally, the theory just cares about the wave function as a whole."

Instead of a stack of sheets of paper, I prefer to think of a 3D object casting different shadows on different planes. For example a 3D cylinder can cast a rectangular shadow on a plane, and a circular shadow on another plane. The cylinder itself, it is not a rectangle or a circle, but a 3D object that can't be captured on a plane. Generalize to a huge number of dimensions, and you get the idea.

On the other hand, Byrne and many of the scientists he consulted defend the MWI picture and claim it's what Everett had in mind.

Everett's used to be my favorite interpretation of quantum mechanics. But Everett assumes the universal validity of quantum mechanics, and perhaps it's too soon to be sure that a theory developed in the early 20th century is the ultimate scientific model of reality. I guess current science will seem very naive from the vantage point of future science. Of course, the core concept of multiple parallel realities could still be part of future scientific models.

I also have an esthetic and emotional objection to the MWI. Everything that can happen does happen in one or another branch of the multiverse, and I don't like to think of all those versions of me in all those words where I am much less happy than here. But there are also [interesting ideas of "quantum resurrection" in MWI worlds] where your life becomes better and better as you move life after life.

An alternative reading of Everett is suggested by "Many Minds" interpretations (of Everett's interpretation) where it's an observer's consciousness, rather than the universe, that splits into parallel streams unaware of each other (see [Byrne 2010] and references therein).

Dieter Zeh, one of the originators of Many Minds interpretations, noted that the MWI "describes one quantum universe" [Joos 2003].

> "Because of its (essential and non-trivial) reference to conscious observers, it would more appropriately be called a 'multi-consciousness' or 'many minds interpretation'."

[Perhaps all your parallel minds are combined in the multimind of a multiversal super-you] that directs this you from behind the scenes.

Variants of Everett's ideas keep popping up. For example, the "Many Interacting Worlds" theory treats a particle's trajectory "as being the outcome of its interactions with other particles that exist in other worlds," explains science writer Anil Ananthaswamy [Ananthaswamy 2018]. For a system of many particles, represented by a point in a many-dimensional configuration space, any given world "interacts with the other worlds in configuration space, and this interaction is local, with nearby worlds influencing each other more than distant worlds." See also [Smolin 2019].

Can Quantum Entanglement Be Used To Send Instant Ftl Messages Across Space And Time?

It turns out that separate quantum particles can have mysterious correlations, known as Einstein-Podolsky-Rosen (EPR) correlations or "quantum entanglement," which seem to operate instantaneously, or at least much faster than light. Einstein never liked entanglement, which he described as "spooky action at a distance." But nature seems to disagree with Einstein, and entangled correlations have been confirmed in the laboratory since the 1980s.

Quantum entanglement is usually introduced using spin states rather than position states. Spin is a quantum property analogous to classical angular momentum (think of a spinning top) that takes discrete values in a given direction, for example up or down in the vertical direction.

Suppose two particles 1 and 2 are created with total spin zero, and then separated. Since the total spin must be zero, the two spins must be opposite. A possible state is 1up-2down (the spin of particle 1 is up and the spin of particle 2 is down). Another possible state is 1down-2up.

But the entangled superposition 1up-2down + 1down-2up is also a possible state. Suppose the two particles in this entangled state are sent to two observers A and B in different locations, perhaps separated by thousands of light years. A can measure the spin of particle 1, and B can measure the spin of particle 2. Quantum mechanics says that the first measurement will collapse the entangled state, randomly, to either 1up-2down or 1down-2up. So if A measures 1up, B will measure 2down, and vice versa.

But wait a sec. Suppose A and B make their measurements at close times, closer than the time it takes for light to travel between them. How can the second particles "know" the result of the spin measurement made on the first? It seems that the two particles are exchanging faster than light (FTL) signals.

Even worse, not all observers would agree on which measurement came first, which shows that there is tension in the peaceful coexistence of relativity and quantum physics.

The question that immediately comes to mind is if quantum entanglement could be used to send FTL messages, or signal backward in time.

The awesome science history book "*How the Hippies Saved Physics*" [Kaiser 2011], by David Kaiser, tells the fascinating story of the Fundamental Fysiks Group, quantum physics and the psychedelic youth culture of the seventies rolled together, with vivid portraits of colorful scientists who dedicated years to developing schemes for FTL messaging via quantum entanglement.

Fundamental Fysiks Group scientists Nick Herbert and Jack Sarfatti "liked to talk about the quantum physics and the possibilities of time travel," wrote Ken Goffman (aka R.U. Sirius of *Mondo 2000* fame) in his book review [Goffman 2011]. "It is clear that hip young scientists in the 1970s broke through an extant taboo against exploring theoretical physics. And even if some may find their theories flakey in the extreme, we can thank them for busting open the exploration of big physics ideas."

"And who knows. Maybe Jack Sarfatti will yet build that time machine."

Nick Herbert's book *"Quantum Reality"* [Herbert 1985] is still very much worth reading 30 years after its first publication. Contrary to some books by other members of the Fundamental Fysiks Group, such as the very successful *"The Tao of Physics"* [Capra 1975] by Fritjof Capra, Herbert's book doesn't emphasize quantum mysticism but sticks to solid - though open-minded and imaginative - physics, including a very clear explanation of [Bell's theorem] (see also [Bell 2004, Gisin 2014]).

Kaiser tells the story of Herbert's imaginative and apparently solid - but ultimately unsuccessful - schemes with names like QUICK and FLASH to use entanglement for FTL communications.

Unfortunately, according to our current understanding of quantum physics, entanglement can't be used to send FTL instant messages. Measuring the spin of one of a pair of entangled particles always gives a random result - even if the results of the two measurements are correlated - and any attempt to pre-set the result would break the entanglement. A good analogy is two decks of "magic" cards that are always in the same order, but the magic only works if both decks are well shuffled first, and cheating breaks the magic.

Another good analogy is due to David Bohm. Two screens in different places seem to show two fish that exhibit weirdly, instantly correlated behaviors - when one turns left the other also turns left - but the screens are really showing two images of the same fish. This analogy illustrates the possibility that two entangled particles might really be different aspects of the same thing, whatever that is.

Of course, an observer at one screen can't send an instant message to an observer at the other screen. Nothing - zooming in, increasing the luminosity, switching the screen off - will work short of persuading the real fish to turn in one direction, which the observer can't do.

In summary, according to our current understanding of the quantum world, entanglement can't be used to send instant FTL messages.

Similarly, physical laws also seem to prohibit the practical utilization of wormholes for FTL signaling and time travel. This doesn't mean these things are impossible in-principle (I suspect future science will pleasantly surprise us), but we aren't clever enough yet.

But FTL fans can still hope that future nonlinear versions of quantum physics might allow for FTL communications, and who knows what else.

"Weinberg's nonlinear quantum mechanics leads either to communication via Einstein-Podolsky-Rosen correlations, or to communications between branches of the wave function," said Joseph Polchinski [Polchinski 1991] referring to a nonlinear variant of quantum mechanics proposed by Nobel laureate Steven Weinberg.

In other words, either FTL instant messages to the stars, or messages to parallel universes. Since other times are special cases of other universes [Deutsch 1997], this implies the possibility of signaling to the past.

In his *"Lectures on Quantum Mechanics"* [Weinberg 2015], Weinberg says:

> "In my view, we ought to take seriously the possibility of finding some more satisfactory other theory, to which quantum mechanics is only a good approximation... Any attempt to generalize quantum mechanics by allowing small non-linearities in the evolution of state vectors risks the introduction of instantaneous communication

between separated observers."

So, prestigious physicists are still considering the possibility of FTL communications. How interesting.

Process 1 And Its Discontents

Is physical reality deterministic? Is physical reality reversible? Is information conserved, or do natural processes destroy and create information? These unanswered questions are, I think, among the most important (perhaps THE most important) philosophical and scientific questions.

Many (probably most) contemporary physicists are staunchly persuaded that the universe is deterministic and reversible, and information is conserved. Determinism means that the future is determined by the present, and reversibility (backward determinism) means that the past is also determined by the present. Information is conserved in a universe that is deterministic and reversible.

In "*The Theoretical Minimum*" [Susskind 2013], Leonard Susskind calls the conservation of information "the minus-first law" of physics (coming before first and zeroth laws) because it "is undoubtedly the most fundamental of all physical laws." In the second *Theoretical Minimum* book, "*Quantum Mechanics*" [Susskind 2014], Susskind underlines again that information is never lost and adds:

> "If two identical isolated systems start out in different states, they stay in different states. Moreover, in the past they were also in different states... Distinctions are conserved. The quantum version of the minus first law has a name - unitarity."

But how to square Susskind's minus-first law with von Neumann's Process 1, the nonunitary, nondeterministic, irreversible collapse of a quantum state upon measurement? "Shouldn't the act of measurement itself be described by the laws of quantum mechanics?," asks Susskind, and his answer is:

> "The answer is yes. The laws of quantum mechanics are not suspended during measurement. However, to examine the measurement process itself as a quantum mechanical evolution, we must consider the entire experimental setup, including the apparatus, as part of a single quantum system."

This is the goal of decoherence theory [Joos 2003]. Things work more or less like this:

In a quantum measurement, a quantum system interacts with a measurement apparatus. Initially, the quantum system is in a superposition of quantum states (for example, a particle can be in a superposition of position states, here AND there). The measurement apparatus must be macroscopic, human-sized, big enough to allow a human to observe the position of a pointer on a scale, or something equivalent.

[Parts of the observer's body] (e.g. the eye, the retina, etc.) can be considered as part of the measurement apparatus [von Neumann 1955].

The interaction between the quantum system and the measurement apparatus pushes the two into an entangled state.

Now, the measurement apparatus is a big thing (remember that it must be large enough to allow a human to observe something), and big things are in constant interaction with the environment. Therefore, the measurement apparatus is always entangled with the environment, and now the quantum system is entangled with the environment as well.

The environment consists of bazillions of particles, which we can't keep track of. The only thing that we can do to build a viable mathematical model of the measurement process is to average out the contributions of the environment.

It can be shown that, in the averaged model, the quantum system and the measurement apparatus are switched, very rapidly, from a superposition of interfering quantum states (for example, here AND there) to a mixture of non-interfering classical states (here OR there). Quantum amplitudes are replaced by classical probabilities. The measurement apparatus indicates that the particle is here, or that the particle is there. Information has leaked into the environment, and is now diluted and dispersed in the environment like a drop of ink in water.

A small quantum systems can be put in an observable quantum superposition by carefully isolating it from environmental decoherence, which is very challenging. Experiments catch decoherence as it happens and confirm the validity and accuracy of the decoherence model for simple, small quantum systems.

Large systems can't be isolated from the environment. Decoherence theory explains why, when we observe a large system, we always find it in a definite state (this OR that) and never find it in a superposition (this AND that).

So, decoherence theory explains a lot. Does it explain all? Does decoherence theory provide a complete explanation of quantum measurement, free of the ugly nonunitary collapse (von Neumann's Process 1)?

It doesn't seem so. Decoherence theory doesn't explain how one of many classical possibilities is selected. Why is the particle found here instead of there, when the possibilities of here and there are both in the mixture produced by decoherence?

In his widely praised book "*Beyond Weird*" [Ball 2018], a book on quantum physics for a wide audience that gives more space to decoherence theory than most popular books, science writer Philip Ball outlines the issue as:

> "How does that selection happen? Why, in any given measurement, do we see this and not that, when both this or that (though no longer 'this and that') are classically possible? Where did the other possibilities go?"

It seems that we still need the ugly Process 1. In "*Decoherence and the Appearance of a Classical World in Quantum Theory*" [Joos 2003], Dieter Zeh, the originator of decoherence theory, states that "it does seem that the measurement problem can only be resolved if the Schrodinger dynamics is supplemented by a nonunitary collapse." In the book's preface, Zeh and his co-authors note that

> "if one is not willing to accept an Everett-type interpretation, an essential element of description, such as an objective collapse, is still missing."

Sean Carroll, a supporter of Everett's Many Worlds Interpretation (MWI) of quantum mechanics, provides a clear explanation of decoherence in the MWI framework [Carroll 2019]. "To the modern Everettian, decoherence is absolutely crucial to making sense of quantum mechanics," says Carroll.

In the MWI, physical reality as a whole, the multiverse of parallel Everett worlds, is unitary (deterministic and reversible). There is no Process 1. There is only decoherence, which distributes possible observed realities in the multiverse.

If it makes sense to think that physical reality is a multiverse of parallel worlds that don't interact or interfere with each other (as noted above, I think this should be taken only as a convenient but simplified picture), then it makes sense to think that the evolution of the multiverse as a whole is unitary, but the evolution of a single world is not.

Quantum Fields, The Standard Model And Beyond

In a formulation of quantum mechanics introduced by Richard Feynman [Feynman 2010], the probability amplitude for a particle to go from A to B is calculated by summing up the amplitudes corresponding to all the paths that the particle could take between A and B.

In general, the amplitude for a quantum system to do something is calculated by summing up the amplitudes corresponding to all the ways to do that thing. Feynman's "path integral" formulation of quantum mechanics is a convenient starting point for quantum field theory.

Quantum field theory, which is the current framework for much of fundamental physics, provides a unified treatment of particles and fields. "In quantum field theory, the primary elements of reality are not individual particles, but underlying fields," explains Nobel laureate Frank Wilczek [Wilczek 2006]. "Thus, for example, all electrons are but excitations of an underlying field, naturally called the electron field, which fills all space and time."

In quantum field theory physical interactions can be represented, using a particle picture, by Feynman diagrams with incoming and outgoing particles joined by short-lived intermediate "virtual" particles. Empty space becomes a dynamic "quantum vacuum" filled by virtual particles that pop in and out of existence. Quantum vacuum fluctuations have important physical effects and provide a background for physics, like a quantum ether.

The current consensus framework for fundamental physics consists of general relativity, quantum mechanics, quantum field theory, and the standard model of particle physics. In the standard model, quantum field theories regulate the interactions of elementary particles, which come in two types: Fermions and bosons. The matter particles, quarks and leptons, are fermions, and the force carriers of the electroweak and strong interactions are bosons.

Then there is the Higgs boson, predicted in the sixties and detected at CERN in 2012. The Higgs field fills the quantum vacuum like a sticky fluid (don't take this too literally). Some particles of the standard model get stuck in the Higgs field and "acquire mass." Think of a fly that gets trapped in a sticky fluid and finds it difficult to move, thus acting as a heavy fly (acquiring mass). Nobel laureate Frank Wilczek promotes the term "core theory" to combine the quantum field theories of the standard model and general relativity [Wilczek 2008, 2015].

A quantum theory of gravity is still elusive [Smolin 2001, Rovelli 2007]. The two main proposals for quantum gravity, string theory [Greene 2003, Susskind 2008, Yau 2010] and loop quantum gravity [Rovelli 2007, 2014, Baggott 2019], aren't experimentally confirmed at this moment and still present unclear theoretical aspects. Both theories introduce radical changes in the concepts of space and time.

Contrary to the bosons that carry forces in the standard model, which have spin 1, the quantum excitations of the gravitational field, called gravitons, would have spin 2, which has a deep impact on the structure of quantum theories of gravity.

Inflationary Cosmology, And Yet Another Multiverse

"*A Big Bang in a Little Room*" [Merali 2017], by science writer Zeeya Merali, provides an accessible introduction to inflationary cosmology.

Here "inflation" refers to the ultra-fast exponential expansion of a patch of empty space that, following the known laws of both general relativity and quantum field theory, tunnels to a temporary "false vacuum" state.

Inflation expands space explosively in very short times. You need a wild imagination here: Think of space expanding by a factor of zillions in zillionths of a second. That space inflates much faster than light doesn't contradict Einstein's relativity: Things in space can't move faster than light, but space itself can.

The universe went through a rapid inflation right after the Big Bang. After a very short inflationary burst the universe, now filled with matter produced by the decay of the false vacuum, continued to expand much more slowly. This is the current mainstream view in cosmology.

In more speculative inflationary theories, there are many (perhaps infinitely many) bubble universes in an ever inflating space. When a region of inflating false vacuum decays back to normal space, a new bubble universe is created with a local Big Bang. Our entire observable universe is but a minute fraction of one of these bubble universes.

It seems to follow that, starting with a little patch of inflating false vacuum, we could create a new universe in the lab. It turns out that the new bubble universe would expand in its own space, initially connected to our space through a wormhole. Perhaps universes with intelligent life make baby universes in an endless cascade? Perhaps we live in a baby universe?

The physical laws of the new bubble universe may be similar to ours, or very different. The inflating space carries the bubble universes away from each other faster than light, and therefore different bubble universes don't interact.

If there are infinitely many (or just a huge lot of) bubble universes of finite complexity, some will be identical to ours. This is a multiverse cosmology, different from but somewhat equivalent to the "Many Worlds" multiverse of quantum mechanics. There's an identical copy of you in another universe very far away, and other more or less similar versions of you in other universes.

If this short outline of some concepts of inflationary cosmology wets your appetite, read Merali's book. Inflationary cosmology is also covered in other accessible books, including "*Our Mathematical Universe*" [Tegmark 2014], by Max Tegmark, and of course "*The Inflationary Universe*" [Guth 1997], by Alan Guth, the originator of inflationary theories.

The concept of a multiverse of worlds with different physical laws is often invoked to explain why the laws of physics seem fine-tuned for the emergence of life. We just find ourselves, the reasoning goes, in a world that happens to have life-friendly physical laws.

I don't consider fine-tuning as much of a problem to solve, because I suspect that some kind of life would emerge in any sufficiently complex universe. Of course, exotic forms of life are likely to be very different from organic life here on Earth, but we shouldn't assume that our still primitive understanding of life is complete.

More Dimensions Than Meets The Eye

Time is considered as a fourth dimension in Einstein's special and general relativity, but there are evident differences between space and time: You can move in all directions in space, but you can't go back in time.

Some contemporary physical theories, and in particular (super)string theory, include extra space dimensions.

The best introduction to higher dimensions is *"The Fourth Dimension"* [Rucker 2014], by mathematician and science fiction writer [Rudy Rucker]. As described in Rucker's book, higher dimensions were often considered as a stage for exotic unknown physics in the 19th and early 20th century, and provided room for all sorts of speculations on paranormal phenomena, the afterlife, and God.

Soon after the publication and first experimental confirmation of Einstein's theory of general relativity, Theodor Kaluza and Oskar Klein extended Einstein's theory to a 5-dimensional spacetime (four space dimensions and one time dimension). We don't see the fourth space dimension because it's "small," rolled up upon itself in a very tiny, submicroscopic circle.

The Kaluza-Klein theory was first considered as very promising because it provided a unified description of gravitation and electromagnetism. Then, it was mostly abandoned until the concept of extra space dimensions resurfaced in string theory.

In a current version of string theory (called superstring theory, but I'll skip the super), space has ten dimensions, nine space dimensions and one time dimension (the related "M-theory" introduces one more space dimension, but I'll stick to ten).

According to string theorists, some of the extra space dimensions could be small, curled up upon themselves in tiny "Calabi-Yau spaces" [Yau 2010], but others could be big like the three space dimensions we know. Theories with one [Randall 2006] or two [Päs 2014] big extra space dimensions have been proposed.

The full 9-dimensional space, or the full 4-dimensional (or 5-dimensional) space when the small Calabi-Yau dimensions are ignored, is called the "bulk." It turns out that sub-spaces in the bulk, called "branes," are dynamical objects that can trap particles and fields, and host complex sub-physics [Randall 2006, Thorne 2014].

To visualize a brane (the name comes from "membrane"), ignore one of our three space dimensions and think of a 2-dimensional surface in a 3-dimensional bulk. Now that you have a mental image, think of our universe as a 3-dimensional brane-world in a 4-dimensional (or 5-dimensional) bulk.

It turns out that the particles and fields of the standard model are trapped in our brane and can't get out (this explains why we perceive only our brane). But gravity can get out, and mediate interactions between our brane and the rest of the bulk, which might include other parallel brane-worlds. Other (hypothetical) particles and fields could also get out.

"New forces confined to distant branes might exist," explains Lisa Randall in *"Warped Passages"* [Randall 2006]. "New particles with which we will never directly interact might propagate on such other branes."

> "If there is life on another brane, those beings, imprisoned in an entirely different environment, most likely experience entirely different forces that are detected by different senses."

"Other branes might be parallel to ours and might house parallel worlds," continues Randall. "But many other types of braneworld might exist too."

> "Branes could intersect and particles could be trapped at the intersections. Branes could have different dimensionality. They could curve. They could move. They could wrap around unseen invisible dimensions. Let your imagination run wild and draw any picture you like. It is not impossible that such a geometry exists in the cosmos."

Besides gravity, other particles and fields might be free to move all over the bulk, perhaps giving rise to higher-dimensional forms of life, which could be intelligent and perhaps super-intelligent [Thorne 2014]. 3-dimensional intelligent forms of life that originate in a brane might, conceivably, explore or migrate to the bulk or to other branes.

Let this sink in. Our world might be one of many parallel brane-worlds, embedded in a master bulk-world with more space dimensions. Our descendants might explore or even migrate to the bulk or to other brane-worlds, which might be very different from our own. Intelligence, and perhaps superintelligence, might exist in the bulk and interact with our world, for example through gravitational signals.

So, contemporary string theory provides room for the spiritual speculations described in Rucker's "*The Fourth Dimension.*"

The bulk is adjacent to our 3-dimensional brane-world, and closer to you than your own skin. A benevolent bulk intelligence might [scan your brain and mind from the bulk] before you die, copy you, and paste you into another brane-world or into the bulk itself.

What if no benevolent bulk intelligence is able to scan you before your death? For example, They (that's the name given to them in "*Interstellar*") might not exist yet. It seems that a solid concept of resurrection needs some sort of time travel, or at least powerful means to interact with the past (time scanning or messaging).

Is time travel possible? Thorne leaves the door open. "If backward time travel is possible in the bulk, it can be achieved only by journeying out through the bulk's space and returning before the journey started while always moving forward in local bulk time," he says [Thorne 2014].

Ways to do just that have been proposed. According to Heinrich Päs, backward time travel is physically possible in an "asymmetrically warped brane universe" with two additional big space dimensions (that is, five big space dimensions in total) [Päs 2009, 2014].

Päs, with his colleagues James Dent, Sandip Pakvasa and Thomas Weiler, proposed to test his theory "by manipulating on our brane initial conditions of gravitons or hypothetical gauge-singlet fermions ('sterile neutrinos') which then propagate in the extra dimensions." Sterile neutrinos are hypothetical particles that, like gravitons, would be able to leave our brane and travel into the bulk.

I remain agnostic on this specific proposal for time travel. Time will tell. My point is this: Gödel demonstrated that general relativity doesn't rule out time travel, and now physicists are suggesting that string theory doesn't rule out time travel.

General relativity is a cornerstone of modern physics, and string theory is widely considered as the most promising framework for new physics. If both general relativity and string theory seem to allow time travel, perhaps we should allow ourselves to consider the possibility that nature allows time travel.

Stephen Hawking agreed. "According to a unifying form of string theory known as M-theory, which is our best hope of uniting general relativity and quantum theory, space–time ought to have eleven dimensions, not just the four that we experience," he said [Hawking 2018].

> "What this would give rise to we don't yet know. But it opens exciting possibilities... In conclusion, rapid space travel and travel back in time can't be ruled out according to our present understanding... science-fiction fans need not lose heart. There's hope in M-theory."

Some imaginative theologians are realizing the implications of string theory.

"In the current version of superstring theory (a conceptual flight of fancy in its way as breath-taking as any idea in eschatology), it is assumed that our universe is located on a 'brane' (a multidimensional membrane) which may be only infinitesimally, but decisively, separated from other universes on other branes," says physicist and Christian theologian John Polking-horne [Polkinghorne 2007], noting that different branes in the overall reality "might draw close together with some form of consequent influence flowing between them."

> "In the theological case, this might be a way to think about sacramental experience and the close presence of the risen Lord. The two creations might sometimes actually intersect, their two times briefly coinciding. I personally think in this way about the resurrection appearances of the risen Christ."

"Perhaps in the distant future, we will evolve so that our consciousness resides in a ball of sterile neutrinos," said Weiler [Ventura 2006]. If so, and if the rest of his theory [Päs 2009] is correct, future humans might be able to migrate outward into the bulk or other branes, travel in time, and resurrect the dead from the past by copying them out.

Superintelligent bulk beings could conceivably design, build, and run a brane-world. Perhaps our universe is a brane-world engineered by advanced higher-dimensional intelligences in the bulk? This is [a physical model for the simulation hypothesis].

The Paradoxes Of Time Travel And Their Solutions

Logical paradoxes are often invoked [Visser 1996] to rule out the physical possibility of backward time travel and messaging.

In the grandfather paradox, you travel back in time and kill your grandfather before he conceived children. But then you were never born, so who went back in time and killed your grandfather? This is an inconsistent causal loop.

In the bootstrap paradox, you travel back in time, meet William Shakespeare, and give him a copy of *"Hamlet"* before Shakespeare wrote it. Shakespeare then copies the text and publishes it. The question is, by whom was *"Hamlet"* created? From your perspective, Shakespeare wrote it. From the perspective of Shakespeare, it was given to him by you.

This bootstrap scenario doesn't necessarily require that you travel backward in time with a physical copy of the book. You could just send information to Shakespeare, perhaps by using signals able to manipulate his brain. In this case, from the perspective of Shakespeare, he writes *"Hamlet"* in a sudden burst of inspiration.

Even so, it seems that *"Hamlet"* appears magically out of nowhere. Yet, the scenario is self-consistent: Consistency is not broken anywhere in the causal loop. This is a self-consistent causal loop.

To me, the bootstrap paradox is not a paradox. If time travel is physically possible, reality contains self-consistent causal loops, and that's just how things work. *"Hamlet"* just exists. Shakespeare wouldn't find this too surprising: He writes (or copies):

> "There are more things in heaven and earth, Horatio, than are dreamt of in your philosophy."

I suspect that self-consistent causal loops are not only allowed, but ubiquitous and necessary for the machinery of reality to work. There are interpretations of quantum mechanics based on self-consistent causal loops [Cramer 2016, Kastner 2012, 2015, 2019]. In theology, there are interpretations of God as an entity that will come into full being only at the end of time, but is still the God of all times, and also created the universe at the beginning [Pannenberg 1994]. [Fred Hoyle] and [Frank Tipler] have developed related ideas based on current physics.

The concept of self-consistent causal loops that involve advanced intelligences in the far future, or God, self-consistently steering the present, plays an important role in many of the following chapters.

Thought experiments with billiard balls that go back in time through a wormhole [Thorne 1994, Everett 2012] illustrate both the grandfather and the bootstrap paradox without bothering Shakespeare and your grandfather.

A billiard ball can go back in time through a wormhole and hit its past self. There are two cases: The ball can hit its past self and push it into the wormhole, in which case we have a self-consistent causal loop. Or, the ball can push its past self away from the wormhole, in which case we have an inconsistent loop.

It turns out that time travel breaks the strict determinism of the Newtonian mechanics of billiard balls, in which there is a unique evolution in time for given initial conditions. The mechanical equations for billiard balls that travel in time have more than one solution for given initial conditions. In particular, it's always possible to find a consistent solution. Perhaps the universe systematically chooses consistent solutions.

Another way to make the grandfather paradox go away is thinking of a causal loop that extends across parallel Everett worlds. See [Everett 2012] (but this is another unrelated Everett, Allen not Hugh). The world in which you are born, and the world in which you kill your grandfather, are two different worlds. Perhaps the physics of the multiverse allows self-consistent causal loops in one world, but spreads inconsistent loops across parallel worlds.

Is Time Real?

Back to the questions discussed above: Is physical reality deterministic? Is physical reality reversible? Is information conserved, or do natural processes destroy and create information?

These questions are, I think, far from settled. I suspect that both views might be valid in a meaningful sense.

A related question: Is time real? Do other times "exist" out there in a block universe (or block multiverse), or does the unfolding of time destroy the old past and create the new future?

In 1922 Henri Bergson and Albert Einstein debated the nature of time and change [Canales 2015], which is still unclear today.

Einstein's universe is pristine, aseptic, mathematical, deterministic, and reversible. Bergson's universe is messy, dirty, living, nondeterministic, and irreversible.

I appreciate both views, and wander chaotically between and around them. When I sit down reading (which I do perhaps too much) I feel close to Einstein, but when I hike in the woods (which I should do much more) I feel close to Bergson.

Thinkers like Alfred North Whitehead and Nobel laureate Ilya Prigogine, a pioneer of irreversible thermodynamics, sided with Bergson, and many biologists side with Bergson as well, but most contemporary mathematicians and theoretical physicists side with Einstein.

To Einstein, time is a mathematical abstraction that appears here and there in the equations of mathematical physics. To Bergson, time is very real. Irreversible processes bring unexpected, unpredictable, non-predetermined novelty to the world.

In "*Order Out of Chaos*" [Prigogine 1984], Prigogine and Isabelle Stengers admit that Bergson misunderstood Einstein's relativity, but support Bergson's view centered on "the basic dimensions of becoming, the irreversibility that Einstein was willing to admit only at the phenomenological level."

Julian Barbour leans toward Einstein, with some twists [Smolin 2019]. Barbour is a renowned physicist who prefers doing theoretical physics for fun, while doing other things for a living. I think Barbour is a really creative scientist also because he can ignore the often vicious politicking of the academy.

In "*The End of Time*" [Barbour 2000], Barbour argues that time doesn't really exist. We never experience the flow of time directly: All that we experience is instantaneous mental states, which contain memories of other instantaneous mental states. So, according to Barbour, reality is a set of "Nows," and the laws of physics favor the occurrence of Nows that contain records (memories) of other Nows.

These special Nows are "time capsules" that contain memories of other time capsules.

Barbour takes the Wheeler-DeWitt equation seriously.

The [Wheeler-DeWitt equation] is a quantum equation, analogous to the Schrödinger equation of quantum mechanics, for the wave function of the universe, which encodes the probability of finding the universe in one or another instantaneous configuration (snapshot) of matter and 3-dimensional geometry (gravitational field). In other words, the Wheeler-DeWitt equation determines the density of snapshots in the multiverse.

The Wheeler-DeWitt equation doesn't contain time explicitly, but in some cases its solutions can be ordered and stacked one on top of another to represent the flow of time. The paths through the multiverse traced by the solutions of the Wheeler-DeWitt equation, with one instantaneous snapshot of the universe followed by another and so forth, represent evolution in time. In this picture, time is not a fixed background, but represents physical change. Other times are just special cases of other universes, as also argued by Deutsch [Deutsch 1997].

Barbour emphasizes that this model also explains why time seems to flow. It's worth noting that a similar model universe was previously proposed by [Fred Hoyle] in his science fiction novel "*October the First is Too Late*" (1966). Hoyle used the terms "pigeon holes" for Barbour's time capsules. [Philosopher Daniel Kolak proposed related ideas].

"Bell also formulated the idea of time capsules (without giving them any name) quite clearly long before me," adds Barbour, referring to John Bell's talk "Quantum mechanics for cosmologists" (published in "*Speakable and Unspeakable in Quantum Mechanics*" [Bell 2004]).

In the talk, following previous work by Nevill Mott in 1929 (republished in "*Quantum Theory and Measurement*" [Wheeler 1983]), Bell analyzed the formation of an alpha particle track in a cloud chamber.

In George Gamow's theory of radioactive decay, an escaping alpha particle is represented by an expanding, spherical wave function. But then, Barbour asks, "why are atoms not ionized at random all over the chamber... How come they are ionized only along one line?"

Mott emphasizes that we shouldn't picture the system's wave function as existing in ordinary three dimensional space, but "we are really dealing with wave functions in the multispace formed by the co-ordinates both of the alpha-particle and of every atom in the Wilson chamber."

It turns out that a rigorous quantum analysis of the alpha particle and the atoms in the cloud chamber confirms that the atoms are ionized along individual tracks. See also the book "*Quantum Dynamics of a Particle in a Tracking Chamber*" [Figari 2014]. "Mott's analysis can be considered the original prototype of the modern approach to the theory of environment-induced decoherence," note the authors.

An instant "track state" configuration of the system contains information about which atoms have been ionized so far. So, an alpha particle in a cloud chamber generates track states that can be considered as records (or time capsules in Barbour's terminology).

Bell suggests that this result can be generalized to more complex systems that include computer memories, or human memories, and notes that "we have no access to the past."

> "We have only our 'memories' and 'records.' But these memories and records are in fact present phenomena."

Barbour suggests a deeper generalization to the whole universe, which contains conscious observers. Time capsules (the "track states" of the whole universe) have a hugely higher probability, and therefore are actually experienced by observers. In other words, you (and all versions of you in other Everett worlds) are experiencing a time capsule that contains records and memories of other time capsules.

According to Barbour, that's all there is. There is no time, only Nows and highly probable Nows (time capsules with records and memories). The theory is still a work in progress, but Barbour presents persuasive arguments. In his approach, "each Now 'competes' with all other Nows in a timeless beauty contest to win the highest probability. The ability of each Now to 'resonate' with the other Nows is what counts." In other words, the global structure of reality selects the time capsules that are experienced.

Barbour notes that there is considerable overlap between his book and the chapter "Time: the first quantum concept" of David Deutsch's "*The Fabric of Reality*" [Deatsch 1997], in which other times are considered as just special cases of other universes. Barbour reiterates:

> "Our past is just another world. This is the message that quantum mechanics and the deep timeless structure of general relativity seem to be telling us."

Back to the question: Is time real? Do other times "exist" out there in a block universe (or block multiverse), or does the unfolding of time destroy the old past and create the new future? Again, I suspect that both views might be valid in a meaningful sense.

Notes

[a physical model for the simulation hypothesis] See "Thoughts experiments in physical theology," "In the beginning was the field," for different (but perhaps related) physical models for the [simulation hypothesis].

[Bell's theorem] Bell analyzed entangled spin systems and derived a theorem that, if confirmed experimentally, would permit ruling out local explanations of quantum entanglement based on "hidden variables." Many laboratory experiments have confirmed Bell's theorem and the intrinsic nonlocality of quantum mechanics. See [Herbert 1985, Bell 2004, Gisin 2014].

[consciousness] See "Transhumanism," "United quantum consciousness," "Eligo, ergo sum, ergo Deus est," and following chapters.

[Frank Tipler] See "Omega Point."

[Fred Hoyle] See "A for Almighty."

[interesting ideas of "quantum resurrection" in MWI worlds] See "The interplay of science fiction, science, and religion."

[looking for Akashic physics] See "The quest for Akashic physics and engineering."

[Parts of the observer's body] See "United quantum consciousness."

[Perhaps all your parallel minds are combined in the multimind of a multiversal super-you] See "The interplay of science fiction, science, and religion."

[Philosopher Daniel Kolak proposed related ideas] See "The lights of Eastern spirituality."

[Rudy Rucker] There is a free online edition of "*The Fourth Dimension*":
http://www.rudyrucker.com/thefourthdimension/
Besides this, I recommend that you read everything that Rucker has written, both fiction and nonfiction. Rudy Rucker is one of my heroes.

[scan your brain and mind from the bulk] Perhaps by using signals carried by gravitons or sterile neutrinos, which can move in both our brane and the bulk.

[simulation hypothesis] See "Sims City."

[There are analogous memory effects for electromagnetic and strong interactions] See "In the beginning was the field."

[Wheeler-DeWitt equation] See also Frank Tipler's explanation in "Omega Point."

References

[Ananthaswamy 2018] Anil Ananthaswamy. *Through Two Doors at Once: The Elegant Experiment That Captures the Enigma of Our Quantum Reality*. Dutton, 2018.

[Ball 2018] Philip Ball. *Beyond Weird: Why Everything You Thought You Knew about Quantum Physics Is Different*. Vintage, 2018.

[Baggott 2019] Jim Baggott. *Quantum Space: Loop Quantum Gravity and the Search for the Structure of Space, Time, and the Universe*. Oxford University Press, 2019.

[Barbour 2000] Julian Barbour. *The End of Time: The Next Revolution in Physics*. Oxford University Press, 2000.

[Bell 2004] John Bell. *Speakable and Unspeakable in Quantum Mechanics*. Cambridge University Press, 2004.

[Byrne 2010] Peter Byrne. *The Many Worlds of Hugh Everett III: Multiple Universes, Mutual Assured Destruction, and the Meltdown of a Nuclear Family*. Oxford University Press, 2010.

[Canales 2015] Jimena Canales. *The Physicist and the Philosopher: Einstein, Bergson, and the Debate That Changed Our Understanding of Time*. Princeton University Press, 2015.

[Capra 1975] Fritjof Capra. *The Tao of Physics: An Exploration of the Parallels Between Modern Physics and Eastern Mysticism*. Shambhala Publications, 1975.

[Carroll 2019] Sean Carroll. *Something Deeply Hidden: Quantum Worlds and the Emergence of Spacetime*. Oneworld, 2019.

[Castelvecchi 2016] Davide Castelvecchi, Alexandra Witze. Einstein's gravitational waves found at last. *Nature News*, 2016.

[Clark 2010] John Clark. The Many Worlds of Hugh Everett, 2010. http://sl4.org/archive/1008/21012.html

[Cramer 2016] John Cramer. *The Quantum Handshake: Entanglement, Nonlocality and Transactions*. Springer, 2016.

[Deutsch 1997] David Deutsch. *The Fabric of Reality: The Science of Parallel Universes - and Its Implications*. Viking Press, 1997.

[DeWitt 1970] Bryce DeWitt. Quantum Mechanics and Reality: Could the solution to the dilemma of indeterminism be a universe in which all possible outcomes of an experiment actually occur? *Physics Today*, 1970.

[DeWitt 1973] Bryce DeWitt, Neill Graham (Eds.). *The Many Worlds Interpretation of Quantum Mechanics*. Princeton University Press, 1973.

[Everett 2012] Allen Everett, Thomas Roman. *Time Travel and Warp Drives: A Scientific Guide to Shortcuts through Time and Space*. University of Chicago Press, 2012.

[Feynman 2010], Richard P. Feynman, Albert R Hibbs. *Quantum Mechanics and Path Integrals*. Dover, 2010.

[Figari 2014] Rodolfo Figari, Alessandro Teta. *Quantum Dynamics of a Particle in a Tracking*

Chamber. Springer, 2014.

[Gisin 2014] Nicolas Gisin. *Quantum Chance: Nonlocality, Teleportation and Other Quantum Marvels.* Springer, 2014.

[Goffman 2011] Ken Goffman. Did "The Hippies" Save Physics? *H+ Magazine*, 2011. http://hplusmagazine.com/2011/08/10/did-the-hippies-save-physics/

[Gott 2002] J Richard Gott, *Time Travel in Einstein's Universe: The Physical Possibilities of Travel Through Time.* Houghton Mifflin Books, 2002.

[Greene 2003 Brian Greene. *The Elegant Universe: Superstrings, Hidden Dimensions, and the Quest for the Ultimate Theory.* W. W. Norton, 2003.

[Guth 1997] Alan Guth. *The Inflationary Universe: The Quest For A New Theory Of Cosmic Origins.* Basic Books, 1997.

[Hawking 2018] Stephen Hawking. *Brief Answers to the Big Questions.* Bantam Books, 2018.

[Herbert 1985] Nick Herbert. *Quantum Reality.* Anchor Books, 1985.

[Joos 2003] Erich Joos et al. *Decoherence and the Appearance of a Classical World in Quantum Theory.* Springer, 2003.

[Kaiser 2011] David Kaiser. *How the Hippies Saved Physics: Science, Counterculture, and the Quantum Revival.* W. W. Norton & Company, 2011.

[Kastner 2012] Ruth Kastner, *The Transactional Interpretation of Quantum Mechanics: The Reality of Possibility.* Cambridge University Press, 2012.

[Kastner 2015] Ruth Kastner. *Understanding Our Unseen Reality: Solving Quantum Riddles.* Imperial College Press, 2015.

[Kastner 2019] Ruth Kastner. *Adventures in Quantumland: Exploring Our Unseen Reality.* World Scientific, 2019.

[Lasky 2016] Paul Lasky et al. Detecting Gravitational-Wave Memory with LIGO: Implications of GW150914. *Physical Review Letters*, 2016.

[Merali 2017] Zeeya Merali. *A Big Bang in a Little Room: The Quest to Create New Universes.* Basic Books, 2017.

[Misner 1973] Charles Misner, Kip Thorne, John Wheeler. *Gravitation.* W. H. Freeman, 1973.

[Pannenberg 1994] Wolfhart Pannenberg. *Systematic Theology.* T & T Clark, 1988–1994.

[Päs 2009] Heinrich Päs, Sandip Pakvasa, James Dent, Thomas Weiler. Closed timelike curves in asymmetrically warped brane universes. *Physical Review D*, 2009. Also available from *arXiv*: https://arxiv.org/abs/gr-qc/0603045

[Päs 2014] Heinrich Päs. *The Perfect Wave: With Neutrinos at the Boundary of Space and Time.* Harvard University Press, 2014.

[Polchinski 1991] Joseph Polchinski. Weinberg's nonlinear quantum mechanics and the Einstein-Podolsky-Rosen paradox. *Physical Review Letters*, 1991.

[Polkinghorne 2007] John Polkinghorne. *Exploring Reality: The Intertwining of Science and Religion.* Yale University Press, 2007.

[Prigogine 1984] Ilya Prigogine, Isabelle Stengers. *Order out of Chaos: Man's new dialogue with nature.* Bantam Books, 1984.

[Randall 2006] Lisa Randall. *Warped Passages: Unraveling the Mysteries of the Universe's Hidden Dimensions.* Harper, 2006.

[Rovelli 2007] Carlo Rovelli. *Quantum Gravity.* Cambridge University Press, 2007.

[Rovelli 2014] Carlo Rovelli. *Covariant Loop Quantum Gravity: An Elementary Introduction to Quantum Gravity and Spinfoam Theory.* Cambridge University Press, 2014.

[Rucker 2014] Rudy Rucker. *The Fourth Dimension: Toward A Geometry of Higher Reality.* Dover, 2014.

[Smolin 2001] Lee Smolin. *Three Roads to Quantum Gravity: A New Understanding of Space, Time and the Universe.* Basic Books, 2001.

[Smolin 2019] Lee Smolin. *Einstein's Unfinished Revolution: The Search for What Lies Beyond the Quantum.* Penguin, 2019.

[Susskind 2008] Leonard Susskind. *The Black Hole War: My Battle with Stephen Hawking to Make the World Safe for Quantum Mechanics.* Little, Brown and Company, 2008.

[Susskind 2013] Leonard Susskind, George Hrabovsky. *The Theoretical Minimum: What You Need to Know to Start Doing Physics.* Basic Books, 2013.

[Susskind 2014] Leonard Susskind, Art Friedman. *Quantum Mechanics: The Theoretical Minimum.* Basic Books, 2014.

[Tegmark 2014] Max Tegmark. *Our Mathematical Universe: My Quest for the Ultimate Nature of Reality.* Knopf, 2014.

[Thorne 1994] Kip Thorne. *Black Holes & Time Warps: Einstein's Outrageous Legacy.* W. W. Norton & Company, 1994.

[Thorne 1998] Kip Thorne. Probing Black Holes and Relativistic Stars with Gravitational Waves. In *Black Holes and Relativistic Stars* (Robert Wald, Ed.). University of Chicago Press, 1998.

[Thorne 2014] Kip Thorne. *The Science of Interstellar.* W. W. Norton & Company, 2014.

[Ventura 2006] Tim Ventura, Heinrich Päs, Thomas Weiler, and Sandip Pakvasa. Through the Looking Glass: Temporal Communications & Time-Travel in Applied Brane Theory Physic. *American Antigravity*, 2006. http://www.americanantigravity.com/files/articles/Time-Travel-Interview.pdf

[Visser 1996] Matt Visser. *Lorentzian Wormholes: From Einstein to Hawking.* Springer, 1996.

[von Neumann 1955] John von Neumann. *Mathematical Foundations of Quantum Mechanics.* Princeton University Press, 1955. (translation of *Mathematische Grundlagen der Quantenmechanik,* Springer, 1932).

[Weinberg 2015] Steven Weinberg. *Lectures on Quantum Mechanics.* Cambridge University Press, 2015.

[Wheeler 1983] John Wheeler, Wojciech Zurek (Eds.). *Quantum Theory and Measurement.*

Princeton University Press, 1983.

[Wilczek 2006] Frank Wilczek. *Fantastic Realities: 49 Mind Journeys And a Trip to Stockholm.* World Scientific Publishing Company, 2006.

[Wilczek 2008] Frank Wilczek. *The Lightness of Being: Mass, Ether, and the Unification of Forces.* Basic Books, 2008.

[Wilczek 2015] Frank Wilczek. *A Beautiful Question: Finding Nature's Deep Design.* Penguin Press, 2015.

[Yau 2010] Shing-Tung Yau, Steve Nadis. *The Shape of Inner Space: String Theory and the Geometry of the Universe's Hidden Dimensions.* Basic Books, 2010.

CHAPTER 12 - SIMS CITY:
LIFE IN A VIDEO GAME

"The Sims" and "Sim City" are two classic video games. In the former, you simulate individual persons, and in the latter you simulate a whole city. What if the entire universe is a simulation, including you and me?

Enter the simulation hypothesis: If video game characters can be intelligent and sentient, perhaps we are sentient and intelligent video game characters? Is our reality, and ourselves in it, a computer simulation? These questions may seem strange at first, but they are not easily dismissed, and philosophers have been asking similar questions for centuries. Today, the simulation hypothesis is a frequent discussion topic in science and philosophy.

Who is running the simulation? Perhaps unknowable alien minds in another level of reality, but a frequent assumption is that it is future humans, our descendants, who run our reality as a historically accurate simulation of their past (our present).

When I first heard of Nick Bostrom's "simulation argument" in 2001, [via the SL4 and Extropians mailing lists], my mind went on fire. I had similar ideas, vaguely conceived, but Nick's was the first solid formulation of the concept that I have seen. [I sent Nick enthusiastic comments].

Bostrom wasn't the first to think of the simulation hypothesis, but his formulation is the best known.

The simulation hypothesis has been further elaborated upon and catapulted to the forefront of public attention by superstar technology entrepreneur Elon Musk, who is persuaded that we are some advanced version of The Sims [Chang 2016].

Musk believes it's almost certain that we are living in a computer simulation: There's only a one-in-billions chance that we're in "base reality" instead of a simulation.

"The strongest argument for us probably being in a simulation is the following: 40 years ago we had Pong - two rectangles and a dot," argues Musk [D'Onfro 2016, Virk 2019]. "That was what games were. Now, 40 years later, we have photorealistic, 3D simulations with millions of people playing simultaneously and it's getting better every year. And soon we'll have virtual reality, augmented reality."

> "If you assume any rate of improvement at all, then games will become indistinguishable from reality. Even if that rate of advancement drops by 1,000 from what it is right now. Then you just imagine 10,000 years in the future, which is nothing in the evolutionary scale. So it's a given that we're clearly on a trajectory to have games that are indistinguishable from reality, and those games could be played on any set-top box or a PC and there would probably be billions of such computers and settop boxes, it would seem to follow that the odds that we're in base reality is one in billions. Tell me what's wrong with that argument?"

Not a watertight argument if you ask me, but it does get the point across. Philosopher Eric Steinhart articulates this counting argument with more detail [Steinhart 2014]:

> "(1) It is highly likely that every civilization like ours will mature further into one that is able to run vast numbers of universe simulations.
> (2) It is highly likely that any civilization able to run vast numbers of universe simulations will want to run them.
> (3) Any civilization that can run simulations and that wants to run them will run them. The engineers in those civilizations will therefore design and create engines that run universes.
> (4) Minds realized by computers are psychologically indiscernible from minds realized by flesh. Consequently,
> (5) there are enormously many more simulated minds than nonsimulated minds.
> (6) Which makes it highly probable that we are simulated minds living in a simulated universe. Our universe is running on some Engine that was designed and created by some Engineers."

This is better, but I am not entirely persuaded of the "highly likely" assumptions. What if creating even one universe simulation, populated by sentient beings like us, would exhaust the resources of the most advanced intergalactic civilization that we can conceive? However, these assumptions are compatible with Steinhart's overall framework outlined below.

As noted above, when I first heard of his simulation argument [I sent Nick enthusiastic comments]. "Perhaps the mathematics of the proof does not work if you allow an infinite number of conscious beings," I said. "This would be the case, for example, if you do not assume that there is a bottom level of reality."

"If there is no bottom then everybody is living in a simulation," replied Nick, which of course is correct. An infinite number of conscious beings could also exist, for example, if there's [a "multiverse" with an infinite number of parallel universes]. But even so, the counting argument works if conscious beings in simulated realities occupy a much bigger (in the mathematical sense of measure) part of the multiverse than conscious beings in physical realities.

I don't think it makes sense to assign a "probability" to the simulation hypothesis. One can only assign probabilities when one has prior applicable information, and we just don't have enough prior information in this case. Pondering whether the probability that we live in a simulation is 7 percent, or maybe 79 percent, is (I think) a waste of time at this moment.

I'm happy enough with noting that there's a possibility that we live in a simulation, with probability between zero and 100 percent. Perhaps we'll be able to say more once we build the first simple simulations that contain arguably sentient simple creatures, which I think could happen in this century.

Popular versions of the simulation hypothesis imagine bored alien teenagers playing us like Sims on a super Xbox in their parents' extra-dimensional basement, or mad alien scientists studying us with ultra-supercomputers in otherworldly facilities, but there are more sophisticated scientific versions.

We shouldn't imagine the "computers" simulating our reality as anything similar to today's computers. No, they won't be slightly more powerful boxes running slightly better future releases of Windows. A computer able to simulate a reality as complex as ours, and containing conscious observers, would have to be orders of magnitude more complex and powerful than anything we can imagine today, and probably be based on very different system software, hardware, and even physics.

Such a computer would likely be sentient and superintelligent in its own way. Therefore, it wouldn't be a what, but a Who: A transcendent Mind in whom "we live, and move, and have our being." [Berkeley 1914, Bruere 2012, Steinhart 2014].

It's worth noting that analogies with computer games can help thinking about [issues in fundamental physics], such as the limit speed of light, quantum entanglement, and quantum collapse. For example, it doesn't make much sense to waste resources to compute something that nobody is looking at. Better to compute it just in time when somebody is looking. In his recently published popular book "*The Simulation Hypothesis*" [Virk 2019], Rizwan Virk gives other examples.

Ben Goertzel notes that Virk's book "is spreading the concept to an even wider audience" [Goertzel 2019]. According to Ben, the simulation hypothesis is "mostly bullshit," but it does highlight some interesting issues. The valuable core concept of the simulation hypothesis is that our physical universe could be embedded in a broader universe, "thus being in some sense a 'simulation' of this greater containing space," says Ben.

> "It's a worthwhile thought experiment but in the end it's most valuable as a pointer toward other, deeper ideas. The reality of our universe is almost surely way crazier than any story about simulations or creators, and almost surely way beyond our current imaginations."

I also consider the "conventional, naive" simulation hypothesis as [a simple intuitive metaphor for a reality that is probably much weirder], but I think that, even if reality is whole, undivided, terminally crazy, and hopelessly beyond our current imaginations, [the simulation hypothesis is a coherent and useful mental picture of reality]. While ordinary reality can be coherently considered as part of a whole undivided reality, it can also be coherently considered as a construct created in a transcendent universe beyond our world, and driven by transcendent agents, which is the essence of the simulation hypothesis.

I often think that the simulation hypothesis is trivially true in the sense that reality is obviously the results of a computation where the universe computes itself according to the (only partly known) physical laws.

The interesting nontrivial questions are if there is a sys-op, agent, intelligence, wholly other mega-consciousness or something like that behind the computation, if that mega-something purposefully intervenes in the computation, and if we could somehow communicate with the simulators or escape from the simulation into their base reality.

It's worth noting that these are independent questions that could have independent answers. There could be a divine sysop that cannot purposefully intervene, or one that can. In either case, communication and exit might or might not be possible. It might turn out that there is a sysop powerless (or unwilling) to intervene, but the characters in the simulation have the power to exit. This possibility would be consistent with the view of human agency and sin adopted by many religions, including Christianity: God gives us choices, but cannot choose salvation for us.

A recent film titled "*The Simulation Hypothesis*" [Forbes 2015], by filmmaker Kent Forbes, blends the simulation hypothesis with interpretations of quantum physics that point to [new digital physics before space and time], from which space and time emerge, and assigns a role to [consciousness] as part of the fundamental fabric of digital physics, and co-creator of reality.

One of the many scientists featured in the film is James Gates, a physicist who found features that look like error-correcting codes in physical laws, a result that suggests the simulation hypothesis [Moskowitz 2016].

This brings me to consider how we could find out that we live in a simulated universe, and how we could somehow communicate with the simulators and join them in their higher reality.

In a delightful short story included in *"Mind Children"* [Moravec 1988], roboticist and transhumanist thinker Hans Moravec imagines cellular automata, called Cellticks, that come to life, consciousness and intelligence in a [Game of Life] simulation operated by a programmer called Newway in our world. The Cellticks study the physics of their world and figure out the cellular automata rules.

Then the Cellticks find out that the laws of their physics are occasionally violated. In fact, there are occasional hardware glitches in Newway's computer. Studying the anomalies, the Cellticks map Newway's computer, decode its system software, and build a message for Newway. A dialog follows. Eventually, the Cellticks copy themselves out of the simulation into dedicated hardware in our world. Together, Newway and the Cellticks can now consider how to move upward into yet another higher reality.

A variation that seems worth considering has been suggested by Extropy co-founder Tom Bell: Those who built our universe included within it certain features - "flaws" as they might first appear - that serve as tests for the insights and agency of those within the simulation.

"Indeed, I sometimes regard the fundamental insight of 're-ecreational theology' [Bell 2016] - that we not only live in an authored universe but that helping it to reproduce will bring joy, happiness, and meaning to our lives - as a kind of tripwire that, once touched, will alert our metaphorical parents that it is time to 'have the talk' with their metaphorical kids about 'where universes come from.'" Tom emailed me. "On that theory, we can all look forward to a sort of cosmological sex-ed class, soon. Indeed, one might say that I've already started the lesson!"

If those who live in a simulated reality can themselves simulate lower level realities, perhaps uppercase Reality is nothing more than an infinite cascade of realities simulated within higher level realities (dreams within dreams, or turtles all the way down). This may well be the simplest explanation of the world, since an infinite regress permits doing without a "base reality" that generates all other realities [Steinhart 2014].

Simulation Theology

The simulation hypothesis has some very desirable features. In his 2003 paper titled "Are You Living In a Computer Simulation?" [Bostrom 2003], published in *Philosophical Quarterly*, Bostrom speculated about parallels with traditional religious conceptions. In the current Simulation Argument FAQ [Bostrom 2011], Bostrom says:

> "These simulators would have created our world, they would be able to monitor everything that happens here, and they would be able to intervene in ways that conflict with the simulated default laws of nature... An afterlife in a different simulation or at a different level of reality after death-in-the-simulation would be a real possibility. It is even conceivable that the simulators might reward or punish their simulated creatures based to how they behave."

Without mincing words, the simulation hypothesis is totally equivalent to Christian cosmology. There's an omniscient and omnipotent God, Who can lift you to Heaven after death if you have been good. What more can you want?

At the same time, the simulation argument is scientifically sound. Even outspoken atheists like Richard Dawkins are forced to concede this point. In "*The God Delusion*" [Dawkins 2006], Dawkins says:

> "Science-fiction authors... have even suggested (and I cannot think how to disprove it) that we live in a computer simulation, set up by some vastly superior civilization. But the simulators themselves would have to come from somewhere. The laws of probability forbid all notions of their spontaneously appearing without simpler antecedents. They probably owe their existence to a (perhaps unfamiliar) version of Darwinian evolution..."

My simple answer to [Dawkins]' point is, so what? If it looks like a God, and it acts like a God, and it thunders like a God, then I call that entity a God.

The [Mormon Transhumanist Association] (MTA) has formulated an explicitly religious version of the simulation hypothesis: "The New God Argument" (NGA) [Cannon 2015], a collaborative work in progress led by Lincoln Cannon, inspired by Bostrom's argument and adapted to Mormon cosmology.

In "*Your Digital Afterlives*" [Steinhart 2014], Eric Steinhart formulates a systematic simulation theology. Steinhart's work is monumental, not for its length - the book has about 250 pages, and Eric is one of my role models for concise writing - but for its breadth and depth.

In Steinhart's simulation theology, there is an endless hierarchy of Gods within universes within Gods. The power of these natural Gods increases without limits, and the ultimate Deity is the unattainable top of an infinite chain (this concept frequently appears in this book). Everything that exists lives in a local universe contained in the Mind of a local God. For example, you exist in the Mind that runs our universe in the level of reality just above ours. But there are infinite higher levels above that.

After you die, you will be endlessly promoted along a progression of universes and Gods. Promotion means implementation at a higher level: You'll be copied out and re-implemented in universes above our current universe, just like the Cellticks in Moravec's story. And so forth. Ascending on this ladder, you'll become a vaster God-like being yourself (theosis). Besides promotions, there will be revisions of your entire life history to happier and better versions.

This very short outline doesn't do justice to Eric's cosmology. See also Lincoln Cannon's more detailed review [Cannon 2016]. My approach is slightly different from those of Eric and Lincoln, in that I openly and cheerfully admit that our ideas are inspired by intellectual fun and wishful thinking, rather than grounded in mathematical necessity.

In particular, I refrain from elaborating too much on the morality of higher level intelligences. I think it would be wonderful if the Gods were nice and kind, and I really hope this is the case, and I can think of analogies (e.g. I am nice and kind to doggies) to persuade myself that this is plausible, but I don't think it can be proven.

I'm happy enough with the essential core of the simulation hypothesis: Perhaps our universe has been designed and is controlled by engineers in a higher level of reality, perhaps the engineers are friendly and nice, and perhaps the friendly and nice engineers can and do intervene in our world.

A few years ago I used to develop virtual reality simulators for industrial machines. I developed the simulators with a commercial game engine, which was the most sophisticated (and expensive) game engine available at the time, and included a realistic physics engine.

But it turned out that the physics engine wasn't realistic enough for some applications. If I had been able to access and modify the underlying source code (I hope the developers did so after seeing all my bug reports), I could have changed the physics of my simulated universe to achieve the results I wanted.

Similarly, perhaps God will one day upgrade the physics engine of our reality to a better, enhanced version. The concept of a new world, the Kingdom, is a cornerstone of Christian theology.

History Of The Simulation Hypothesis

In *"Apocalyptic AI"* [Geraci 2010], Robert Geraci forcefully notes that Moravec has been the first to formulate (in modern terms) the idea that our reality could be a simulation, much before Bostrom:

> "Bostrom credits himself for having published the simulation argument rather than specifying that he published an essay about the simulation argument, which was presented by Moravec more than a decade before Bostrom."

Geraci is referring to Moravec's 1992 essay titled "Pigs in Cyberspace" [Moravec 1992].

"An evolving cyberspace becomes effectively ever more capacious and long lasting, and so can support ever more minds of ever greater power," said Moravec. "If these minds spend only an infinitesimal fraction of their energy contemplating the human past, their sheer power should ensure that eventually our entire history is replayed many times in many places, and in many variations."

> "The very moment we are now experiencing may actually be (almost certainly is) such a distributed mental event, and most likely is a complete fabrication that never happened physically."

By "almost certainly" Moravec (pre-echoing Musk) refers to the idea that observers living in simulated realities may vastly outnumber observers living in original physical realities.

Actually, the simulation hypothesis is already hinted at in *"Mind Children"* [Moravec 1988], for example in the Cellticks story outlined above. Moravec formulated the simulation hypothesis in clearer terms in an interview with Charles Platt [Platt 1995]:

> "Moravec foresees a kind of happy ending, though, because the cyberspace entities should find human activity interesting from a historical perspective.
> We will be remembered as their ancestors, the creators who enabled them to exist.

> As Moravec puts it, 'We are their past, and they will be interested in us for the same reason that today we are interested in the origins of our own life on Earth.'
> Assuming the artificial intelligences now have truly overwhelming processing power, they should be able to reconstruct human society in every detail by tracing atomic events backward in time. 'It will cost them very little to preserve us this way,' he points out. 'They will, in fact, be able to re-create a model of our entire civilization, with everything and everyone in it, down to the atomic level, simulating our atoms with machinery that's vastly subatomic. Also,' he says with amusement, 'they'll be able to use data compression to remove the redundant stuff that isn't important.'

> But by this logic, our current 'reality' could be nothing more than a simulation produced by information entities.

> 'Of course.' Moravec shrugs and waves his hand as if the idea is too obvious. 'In fact, the robots will re-create us any number of times, whereas the original version of our world exists, at most, only once. Therefore, statistically speaking, it's much more likely we're living in a vast simulation than in the original version. To me, the whole concept of reality is rather absurd. But while you're inside the scenario, you can't help

but play by the rules. So we might as well pretend this is real - even though the chance things are as they seem is essentially negligible.'

And so, according to Hans Moravec, the human race is almost certainly extinct, while the world around us is just an advanced version of SimCity."

I don't care too much about who was the first contemporary thinker to formulate the simulation hypothesis in modern terms. Kudos to both Moravec and Bostrom. The idea is much older.

In "*Three Dialogues Between Hylas and Philonous in Opposition to Sceptics and Atheists (Third Dialogue)*" [Berkeley 1914], Bishop George Berkeley quoted Paul (Acts 17:28) and argued that everything in the universe is but a perception, a thought in "the infinite mind of God, in whom 'we live, and move, and have our being.'" According to Berkeley, we are thoughts in the mind of God.

It is easy to see that Berkeley and Moravec are saying very similar things, each in the language of his philosophy and age. It's also worth noting that, [if we think of the physical universe as the Mind of God], Berkeley's idea is trivially true.

Apparently, there is an important difference between Berkeley and Moravec: Berkeley, an 18th century Christian and a representative of the Church, believed in supernatural phenomena not understandable by science, while Moravec, a modern engineer, believes reality is fully understandable and explainable by science. Moravec's simulated realities will be developed by future engineers, within the framework of future science.

If our reality itself is a simulation, everything in our universe can be understood in terms of the physical laws of the higher level reality in which our universe is simulated. Everything is natural, and nothing is supernatural.

But... this is only true from the perspective of those who are running the simulation. They can't violate the laws of their own physics, but they can violate the physics of the universe that they are simulating, bypassing or modifying the physics engine, anytime. From the perspective of those who live in the simulation, supernatural phenomena can happen: The reality engineers who run the simulation may choose to violate the rules of the game.

Make this simple experiment: Run a [Game of Life] program, choose an initial pattern, and let it evolve for a while. Now, stop the program, flip a cell, and resume the program. You have just violated the physical laws (the simple cellular automata evolution rules of Life) of the lower level of reality that you are simulating. Hypothetical observers within the simulation would observe a supernatural event that can't be understood in terms of the physical laws of their universe.

Similarly, if our own reality is a simulation, the engineers who control the simulation can't violate the laws of THEIR physics, but they can violate the laws of OUR physics anytime.

It's worth noting that, instead of violating our physics, the engineers could steer our reality more subtly, through [gaps in the causally open laws of our physics]. In fact, nondeterminism and randomness seem built in the fabric of our reality. If so, the engineers could intervene in our world by choosing the (apparently random) outcomes of quantum and chaotic collapse events.

Notes

[a "multiverse" with an infinite number of parallel universes] See "Exotic space, mysterious time, magic quantum."

[a simple intuitive metaphor for a reality that is probably much weirder] See "Thought experiments in physical theology," "In the beginning was the field."

[consciousness] See "United quantum consciousness," "Eligo, ergo sum, ergo Deus est," "Thought experiments in physical theology," "In the beginning was the field."

[Dawkins] See "Little green Gods."

[Game of Life] See "The Life of Glider."

[gaps in the causally open laws of our physics] See "There's plenty of room at the bottom," "Eligo, ergo sum, ergo Deus est," "Thought experiments in physical theology," "In the beginning was the field."

[if we think of the physical universe as the Mind of God] See "In the beginning was the field."

[I sent Nick enthusiastic comments] I interpreted Nick's arguments in a theistic way, and commented: "Thanks Nick for this idea, one of the most interesting I have seen recently... Another way to state the conclusions is that, given the assumptions, the probability that I live in a universe created and run by a god is very high..." An archived copy of my post can be found at:
http://extropians.weidai.com/extropians.4Q01/3873.html
An archived copy of Nick's reply can be found at:
http://extropians.weidai.com/extropians.4Q01/3918.html

[issues in fundamental physics] See "Exotic space, mysterious time, magic quantum," and following chapters.

[Mormon Transhumanist Association] See "Man will become like God, say Mormons and transhumanists."

[new digital physics before space and time] See "The quest for Akashic physics and engineering."

[the simulation hypothesis is a coherent and useful mental picture of reality] See "Thought experiments in physical theology," "In the beginning was the field."

[via the SL4 and Extropians mailing lists] An archived copy of Nick's post, titled "New website: The Simulation Argument," can be found at:
http://extropians.weidai.com/extropians.4Q01/3654.html

References

[Bell 2016] Tom Bell. Seven Steps Toward an Authored Universe. YouTube, 2016.
https://www.youtube.com/watch?v=swidctE3h2U

[Berkeley 1914] George Berkeley. *Three Dialogues Between Hylas and Philonous in Opposition to Sceptics and Atheists*. P.F. Collier & Son, 1909–14.

[Bostrom 2003] Nick Bostrom. Are You Living In a Computer Simulation? *Philosophical Quarterly*, 2003.
http://www.simulation-argument.com/simulation.html

[Bostrom 2011] Nick Bostrom. The Simulation Argument FAQ, 2011.
https://www.simulation-argument.com/faq.html

[Bruere 2012] Dirk Bruere. *The Praxis*. Amazon Digital Services, 2012.

[Cannon 2015] Lincoln Cannon. What is Mormon Transhumanism? *Theology and Science*, 2015. See also:
https://new-god-argument.com/

[Cannon 2016] Lincoln Cannon. Your Digital Afterlives: Computational Theories of Life after Death, 2016.
https://lincoln.metacannon.net/2016/03/your-digital-afterlives-computational.html

[Chang 2016] Alvin Chang. This cartoon explains why Elon Musk thinks we're characters in a computer simulation. He might be right. *Vox*, 2016
https://www.vox.com/technology/2016/6/23/12007694/elon-musk-simulation-cartoon

[Dawkins 2006] Richard Dawkins. *The God Delusion*. Houghton Mifflin Harcourt, 2006.

[D'Onfro 2016] Jillian D'Onfro. Here's the question Elon Musk talked about so much that he now refuses to discuss it in hot tubs. *Business Insider*, 2016.
http://www.businessinsider.com/the-question-elon-musk-refuses-to-talk-about-in-hot-tubs-2016-6

[Forbes 2015] Kent Forbes. *The Simulation Hypothesis*. Fair Wind Films, 2015.
https://vimeo.com/126833477

[Geraci 2010] Robert Geraci. *Apocalyptic AI: Visions of Heaven in Robotics, Artificial Intelligence, and Virtual Reality*. Oxford University Press, 2010.

[Goertzel 2019] Ben Goertzel. The Simulation Hypothesis - Not Nearly Crazy Enough to Be True. *The Multiverse According to Ben*, 2019.
http://multiverseaccordingtoben.blogspot.com/2019/07/the-simulation-hypothesis-is-mostly.html

[Moravec 1988] Hans Moravec. *Mind Children: The Future of Robot and Human Intelligence*. Harvard University Press, 1988.

[Moravec 1992] Hans Moravec. Pigs in Cyberspace. In *The Transhumanist Reader: Classical and Contemporary Essays on the Science, Technology, and Philosophy of the Human Future* (Max More, Natasha Vita-More, Eds.). Wiley-Blackwell, 2013.

[Moskowitz 2016] Clara Moskowitz. Are We Living in a Computer Simulation? *Scientific American*, 2016.
https://www.scientificamerican.com/article/are-we-living-in-a-computer-simulation/

[Platt 1995] Charles Platt. Superhumanism. *Wired*, 1995.
https://www.wired.com/1995/10/moravec/

[Steinhart 2014] Eric Steinhart. *Your Digital Afterlives: Computational Theories of Life after Death*. Palgrave Macmillan, 2014.

[Virk 2019] Rizwan Virk. *The Simulation Hypothesis: An MIT Computer Scientist Shows Why AI, Quantum Physics and Eastern Mystics All Agree We Are In a Video Game*. Bayview Books, 2019.

CHAPTER 13 – THE LIFE
OF JOE GLIDER

The Game of Life, a cellular automaton devised by the British mathematician John Conway in 1970, is a rich mental laboratory to think about computational universes, and perhaps about the physical universe as well.

Cellular automata are mathematical systems of cells arranged in a grid, which can be one-dimensional, two-dimensional, or multi-dimensional. The evolution of a cellular automaton from one instant of discrete time to the next is governed by simple rules to update the state of all cells as a function of their current state and that of nearby cells.

The chief evangelist of cellular automata is Stephen Wolfram, and the Bible of the discipline is Wolfram's "*A New Kind of Science*" [Wolfram 2002]. See also Wolfram's collected papers on cellular automata and complexity [Wolfram 1994] and Rudy Rucker's insightful thoughts on cellular automata [Rucker 2016].

Cellular automata show that very complex behavior can emerge from very simple rules. The Game of Life (just "Life" hereafter) is a two-dimensional cellular automaton with very simple rules that produce strikingly complex, lifelike patterns.

The computational universe of Life shares important properties with our universe, including emergent complexity, computational irreducibility, and Turing-completeness. The main difference is that Life is fully deterministic, which might not be the case of our universe. While Life is (evidently) deterministic and irreversible, [determinism and reversibility in our universe are open issues].

Another important difference is that, though Life can give rise to very complex phenomena, perhaps as complex as anything in our universe, the fundamental physics of Life (the cellular automata evolution rules) is fully known (we put it there) and very simple.

The rules are VERY simple indeed: Life unfolds in a two-dimensional array of square cells. A cell can be in one of two states: on and off. The two states can also be indicated as black and white, or alive and dead. Life evolves in discrete time steps, from one instant of time to the next.

The next state of a cell depends only on its current state and that of the eight nearby cells. A dead (off) cell becomes alive (on) if exactly three of its neighbors are alive. An alive cell stays alive if two or three of its neighbors are alive, otherwise it dies off. That simple.

In fact, Life is so simple that you could follow the evolution of a simple pattern of cells with pencil and paper, or even in your head. More realistically, there are excellent free Life programs like [Golly].

The Turing Church logo, featured on the cover of this book, is a stylized version of one of the smallest infinite-growth patterns in Life, patterns that keep growing forever.

This pattern leaves a wake behind, a permanent memory trace, a stairway to infinity that looks like a stylized DNA helix (try it in Golly). Unlimited growth, cosmic memory, evolution of life toward transcendence - all the symbols that I wanted are here. [This Life pattern was found by mathematician Paul Callahan] [Adamatzky 2010], but I used a specular reflection of the pattern that goes up and forward (instead of up and back).

"*The Recursive Universe*" [Poundstone 2013], by William Poundstone, first published in 1985, is a classic treatise on Life (the universe, and everything), with an encyclopedic coverage of Life (as known in 1985) and intriguing parallels with physics, thermodynamics, computation, and life in our universe. Poundstone's Afterword to the 2013 edition briefly covers important developments in Life since 1985.

The construction of a Universal Turing Machine (UTM) within Life, by mathematician Paul Rendell [Rendell 2014, 2016], is an especially interesting recent development.

A Turing Machine is a simple conceptual model of computing machine with a fixed program and infinite storage, introduced by Alan Turing. In practice, infinite storage can be interpreted as storage large enough for executing the program. Computability by a Turing Machine is often considered as a definition of computability. "In simple terms," notes Rendell, "everything algorithmically computable is computable by a Turing Machine." This is a simplified formulation of the Turing-Church thesis (more often indicated as Church-Turing thesis, or conjecture) that lends its name to this book.

A Universal Turing Machine is a Turing Machine that can be programmed to emulate any Turing Machine. In other words, a UTM with sufficient storage space can compute all that can be computed. Rendell showed that UTMs exist in the Life universe, and implemented a simple UTM in Life. Therefore, Life can be programmed to solve any computable problem, by setting up an appropriate initial configuration of cells.

Now, the computability of intelligence and consciousness is an open issue, with strong arguments presented from both sides. But if intelligence and consciousness are computable (that is, if a UTM can be intelligent and conscious), it seems to follow that intelligent, conscious life can exist in Life.

Is There Life In Life?

The chapter "Self-Reproducing Life Patterns" of Poundstone's book [Poundstone 2013] details Conway's analysis of true, lifelike self-reproduction in the Life universe. Poundstone and Conway think that life and consciousness would eventually emerge in a sufficiently large (actually, unthinkably huge) Life field, initially in a random state.

An important condition is that the random initial Life field should be sparse (with a very low density of on cells) to give enough time to self-reproducing patterns to propagate, evolve and learn new tricks without being untimely destroyed.

Besides huge size and vanishingly small density, no conditions are imposed on the initial random configuration. Poundstone and Conway believe that the laws of Life physics are "stronger" than any specific initial conditions and similar outcomes will eventually emerge from different initial random fields (this may well be a property of our own universe as well). Poundstone explains:

> "Eventually, self-reproducing patterns must tend to fill the Life plane. The most common, most natural large objects in a thin random Life field might - ultimately - be self-reproducing patterns. The fate of any typical region of the plane could be to become populated with self-reproducing patterns, all the offspring of an accidental creation that probably took place in a distant part of the infinite plane.
>
> A self-replicating Life pattern that moves might benefit from sensory and nervous systems to deal with new environments. Double side-tracking can send a glider out and bring it back. Gliders that fail to return would indicate an obstacle ahead. Thus a pattern could have 'eyes' or 'antennae' of sorts.
>
> Presumably, the long-term evolution of an infinite Life field would proceed somewhat like biologists imagine the evolution of life on the early earth proceeded.
>
> First the Life plane would become populated with colonies of first-generation self-replicating patterns. Each colony would derive from a single seed pattern that arose purely by chance. The odds against a pattern arising by chance grow even steeper for more complex patterns, so practically all of the first-generation patterns would possess only the minimum level of organization necessary to reproduce. They would be the Life version of Von Neumann's machine - a mindless self-replicator.
>
> From time to time, mutations would occur. A pattern might be constructed in a site containing other Life objects. A stray glider might wander into a pattern's works. Most such mutations would be harmful. But rare cases would produce patterns better able to survive than their neighbors. Natural selection would favor the mutated patterns."

Conway himself notes that some forms of life might emerge in Life [Conway 2004]. In Conway's words:

> "It's probable, given a large enough Life space, initially in a random state, that after a long time, intelligent self-reproducing animals will emerge and populate some parts of the space.
>
> "Moreover, it is presumably possible to design such patterns which will survive in-

side the typical Life environment (a sort of primordial broth made of blocks, blinkers, gliders, ...). It might for instance do this by shooting out masses of gliders to detect nearby objects and then take appropriate action to eliminate them. So one of these 'animals' could be more or less adjusted to its environment than another. If both were self-replicating and shared a common territory, presumably more copies of the better adapted one would survive and replicate.

Analogies with real life processes are impossible to resist... There is even the very remote possibility that space-time itself is granular, composed of discrete units, and that the universe, as Edward Fredkin of M.I.T. and others have suggested, is a cellular automaton run by an enormous computer."

Poundstone notes that the existence of universal computers in Life implies that the nervous systems of self-reproducing patterns can be arbitrarily complex.

"Eventually, 'intelligent' species might evolve from the same sort of selective pressures that operated on earth."

Of course, there is no reason to stop at human-level intelligence. We are starting to boost our evolution by developing superintelligent technology, and the same could happen in a Life universe.

Poundstone ponders how big are Life self-reproducing patterns, and how big are the smallest Life random fields that spontaneously form self-reproducing patterns, and arrives at unthinkably huge sizes. My own analysis below is based on typical scales in Life and in our physical universe, and also arrives at hyper-astronomical numbers.

Let's consider one nanometer (10^{-9} m) as the size of the smallest forms of life in our universe (the smallest known forms of life are bigger than that, but let's leave some room for new findings). Let's consider the Planck length (10^{-35} m) as the fundamental scale (the smallest meaningful size) in our universe.

In the framework of this rough analogy, on a display where one Life cell is 1 cm across, the size of the smallest life form would be 10^{24} m. How big is that? One light year is 10^{16} m, so the smallest life form in Life is 10^{8} (100 million) light years across (that is the space occupied by thousands of galaxies).

Of course, that is not big enough, because life doesn't exist in isolation but needs a whole ecology to support it. Considering the size of a small planet (1000 kilometers) as a typical size for a whole ecology, we must multiply the size of the smallest life form in Life by the size of the planet expressed in nanometers (10^{15}). The result is 10^{23} light years. The size of the observable universe is 100 billion (10^{11}) light years. In conclusion, the smallest random Life board that eventually produces life is a trillion (10^{12}) times bigger than the universe.

Based on these numbers, we are not likely to build a Life computation with sentient and intelligent inhabitants anytime soon. But perhaps one may be built in the (far) future, and/or alien super-civilizations out there create intelligent Life computations based on some kind of weird quantum technology.

Also, perhaps all consistent realities exist in some sense, and Life is certainly consistent. If so, mathematical universes populated by superintelligent forms of life (aka Gods) exist somewhere, and in principle we know of a very short recipe to build one: take a random

Life field with size X and density Y, and let it evolve until it develops life, intelligence, and superintelligence.

I find this topic totally fascinating, and a few years ago I used to think that life, intelligence, and superintelligence could exist in a Life universe. Now, I'm not so sure.

In the totally deterministic mathematical universe of Life, everything is uniquely determined by the simple rules of Life physics and the initial state of the grid. This can be hugely complex, but it's really a finite body of information that can be coded in an integer number. I don't think a number can have conscious experiences.

My intuition tells me that, for consciousness to be present, something has to happen, but nothing happens to an abstract number. It isn't like the number nineteen, or the factorial of the factorial (iterate a zillion times) of nineteen can fall in love, or be in a bad mood.

I tend to consider [consciousness as a state of matter], which is physically realized in the biological brain and, I guess, in other physical systems. A futuristic computer running a huge Life universe might contain conscious experiences, encoded in the state of the computer's matter substrate.

But what about free will? I suspect that free will can only arise in systems that exhibit the causal openness of our physical universe, with [quantum or chaotic collapse events] that are compatible with but not uniquely determined by the physical laws and initial conditions. See [Ilachinski 2001] for fascinating speculations on cellular automata with probabilistic and quantum-like evolution rules.

So, I do NOT think that active consciousness and free will can arise in a Life universe. However, I think passive consciousness, able to observe the world with a delusion of free agency, could well arise in Life.

In the following I will suspend disbelief and assume that Life patterns can think and feel.

Meet Joe Glider

Gliders are among the simplest patterns in Life. If you run Golly with an initial pattern of a few tens of cells, you'll notice little groups of pixels that wiggle and move diagonally with constant speed, retaining their dynamic individuality until they bump into other patterns. These are the gliders.

Here I'm assuming that conscious, thinking and feeling patterns can exist in Life, but of course a glider is too simple to think or feel. At the same time, gliders can be considered "alive" in some sense, just like a molecule may be considered alive.

In "Being a Glider in the Game of Life," by Markus Echterhoff [Echterhoff 2011], and "Autopoiesis and Cognition in the Game of Life," by Randall Beer [Beer 2004], the authors describe the life of a glider. A glider can move in one of four directions (SE, SW, NW, NE), and be in one of four phases.

These possible glider states and their transformations into other glider states according to the cellular automata laws of Life physics constitute "gliderness" and can be thought of as simple "mental states" in the life of a glider.

Therefore, let's suspend disbelief and think of a glider, let's call him Joe Glider, as a conscious living being in Life. At any time, Joe is in a certain position and in one of the 16 possible mental states (four directions and four phases).

I Will Fear No Evil

This section is adapted from a talk on "The Computational Problem of Evil" [Prisco 2013] that I gave at the 2013 Conference of the [Mormon Transhumanist Association] (MTA). I analyzed the problem of evil in a computational Life universe, and I used animations featuring Joe Glider to illustrate my argument.

I had previously outlined these ideas in a *Fast Forward Radio* interview [Bowermaster 2012].

I wish to thank Lincoln Cannon and James Carroll for helping me to elaborate and clarify my thoughts, which of course is a work in progress.

[If an omnipotent and benevolent God permits evil and suffering, then God is either not omnipotent, or not benevolent, or neither, or perhaps God doesn't exist at all]. This, known as the problem of evil, is one of the main reasons why former believers become atheists.

It turns out that the problem of evil has a simple solution when examined with a rigorous approach based on the physics of computation.

The medieval philosophers, who were as smart as contemporary philosophers and thought a lot about these things, knew that "omnipotent" is a concept that needs to be defined and limited. Could an omnipotent being create a stone too heavy to be lifted, even by the same omnipotent being?

If God could lift the stone, then it seems that God would cease to be omnipotent, since the stone was not heavy enough; if God couldn't lift the stone, it seems that God was not omnipotent to begin with.

But a stone so heavy that it cannot be lifted by an omnipotent being cannot exist, because an omnipotent being is defined as a being that can lift all stones. The stone is a contradiction in terms and a logical impossibility, like a triangle with four sides (a triangle is defined as a polygon with three sides). God can't draw a triangle with four sides, because a triangle with four sides cannot exist by definition.

I will use a computational metaphor where the universe, the physical reality that we inhabit, is seen as a "program" running on a "computer." Several philosophers and researchers have proposed that this metaphor may be literally "true," but of course we should not imagine anything like a simple computer running a simple program that we can understand. If we consider elementary particles and fields as circuitry, and the laws of physics as a program, then the reality-as-computation metaphor becomes trivially true.

Conway's Game of Life is a simple example of computational universe, much simpler than our physical reality, but complex enough to illustrate my argument. The universe of Life is an infinite two-dimensional orthogonal grid of square cells, each of which is in one of two possible states, alive or dead.

Every cell interacts with its eight neighbors, which are the cells that are horizontally, vertically, or diagonally adjacent. At each step in time, the new state of the cell is computed as a simple function of the previous states of the cell and its neighbors.

Despite the apparent simplicity of the rules, surprisingly complex and lifelike patterns have been shown to exist in Life, notably a Universal Turing Machine. I will use Joe Glider, a hypothetical inhabitant of Life, to illustrate my argument.

God, the faithful believe, observes reality from the privileged point of view of the "system administrator" who started the computation, and may choose to intervene.

Most believers make the additional assumption that God is benevolent, and lovingly cares about the welfare and happiness of the conscious beings who live in the universe.

To see how God can steer reality, make this simple experiment: Run a Life program like Golly, choose an initial pattern, and let it evolve for a while. Now, stop the program, flip a cell, and resume the program.

You have just performed a miracle: something that violates the physical laws (the simple rules of Life). Hypothetical observers within Life would observe an event that cannot be understood in terms of the physical laws of their universe.

Perhaps God has also subtler means to steer reality, which do not require violating the laws of physics. [Irreducibly random phenomena] seem to happen at the quantum scale (collapse of the wavefunction) and can be amplified to the macroscopic scale (Schrödinger's cat). Irreducibly random phenomena and chaotic collapse events are also found in non-quantum mathematical physics. A God able to tweak apparently random collapse events to achieve a desired outcome could intervene in the universe and steer reality without violating the physical laws.

But then, why didn't God prevent Auschwitz?

To answer this question, let's go back to the simple computational reality of Life. Besides some very simple initial configurations, Life is computationally irreducible: If you want to know what happens in the future, you must run the program through all intermediate iterations. There is no shortcut that permits predicting, with total certainty, what will happen in the future, without actually running the program. Stephen Wolfram explains [Durham 1985]:

> "There are some cellular automata whose behaviour can never be reduced to a formula. The only way to find out what they do is to simulate them step by step. No simpler computation provides a significant short cut. This property is known as computational irreducibility. Universal computers such as general Turing machines are among the systems which possess it."

The computational irreducibility of Life is shared by all really interesting computations (actually, it can be taken as a definition of really interesting computation). In particular, our physical reality is computationally irreducible: The universe is the fastest computer that can compute itself. In other words, a 100 percent complete and accurate prediction of tomorrow's weather cannot be done in less than 24 hours, and the only way to predict the future with complete accuracy is waiting for the future to happen.

This makes sense because the existence of a computer faster than the universe, within the universe, would lead to logical contradictions. Suppose you could compute the state of the universe tomorrow faster than the universe itself. The results of the computation will include the color of the shirt that you wear tomorrow. Then you could invalidate the prediction by simply choosing to wear, tomorrow, a shirt of another color.

Many times in history, for example in the 1930s, millions of people have been brutalized by evil regimes, and suffered a lot. Surely a benevolent and omnipotent God would try to do something to avoid that.

But there are no computational shortcuts. The only way to predict, with complete accuracy, that certain events would lead to Auschwitz, is to let the computation unfold until Auschwitz.

Perhaps, even if God can't predict the future with complete accuracy to identify subtle non-invasive interventions in the universe that would prevent evil, God could keep intervening unsubtly, massively, continuously, and systematically, to prevent bad things from happening.

But this strategy doesn't seem to work very well, as illustrated by this Life analogy:

Joe Glider can "feel" as in one of 16 mental states (travelling SE, SW, NW or NE and cycling through four phases per direction). The "consciousness stream" of Joe Glider is in the phase changes that Joe experiences while moving along its path, and occasional non-lethal interactions with other Life patterns.

Suppose Joe is travelling SE, on a collision course with a pattern that will destroy him, in the sense that after the collision there won't be any glider that can be identified with Joe. Some patterns won't destroy Joe (depending on the relative phases), but most patterns will.

If there is enough room to maneuver, God can protect Joe by placing a reflector (a Life pattern that switches an incoming glider to a new direction and phase) on Joe's path, and then destroying the reflector when Joe is on a new safer path. This intervention is sort of compatible with Life physics since it can't be detected by observers in the Life universe, not even by Joe himself. It's worth noting the analogy with the quantum tweaks mentioned above.

If there isn't enough room for this maneuver, God can subtly tweak and steer Joe by switching on [two off cells close to Joe] to change Joe's travel direction to SW. If no other patterns are too close, this slightly more invasive intervention switches Joe to a new direction and phase, but leaves the rest of the Life universe unchanged.

From Joe's point of view, this is a small and respectful intervention, because it doesn't violate the glider-ness and Joe-ness of Joe except for a small discontinuity (the temporary addition of two cells). To Joe, the discontinuity would feel like a sudden hunch or something like that.

If Joe finds himself in a region densely populated by many other patterns, God can still steer Joe carefully on a safe path. But now God should flip a lot of cells very often, including Joe's own cells. Then, Joe would stop feeling like himself, and the glider-ness and Joe-ness of Joe would be destroyed.

With this massive and invasive intervention, God has not saved Joe, but destroyed Joe and created a new pattern, a zombie that does not follow the physics of consciousness and therefore is not able to have any conscious experience at all.

Even in the safer cases outlined above, God has no way to know what the long term results of an intervention will be.

Perhaps God could just use a faster computer to make the prediction? You can predict the evolution of Life on your computer, faster than just waiting for the results, by simply running Golly on a faster computer.

If you see that something bad will happen to the version of Joe Glider in the faster computer, you can try to flip some cells so that the same bad things don't happen to the original Joe.

Unfortunately this wouldn't work, because we are dealing with very complex computations, so complex that they contain thinking and feeling persons like you and me. If God uses a faster computer to predict Auschwitz before it happens in our own reality, Auschwitz will happen in the faster computer, and people will suffer in the faster computer.

In conclusion, God is unable to predict with complete accuracy the future of a computation that includes thinking and feeling creatures. God can only work with incomplete resources and information, just like us.

When we are children, we think that our parents are omniscient, omnipotent, and supremely wise. When we find out that it is not so, we are very disappointed. Perhaps our parents didn't protect us from painful things, and we may think that they didn't love us.

But when we grow up and become ourselves adults, and parents, we understand that some things were beyond the power of our parents to change. We do our best for our children, but sometimes our best is not good enough.

According to the interpretation of Mormon scriptures promoted by the MTA [Cannon 2015], we will become Gods ourselves, and we will create worlds inhabited by sentient, thinking and feeling creatures. We will love our creations - what parent doesn't? - but sometimes we will be unable to protect them from suffering, and pain. We will, however, do our best, and learn from our mistakes.

Notes

[consciousness as a state of matter] See "Into the deep waters."

[determinism and reversibility in our universe are open issues] See "Exotic space, mysterious time, magic quantum," "There's plenty of room at the bottom," and following chapters.

[Golly] Golly is a standard, free, open source life simulator. See:
http://golly.sourceforge.net/

[If an omnipotent and benevolent God permits evil and suffering, then God is either not omnipotent, or not benevolent, or neither, or perhaps God doesn't exist at all] I realize that this and similar passages may sound awkward, but I'm trying to avoid referring to God with gendered pronouns. Not for "political correctness" (I really don't care about that), but because gendered pronouns would be too anthropomorphic for my conception of God. This rules out "he" and "she." The neutral "it" sounds disrespectful, and seems to negate the personal nature of God. Using the currently fashionable "they" seems a theological statement (more Gods than one) in this context. So, I am just repeating "God" as many times as I need to.

[Irreducibly random phenomena] See "Exotic space, mysterious time, magic quantum" for irreducibly random phenomena in quantum physics. See "There's plenty of room at the bottom," "Eligo, ergo sum, ergo Deus est," "Thought experiments in physical theology" for irreducibly random phenomena in non-quantum mathematical physics.

[Mormon Transhumanist Association] See "Man will become like God, say Mormons and transhumanists."

[quantum or chaotic collapse events] See "There's plenty of room at the bottom," "Eligo, ergo sum, ergo Deus est," "Thought experiments in physical theology."

[This Life pattern was found by mathematician Paul Callahan] See "Infinite growth," Conway-Life wiki:
https://www.conwaylife.com/wiki/Infinite_growth

[two off cells close to Joe] Adding two diagonal cells in the direction of motion to a glider in a certain phase reflects the glider by 90 degrees. See "Smallest glider reflector ever," Conway-Life forums:
http://www.conwaylife.com/forums/viewtopic.php?p=1282

References

[Adamatzky 2010] Andrew Adamatzky (Ed.). *Game of Life Cellular Automata*. Springer, 2010.

[Beer 2004] Randall Beer. Autopoiesis and Cognition in the Game of Life. *Artificial Life*, 2004.
https://cepa.info/fulltexts/1143.pdf

[Bowermaster 2012] Phil Bowermaster, Stephen Gordon. The Physics of Miracles. *Fast Forward Radio*, 2012.
http://www.blogtalkradio.com/worldtransformed/2012/08/16/religion-for-robots--fast-forward-radio

[Cannon 2015] Lincoln Cannon. What is Mormon Transhumanism? *Theology and Science*, 2015.
https://new-god-argument.com/

[Conway 2004] John Conway. What is Life? *Winning Ways for Your Mathematical Plays*, Volume 4. Elwyn Berlekamp, John Conway, Richard Guy, Eds. A. K. Peters, 2004.

[Durham 1985] Tony Durham. Explorations in the Cellular Microworld. *Computing*, 1985.
http://www.stephenwolfram.com/media/explorations-cellular-microworld/

[Echterhoff 2011] Markus Echterhoff. Being a Glider in the Game of Life, 2011.
https://www.markusechterhoff.com/papers/echterhoff2011_-_being_a_glider_in_the_game_of_life/

[Ilachinski 2001] Andrew Ilachinski. *Cellular Automata: A Discrete Universe*. World Scientific, 2001.

[Poundstone 2013] William Poundstone. *The Recursive Universe: Cosmic Complexity and the Limits of Scientific Knowledge*. Dover, 2013.

[Prisco 2013] Giulio Prisco. The Computational Problem of Evil. YouTube, 2013.
https://www.youtube.com/watch?v=fiTb6zhqHLI

[Rendell 2014] Paul Rendell. *Turing Machine Universality of the Game of Life*. Thesis, UWE Bristol, 2014.
http://eprints.uwe.ac.uk/22323/

[Rendell 2016] Paul Rendell. *Turing Machine Universality of the Game of Life*. Springer, 2016.

[Rucker 2016] Rudy Rucker. *The Lifebox, the Seashell, and the Soul: What Gnarly Computation Taught Me About Ultimate Reality, The Meaning of Life, And How to Be Happy*. Transreal Books, 2016.

[Wolfram 1994] Stephen Wolfram. *Cellular Automata and Complexity: Collected Papers*. Westview Press, 1994.

[Wolfram 2002] Stephen Wolfram. *A New Kind of Science*. Wolfram Media, 2002.
Online version: http://www.wolframscience.com/nks/

CHAPTER 14 - A FOR ALMIGHTY: FRED HOYLE'S COSMIC THEOLOGY

Sir Fred Hoyle (1915 - 2001) was both an accomplished science fiction writer - his novels "*A for Andromeda*" [Hoyle 1962] and "*The Black Cloud*" [Hoyle 2010] are rightly placed among the masterpieces of science fiction of all times - and a Nobel Prize level scientist. It's well known that Hoyle was denied a Nobel Prize in Physics [Gregory 2005] that should have been rightfully his for his pioneering work on nucleosynthesis processes in stars.

Hoyle's collaborator William Alfred Fowler received the Nobel prize in 1983, but Hoyle's fundamental contributions - later acknowledged by Fowler - were overlooked by the Nobel committee. That has been attributed to Hoyle's brash personality and penchant for politically incorrect statements, including - I guess - daring to suggest that the universe is controlled by a cosmic God.

Hoyle first came to the God conclusion by reflecting on what would later be known as "Anthropic Principle" - the amazing coincidences and fine-tuning of the physical constants that appear to favor the emergence of carbon-based life. "Some supercalculating intellect must have designed the properties of the carbon atom," he said [Hoyle 1981].

> "A common sense interpretation of the facts suggests that a superintellect has monkeyed with physics, as well as with chemistry and biology, and that there are no blind forces worth speaking about in nature. The numbers one calculates from the facts seem to me so overwhelming as to put this conclusion almost beyond question."

In a video clip titled "Fine Tuning" [Polkinghorne 2009], physicist and theologian John Polkinhorne tells the story of Hoyle's discovery of how carbon atoms are formed in the stars. "The chemistry of life is the chemistry of carbon," says Polkinghorne. Where does carbon come from? The only place in the whole universe where carbon can be made is in the interior of stars. "Every atom of carbon inside our bodies was once inside a star," continues Polkinghorne. "We are people of stardust."

Stellar nucleosynthesis can create carbon atoms if and only if the carbon atom has an excited state with a very specific energy level (resonance). With "anthropic reasoning" - the universe must be able to produce carbon-based life such as ourselves - Hoyle predicted this resonance before it was found experimentally. "If the laws of nuclear physics had been a tiny bit different, either there would be no resonance at all, or it would be at some other energy, which would be no good," explains Polkinghorne. "And Fred, who had a lifelong commitment to atheism, is reported to have said (in a Yorkshire accent):"

> "The universe is a put-up job."

"In other words, this can't be just a happy accident, it's too significant for that," concludes Polkinghorne. "There must be something behind all this. Because Fred didn't like the word 'God', he says some (capital I) Intelligence has monkeyed with the laws of the universe."

Though Hoyle didn't like the word "God," his ultimate Intelligence looks very much like God to me. The loving, personal aspect of God, and the concept of personal resurrection, aren't part of Hoyle's "theology," but they aren't necessarily incompatible with it either (see below). Therefore, I hope Sir Fred will forgive me for using the G word in this review.

Jane Gregory's biography "*Fred Hoyle's Universe*" [Gregory 2005] offers a fascinating portrait of the life and work of a visionary scientist and politically incorrect thinker who threw stones at too many sacred cows to be rewarded with a Nobel Prize. In fact, Hoyle dared to publicly and vigorously oppose parts of Darwin's theory of evolution, because he considered the probability of inorganic matter spontaneously assembling into organic life, and continuing to evolve through random mutations alone, as far too small to be credible. As an alternative to Darwinism, Hoyle proposed his own highly imaginative version of Intelligent Design (ID). Supporting ID is guaranteed to attract rabid hostility in "liberal" academic circles, but Hoyle made things even worse by using the forbidden G word. A scientist who finds God, of all things. That's probably why Hoyle was denied a well-deserved Nobel Prize.

"Many in the scientific community had felt for a while that stellar nucleosynthesis was an achievement worthy of a Nobel Prize," Gregory reports. "*The Observer* newspaper, commenting on Hoyle's recent thinking on a cosmic deity, suggested that this 'unexpected conversion may bring him some comfort during a vexing time - for the diminutive, mercurial physicist has just been soundly snubbed by the world of science.' *New Scientist* published an article subtitled 'a defence for Sir Fred Hoyle,' which pondered the paradox of a likeable, inventive scientist who manages nevertheless to repeatedly raise the hackles of the scientific establishment, and suggested that Hoyle's 'breadth of vision' made other scientists uneasy." In 1997 Hoyle was awarded the prestigious Crafoord Prize for his work on stellar nucleosynthesis, which other scientists interpreted as a redress for having been excluded from the Nobel.

Hoyle started as an atheist, but through science he came to cosmic visions essentially similar to - actually indistinguishable from - those found in the world's religions. He imagined a hierarchy of Gods in the universe, from lowercase local gods all the way to an asymptotic cosmic God that emerges from the physical universe, comes into full being in the infinitely distant future beyond time, controls space and time, seeds the universe with life, and keeps tweaking and fine-tuning the whole of space-time with subtle quantum messages and self-consistent causal loops in time. A for Almighty, indeed.

But Sir Fred wasn't a mystic. He was a scientist, and a top class physicist. Therefore, he didn't stop at inspiring poetic visions, but dared to try and propose physical models for both the local gods, aka Intelligent Designers, and the ultimate cosmic God.

Intelligent Designers

In *"The Intelligent Universe"* [Hoyle 1984], a thoughtful and beautifully illustrated popular science book published in 1984, Hoyle set forth his unconventional views of life, the universe, and everything. According to Hoyle, life on our planet was seeded by cosmic organic spores that pervade the universe, perhaps engineered by ancient intelligences to create a new material substrate - carbon-based biology - able to continue hosting intelligent life in an evolving universe, with changing physical constant, which was becoming hostile to the old material substrate - whatever that was - of intelligence.

Intelligence "continually has to modify and adapt the material by which it is expressed in order to keep in step with an ever-changing Universe," says Hoyle. "Success is always temporary, yet because intelligence is at work, somewhere in the Universe living matter is keeping ahead... Suppose also that our species continues into the future for many thousands of millions of years, and that the understanding of the world by our descendants advances throughout such an immense span of time at a rate similar to the advance of our ancestors over the past million years. Suppose also that our remote descendants become aware that the critical tunings in carbon and oxygen are changing, a situation which even their greatly advanced technology is powerless to prevent."

> "Driven by an innate conviction in their survival, they could set about the problem of finding an entirely new material structure to which the store of knowledge that constituted themselves might be transferred. This it seems to me explains why another intelligence, an intelligence which preceded us, was led to put together, as a deliberate act of creation, a structure for carbon-based life."

Hoyle's vision of super-intelligent civilizations engineering new forms of life able to continue the cosmic march of intelligence is very transhumanist to say the least. However, Hoyle doesn't have cultural survival in mind, let alone personal survival, but only the continuation of intelligent life as a whole.

Hoyle suspects that, as far as individuals are concerned, the "software" doesn't survive the destruction of the "hardware." However, he says, for life as a whole, the survival of the software "is probably much more firmly grounded."

But perhaps our creators were able to do a little more than that. Perhaps they were able to build into carbon-based life some kind of awareness of its origins. Perhaps our religious impulses are firmware instructions to continue the march of intelligent life out there among the stars. In Hoyle's words:

> "You are derived from something 'out there' in the sky. Seek it, and you will find much more than you expect."

Let's recap things so far. Hoyle attacked Darwin and put the Intelligent Designers in his place, and added to his previous cosmological heresies, such as replacing the Big Bang with one or another form of steady-state model, the suggestion that the physical constants could [change with time]. That by itself was more than enough to earn the wrath of the bureaucrats of science in the eighties (I guess today's "Scientific Justice Warriors" (SJWs) would burn Hoyle just like their predecessors burned Giordano Bruno). But let's come to the G word.

In an Afterword to the Penguin Classics edition of Hoyle's *"The Black Cloud"* [Hoyle 2010],

Richard Dawkins praises the novel as one of the greatest works of science fiction ever written.

I totally agree with Dawkins. In "*The Black Cloud*" we (actually, our fathers - the book was first published in 1957) are confronted with a fundamentally alien entity, with knowledge and powers vastly exceeding our own. Dawkins says:

> "The Black Cloud vividly conveys to us what it would be like to be visited by an extraterrestrial being whose intelligence would seem god-like from our lowly point of view. Indeed, Hoyle's imagination far outperforms all religions known to me. Would such a super-intelligence then actually be a god? An interesting question, perhaps the founding question of a new discipline of 'Scientific Theology.'"

> "The answer, it seems to me, turns not on what the super-intelligence is capable of doing, but on its provenance. Alien beings, no matter how advanced their intelligence and accomplishments, would presumably have evolved by something like the same gradual evolutionary process as gave rise to our kind of life."

I agree with the second part of the last paragraph of Dawkins' quote, but not with the first. The color of the cat, or its provenance, doesn't matter if the cat is still able to catch mice and all that. If it acts like a god, and it thunders like a god, then I call an entity a god.

But the Black Cloud and the Intelligent Designers are just little local lowercase gods. Their powers are awesome from our perspective, but insignificant from a cosmic perspective. They live and act within the universe, and must obey its laws that they are powerless to change. In "*The Intelligent Universe*," Hoyle notes that the Intelligent Designers are like the Greek gods, extremely powerful but nonetheless limited beings, rather than the Almighty Christian God.

"'God' is a forbidden word in science, but if we define an intelligence superior to ourselves as a deity, then in this book we have arrived at two kinds - the intelligences of Chapter 9 and the 'God' of the infinite future," says Hoyle (the intelligences of Chapter 9 are the Intelligent Designers). "Interestingly, these two very different forms of intelligence correspond closely with the Greek idea of deities as managers of an already existing Universe on the one hand, and the Judaeo-Christian idea of a deity outside the Universe on the other."

In "*Evolution From Space*" [Hoyle 1982b], Sir Fred considers the sequence:

... - ???? - ??? - ?? - ? - man.

God is the never reached limit at the left.

So let's come to God.

The Ultimate Cosmic God

In "*The Intelligent Universe*" [Hoyle 1984] Hoyle ponders the weirdness of quantum mechanics with the example of a particle that can be in the left half (A) or in the right half (B) of a box. His observations, however, apply to the general case of a quantum system that can be in two possible states, for example spin-up or spin-down. "The chance of A is half and the chance of B is half," says Hoyle. "Quantum physics states that before we look into the box, the electron does not actually have a position - this is only fixed the instant we look at it, by our consciousness in some strange way being part of the experiment itself."

Hoyle subscribes to a "consciousness interpretation" of quantum physics, where one of the states of a quantum system - initially in a superposition of states - becomes real when it's inspected by a conscious observer, while [the other states vanish]. "Quantum physics states that until it has actually been observed, it does not have a distinct position at all," says Hoyle. "Only at the moment that the consciousness of the experimenter intervenes is the position of the electron suddenly 'decided'."

Quantum weirdness isn't too worrisome if it remains confined to microevents at the quantum scale. But Hoyle tells the story of how, one day, he was shocked by suddenly realizing that quantum superpositions can be amplified to the macroscopic scale of everyday experience. "Macroevents are represented as being completely predictable, whereas the microevents that make them up are not," he says. "But this separation seems quite arbitrary."

> "Taken to its logical conclusion, quantum mechanics should lead to a spreading vagueness in the world, even to the extent of making vague the events of everyday life. But apparently this does not happen. If you hold a match to this page, it will bum, an event which is completely predictable. Hence in some way there must be a sharpening of the picture which compensates for the uncertain fuzziness which quantum mechanics predicts."

Hoyle is persuaded that the sharpening of the picture - the choice of one of the possible outcomes of a quantum event - happens in the mind of the observer. This seems to validate free will - snap decisions reached on the spur of the moment, prompted by an "inner voice" as a result of quantum events in the brain amplified to the macroscopic scale. But a random sharpening of the picture seems a very poor form of free will, even if we manage to persuade ourselves that a random decision is really "our" decision. Free will requires more than randomness, and Hoyle proposes an imaginative way out:

> "Imagine the quantum event in question being repeated many times under identical conditions. Sometimes A will happen and sometimes B, creating a sequence - B B A B A A A B A B B A B B A B ... in which the ratio of As and Bs is known for a sufficiently long sequence. Although this ratio is itself thoroughly predictable, the actual sequence of As and Bs is not. It is usual to suppose that the sequence is random, and in some situations it may indeed be so, but to suppose that all such sequences are random is itself purely speculative. The effect of reversing this thinking is remarkable. Imagine now that some sequences are non-random. Let us represent A by a dash and B by a dot... The Morse code springs instantly to mind."

> "It is evident that such a sequence could carry a message, it could carry information. Suppose our brains contain a quantum 'experiment', an experiment repeated many

times under similar initial conditions, each with the equivalent of a dot or a dash as its result. The outcome could be a potential message available for permanent storage in the memory, ready to be acted upon, an injection of information that could form the basis for the behaviour that we call free will."

According to Hoyle, complex arrangements of matter can decode "Morse code" messages encoded in quantum randomness. In particular, life - a very complex and organized form of matter - can decode and execute these messages.

"The atoms in living material are arranged in more complex ways than in non-living matter, but why then should complex arrangements of atoms be so crucially different from simple arrangements?," wonders Hoyle. "Because complex arrangements can set up situations of the A or B type, and can then proceed to recognize the information contained in the resulting sequences of As and Bs, dots and dashes, which simple arrangements of atoms are unable to do."

> "We can also add that it is the process of recognition of such sequences that constitutes the phenomenon of consciousness... The information sequences, the Morse code messages if you like, are there at all stages, just as the books in a school are there for any child competent to read them."

So, according to Hoyle, our thoughts and decisions are driven by complex, non-random information delivered to specialized quantum decoders in the brain, and consciousness itself is a byproduct of decoding "Morse messages" encoded in quantum noise. If consciousness is involved in a fundamental, not entirely passive way, free will seems to come back into the equation ([too bad Hoyle doesn't develop this point]). Hoyle continues:

> "The problem now is to understand where the coded information sequences might come from..."

The Maxwell's equations of electromagnetism have two sets of solutions, one with radiation traveling from the past to the future, and another with radiation traveling from the future to the past. Hoyle notes that solutions in the second set - the "advanced wave" solutions - are usually discarded without thinking twice, but there are no fundamental reasons to do so. On the contrary, the advanced wave solutions could be physically meaningful. In fact, Hoyle himself and Jayant Narlikar, extending previous works of Wheeler and Feynman, developed "a time-symmetric local quantum theory augmented by a cosmological response from the future that reproduced exactly all the practical results of normal quantum electrodynamics" [Hoyle 1982a].

"The quantum version of the Wheeler-Feynman theory involves an influence functional through which the local system interacts with the large scale cosmological boundary conditions," noted Narlikar in the proceedings of a 2002 conference dedicated to Hoyle's work [Narlikar 2003]. "This local+cosmological interaction appears as transition probability for a local system, wherein all cosmological variables are integrated out. Phenomena like spontaneous transition or a collapse of the wavefunction are seen to arise from this interaction. This suggests that, the attempts to explain some of these phenomena through local hidden variables having failed, the real clue to the mystery may lie in the response of the universe in the above fashion."

Now Hoyle drops a theological bomb: the information-rich quantum messages that drive living organisms come from an Intelligence (capital I) in the infinitely distant future. The ultimate Intelligence ensures that complexity, information, and life advance in a universe that otherwise would be doomed to decay by entropy.

"Quantum mechanics is based on the propagation of radiation only from past to future, and as we have seen leads only to statistical averages, not to predictions of the nature of individual quantum events. Quantum mechanics is no exception to general experience in physics, which shows that the propagation of radiation in the past-to-future time-sense leads inevitably to degeneration, to senescence, to the loss of information... But in biology this situation is reversed, because as living organisms develop they increase in complexity, gaining information rather than losing it."

"Biological systems are able in some way to utilize the opposite time-sense in which radiation propagates from future to past. Bizarre as this may appear, they must somehow be working backwards in time. If events could operate not only from past to future, but also from future to past, the seemingly intractable problem of quantum uncertainty could be solved. Instead of living matter becoming more and more disorganized, it could react to quantum signals from the future - the information necessary for the development of life. Instead of the Universe being committed to increasing disorder and decay, the opposite could then be true."

"On a cosmic scale the effect of introducing information from the future would be similarly far-reaching. Instead of the Universe beginning in the wound-up state of the big bang, degenerating ever since, an initially primitive state of affairs could wind itself up gradually as time proceeds, becoming more, not less sophisticated, from past to future. This would allow the accumulation of information - information without which the evolution of life, and of the Universe itself, makes no logical sense."

"...the ultimate cause being a source of information, an intelligence if you like, placed in the remote future."

As Polkinghorne noted, Hoyle prefers not to call the ultimate Intelligence "God," but it's difficult to call it something else. Hoyle emphasizes that the ultimate Intelligence does not operate from some particular time-location in the future - if so, it would be itself driven by signals from its own future - but from infinitely far in the future. The concept of eternity figures large in many religions, "with the notion that there is a controlling force that lies at an unattainable distance," concludes Hoyle. "Perhaps here we have a vaguely perceived truth masked by the adornment of ritual and ceremony, obscured by the trappings of our earthly existence?"

"For those with a taste for mathematics, I have sought to follow the trail a little further in a recently published article," says Hoyle. He is referring to (I guess) the article titled "The Universe: Past and Present Reflections" [Hoyle 1982a] published in *Annual Review of Astronomy and Astrophysics* in 1982, not to be confused with the 1981 article with the same title [Hoyle 1981]. Some passages in the 1982 article shed more light on Hoyle's thinking.

According to Hoyle, it's possible to see in rather precise mathematical terms how the ultimate Intelligence could establish intelligence throughout the Universe by imposing information sequences on finite material systems. Referring to Hugh Everett's seminal 1957 paper "'Relative State' Formulation of Quantum Mechanics" [Everett 1957, DeWitt 1973], Hoyle outlines and interprets Everett's ideas - often indicated as [Everett's Many-Worlds Interpretation" (MWI)] - directly from the original source.

Quantum mechanics seems to lead to a proliferation of subobservers, each one considering "himself as being identified with a definite state of the quantum mechanical system." Hoyle recalls that, much before Everett, he and his fellow students used to lightly speculate about "alter egos" in parallel universes, and suspects that the concept may have been speculated about since the earliest days of quantum mechanics.

However, Hoyle doesn't buy the MWI. He considers the branching, enormously complex "Everett tree" of quantum mechanics as a reference map of possibilities, but thinks it must be complemented by an explanation of how the "special subobserver wavefunction" that represents consciousness chooses a specific route in the reference map. According to Hoyle, consciousness itself is a byproduct of the process of choosing a route - or, using Sir Fred's analogy, lopping the unrealized branches of the Everett tree. The process is controlled by "signals that propagate future-to-past, opposite to the branching of the tree itself, which goes past-to-future." The signals are directed by the ultimate Intelligence at the end of time.

> "In analogy to a two-stroke engine, quantum mechanics is just one of the cylinders, stroking from past-to-future. The other cylinder serves to condense the wavefunction, and it strokes from future-to-past."

A future end-point, situated at an infinite time distance in the Everett tree, imposes a deterministic reality on an observed quantum system, causing the observer's consciousness to choose the path that will lead to the end-point. If we were to start "with deterministic reality at the limit, arguing backwards from future to past, there would be deterministic reality at every link of the chain."

Thoughts On Hoyle's Cosmic Theology

More than 30 years after the publication of *"The Intelligent Universe,"* quantum physics is still a mystery, but there have been interesting and relevant theoretical developments.

Hoyle's theory is based on a consciousness interpretation of quantum physics - the observer's consciousness chooses the outcome of quantum events. In *"Mathematical Foundations of Quantum Mechanics"* [von Neumann 1955], the reference quantum mechanics text used by Hoyle and Everett, von Neumann distinguished between two fundamental quantum processes – Process 2, the deterministic evolution of the wavefunction predicted by the equations of quantum mechanics, and Process 1, the random collapse of the wavefunction upon observation. According to Hoyle, Process 1 is the action of consciousness upon the universe, and the explanation of consciousness itself.

Today, a popular alternate view is that ultimate quantum reality is deterministic, but the unavoidable interactions and entanglement with the rest of the world force (apparently) individual quantum systems to (apparently) undergo a rapid collapse, upon measurement, in a process called "environmental [decoherence]." [Joos 2003]. In the decoherence approach, the apparently discarded information is not lost but transferred to the environment, where it is rapidly "lost in translation" into less and less accessible degrees of freedom and eventually becomes indistinguishable from noise.

However, observation outcomes for apparently individual quantum systems are still effectively random. Decoherence seems to force a quantum state to collapse into one of the possible outcomes, but we can't tell which one.

Decoherence explains how the wavefunction of a quantum system Q, as a result of the inevitable interactions and entanglement with the environment, appears to collapse upon measurement (von Neumann's Process 1). According to some physicists, decoherence explains everything without needing a "real" collapse. The total system (Q plus the measurement equipment and the environment) continues to evolve according to the deterministic equations of quantum mechanics (von Neumann's Process 2), and the total information is conserved, but Q taken alone appears to undergo a collapse and lose information, they say. The evolution of Q taken alone appears as effectively random, but "Q taken alone" is an approximation, and the evolution of the total entangled system (Q + the rest of the world) is not random.

According to some physicists, decoherence explains why the macroscopic world seems classical instead of quantum (with the exception of very carefully prepared cases difficult to realize), without requiring ad-hoc additions to the equations of quantum mechanics (such as von Neumann's Process 1). There is no Process 1, only Process 2, they say. Therefore, some physicists, including Dieter Zeh, who first described decoherence, think decoherence lends support to Everett's ideas [Joos 2003].

It must be noted, however, that [decoherence] theory doesn't explain how one of many possible outcomes is selected. Therefore, the choice seems to be between von Neumann's Process 1 and [Everett's Many-Worlds Interpretation" (MWI)].

A new interpretation of quantum mechanics, called "Transactional Interpretation" [Cramer 2016] has been proposed by John Cramer in 1986. Cramer's interpretation is based on a "quantum handshake" between retarded wave and advanced wave solutions of the equations of relativistic quantum mechanics. The retarded waves propagate forward in time, and the advanced waves - analogous to Hoyle's advanced waves - propagate backward in time. The collapse of the wavefunction is "two-way in time and atemporal" [Cramer 2016]. Though controversial, Cramer's Transactional Interpretation - which is at least strongly resonant with Hoyle's ideas - has been accepted by a minority of physicists as the most promising interpretation of quantum mechanics that has been proposed to date.

It's interesting to think of how to update Hoyle's ideas in light of the new developments in quantum physics since the eighties, in particular decoherence, the renaissance of Everett's ideas, and Cramer's Transactional Interpretation.

Hoyle's ultimate Intelligence can be thought of as a God that emerges asymptotically from the evolution of life in the universe, and controls the universe across space and time by influencing living organisms, anytime and anywhere. God controls the past by creating and sustaining the conditions for God's ultimate emergence through self-consistent causal loops in time.

It's worth noting that Hoyle's God works through people. In fact, according to Hoyle, only living beings are able to decode and act upon God's messages from the far future. Other complex arrangements of matter are also able to do so, but since Hoyle identifies consciousness with the process of decoding God's messages, any such complex arrangement of matter qualifies as a conscious, living being.

Hoyle's cosmic God may seem cold and distant, very different from the loving and caring Christian God that answers our prayers and will resurrect us after death, in a new and better world. As noted above, Hoyle preferred to distance himself from the Christian God, but is his God that different? Don't forget that Hoyle's God - the ultimate Intelligence at the end of time - is present in our mind and active in the world, through us.

In fact, in Hoyle's cosmic theology, we are the agents of God's divine action in the world.

God can send us directed messages and "revelations," which will be translated by our minds into messages that we are able to more or less understand - remember that "the information sequences... are there at all stages, just as the books in a school are there for any child competent to read them." Perhaps some revelations are really coming from God? The possibility can't be excluded in Hoyle's model.

God is also active elsewhere in the universe, through alien intelligences, including intermediate lowercase gods.

Though Hoyle is skeptical of personal resurrection, it seems evident that his God, omniscient, omnipresent and omnipotent, could easily resurrect us if He so wishes.

The question remains of whether the ultimate Intelligence, a "wholly other" entity inconceivably different from us and infinitely higher than us, could ever care enough about tiny unimportant beings like us on a tiny planet lost in the immensity of the universe. But the same question can be asked of the Christian God, and the Christian answer is that, yes, God does care. Why and how? The question must remain unanswered, because we can't understand God.

But for a simple analogy, consider this: I am much higher than my doggy, but I love her deeply and try to do my best to keep her happy. I understand (more or less) what she wants and "answer her prayers" to the best of my ability. In many cases I am able to "descend to her level" and communicate with her in a way that is (more or less) understandable to her. If you have a pet, you know what I am talking about. Why shouldn't God love me, too?

I remember that once in the nineties I went back home to feed my Tamagotchi (remember those plastic toys with a virtual pet inside?) because I didn't want it to be unhappy. Why shouldn't God love you, too?

Notes

[change with time] The idea that the physical constants and the physical laws could change with time has been recently suggested by top physicists and philosophers of science, notably including Lee Smolin and Roberto Mangabeira Unger.

[decoherence] See "Exotic space, mysterious time, magic quantum," "United quantum consciousness."

[the other states vanish] The reduction of a superposition of quantum states to a single quantum state upon measurement is often indicated as "collapse of the wavefunction." Hoyle and others think it's the observer's consciousness that causes the collapse of the wavefunction.

[Everett's Many-Worlds Interpretation" (MWI)] See "Exotic space, mysterious time, magic quantum." The popular "Many Worlds" interpretation of Everett's ideas is to be considered as an oversimplified picture. H. Dieter Zeh wrote: "While also called a 'many worlds interpretation', it describes one quantum universe. Because of its (essential and non-trivial) reference to conscious observers, it would more appropriately be called a 'multi-consciousness' or 'many minds interpretation." [Joos 2003].

[too bad Hoyle doesn't develop this point] The idea that consciousness is involved in the unfolding of physical processes in a fundamental, not entirely passive way, is discussed in other chapters. See "United quantum consciousness," "Eligo, ergo sum, ergo Deus est," "In the beginning was the field."

References

[Cramer 2016] John Cramer. *The Quantum Handshake: Entanglement, Nonlocality and Transactions.* Springer, 2016.

[DeWitt 1973] Bryce DeWitt, Neill Graham (Eds.). *The Many Worlds Interpretation of Quantum Mechanics.* Princeton University Press, 1973.

[Everett 1957] Hugh Everett. 'Relative State' Formulation of Quantum Mechanics. *Review of Modern Physics*, 1957. Republished in [DeWitt 1973].

[Gregory 2005] Jane Gregory. *Fred Hoyle's Universe.* Oxford University Press, 2005.

[Hoyle 1962] Fred Hoyle and John Elliott. *A for Andromeda.* Harper & Row, 1962.

[Hoyle 1981] Fred Hoyle. The Universe: Past and Present Reflections. *Engineering and Science*, November, 1981.

[Hoyle 1982a] Fred Hoyle. The Universe: Past and Present Reflections. *Annual Review of Astronomy and Astrophysics*, 1982.

[Hoyle 1982b] Fred Hoyle and Chandra Wickramasinghe. *Evolution From Space: A Theory of Cosmic Creationism.* Littlehampton Book Services Ltd., 1982.

[Hoyle 1984] Fred Hoyle. *The Intelligent Universe - A new view of creation and evolution.* Holt, Rinehart and Winston, 1984.

[Hoyle 2010] Fred Hoyle. *The Black Cloud.* Penguin Classics, 2010. (First published by Heinemann, 1957).

[Joos 2003] Erich Joos et al. *Decoherence and the Appearance of a Classical World in Quantum Theory.* Springer, 2003.

[Narlikar 2003] Jayant Narlikar. Working with Fred on action at a distance. *Fred Hoyle's Universe - Proceedings of a Conference Celebrating Fred Hoyle's Extraordinary Contributions to Science.* Springer, 2003.

[Polkinghorne 2009] John Polkinghorne. Fine Tuning (video).
https://www.youtube.com/watch?v=ncsuh_5l6Hw

[von Neumann 1955] John von Neumann. *Mathematical Foundations of Quantum Mechanics.* Princeton University Press, 1955.

CHAPTER 15 - OMEGA POINT: FRANK TIPLER'S PHYSICS OF IMMORTALITY AND CHRISTIANITY

In "*The Physics of Immortality*" [Tipler 1994], physicist and cosmologist Frank Tipler suggests that everyone who has ever lived will be resurrected to eternal life in a new world at the end of time.

"I shall describe the physical mechanism of the universal resurrection," says Tipler. "I shall show exactly how physics will permit the resurrection to eternal life of everyone who has lived, is living, and will live. I shall show exactly why this power to resurrect which modern physics allows will actually exist in the far future, and why it will in fact be used."

> "If any reader has lost a loved one, or is afraid of death, modern physics says: 'Be comforted, you and they shall live again.'"

Did you say something? Did I hear "wishful thinking" or something like that?

Why, yes. The wishful thinking of Columbus, who stubbornly pursued his dream to sail to a new world. The wishful thinking of the poor young man who decides to become a rich man, and eventually succeeds.

I was very impressed and influenced by Tipler's book when I first read it more than 20 years ago. I read the book as a call to action: Tipler puts forward credible arguments to show that universal resurrection is compatible with science, and now it's up to future scientists and engineers to develop resurrection science and implement resurrection technology. It's a plan, a project - and when you embark on a challenging project, wishful thinking helps. If you don't believe that you can reach the destination, why should you start the journey?

In "*The Physics of Immortality*," Tipler proposes a high level concept: Future technology might be able to resurrect the dead by somehow "copying them to the future."

Besides this high level concept, Tipler also proposes a specific resurrection mechanism:

Our descendants in the far future, close to the end point of the gravitational collapse of the universe (the so called Big Crunch), will steer the dynamics of the collapsing universe in such a way as to make unlimited subjective time, energy, and computing power, available to them before reaching the final singularity. Having done so, they will restore to consciousness all sentient beings of the past, perhaps through a "brute force" computational emulation of the past history of the universe. So after death we will wake up again, perhaps in a simulated environment with many of the features assigned to the afterlife world by the major religions.

In "*The Fabric of Reality*" [Deutsch 1997], physicist and quantum computing pioneer David

Deutsch offers a compact and insightful outline of Tipler's ideas. Deutsch explains:

> "The key discovery in the omega-point theory is that of a class of cosmological models in which, though the universe is finite in both space and time, the memory capacity, the number of possible computational steps and the effective energy supply are all unlimited. This apparent impossibility can happen because of the extreme violence of the final moments of the universe's Big Crunch collapse."

"Matter as we know it would not survive: all matter, and even the atoms themselves, would be wrenched apart by the gravitational shearing forces generated by the deformed space-time," continues Deutsch. "However, these shearing forces would also provide an unlimited source of available energy, which could in principle be used to power a computer. How could a computer exist under such conditions? The only 'stuff' left to build computers with would be elementary particles and gravity itself, presumably in some highly exotic quantum states."

> "If suitable states of particles and the gravitational field exist, then they would also provide an unlimited memory capacity, and the universe would be shrinking so fast that an infinite number of memory accesses would be feasible in a finite time before the end."

Tipler and Deutsch make the assumption that intelligent life will continue to exist until the end of time. Of course, it won't be organic life as we know it, which couldn't exist in the extremely violent environment of the final moments of the collapsing universe, but strange and superintelligent life implemented directly on the exotic fabric of high-energy quantum reality. In fact, ultimate intelligent life and ultimate computers will be one and the same thing.

It's worth emphasizing that, if the superintelligent inhabitants of the end of time will have an infinite computing capacity at their disposal, they will experience an infinite subjective time in the finite time left before the end of the universe. "They will be in no hurry, for subjectively they will live for ever," says Deutsch.

> "With one second, or one microsecond, to go, they will still have 'all the time in the world' to do more, experience more, create more - infinitely more."

In the words of Christian transhumanist thinker Micah Redding, intelligent life "would be endlessly manufacturing time" [Redding 2016b].

The end, the limit point of the gravitational collapse of the universe, is what Tipler calls the Omega Point. It's important to note that an Omega Point with the desired property that intelligent life continues to exist until the end with infinite subjective time ahead doesn't happen spontaneously, but requires the continuous, relentless, purposeful intervention of intelligent life itself.

To attain an omega point, "the universe would have to be continually 'steered' back onto the right trajectories," explains Deutsch. "Tipler has shown in principle how this could be done, by manipulating the gravitational field over the whole of space."

The technology used for the stabilizing mechanisms, and for storing information, "would have to be continually improved - indeed, improved an infinite number of times - as the density and stresses became ever higher without limit."

> "And so he claims that at the omega-point limit there is an omniscient, omnipotent,

omnipresent society of people. This society, Tipler identifies as God."

In fact, according to Tipler and Deutsch, the strange and exotic forms of superintelligent life (in other words, the people) at the end of time will have to be everywhere (omnipresent) and act on the universe (omnipotent) based on their unlimited knowledge (omniscient) to ensure the continuation of their own existence.

Strictly speaking, the omni- properties apply only to the limit and not to the process before the limit, but any degree of omni-ness will be reached and exceeded at some finite time before the limit. Tipler goes on to establish interesting parallels and correspondences between the Omega Point cosmology and traditional religions.

In particular, the Omega God will be able to resurrect the dead of the past - everyone who has ever lived - using ultra-advanced technology.

How can the Omega God resurrect the dead? Of course we don't know the ultra-advanced science and technology available to the superintelligent life near the Omega Point, and there could be ways that we can't even begin to imagine. However, Tipler and Deutsch focus on one specific resurrection mechanism.

Both Tipler and Deutsch support [Hugh Everett's interpretation of quantum mechanics], which is often (and perhaps misleadingly) referred to as "Many Worlds Interpretation" (MWI).

In the MWI, different universes compatible with the laws of physics co-exist in a "multiverse" where all possibilities are realized in different branches. Think for example of a huge stack of cards, where every one of the cards is a separate universe. Our universe is but one card in the multiverse stack, and different copies of you and I exist in other cards.

"Once one has enough computer power (and remember that eventually any desired amount will be available), one can run a virtual-reality rendering of the entire universe - indeed, the entire multiverse starting at the Big Bang, with any desired degree of accuracy," explains Deutsch. "All the human beings who have ever lived anywhere in the multiverse (that is, all those whose existence was physically possible) will appear somewhere in this vast rendering. So will every extraterrestrial and artificial intelligence that could ever have existed."

> "The controlling program can look out for these intelligent beings and, if it wants to, place them in a better virtual environment - one, perhaps, in which they will not die again, and will have all their wishes granted (or at least, all wishes that a given, unimaginably high, level of computing resources can meet)."

In other words, the Omega God can grant an afterlife in a huge [simulated reality], indistinguishable from the afterlife promised by traditional religions. It's interesting and instructive to compare the scientific outline of Tipler's ideas given by Deutsch to the outline given by Christian theologian Wolfhart Pannenberg [Pannenberg 1995].

"Tipler conceives the Omega Point as all-knowing and all-powerful and therefore considers it to be factually identical with the Creator God of religion," says [Pannenberg].

> "As the locus of maximum information, the endpoint of the universe cannot be conceptualized simply as a product of cosmic process; rather, it is much more to be thought of as the creative origin of the universe, and the history of the universe is to be conceived from the perspective of this origin."

TALES OF THE TURING CHURCH

"This insight presupposes that the Omega Point is distinct from the processes of the universe, which are in fact dependent upon the Omega Point for their continuation," continues Pannenberg. "It is precisely with respect to this view of the reality of the world that Tipler has permitted himself to be stimulated and encouraged by Christian theology, which conceptualizes the Creator God of the universe as a God whose existence is bound up with the future of his kingdom."

Soft Tiplerianism

I will use the term "soft Tiplerianism" to indicate a general, high level, conceptual adaptation of Tipler's ideas, without proofs, details, or specific implementation proposals. I subscribe to soft Tiplerianism in the sense that I am persuaded that Tipler is essentially right in spirit, and future scientists will have all the time to work out the details.

Tipler has been criticized, from both sides, for mixing religion with science. He has also been criticized for some scientific assumptions. For example, it appears that the expansion of the universe is accelerating and that the universe, left to itself, will never enter the gravitational collapse phase which is a prerequisite for the Omega Point scenario.

But even if this is the case (that is, even if the Universe "left to itself" would not spontaneously evolve to an Omega Point -like cosmology), Tipler thinks that we may be able to do something about it: The expansion of life to engulf the universe "is exactly what is required to cancel the positive cosmological constant" (see the 2002 interview below). This "fix what you don't like" transhumanist attitude is summarized in Ray Kurzweil's last sentence in "*The Age of Spiritual Machines*" [Kurzweil 1999]:

> "So will the Universe end in a big crunch, or in an infinite expansion of dead stars, or in some other manner? In my view, the primary issue is not the mass of the Universe, or the possible existence of antigravity, or of Einstein's so-called cosmological constant. Rather, the fate of the Universe is a decision yet to be made, one which we will intelligently consider when the time is right."

We shouldn't take nature (lower case n intended) as an absolute that cannot be modified or as something "superior" that must be revered, but rather as a plastic material that can be shaped and modified once we develop the capability to do so. Which is, in my opinion, what transhumanism is all about.

Past generations were used to considering human biology, with all its undesired accidents such as blindness, cancer, aging, mortality, and stupidity, as an absolute. We are beginning to see that, after all, our bodies and minds are just machines that can be fixed, improved and re-engineered once we develop the needed knowledge and tools.

Tipler is just proposing to apply the same concept to the entire universe, that's all.

I don't know whether, when, and how megascale cosmic engineering and fundamental reality hacking could become actual possibilities. But I allow myself to contemplate this vision, which gives me hope and motivation.

It is worth noting that maverick Christian thinker Pierre Teilhard de Chardin, who used the term "Omega Point" before Tipler, has also been often criticized (even by Tipler himself!) for not getting some scientific facts right.

But that's really like dismissing Leonardo as a crank because the aircraft models that he sketched wouldn't fly, which is just stupid. Leonardo was a genius who got the concepts right, and later engineers equipped with more detailed knowledge have realized his visions.

While I find speculations on megascale cosmic engineering and fundamental reality hacking in the very far future interesting, I don't think we can take too seriously our speculations on the capabilities and motivations of superintelligent entities that are millions of years more advanced than us. So, I am quite agnostic on the specific resurrection mechanism proposed by Tipler.

I don't think we know enough physics to imagine how our descendants in the far future could hack reality and re-engineer spacetime, and I don't think we can guess the motivations of beings very different from us, and smarter than us like we are smarter than a beetle.

In other words we cannot know HOW advanced life forms at the Omega Point will hack spacetime, and we cannot know WHY they will choose to resurrect sentient beings of past ages.

But I think in "*The Physics of Immortality*" Tipler makes a good case THAT future sentient beings may be capable of spacetime engineering at the grandest scale. Tipler shows that some high level visions of religions, such as the cosmic role of life and consciousness and the possibility of the resurrection of the dead, are essentially compatible with science.

I am also open to the idea that we could find ways to resurrect the dead much before the end of the universe, regardless of a Big Crunch that may or may not take place. A fictional example of resurrection technology can be found in the novel ["*The Light of Other Days*"], by Arthur Clarke and Stephen Baxter [Baxter 2000].

In the Clarke-Baxter "theory," micro-wormholes naturally embedded with high density in the fabric of spacetime permit looking back in time and downloading a copy of a person's mind, which can then be uploaded to the future. In "*The Light of Other Days*," that happens only a couple of centuries in our future.

Many other thinkers and writers, including [Nikolai Fedorov] and Hans Moravec, have dared contemplating technological resurrection. See also "*Technological Resurrection*" [Jones 2017], a delightful and easy to read book by Jonathan Jones.

While I prefer to remain open-minded on future science, I do relate deeply to Tipler's high level concept that future technology may be able to resurrect the dead of past ages by somehow "copying them to the future" and, in the spirit of Shakespeare's immortal words "There are more things in Heaven and Earth...," I allow myself to contemplate this vision.

Tipler's ideas can provide some degree of hope, grounded in science, in some of the promises of traditional religions, without the rigid dogmatism and intolerance that have plagued traditional religions.

Our descendants could become a key factor in the destiny of the universe, develop the ability to choose and build the universe they want to inhabit, and invite the dead of past ages to join the party by copying them to the future. I hope these high level and still fuzzy concepts will be detailed and realized by future scientists and engineers.

We should take the first small steps on this cosmic path, while at the same time trying to ensure our immediate survival. One of the first small steps that should be taken, I think, is making transhumanism more appealing to more people in a more immediate way.

Therefore, I am proposing to include soft Tiplerianism, defined here as "future technology may be able to resurrect the dead of past ages by somehow copying them to the future," as a cornerstone of the transhumanist cultural package.

I am persuaded that this vision could reach far beyond the original transhumanist subculture, give many more people hope and sparkling transcendent visions, and motivate them to roll up their sleeves and try to do something good.

Another reason why I prefer a softer approach is that I don't really buy Tipler's claim that we already have a working Theory of Everything (see below).

I love Tipler's Omega Point concept, but I think Tipler is mistaken in thinking that we know all the physics that we need, and I prefer to keep the door open to radical surprises and unexpected breakthroughs that, as shown by the history of science, always come up sooner or later.

However, it has to be said in Tipler's praise that he tries to go beyond scientific poetry into the territory of actual, quantitative science, and puts his hands in the mud to develop detailed physical models. If his models are not good enough, future scientists inspired by his work will develop better models.

It's interesting to note that a soft version of Tipler's ideas is already present in his first book, "*The Anthropic Cosmological Principle*" [Barrow 1986], written in collaboration with John Barrow.

"*The Anthropic Cosmological Principle*" makes a case that our descendants in the far future will colonize the universe and become cosmic engineers, masters of space and time, with God-like abilities. What is missing from "*The Anthropic Cosmological Principle*" is the resurrection idea and the more explicit parallels with religion.

"I wanted to discuss the connection with religion in some detail, but my co-author was rather frightened of that," says Tipler [Prisco 2016]. "In my second book I decided to follow that through in great and gory detail."

The Physics Of Christianity: From Cosmology To Geography

In his third book, "*The Physics of Christianity*" [Tipler 2007b], Tipler tries to show that a specific religion, Christianity, is not only compatible with but even derivable from physics.

While in his previous books Tipler described himself as a scientist who found himself forced to consider parallels with religion as a result of his research, Tipler's third (and so far last) book has been written by a Christian believer.

Tipler describes his "conversion" to Christianity as a result of his dialogue with Pannenberg: "This German theologian, Wolfhart Pannenberg, certainly spent fifteen years in a finally successful attempt to persuade an American physicist (me) that Christianity, undiluted Chalcedonian Christianity, might in fact be true and might even be proven to be true by science."

It's interesting to compare the reactions of the science establishment to Tipler's three books. The first, "*The Anthropic Cosmological Principle*," has been mostly praised. The second, "*The Physics of Immortality*," has been both praised and criticized. The third, "*The Physics of Christianity*," has been mostly criticized and dismissed. The reactions seem proportional to the degree of "softness" of the books.

After the publication of "*The Physics of Christianity*," Tipler has been accused of a number of scientific sins, first and foremost that of wishfully assuming his conclusions. But it's easy to see that most of Tipler's critics are guilty of exactly the same sin: If Tipler stretches physics to adapt it to Christianity, they stretch physics to adapt it to the politically correct (PC) atheism which is now fashionable in the scientific mainstream.

If I have to choose between Tipler and his critics, I'll take Tipler anytime, at least he is intellectually engaging in an inspiring way.

James Redford, who self-describes as a scientific rationalist and a born-again Christian converted from atheism, has written a freely downloadable book [Redford 2012] to promote Tipler's ideas. Redford's book is more focused on the theological aspects of Tipler's work, but provides a long list of references (almost 500 entries) that includes scientific references not listed in Tipler's own works.

The first part of "*The Physics of Christianity*" is a concise summary of fundamental physics as understood at the time of writing (Tipler considers it as a concise summary of fundamental physics, without qualifications).

It's worth noting that even ferocious critics are forced to acknowledge Tipler's stellar qualifications and "reasonable descriptions of various aspects of modern physics" [Krauss 2007].

Tipler assumes Everett's MWI as the only viable and valid interpretation of quantum physics, and claims that, contrary to the opinion of most theoretical physicists, we already have a valid theory of quantum gravity - a "Theory of Everything" (ToE).

After his summary of modern physics, Tipler refines his Omega Point model of the far future history of the universe and suggests that, by purposefully annihilating baryonic matter, sentient life will be able to stop the accelerating expansion of the universe and start its gravitational collapse (Big Crunch), which is a necessary prerequisite for the Omega Point scenario.

In a diagram that summarizes Tipler's Omega Point cosmology, time is on the vertical axis and the radius of the universe is on the horizontal axis. Reality is a multiverse in Everett's

MWI sense, and different branches of the multiverse (different universes) are represented by different curves in the diagram.

All universes begin and end in singularities, which are the common start and end points of all curves. Intelligent life will be able to trigger a gravitational collapse in all universes. The vertical line connecting the two singularities at the beginning and the end is another singularity at the edge of the multiverse.

Tipler identifies the three singularities in the diagram with the three persons of the Trinity of Christian theology. The singularities at the end and the beginning of the multiverse are identified, respectively, with the Father and the Holy Spirit. The Son is identified with the singularity at the edge of the multiverse.

"I realized that I had a third Singularity in my drawings representing the Many Worlds picture in *The Physics of Immortality*," explains Tipler [Prisco 2016]. "There actually was a singularity that connected the final singularity with the initial singularity, and you could say that all these singularities therefore are really one."

> "So, you have three singularities, which are really the same singularity, which obviously suggests a Trinity.
>
> I found natural to identify the final singularity with God the father, because in the passage Exodus 3:14 Moses asks God for His name and God replies 'I will be what I will be.' Aha! Ultimate future!
>
> What about the initial singularity? Well, if you look at the beginning of time as pictured in Genesis, Chapter 1 verse 2, you have a phrase that is 'The spirit of God hovered over the waters,' and the great Christian theologian Augustine said that this is indeed a reference to God the Holy Spirit.
>
> So, I've got natural identifications from the leading theologians about which God is which, and there's only the third singularity to identify, and so I identified the third Singularity with God the Son. That's how the theology is following on from the physics."

In the second part of "*The Physics of Christianity*," the virgin birth of Jesus, his incarnation, his resurrection, and several specific miracles are discussed and "explained" in terms of contemporary physics in the framework of Tipler's cosmology.

Armed with his encyclopedic knowledge of physics and theology, Tipler tries to show that his conclusions are plausible and even proposes falsifiable experiments to prove them. But I think the second part of the book is "not in the same universe" as the first one, and less interesting.

I find it off-topic like, say, describing in detail the provincial [geography] of the Earth in a cosmology essay on the large scale structure of the universe.

While I am very interested in Tipler's cosmology and visions of spacetime engineering and technological resurrection in the far future, I just don't find "geographical details" like the virgin birth interesting enough. Perhaps Tipler is right, but so what? Doesn't make much of a difference to me.

Of course I realize that many Christians do find these "geographical details" very important and central to their faith. Therefore, I praise Tipler for trying to build bridges. To those who care about geography and a literal interpretation of the Bible, the second part of *"The Physics of Christianity"* offers a framework that permits considering everything in the Bible as entirely compatible with known science.

I'll focus on the first part of *"The Physics of Christianity,"* a revised and streamlined version of *"The Physics of Immortality"* with new interesting insights and more intuitive metaphors. The first part of the book can be appreciated independently of the second part.

Tipler's theory is so coherent and consistent that it doesn't leave much room for flexibility: All assumptions are necessary. A key assumption, from which all the rest follows, is that we already have a final Theory of Everything (ToE), and better mathematical techniques will enable future scientists to achieve more and more detailed understanding (and mastery) of the universe in the essentially known framework of [general relativity, quantum mechanics, quantum field theory, and the standard model].

I don't buy Tipler's assumption that we already have a final ToE. On the contrary, I suspect that [science is still far from ultimate reality]. My reading of Tipler's works is that current physics already offers some support for the promise of universal resurrection in a new world. Future physics could, and I think will, offer more.

I enthusiastically buy Tipler's ideas as a project for the future of our species. Our descendants in the far future will master spacetime, steer the universe toward good outcomes (states favorable to intelligent life), and bring back the dead, and even current physics shows that we can do all that. By all means, let's go out there and do all that!

Tipler's Theory Of Everything

"The quantization of Einstein's gravity theory was actually achieved in the 1960s by two American Nobel Prize-winning physicists, Richard P. Feynman and Steven Weinberg, who, remarkably, did not realize they had solved the problem of quantum gravity (most physicists don't realize this even today)," claims Tipler in "*The Physics of Christianity*."

However, Tipler explains that this known theory of quantum gravity requires summing an infinite number of terms of exploding complexity, with derivatives of higher and higher orders. We "cannot even determine, or write down, even in principle, the ultimate equations the particle will follow!"

> "In fact, if we consider an equation to consist of an infinite number of terms, there are no ultimate equations. This does not mean that the history of the particle and its analogues in the multiverse is not subject to, and completely determined by, physical law. It is, even in the Feynman-Weinberg theory. But we humans will never know this theory."

In other words, we have a ToE, but we will never be able to calculate all its consequences. It's worth noting that this neatly resonates with deterministic [chaos theory], where we know the equations but we also know that we can't solve them. Tipler emphasizes that, even though no scientist will ever be able to understand all the implications of the ToE at a given time, future scientists will understand and use the ToE with ever-increasing precision.

Tipler's claims have been criticized by other quantum gravity researchers. In the brief history of quantum gravity research included in "*Quantum Gravity*" [Rovelli 2007] (another version of this historical sketch is freely available from *arXiv* [Rovelli 2001]), Carlo Rovelli refers to the quantum gravity works of Feynman, DeWitt, and others in the sixties as important milestones, but hardly the last word. On the contrary, the decade "closes with the main lines of the covariant and the canonical theory clearly defined," says Rovelli. "It will soon become clear that neither theory works."

Feynman's approach to quantum gravity is detailed in "*Feynman Lectures on Gravitation*" [Feynman 1995], a book based on a course on gravitation that Feynman taught at Caltech in 1962-63.

"Feynman aimed the course at advanced graduate students and postdoctoral fellows who were familiar with the methods of relativistic quantum field theory - in particular, with Feynman-diagram perturbation theory in quantum electrodynamics," note John Preskill and Nobel laureate Kip Thorne in the introduction. Feynman "develops the theory of a massless spin-2 field (the graviton) coupled to the energy-momentum tensor of matter, and demonstrates that the effort to make the theory self-consistent leads inevitably to Einstein's general relativity..."

> "Feynman views the quantum theory of gravitation as 'just another quantum field theory' like quantum electrodynamics."

Many experts consider quantized general relativity, as developed in the sixties, as a good theory of quantum gravity, but they take it as valid only for weak fields, an [effective field theory] that is likely to be eventually superseded by new theories. According to Nobel laureate Frank Wilczek [Wilczek 2006]:

"There is a perfectly well-defined quantum theory of gravity that agrees accurately with all available experimental data. Here it is. Take classical general relativity as it stands: the Einstein-Hilbert action for gravity, with minimal coupling to the standard model of matter. Expand the metric field in small fluctuations around flat space, and pass from the classical to the quantum theory following the canonical procedure. This is just what we do for any other field."

Wilczek uses the term "Core Theory" to indicate the combination of the standard model and general relativity, with its weak-field quantum version, and considers the Core Theory as the current framework for fundamental physics [Wilczek 2008, Wilczek 2015].

A problem with quantized general relativity is that it doesn't seem renormalizable. Renormalization is a sort of "emergency surgery" that one has to perform on quantum field equations to avoid getting infinite results, and renormalizability is often considered as a necessary feature of viable quantum field theories.

However, "Weinberg published a paper showing in detail that with all terms in the Lagrangian, the Feynman theory is renormalizable [Gomis 1996]," Tipler explained to me. "I would say that the reason most don't follow Weinberg is because he doesn't solve the divergent power series problem. My way of eliminating the infinities in the power series, and making the individual integrals finite, doesn't need renormalizability. The integrals are finite to start with; they don't have to be renormalized."

To those with a background in theoretical physics, I recommend reading also Tipler's detailed outlines of the physics on which "*The Physics of Christianity*" is based: "The structure of the world from pure numbers" [Tipler 2005] and "Feynman-Weinberg Quantum Gravity and the Extended Standard Model as a Theory of Everything" [Tipler 2007a]. These are two different versions of essentially the same paper.

Tipler is persuaded that we already know enough physics to understand how the universe works, and we already have the much sought after Theory of Everything (ToE).

Why should we expect the laws of physics we know about "to be the ultimate laws of physics?," is the question asked and answered in [Tipler 2012]. "After all, was not the classical mechanics of Newton replaced in the early twentieth century by relativity and quantum mechanics?"

To answer this question, Tipler argues that the new physics - Einstein's general relativity, quantum physics, and the standard model of particle physics - developed in the 20th century, spectacular and revolutionary as it's usually described, is really but a continuation of the classical physics of Newton and Maxwell.

There was "no scientific revolution in twentieth century physics. So we have no reason whatsoever for believing that our knowledge of physics is incomplete," says Tipler. "We already have a Theory of Everything." In particular, we have a theory of quantum gravity, developed in the sixties by Feynman [Feynman 1995], Wheeler and DeWitt [DeWitt 1967].

"I have been able to show [Tipler 2005] that, when constrained by observations, the two theories are mathematically equivalent, and that the Wheeler-DeWitt equation has only one solution: the collection of universes that make up the multiverse of which our own universe is one," says Tipler [Tipler 2012].

"There are actually two theories out there for quantized gravity," explains Tipler in [Prisco

2016].

> "The Feynman quantum gravity theory is just a very straightforward quantization procedure. We all know, from the properties of gravitational radiation of classical gravity itself, that gravity is a spin 2 field. So what Feynman did was quantize a spin 2 field. It was an obvious thing to do.
>
> There was another approach, which was taken at the suggestion of John Wheeler and worked on in detail by Bryce DeWitt, so the resulting equation is called the Wheeler-DeWitt equation, which is another way to quantize gravity."

The [Wheeler-DeWitt equation] is a quantum equation, analogous to the Schrödinger equation of quantum mechanics, for the wave function of the universe, which encodes the probability of finding the universe in one or another instantaneous configuration (snapshot) of matter and 3-dimensional geometry (gravitational field). In other words, the Wheeler-DeWitt equation determines the density of snapshots in the multiverse.

The Wheeler-DeWitt equation doesn't contain time explicitly, but in some cases its solutions can be ordered and stacked one on top of another to represent the flow of time. The paths through the multiverse traced by the solutions of the Wheeler-DeWitt equation, with one instantaneous snapshot of the universe followed by another and so forth, represent evolution in time. In this picture, time is not a fixed background, but represents physical change. Other times are just special cases of other universes, as also argued by Deutsch [Deutsch 1997].

Tipler solves the Wheeler-DeWitt equation for a model multiverse, with [boundary conditions] designed to ensure that mathematical singularities where the laws of physics fail, which would invalidate the unitarity of quantum mechanics (that is, the deterministic evolution of the multiverse), do not exist in the observable multiverse.

In Tipler's solution, the nasty observable singularities are sort of pushed out to the edge of the multiverse outside space and time, where they are absorbed by the Trinity singularity.

In *"The Physics of Immortality,"* Tipler derived the existence of the Omega Point singularity from the requirement that life continues to exist forever. But in *"The Physics of Christianity,"* he says:

> "I have since improved my argument: the existence of the Omega Point singularity is an automatic consequence of the most fundamental laws of physics, specifically quantum mechanics and relativity. Life has not come into the argument."

It seems to me that Tipler has not only improved but also reversed his argument: Now it's the Omega Point singularity that forces life to exist forever and provide the manpower to ensure the consistency of physics at all times.

I have to say that my esthetic preference goes to Tipler's original formulation. Regardless of whether the Omega Point scenario will inevitably happen, I am happy enough with knowing that it CAN happen, IF we and our descendants work to make it happen.

Interview With Frank Tipler (2002)

This interview with Frank Tipler was published in the late lamented *Transhumanity Magazine* of the [World Transhumanist Association] (WTA, then rebranded as Humanity+) in November 2002. I was the editor of *Transhumanity* at the time, and Tipler was a member of the WTA.

In fact, the interview shows that Frank Tipler is a radical transhumanist, unconcerned with the "pedestrian" transhumanism of cryonics and anti-aging pills, and focused on the visionary transhumanism of mind uploading, strong Artificial Intelligence (AI), space expansion, and the cosmic future of humanity in the framework of his Omega Point cosmology.

The interview provides a snapshot of Tipler's thinking between his second and third books. Therefore, I have included the full text of the interview here, with some typos fixed.

Q) In "*The Physics of Immortality*" you make very specific predictions for the masses of the top quark and the Higgs boson, and say that an experimental confirmation would be a very clear indication that the Omega Point Theory is correct. Do you see any indications from recent experiments that your predicted masses for these particles are more likely, or less likely, to be confirmed?

A) The top quark was found shortly after my book was published. The current value the experimenters give is 170 GeV. I predicted 185 +/- 20 GeV. So (unless the experimenters drop the value) my prediction seems to agree with reality. My Higgs prediction of 220 +/- 20 GeV is still open. The current lower bound quoted for a Standard Model Higgs is about 100 GeV ("lower bound" means that the actual value must be above the "lower bound"). I imagine that we will have to wait for the Large Hadron Collider to go online in 2005 before we see the Higgs. My prediction of the top and Higgs came from my deduction that the Higgs field would be only marginally stable. (I inferred marginal stability from acceleration in the collapse phase of the universe.) I then used the standard stability curve to get the particle masses. Given that the top quark is in the correct position for marginally stability, the Higgs boson pretty well has to have the marginally value also, given the shape of the stability curve. Since my book was written, the stability curves have been improved, and I think 190 +/- 20 GeV would be a better estimate for the Higgs mass, using these improved stability curves.

Q): The Omega Point Theory requires a "closed" universe, where at some point the cosmic expansion is reversed by a contraction phase terminating in a gravitational collapse. What do you think of recent measurements from novae in distant galaxies indicating that cosmic expansion is accelerating?

A) I think the evidence that the universe is currently accelerating is VERY strong. Besides the direct evidence for acceleration from the supernovae which you mention, we have observations of flatness from the acoustic peaks in the Cosmic Microwave Background Radiation (CMBR). Recall my predictions 1 and 5: the first is for closure, and the 5th for near flatness, so my prediction (and inflation's) for flatness is looking good. Near flatness plus insufficient Dark Matter to close the universe means that there HAS to be Dark Energy, hence the acceleration.

I unfortunately overlooked the possibility that acceleration could occur in the expanding phase of the universe. Acceleration in the expanding phase of universal history invalidates my prediction of Hubble's constant (Second half of prediction 5) The current value of Hub-

GIULIO PRISCO

ble's constant is 70 km/sec-Mpc rather than the 45 km/sec-Mpc I predicted.

I SHOULD have predicted acceleration in the expanding phase, since the existence of a net number of baryons in the universe implies the Higgs field would not be in its true vacuum, where we would expect the positive cosmological constant (which is the mechanism for acceleration in the collapsing phase of universal history) would be exactly cancelled.

So, if the observed acceleration were to continue forever, the Omega Point Theory would be refuted. But the expansion of life to engulf the universe is EXACTLY what is required to cancel the positive cosmological constant (a.k.a. the Dark Energy): as life expands outward, life will require energy, and before the collapse of the universe provides gravitational collapse energy, the energy source will be the conversion of baryons and leptons into energy via electroweak quantum tunnelling, a process I describe in Section N (relativistic spacecraft) of the Appendix for Scientists. What I did not realize when I wrote my book a decade ago is that this electroweak process would also act to cancel any positive cosmological constant today, and that the net baryon number in the universe would REQUIRE such Dark Energy today.

Q) What are the implications for the Omega Point Theory of dark matter and dark energy?

A) The Omega Point Theory suggests that the particle physics Standard Model (SM) is sufficient to explain both: the Dark Energy is just the currently uncancelled part of the positive cosmological constant, and the Dark Matter is just the Standard Model SU(2)_{left} field, coupled to the SM Higgs field. I was very worried when I wrote "The Physics of Immortality" that the entropy in the CMBR would make an acceleration in the collapsing phase of universal history impossible. I propose to solve this problem by claiming the temperature of the CMBR - currently "measured" to have a temperature of 2.2726 degrees Kelvin - is actually at absolute zero! I show in a paper I put on the lanl data base (xxx.lanl.gov) last November that such an apparently ridiculous claim is possible, because any quantized gauge field in a homogeneous and isotropic universe would NECESSARILY have a Planckian spectrum, even at zero temperature! What the measurements of CMBR showing that it is Planckian - which it most certainly is - are really measuring is not the temperature, but the size of the universe. In my paper, I show how to convert the quoted "temperature" of 2.2726 into the size of the universe.

I describe a simple experiment to check my claims. Such an experiment would be important because it would check three things simultaneously: (1) it would show what the Dark Matter is, (2) it would show what the Dark Energy is, and (3) it would provide another test of the Omega Point Theory: it would test the idea of computers taking over the universe. My proposed experiment could in principle be done by anyone familiar with microwave techniques, using very cheap equipment. An accelerator like the billion dollar machines at Fermilab or CERN would not be required. A few thousand dollars worth of equipment would do it. Any takers?

As an added inducement, I point out in the above-mentioned paper that the effect I'm predicting has probably already been seen! An outstanding anomaly in astrophysics has been the existence of Ultra High Energy (UHE) cosmic rays: they shouldn't be able to propagate through the CMBR, yet they do. If the CMBR has the properties I claim, UHE Cosmic Rays WOULD be able to propagate through the CMBR.

Q) In "The Age of Spiritual Machines" Ray Kurzweil suggests that perhaps even a universe that left to itself would expand forever can be engineered into a collapse by future civilizations, or the other way around. This would be some amazing cosmic spacetime engineering in-

288

deed! Do you think this may be possible, and can you imagine any plausible mechanism?

A) The universe would collapse even if spatially open, if a negative cosmological constant were to exist, and could be turned on. But only if a negative cosmological constant already existed could this engineering be done. The experimental evidence is strong that the cosmological constant is POSITIVE, not negative. Furthermore, no engineering could change the spatial topology of the universe. This would violate a fundamental law of quantum mechanics called unitarity.

But note that what I have suggested above to cancel the observed acceleration would in effect be a universal engineering project to force a collapse, where without the action of life, there would be no collapse.

In another paper (also available on the lanl, and in the published technical literature) I have argued that the known laws of physics REQUIRE life to engage in this engineering project.

Q) Andrei Linde has recently theorized that the universe may indeed collapse rather than expanding forever. But in Linde's theory the collapse comes a mere 10 to 20 billion years from now. How would this affect the Omega Point Theory's requirement for intelligent life to expand relatively quickly and manipulate the contraction into a Taub collapse?

A) Linde and I have different approaches to physics. I refuse to use anything other than the known laws of physics. I assume that these laws are correct, until an experiment shows that they have a limited range of applicability. Linde decides what he wants the universe to be like, and invents whatever laws are required to give him what he wants. Linde's laws are invented to eliminate anything like the Omega Point Theory, so it is likely that the Taub collapse won't work.

Notice in particular that Linde's Eternal Chaotic Inflation theory is played out in a spatially infinite universe. It is a mathematical theorem that the universe has to be spatially FINITE if it is to end in an Omega point.

Q) In the Omega Point Theory, humans colonize the universe via space probes that travel to distant planets and literally synthesize human beings on the spot rather than carrying them the whole way as full-grown, oxygen-breathing passengers. How can we be sure that each Adam and Eve (so to speak) that are placed on all of those distant worlds will cooperate in the grand effort to engineer a Taub collapse of the universe?

A) It is in their selfish interests to act locally to force the universe into a Taub collapse. If they cooperate they live, if they don't cooperate, they die. Also, I have argued, as I said above, that the laws of physics will ensure that they cooperate.

Q) In their SF novel "*The Light of Other Days*" Sir Arthur Clarke and Stephen Baxter imagine a near future civilization resurrecting the dead of past ages by reaching into the past, through micro wormholes, to download full snapshots of brain states and memories. Do you think that some of us might be restored to life, much before the Omega Point, by similar means?

A) No. Wormholes involve a violation of unitarity, because they involve topology change. Can't happen, unless the laws of physics are wrong. Where is the experiment showing that they are? Until I see the experiment, I will continue to believe in the known laws of physics.

Q) Have you, or Prof. Wolfhart Pannenberg [NOTE: he is a well known theologian who supports Tipler's views], managed to convince any religious leaders to accept all, most, or any significant portion of the Omega Point Theory?

A) No. I ascribe this rejection to the same reason that no religious leader has ever accepted "any significant portion" of the Transhumanist Credo. Most if not all religious leaders reject the idea that we humans are just special types of computers, and that human downloads and/or artificial intelligences are possible. Most, if not all, religious leaders reject the idea that the human mind (or soul) is just a program running on the wet computer we call the brain. Instead, they believe in an "immortal soul" which appears to be some sort of "stuff" not subject to the laws of physics.

In theology, this belief is connected with the gnostic (or Manichean) heresy, which holds that there is a "spiritual realm" superior to the material realm, which, since inferior, is uninteresting, or evil, or both. The goal in the gnostic heresy is to escape from the world of matter into the spirit world. Unfortunately, this heresy is widespread even among Christians (who should know better), and it prevents the Omega Point Theory - or transhumanism - from being taken seriously.

But I expect this to change in the future. I have just come back from a conference on Christianity, and when I pointed out the connection between the gnostic heresy and their rejection of transhumanism, the Christians at the conference began - for the first time, I think - to take transhumanism (and hence the Omega Point) seriously.

I was also told by a German reporter that the Lutheran Bishop of Hamburg has accepted the Omega Point Theory. Is a bishop a "religious leader," or should I hold out for an archbishop or cardinal?

Q) You point out that many of the tenets of Christianity and Islam are similar, perhaps even identical in a fundamental way. Yet many bloody wars have been fought between Christians and Muslims, and now these two worlds seem headed for another major clash, perhaps much worse than the previous. Any thought that you wish to share?

A) I discussed the problem which Islam faces on pages 302-304 (the last part of the "Garden of Islam" section of Chapter 11) of *The Physics of Immortality*." There are tolerant Muslims, and always have been, but throughout Islamic history, these tolerant Muslims are almost always dominated by Muslims who hate anything other than Islam. So Islam is almost always accompanied by war against non-Muslims. But there are encouraging signs that if given a democratic government, the good Muslims will take control from the evil Muslims. Iran is a "semi-democracy" in the sense that a parliament elected by the Iranian people have real, even if not complete, power. This parliament passes progressive laws, and if the Mullahs were also elected, I would predict that Iran would be a tolerant, liberal society, even if formally a theocracy.

Q) Suppose the human race becomes extinct before colonizing the universe. Then it is up to some other race to build the Omega Point scenario. Why should these superaliens want to resurrect us, today's humans?

A) We are so close to beginning the colonization - after colonization begins, our descendants would be too spread out to be completely wiped out - that I would claim the laws of physics would make it impossible for us to become extinct before giving rise to our descendants (human downloads and/or AI's). If the laws of physics be for us, who can be against us!

Q) You seem to accept the Many Worlds Interpretation (MWI) of quantum physics. Does the MWI mean that the universe splits into separate branches when a measurement is made, or that our mind splits into separate branches when the result of a measurement is observed?

A) I definitely accept the MWI. The MWI is not an option, but as I show in my book, a necessary mathematical consequence of quantum mechanics applying at all levels: not just atoms, but also humans are quantum mechanical objects. So if the MWI is actually false, then quantum mechanics must also be false at some level of complexity. All competent mathematical physicists know this perfectly well. Roger Penrose in his *"The Emperor's New Mind"* makes this point. It's just that Penrose explicitly rejects linear quantum mechanics at the level of the human brain. But as I have mentioned, I accept the known physical laws as being true, until an experiment shows them to be false.

It is better to think of parts of the universe as splitting. As Everett once said (roughly), if a mouse observes the universe, the mouse, not the universe, is changed. I would say, if a human mind observes the universe, the mind, not the universe, is split.

Q): After the tremendous amount of thought, research and writing that you put into your book, how do you feel about the hostile reception it received? Does the criticism bother you? Do you ignore it as much as possible? Or are you just waiting to be resurrected at the Omega Point so you can say "See, I told you so!"?

A) "Sticks and stones may break my bones, but words will never harm me." Criticism is the driving force of science. Much of the criticism has consisted of insults, and hence not useful. But my improvements in the Omega Point Theory, described above, are due in large part to technical criticisms. My explanation of the Dark Matter and Dark Energy, and the simple experiment to test it, derive from criticisms I received from Gordon Kane, a professor of physics at the University of Michigan, after I gave a seminar at the University of Michigan a few years ago.

What I was unprepared for was the hostile "stone throwing" I received at Tulane University. I was actually formally tried for heresy (this word was not used by the panel convened to try me. Instead, I was told that I "didn't think like everyone else in the department"). I was not fired - it's difficult to fire a tenured full professor, especially for unorthodox thinking, exactly what tenure is supposed to protect. But my salary was frozen: since my work was "worthless," it is clear to University officials that I should receive no raise. So now my pay is some $30,000 less than the Tulane full professor average, almost at the level of a starting assistant professor at Tulane, and definitely less than the assistant professor at a place like Cal Tech.

In the past I could have made up the salary shortfall by writing books. But Tulane changed the terms of my employment (the Louisiana courts have ruled that the University can do this to any faculty member), and now Tulane claims to own the copyright to any book I may write. So it looks as if I may depend on others elsewhere to develop the OPT. Fortunately, transhumanists exist, and eventually some will be trained in cosmology.

Q): If the Omega Point Theory is true, we shall be resurrected at the end of time and live in a very pleasant world. So why shouldn't we just relax and enjoy life instead of working hard to improve our life in today's world?

A) The selfish answer is that we don't know what the far future people will know about us. If they record that we slack off now, this slacker will be the only version of us emulated in the far future computers. With a slacker personality, we cannot enjoy the future to the fullest extent, to say nothing of the trouble we would be in for if we adopt an evil attitude, and THIS info make it to the far future.

The unselfish answer is that it is our duty. Buy working hard now, we can reduce the amount of suffering between now and the resurrection time. So in spite of my difficulties at Tulane, I'll keep trying to develop the OPT: if I succeed, human knowledge will be advanced - especially if I can persuade someone to do the simple experiment I describe!

Q) The Omega Point Theory deals with the far future. Most of our readers are more interested in the short and medium term future, and in particular in the possibility to improve the human physical and mental characteristics by applying nano/bio/info technologies. What timeline do you imagine for the gradual merging of biological and machine intelligences that many contemporary thinkers foresee? For example, when do you think we may develop working interfaces between biological brains and machines, or technologies to upload minds to machines?

A) I think we'll see AI's and/or human downloads some time this century.

Frankly Speaking About Physics, Transhumanism And Theology

After the 2002 interview I have remained in contact with Tipler. Surprisingly for such a visionary thinker, Frank comes out as a hard-nosed, old-school physicist. He reminds me of one of my favorite university professors, a man with an encyclopedic knowledge of physics who spoke plainly and frankly, didn't suffer fools, and often seemed on the verge of physically attacking students (and colleagues) guilty of sloppy thinking.

Tipler gave a summary of his ideas at a Turing Church online workshop that I organized in 2011 [Prisco 2011]. James Redford provided a partial transcript in [Redford 2015]. In the talk, Frank gave what I consider as the best description of radical, visionary transhumanism:

> "I expect that the human race and its artificial intelligences and downloads will eventually move out into space and ultimately take over the universe."

Tipler is a member of the Academic Advisory Council of the [Christian Transhumanist Association] (CTA), which was formally established in 2014. In June 2016 Micah Redding, Executive Director of the CTA, interviewed Tipler for the Christian Transhumanist Podcast [Redding 2016a]. Micah then wrote a very clear and inspiring summary of Frank's ideas for a Christian audience [Redding 2016b].

In July 2016, Micah and I interviewed Frank again [Prisco 2016] in the context of the [India Awakens Conference]. These two long interviews, the first more focused on theology and transhumanism (with some physics as well), and the second more focused on physics and theology (with transhumanism in the background), provide a detailed recent overview of Frank's ideas.

The July 2016 interview is much too long (more than two hours) to include a full transcript here, but I have used selected quotes in this chapter, and the original video is available online.

One of the most interesting discussions in the interview is about alien life. I have mostly used the term "intelligent life" here, but Frank is more specific: He thinks it is our descendants who will trigger the gravitational collapse of all universes and steer the multiverse toward the Omega Point.

Frank's argument is based on the consideration that independent civilizations, unable to communicate faster than the speed of light, could not coordinate their interventions with the required high precision. Too much annihilation of baryonic matter too fast, and the Omega Point is gone. Therefore, we are probably alone, or one of very few civilizations in the entire universe.

I think this argument is too pessimistic, because independent civilization could act collectively in a responsible way without exchanging messages.

For example, we can assume that any sufficiently advanced civilization will independently develop the Omega Point theory and act accordingly. We can also assume that, by the time it is able to annihilate baryonic matter, any advanced civilization is also able to study some close stars and make sure that there are no other civilizations nearby, say in a volume of 1,000 cubic light years. Then, they could set a safe limit to spacetime engineering, which could be increased over time.

Another interesting discussion is about whether the Omega Point singularity is the personal, loving and caring God of Christianity. A mathematical singularity around the multiverse seems too abstract and impersonal, but Frank insists that the Omega Point singularity is the trinitarian God of Christianity. God is outside spacetime, but at the same time God is "closer to you than your own skin," and wants to talk to you. Prayer is but a means to open yourself to the silent voice of God.

In Volume 2 of his *"Systematic Theology"* treatise [Pannenberg 1994], Pannenberg argues that the Omega God, which will come into being at the end of time, is the God of all times, and also created the universe at the beginning: The divine reality, "according to Tipler, does not come into being only at the omega but is to be thought of as free from all the restrictions of time at the omega."

> "Therefore, in terms of the eschatological future, this divine reality is present at each phase of the cosmic process, and hence as already the creative origin of the universe at the beginning of its course."

"I agree with what Pannenberg says and I think that's a very nice short description of the view that I've been expounding today and I have expounded in my books," says Frank.

Frank also said that he is working on a new book, which I can't wait to read.

Notes

[boundary conditions] In Tipler's words [Prisco 2016]: "The correct boundary conditions are, there can not be any event horizons at any level of size. Not only can event horizons not exist around astrophysical black holes, they can not appear in the microcosm. Now what that means mathematically, no event horizon is mathematically equivalent to the statement that the final singularity is a single point in the Penrose c-boundary topology, and that, remember, is my fundamental starting point for my Omega Point theory, which says that the universe will end in a singularity which has no event horizons. What I have done in order to solve the problems of quantum field theory, is impose the condition that event horizons do not exist at any level. That does not mean black holes do not exist. Astrophysical black holes certainly do exist, we have seen them. But mathematical black holes do not exist, because what is a mathematical black hole? A mathematical black hole is one in which if you fall in you never ever get out. But how would you ever know that you'll never get out until you look at the entire future of the universe? Now, if the universe is closed, spatially closed, the mathematical term is spatially compact, then it is possible to have a universe with no event horizons. If the universe is spatially non-compact, we say it's open or flat, than you have to have event horizons, that is a theorem. So I conclude from this that the universe has to be spatially closed, which means that it is finite in size spatially. You can also use more complicated considerations in physics and conclude that, not only is it spatially compact, but spatially it must be a 3 dimensional sphere. That gives you some info on boundary conditions."

[chaos theory] See "There's plenty of room at the bottom," "Eligo, ergo sum, ergo Deus est," "Thought experiments in physical theology."

[Christian Transhumanist Association] See "Christianity and transhumanism are much closer than you think."

[effective field theory] See "Into the deep waters."

[general relativity, quantum mechanics, quantum field theory and the standard model] See "Exotic space, mysterious time, magic quantum."

[geography] - See "Turing Church."

[Hugh Everett's interpretation of quantum mechanics] See "Exotic space, mysterious time, magic quantum."

[India Awakens Conference] See "The lights of Eastern spirituality."

[Nikolai Fedorov] See "Knocking on Heaven's door."

[Pannenberg] - See "Christianity and Transhumanism Are Much Closer Than You Think" for other related ideas of Pannenberg.

[science is still far from ultimate reality] See "Into the deep waters."

[simulated reality] See "Sims City."

["*The Light of Other Days*"] See "The interplay of science fiction, science, and religion."

[Wheeler-DeWitt equation] In "*The Physics of Immortality*," Tipler gives a good conceptual explanations. Also listen to Tipler's explanation in [Prisco 2016], which begins with: "As you have correctly pointed out, the Wheeler-DeWitt equation is an equation for quantum gravity. All quantum mechanical equations are equations for wave functions. What are the argument of the wave function, that is, what is the wave function a function of? In the Wheeler-DeWitt equation, it is a function of the 3-metric, that means, not 4-dimensional but 3-dimensional, the spatial metric only. It does not contain time, at least not directly. The wave function in the Wheeler-DeWitt equation is not only a function of the 3-metric, but also a function of whatever matter variables you have around, which are controlling the spatial metric..."

[World Transhumanist Association] See "Transhumanism."

References

[Barrow 1986] John Barrow, Frank Tipler. *The Anthropic Cosmological Principle*. Oxford University Press, 1986.

[Baxter 2000] Stephen Baxter, Arthur Clarke. *The Light of Other Days*. Tor, 2000.

[Deutsch 1997] David Deutsch. *The Fabric of Reality: The Science of Parallel Universes - and Its Implications*. Viking Press, 1997.

[DeWitt 1967] Bryce DeWitt. Quantum theory of gravity (I, II, and III). *Physical Review*, 1967.

[Feynman 1995] Richard Feynman. *Feynman Lectures on Gravitation*. Addison-Wesley, 1995.

[Gomis 1996] Joaquim Gomis, Steven Weinberg. Are Nonrenormalizable Gauge Theories Renormalizable?. *Nuclear Physics B*, 1996.

[Jones 2017] Jonathan Jones. *Technological Resurrection: A Thought Experiment*. Amazon Digital Services, 2017.

[Krauss 2007] Lawrence Krauss. The Physics of Christianity by Frank Tipler. *New Scientist*, 2007.

[Kurzweil 1999] Ray Kurzweil. *The Age of Spiritual Machines*. Viking Press, 1999.

[Pannenberg 1994] Wolfhart Pannenberg. *Systematic Theology*. T & T Clark, 1988–1994.

[Pannenberg 2005] Wolfhart Pannenberg. Breaking a Taboo: Frank Tipler's The Physics of Immortality. *Zygon*, 2005.

[Prisco 2011] Giulio Prisco. FT Turing Church Online Workshop. YouTube, 2011.
https://www.youtube.com/watch?v=__tx3UXWigM

[Prisco 2016] Giulio Prisco. Q/A with Frank J. Tipler. YouTube, 2016.
https://www.youtube.com/watch?v=w1lm4HmVfs4

[Redding 2016a] Micah Redding. Ep 19: Frank Tipler & The End of the Universe. *Christian Transhumanist Podcast*, 2016.
https://www.christiantranshumanism.org/podcast/19

[Redding 2016b] Micah Redding. The Omega Point Theory, 2016.
http://micahredding.com/blog/omega-point-theory

[Redford 2012] James Redford. The Physics of God and the Quantum Gravity Theory of Everything. *Social Science Research Network*, 2012.

[Redford 2015] James Redford. Commentary on Frank Tipler's Presentation at the Turing Church Online Workshop 2. *Theophysics*, 2015.
http://theophysics.host56.com/tipler-turing-church-workshop-2011.html

[Rovelli 2001] Carlo Rovelli. Notes for a brief history of quantum gravity. *arXiv*, 2001.
http://arxiv.org/abs/gr-qc/0006061

[Rovelli 2007] Carlo Rovelli. *Quantum Gravity*. Cambridge University Press, 2007.

[Tipler 1994] Frank Tipler. *The Physics of Immortality: Modern Cosmology, God and the Resurrec-*

tion of the Dead. Doubleday, 1994.

[Tipler 2005] Frank Tipler. The structure of the world from pure numbers. *Reports on Progress in Physics*, 2005.

[Tipler 2007a] Frank Tipler. Feynman-Weinberg Quantum Gravity and the Extended Standard Model as a Theory of Everything. *arXiv*, 2007. http://arxiv.org/abs/0704.3276

[Tipler 2007b] Frank Tipler. *The Physics of Christianity*. Doubleday, 2007.

[Tipler 2012] Frank Tipler. Inevitable Existence and Inevitable Goodness of the Singularity. *Journal of Consciousness Studies*, 2012.

[Wilczek 2006] Frank Wilczek. *Fantastic Realities: 49 Mind Journeys And a Trip to Stockholm*. World Scientific, 2006.

[Wilczek 2008] Frank Wilczek. *The Lightness of Being: Mass, Ether, and the Unification of Forces*. Basic Books, 2008.

[Wilczek 2015] Frank Wilczek. *A Beautiful Question: Finding Nature's Deep Design*. Penguin Press, 2015.

CHAPTER 16 - UNITED QUANTUM CONSCIOUSNESS: AMIT GOSWAMI'S SELF-AWARE UNIVERSE

"Quantum physicists have been unable to eliminate the concept of collapse from the theory," says physicist Amit Goswami in "*God Is Not Dead*" [Goswami 2012]. "The truth is, an understanding of collapse requires consciousness."

Goswami, a sometimes controversial scientist who wrote an excellent textbook on quantum physics and many popular books, and was prominently featured in the cult film "*What the Bleep Do We Know!?*" [Arntz 2007], is persuaded that consciousness shapes physical reality.

According to Goswami, John von Neumann was the first to propose that the observer's consciousness is what causes the [collapse] of the [quantum] wave function.

Von Neumann argued that "quantum mechanics has two distinct laws of time evolution," explains Goswami in "*Quantum Mechanics*" [Goswami 2003], a good textbook that, besides teaching college-level quantum mechanics, gives more space and emphasis than usual to interpretative issues.

> "The first is the Schrödinger equation, which gives a deterministic continuous prediction of the future states of the system if the initial state is known. The second is the reduction postulate, which operates whenever the system is subjected to measurement; now probability enters, for the reduction postulate is a probabilistic statement describing a discontinuous, acausal change in the system. Before measurement there is the coherent superposition, after measurement only the eigenstate of the measured observable. But this reduction cannot be described by the Schrödinger equation."

The reduction - aka [collapse] - postulate says that a typical [quantum] state "collapses" upon measurement into one of several possible outcomes. The actual outcome of the collapse seems random, and only the probabilities of different possible outcomes are predicted by the Schrödinger equation.

Interestingly, John von Neumann used the opposite order in his seminal book "*Mathematical Foundations of Quantum Mechanics*" [von Neumann 1955]. "We therefore have two fundamentally different types of interventions which can occur in a quantum system," said von Neumann.

> "First, the arbitrary changes by measurements (Process 1)... Second, the automatic changes which occur with passage of time (Process 2)."

Von Neumann indicated with Process 2 the ordered, deterministic evolution of a quantum system predicted by the equations of quantum mechanics, and with Process 1 the unpredictable, random collapse that happens upon measurement.

The order used by von Neumann seems to indicate a special concern with measurement (What is a measurement? Where and when does it happen? Does it require a conscious observer?). In fact, the last two chapters of von Neumann's book are dedicated to problems and issues in the quantum theory of measurement.

As von Neumann first argued, "if a chain of material machines measures a dichotomic quantum object such as Schrodinger's cat in the coherent superposition of live and dead cats, they all in turn pick up the dichotomy of the object, ad infinitum," continues Goswami.

> "How do we get out of such a logjam? The answer is startling. By jumping out of the system! We know that an observation by a conscious observer ends the dichotomy. Thus, said von Neumann - and later other authors such as London and Bauers, and Wigner supported his idea - it is our consciousness, acting from outside of the system, that collapses the quantum wave function."

Von Neumann considered a chain of measuring devices starting with a thermometer and extending all the way into the observer's body and mind, with each device measuring the output of the previous one, and argued that the collapse of the wave function (Process 1) can be placed anywhere in the chain, from the first measuring device to the observer's conscious perception of the measurement result:

> "That is, we must always divide the world into two parts, the one being the observed system, the other the observer. In the former, we can follow up all physical processes (in principle at least) arbitrarily precisely. In the latter, this is meaningless. The boundary between the two is arbitrary to a very large extent... Now quantum mechanics describes the events which occur in the observed portions of the worlds so long as they do not interact with the observing portion, with the aid of the process 2, but as soon as such an interaction occurs, i.e., a measurement, it requires the application of process 1. The dual form is therefore justified."

> "In order to discuss this, let us divide the world Into three parts: I, II, III. Let I be the system actually observed, II the measuring Instrument, and III the actual observer. It is to be shown that the boundary can just as well be drawn between I and II + III as between I + II and III. (In our example above, in the comparison of the first and second cases, I was the system to be observed, II the thermometer, and III the light plus the observer; in the comparison of the second and third cases, I was the system to be observed plus the thermometer, II the light plus the eye of the observer, III the observer, from the retina on; In the comparison of the third and fourth cases, I was everything up to the retina of the observer, II his retina, nerve tracts and brain, III his abstract 'ego.')"

From these quotes we see that von Neumann implicitly suggested that the observer's consciousness ("his abstract 'ego'" - "sein abstraktes 'Ich'" in the German original) could be where Process 1 happens, but didn't explicitly conclude that it is so. However, the reader is left with the impression that von Neumann did have stronger claims in his mind, but just didn't write them down.

Stronger claims were then made by London and Bauer ("The Theory of Observation in Quantum Mechanics"), and Wigner ("Remarks on the Mind-Body Question"). Both essays are included in the "*Quantum Theory and Measurement*" collection [Wheeler 1983], edited by John Wheeler and Wojciech Zurek.

A visual example frequently used by Goswami is "My Wife and My Mother-in-Law," an optical illusion created by British cartoonist William Ely Hill in 1915 and published in *Puck* magazine with the caption "They are both in this picture - Find them." In fact, the sketch contains both a young woman and an old woman, and the viewer can bring one or the other to the forefront of perception. Interestingly, different people see one or the other first: I saw the old woman immediately but it took a few minutes to find the young woman. Goswami uses the sketch - an artistic version of the Necker cube - to illustrate how consciousness can choose to make "real" one of many possible outcomes of a quantum event.

The von Neumann-Wigner "consciousness causes collapse" interpretation of quantum mechanics enjoyed a certain popularity in the past, but today many physicists consider it outdated.

Some physicists are also persuaded that von Neumann's Process 1 is only apparent. They argue that pure quantum states are found to be very delicate and vulnerable to disruption (and more so for large systems): [Decoherence] effects [Joos 2003] caused by interactions with the rest of the world cause the apparent collapse of a quantum system upon measurement.

No real physical system can be considered as isolated from the environment, and even the cosmic microwave background is sufficient to rapidly cause decoherence. The collapse of a quantum system upon measurement is only apparent, some physicists say, because the total system (which includes the measurement equipment and the environment) continues to evolve according to the deterministic equations of quantum mechanics (von Neumann's Process 2). The measured quantum system, taken alone, appears to undergo a quantum jump upon measurement, which appears as effectively random.

Decoherence explains why the world seems classical instead of quantum - why we never see quantum superpositions of macroscopic everyday objects. Some physicists argue that decoherence explains everything without requiring ad-hoc additions to the equations of quantum mechanics (such as von Neumann's Process 1). The collapse of the wave function, they say, is apparent but not real: There is no Process 1, only Process 2, and the apparently lost information is not lost but "leaked into the environment," sort of.

Therefore, emphasizing that decoherence is not a separate theory, or an interpretation of quantum mechanics, but a mathematical consequence of the known equations, some physicists claim that decoherence invalidates the "consciousness causes collapse" interpretation of quantum mechanics, as well as other interpretations that invoke Process 1.

Other physicists, including Goswami, don't consider decoherence as a complete account of quantum measurement, but incorporate it in other theories. The issue is far from being settled. I think decoherence goes only halfway: It explains how quantum superpositions of macroscopic everyday objects are rapidly washed out, leaving only one outcome in place, but doesn't explain how the single outcome is chosen and realized. For that, we still need Process 1.

"Decoherence is a decoy," says Goswami in [Prisco 2016]. I tend to agree.

Who Makes The Choice?

If the observer's consciousness is what causes the collapse of the wave function, the questions that come to mind are: Which observer? Whose consciousness? Consider the poor Schrödinger's cat, placed in a box with a device triggered by a random quantum event in such a way as to kill the cat with a probability of 50 percent in one hour.

According to the equations of quantum mechanics, the cat is in a superposition of alive and dead states - yes, that's what the equations of quantum mechanics (Process 2) say - until a conscious observer opens the box and takes a look.

Wigner placed a second conscious observer (Wigner's friend) between the box and the first observer. Wigner's friend opens the box, checks if the cat is alive or dead, and tells the first observer. It seems evident that now the observer that collapses the wave function is Wigner's friend, and the cat is definitely alive or definitely dead before the first observer becomes aware of the cat's state.

But what if the two observations are simultaneous? Who collapses the wave function, the first observer or the friend? What if the friend is in the box instead of the cat? Now there is a conscious observer in the box, who presumably is always in a definite alive or dead state.

What if we consider the cat as a conscious observer? To me, and to all other pet owners (I prefer to consider myself as my doggy's daddy, not owner), it's evident that dogs and cats are conscious. So, the cat is always in a definite alive or dead state.

But now replace the cat with an inanimate device. A computer? But why a sufficiently sophisticated computer shouldn't be conscious? Let's make it a simple dumb device. But now the question presents itself again: if two observers open the box and look inside simultaneously, which one collapses the wave function?

I often think about this problem with the help of the following example:

Consider two particles in an entangled state where the two particles exhibit correlated spins upon measurement. Indicating the two particles as 1 and 2 and the possible spins as up and down, the quantum state Q of the two-particle system could be the superposition 1up-2down + 1down-2up. In this case, measuring the spin of one of the particles would collapse Q to either 1up-2down or 1down-2up, and the measured spins of the two particles would always be in opposite directions.

Experimental evidence confirms that entangled correlations are still observed when the separation between the two particles is "space-like," which means that the two particles are out of each other's light cone: There is not enough time for light to travel from one particle to the other.

This "spooky action at a distance" found in quantum entanglement has excited the imagination of physicists for decades, as a hypothetical means to achieve faster than light communication. Unfortunately, it appears that the randomness of the collapse upon measurement makes it impossible to use entanglement to send messages.

However, the entangled correlations themselves don't seem limited by the speed of light, and the two particles in the entangled state Q can be considered as one quantum "thing" in a fundamental sense. The correlations between two entangled particles with a space-like separation, which cannot be explained by speed-of-light signaling between two separate parts of the physical universe, tell us that the two particles are really one in some sense that our everyday intuition is not equipped to visualize.

Suppose two observers A and B measure the two entangled particles. The first measurement collapses the system to either 1up-2down or 1down-2up. So the first observer (for example A) defines the result that the second observer will measure. But if the separation between A and B is space-like, according to Einstein there is another, equally valid frame of reference, where the observation of B comes first. So we cannot say which observer, A or B, collapses the system.

In other words, if the separation between the A and B observations is space-like, then there are equally valid frames of reference where A or B come first. Therefore, if we assume both the ontological reality of the wave function and the "consciousness causes collapse" hypothesis, then it's impossible to answer the question "who collapses the wavefunction, A or B?" consistently.

The simplest way out seems to consider also the two observers A and B as one and the same observer. If the observed defines the observer, than two observers of the same thing are really one and the same.

This is also the conclusion reached by Goswami. Quantum physics seems to say that it's consciousness that chooses the outcome of quantum collapse events. Now, different conscious observers could make different individual choices, which seems incompatible with the existence of objective reality. But we can make sense of this apparent incompatibility between quantum physics and objective reality by thinking of the consciousness that chooses not as a local individual consciousness, but as a nonlocal, cosmic "unitive consciousness" that all observers share. Here's how Goswami puts it [Goswami 2003]:

> "But a consciousness that can collapse the wave function of a photon at a distance instantly must itself be nonlocal... What collapses the quantum wave function? A nonlocal, unitive consciousness."

"How can reality be so subjective that each of us observers can choose our own realities from quantum possibilities?," wonders Goswami [Goswami 2012]. "How can there be any consensus reality in that case? Without consensus reality, how can there be science?" Here's the surprising answer:

> "Surprise, surprise. We don't choose in our ordinary state of individual consciousness that we call the ego, the subjective aspect of ourselves that the behaviorist studies and that is the result of conditioning. Instead, we choose from an unconditioned, objective state of unitive consciousness, the non-ordinary state where we are one, a state we can readily identify with God."

Here, there are interesting parallels with Daniel Kolak's philosophy of [Open Individualism] [Kolak 2004]: Every consciousness is fundamentally the same, and we are all the same person. Goswami continues:

> "In the state from which we choose, we are all one: we are in God-consciousness. Our exercise of choice, the event quantum physicists call the collapse of the quantum possibility wave, is God's exercise of the power of [downward causation]. And the way God's downward causation works is this: for many objects and many events, the choice is made in such a way that objective predictions of quantum probability hold;

yet, in individual events, the scope of creative subjectivity is retained."

Scientific materialism is a monist worldview that sees matter and energy, the particles and fields known to current science, as the primary stuff of reality. Scientific materialists see the conscious mind as an "epiphenomenon" - a by-product of the material activity of the physical brain.

It may seem that Goswami is proposing a dualist worldview in which both mind and matter are primary. But actually Goswami is proposing to consider consciousness as primary. In his best-known book, *The Self-Aware Universe* [Goswami 1995], Goswami sums up his monist worldview as:

> "In the past few years it has become increasingly clear to me that the only view of the brain-mind that is complete and consistent in its explanatory power is this: The brain-mind is an interactive system with both classical and quantum components. These components interact within a basic idealist framework in which consciousness is primary."

It's worth noting that the collapse happens also in the brain of an observer like you, which is entangled with the quantum system observed. In fact, your mental state after an observation contains the awareness of having observed one specific outcome, rather than a superposition of states in which you are aware of having observed different outcomes.

It seems very likely that such a superposition would feel quite different from ordinary states of awareness. Therefore, consciousness defines the physical world by collapsing the quantum wave function, but it's the collapse of the quantum wave function that makes ordinary awareness possible. As in Escher's sketch where the right hand draws the left hand, which draws the right hand in turn, mind and matter generate each other in turn in a "tangled hierarchy."

Life Is Special

Goswami didn't talk about God in his first books, but he does in later books. However, his God is different from the "personal" God of popular Christianity.

In September 2016 I hosted an online interview with Goswami [Prisco 2016]. The interview was organized in preparation for the [India Awakens conference] in Kolkata, India, and was published in the video proceedings of the conference [Prisco 2017]. Amit Goswami, who was born in India and studied at the University of Kolkata before becoming a professor of physics at the University of Oregon, is prominent among the Indian scientists who are blurring the lines between science and spirituality.

Speaking about whether the God of quantum physics is the personal Christian God or an impersonal abstract God, Goswami noted that, contrary to the Old Testament, Jesus never claimed that God is personal. According to Goswami, Jesus "understood quantum physics" (all great mystics did) and described - in a format accessible to his contemporaries - God as a transcendent consciousness beyond conventional space and time.

Our memories are stored in our physical brains, but quantum non-locality implies that our memories are also stored in the non-local quantum reality beyond space and time. Therefore, according to Goswami, quantum physics supports a diffuse, ethereal version of reincarnation: others will be able to use those memories and inherit what we have learned in this life, including aspects of our personality.

I am especially interested in "Akashic Engineering" - the possibility that future scientists could learn how to "read" quantum reality and develop technologies able to precisely control quantum phenomena and even, in the far future, to bring the dead back to life, with their memories intact. I probed Goswami's imagination about Akashic Engineering, but he doesn't think we can say much about long-term developments in science and technology - as he correctly points out, many technologies that we have today wouldn't be understandable to people alive only a few centuries ago.

Goswami is persuaded that life is special. For example, while it seems impossible to use quantum entanglement to transmit information, living systems can exploit the vantage point of the non-local unitive consciousness to exchange information behind the scenes of material reality. This could be the physical basis of "paranormal" phenomena and the "morphic fields" studied by Rupert Sheldrake [Sheldrake 2009].

Therefore, according to Goswami, there are limits to what "material" technologies based on the manipulation of inanimate matter can achieve, and those limits will be especially evident when facing the subtler aspects of quantum reality. On the other hand, the possibilities of living systems are much wider, and we could (and should) learn how to work with living systems, develop human potential, and make better use of the intrinsic "spiritual" abilities of humans. We can, in fact, think of spirituality and human potential in the context of our upcoming evolution from human to superhuman.

Goswami's position is certainly coherent, but I don't share his conviction that only life as we know it - the carbon-based organic forms of life that exist on this planet - can use quantum weirdness to work around the limitations of ordinary space, time, and causation. On the contrary, I am persuaded that, if quantum weirdness plays a critical role in the "paranormal" abilities of the human brain (I am thinking of the ideas of Hameroff and Penrose [Penrose

1994]), future scientists will be able to engineer materials that exhibit the same quantum behavior. Of course, the best way to describe such materials could well be "living."

What The Bleep Is Quantum Mysticism?

Amit Goswami is a prominent spokesman for quantum consciousness research and "quantum mysticism," which are considered as fringe, cranky "pseudoscience" (whatever that means) by those "bureaucrats of science" who hate highly imaginative scientific speculations.

The core idea of quantum consciousness research is that subtle quantum effects could play a key role in how the conscious mind emerges from the physical brain. This is only borderline fringe, almost respectably mainstream, but quantum mysticism steps beyond the line to explore ultimate reality, mind-over-matter, frontier theology and all that. A recent *BBC* review [Ball 2017] notes that:

> "'Quantum consciousness' is widely derided as mystical woo, but it just will not go away... it would transform our ideas about both physics and the mind. That seems a chance worth exploring."

Goswami is featured in the 2004 quantum mysticism cult film *"What the Bleep Do We Know!?"* [Arntz 2007], a very good non-mathematical introduction to the weirdest, counter-intuitive aspects of quantum physics, with excellent examples and special effects, and intriguing hints at the possibility that weird quantum effects might eventually provide a solid scientific framework for mind-over-matter phenomena.

But of course the film has been demonized by the bureaucrats of science as "pseudoscience." For example, science writer Annalee Newitz (a good science writer who unfortunately shares the mindset of the bureaucrats of science and often condemns imaginative speculations) refers to the "widely-condemned pseudoscience documentary *What the Bleep Do We Know*" [Newitz 2014].

It was surprising, the filmmakers say [Arntz 2007], that the film received very little criticism from religious groups, and a lot of criticism from the science establishment:

> "We were slammed by the scientific community. There are some very vocal and energized skeptics out there who are outraged when anything beyond the materialistic worldview is put forth... We (naively) thought the response would be, well, scientific. It's been mostly name calling."

I have been reading through some of that name calling, and I am not surprised at all: Name calling is exactly what I expect from the bureaucrats of science.

Of course I like some parts of the film less than other parts. But, all things considered, I think the film is very good. It explains well enough some interesting aspects of contemporary research in physics and consciousness, and brilliantly suggests that perhaps, just perhaps, there's more to reality than meets the eye.

I have no problem with the possibility that the human mind (the most complex physical system in the known universe) may have unexpected and currently unexplained influences on the rest of reality. Besides being considered by many top class scientists with an open mind, exotic mind-over-matter phenomena have been reported since the dawn of history in all known cultures. That doesn't make them "true," whatever that means, but it does make them worth of scientific investigation. But no, the bureaucrats of science call all that "pseudoscience."

What is pseudoscience? It must be something that looks like science, but is not science. So what is science? Like most things, science can only be defined operationally, as a process and a method - science is how you look at something, not what you look at. The scientific method is a time-tested mental framework with an ever evolving toolbox for theoretical model-making, design and execution of experiments, and data analysis. If something is science or "pseudoscience" is independent of the phenomena under investigation, and depends only on whether the scientific method is properly followed. You can study a poltergeist scientifically, and a chemical reaction unscientifically.

I am persuaded that scientific quantum mysticism will spawn awesome science and transhumanist engineering.

Notes

[collapse] See "Exotic space, mysterious time, magic quantum."

[Decoherence] See "Exotic space, mysterious time, magic quantum," "A for Almighty."

[downward causation] See "There's plenty of room at the bottom."

[India Awakens conference] See "The lights of Eastern spirituality."

[Open Individualism] - See "The lights of Eastern spirituality."

[quantum] See "Exotic space, mysterious time, magic quantum."

References

[Arntz 2007] William Arntz, Betsy Chasse, Mark Vicente. *What the Bleep Do We Know!?: Discovering the Endless Possibilities for Altering Your Everyday Reality*. Health Communications, 2007.

[Ball 2017] Philip Ball. The strange link between the human mind and quantum physics. *BBC*, 2017.
http://www.bbc.com/earth/story/20170215-the-strange-link-between-the-human-mind-and-quantum-physics

[Goswami 1995] Amit Goswami. *The Self-Aware Universe: How Consciousness Creates the Material World*. TarcherPerigee, 1995.

[Goswami 2003] Amit Goswami. *Quantum Mechanics*. Waveland Press, 2003.

[Goswami 2012] Amit Goswami. *God Is Not Dead: What Quantum Physics Tells Us About Our Origins and How We Should Live*. Hampton Roads Publishing, 2012.

[Joos 2003] Erich Joos et al. *Decoherence and the Appearance of a Classical World in Quantum Theory*. Springer, 2003.

[Kolak 2004] Daniel Kolak. *I Am You: The Metaphysical Foundations for Global Ethics*. Springer, 2004.

[Newitz 2014] Annalee Newitz. Stop Putting New Age Pseudoscience in Our Science Fiction. *io9*, 2014.
https://io9.gizmodo.com/stop-putting-new-age-pseudoscience-in-our-science-ficti-1656432047

[Penrose 1994] Roger Penrose. *Shadows of the Mind: A Search for the Missing Science of Consciousness*. Oxford University Press, 1994.

[Prisco 2016] Giulio Prisco. Q/A with Amit Goswami. YouTube, 2016.
https://www.youtube.com/watch?v=UQirNMTcNG8

[Prisco 2017] Giulio Prisco. India Awakens Conference: Video proceedings. *Turing Church*, 2017.
https://turingchurch.net/india-awakens-conference-video-proceedings-1c7bab279d5c

[Sheldrake 2009] Rupert Sheldrake. *A New Science of Life: The Hypothesis of Formative Causation*, 3rd edition. Icon Books, 2009.

[von Neumann 1955] John von Neumann. *Mathematical Foundations of Quantum Mechanics*. Princeton University Press, 1955. (translation of *Mathematische Grundlagen der Quantenmechanik*, Springer, 1932).

[Wheeler 1983] John Wheeler, Wojciech Zurek (Eds.). *Quantum Theory and Measurement*. Princeton University Press, 1983.

CHAPTER 17 - THE QUEST
FOR AKASHIC PHYSICS
AND ENGINEERING

Perhaps everything that ever happens, including our thoughts and memories, is stored in permanent "Akashic records," a cosmic memory field hidden in yet unknown aspects of reality.

In "*Esoteric Buddhism*" [Sinnett 1883], Alfred Percy Sinnett noted that early Buddhism "held to a permanency of records in the Akasha, and the potential capacity of man to read the same when he has evoluted to the stage of true individual enlightenment."

The Akasha, a Sanskrit word for ether or space, was popularized in the West by Theosophy writers [Abraham 2017] including Helena Blavatsky and Rudolf Steiner. Blavatsky thought of the Akasha as "indestructible tablets of the astral light" recording both the past and future of human thought and action. In modern terminology, we can think of the Akasha as a cosmic memory field that stores permanent records of everything that ever happens in the universe.

In "*Demystifying the Akasha*" [Abraham 2010], Ralph Abraham and Sisir Roy quote the polymath genius Ervin László [László 2009]:

> "A universal information and memory field could exist in nature, associated with the fundamental element of physical reality physicists call the unified field... Honoring an ancient insight, this is the aspect or dimension of the unified field that I have called the Akashic Field."

Sisir Roy, the author of "*Statistical Geometry and Applications to Microphysics and Cosmology*" [Roy 1998], is a physicist interested in the geometry of quantum spacetime near the Planck scale.

Ralph Abraham is a top mathematician and maverick scientist who, besides the acclaimed textbook "*Foundation of Mechanics*" [Abraham 1987] on advanced mathematical physics, wrote about esoteric aspects of mind and physical reality with Terence McKenna and Rupert Sheldrake [Sheldrake 2001].

In his preface to László's "*The Connectivity Hypothesis*" [László 2003], Abraham says: "When a great grand unified theory will appear it will very likely conform to the prophetic vision of Ervin László." After "*The Connectivity Hypothesis*," László wrote a simplified but thoughtful account of his ideas in "*Science and the Akashic Field*" [László 2007], and then several related books. The last book in László's Akashic series is "*The Self-Actualizing Cosmos*" [László 2014].

"*Demystifying the Akasha*" is a short and compact book that covers a huge territory including Western and Eastern philosophies and religions, the foundations of quantum physics, recent advances in quantum gravity research, and the digital physics of discrete spacetimes.

Fully understanding everything requires specialized knowledge of all those fields, but the book is readable and has something for everyone. The references, a careful selection of the best related writings, fill the gaps in the book.

"We have repurposed a mathematical model for the quantum vacuum, originally due to Requardt and Roy, as a model for consciousness," note the authors. "*Demystifying the Akasha*" includes the full text of a 2001 article by Roy and Manfred Requardt [Requardt 2001], which is a precursor of the book.

Contemporary quantum physics shows that the vacuum, the simplest configuration of spacetime, has a complex dynamic structure. "The quantum vacuum is a seething froth sparkling with elementary particles emerging from nowhere in pairs, and after a very short time, vanishing again as they came," explain Abraham and Roy. A fundamental information field associated with the quantum vacuum is, according to László, "the deepest and most fundamental level of physical reality in the universe."

In a recent book titled "*Understanding Space, Time and Causality*" [Sreekantan 2019], which provides an insightful summary of the intersections of contemporary physics and traditional Indian thinking, Roy and physicist B. V. Sreekantan note that the contemporary scientific conception of the quantum vacuum, described by quantum field theories in terms of underlying space and time, can't be directly compared to the traditional conception of the Akasha, which is beyond space and time.

However, Sreekantan and Roy emphasize that Abraham and Roy have defined a "subtle" substrate underneath space and time, "from which one gets physical space-time or quantum vacuum, and hence the comparison appears to be a meaningful one." In the Abraham-Roy (AR) model, outlined below with more detail, the notions of space and time are built up from pre-geometric networks "that give rise to a space-time continuum with well-defined structure. Here, each entity is interconnected may be due to the existence of 'non-locality' - one of the fundamental tenets of quantum theory."

Worth noting, mainstream physics is warming up to the idea that [space and time might emerge from the non-local entanglement structure of a fundamental field beyond space and time].

Abraham and Roy build a model for the fundamental field based on a "pre-geometry" of dynamical cellular networks - huge graphs with internal dynamics similar to [cellular automata] - that exist beyond spacetime, and from which the geometry of spacetime is derived.

Abraham and Roy don't intend to propose a "final" unified Theory of Everything (there is no "final" in science). Rather, they intend to show a template mathematical model of reality, compatible with current scientific knowledge, which includes an Akashic information and memory field able to explain paranormal phenomena. They say:

> "Our intention is to contribute a theory, more precisely a mathematical model, in which all paranormal phenomena may be understood, including quantum entanglement and the measurement problem."

I had always realized that Akashic field theories are related to my own ideas on technological resurrection, but further reflections and research led me to realize that they are essentially equivalent.

Following [Fedorov and the Russian Cosmists], I have often argued that future scientists equipped with "magic" spacetime technologies will be able to resurrect the dead by "copying them to the future." For such a thing to be possible, it's necessary that the information needed to resurrect the dead - life events, memories, thoughts, and feelings - exists somewhere out there in a somehow retrievable form. In other words, there must be an Akashic memory field. Conversely, if the Akashic field exists, future scientists could resurrect the dead by solving the engineering problem of how to read the Akashic records.

Therefore, following László, I will honor the ancient Akashic insights and use the term "Akashic physics" for the yet unknown physical theories upon which future resurrection technologies could be based. It seems very plausible that, as Abraham and Roy argue, future Akashic physics will be able to explain all sorts of "paranormal" phenomena. I will use the term "Akashic engineering" for new technologies able to leverage and exploit Akashic physics.

In passing, I think the term "paranormal" is misleading because, if something happens, then it is normal. However, "paranormal" is frequently used and easily understandable: It includes telepathy, remote viewing, precognition, reincarnation and related phenomena, which can be physically explained if the mind can somehow extract information from the cosmic Akashic records.

There is a roadblock in the quest for Akashic physics and engineering. Apparently, information is irreversibly erased from the universe all the time. In some mainstream formulations and interpretations of quantum physics, [information is fundamentally and irretrievably erased by the collapse of the wavefunction]. Even in classical (non-quantum) physics information is erased in practice (hidden and scrambled beyond recognition) by chaotic dissipation. Viable theories of Akashic physics should include explanations of how the apparently lost information is safely stored.

For example, in [Everett's "Many-Worlds Interpretation" of quantum physics (MWI)] the collapse of the wavefunction is local to the single branch of the multiverse that our senses perceive, and the apparently lost information is still available in the multiverse at large. Therefore, information is preserved in Everett's multiverse, which is a possible stage for Akashic physics.

In "*The Fabric of Reality*" [Deutsch 1997] David Deutsch shows that other times are just special cases of other universes. Therefore, the apparently lost information - including the life events, memories, thoughts, and feelings of everyone who ever lived - is out there in the Akashic multiverse, and future scientists could search for - and find - ways to retrieve it.

In the passage quoted above, Sinnett was (probably) thinking of spiritual rather than technological means to read the Akashic records, but Robert Pirsig's words come to mind [Pirsig 1974]:

> "The Buddha, the Godhead, resides quite as comfortably in the circuits of a digital computer or the gears of a cycle transmission as he does at the top of the mountain, or in the petals of a flower."

The scientific literature is full of ideas that could be useful in the quest for Akashic physics and engineering. Which ideas will break through? I think it's much too early to tell.

Of course the ideas of László, Abraham and Roy are attacked by militant atheists because they sound like religion. Most professional scientists take special care to hide the more "mystical" implications of their work behind layers of aseptic and innocuous scientific jargon to protect themselves from the academic thought police.

Mathematics, Cyberculture, And The Resacralization Of The World

Ralph Abraham was a frequent contributor to *Mondo 2000*, the legendary cyberculture magazine edited by R.U. Sirius in the 1980-90s and [recently revived as an online magazine].

I hope the new online magazine will be as epoch-making as the original printed *Mondo*. In the meantime, we can find some old *Mondo* issues collected in the Mondo 2000 History Project and other archives [Prisco 2017b]. This section dedicated to Ralph includes excerpts from my first contribution to the revived *Mondo* [Prisco 2017c], with minor edits.

In my student days I spent many hours reading Ralph's *"Foundations of Mechanics"* [Abraham 1987], instead of my boring college textbooks, to try and understand some of the magic of differential geometry and its applications to Einstein's cosmology. I understood maybe ten percent, but that ten percent was useful.

Another highly recommended book is Abraham's *"Dynamics: The Geometry of Behavior"* [Abraham 1992], a treatise on advanced mathematics and physics that, using diagrams and cartoons in place of mathematical formulas, builds a visual understanding of advanced mechanics and chaos theory.

I think developing a visual understanding of complex mathematics and physics is important, and I am persuaded that the lack of intuitive visual models is a major roadblock in the quest to understand modern physics, especially quantum physics.

Ralph seems to consider his life as a square university professor as a boring prelude to his real and very unsquare life as a cyberculture icon and explorer of the wildest fringes of mathematics, physics, history, society, life, the universe, and everything.

"There was a period of six or seven years that included psychedelics, traveling in Europe, sleeping in the street, traveling to India and living in a cave, and so on - these were all parts of what I call my 'walkabout'" said Ralph in a 1991 interview published in *Mondo* 3. "It was between my first, more prosaic period of mathematical work and all that has followed in the past fifteen years."

"Demystifying the Akasha" includes a detailed story of Ralph's time in India and his adventures in Eastern spirituality, study of consciousness, and appreciation of the wholeness of reality.

"We need to understand whole systems, and whole systems can't be understood by reduction - though the terrific gains in understanding made by the reductionist scientist will have a role to play in understanding whole systems," explained Ralph in *Mondo*. "The technology for modeling whole systems is on the frontier of science at the moment. It's the crucial frontier for solving our crisis."

Understanding whole systems is the goal of [dynamical systems theory, aka chaos theory], of which Ralph is best known as one of the pioneers. In *"The Chaos Avant-Garde"* [Abraham 2001], Ralph gives a personal view of the early days of chaos theory, which he considers as one of the most important transformations of all times, not only in science but also in culture [Sheldrake 2001].

"And due perhaps to the occurrence of my name in an extraordinarily popular book by a journalist [Gleick 1987], I have been consulted by many scientists involved in the paradigm shift from order to chaos when it first appeared in their own fields," he says.

The emergence of the internet was, according to Ralph, a momentous phenomenon with a major cultural impact and full of promises. But sadly the promises of cyberspace remain un-realized. I totally agree.

"By 1990 I had essentially given up on the fate of the biosphere and noosphere," Ralph told me. "We had all done our best, nothing seemed to work."

> "Then, in 1994, I became aware of the innovation of the World Wide Web. This seemed to give us new hope, as the connectivity of the noosphere was getting this major bump. I poured all my creative energy into cyberspace. My optimism lasted a decade or so, until it seemed the forces of evil were once again pulling ahead. Now it seems we need another miracle."

I think the prospect of Akashic physics and engineering could re-enchant the world and re-connect us to the sacred. This could be, I think, the miracle Ralph is looking for.

"I believe that the most important activity to save the world, or at least to move toward hope in that direction, is to recreate for some larger portion of humanity the lost thread of our connection to the sacred," says Ralph in [Sheldrake 2001]. "This is the program that I call 'the resacralization of the world.'"

The Ar Model: Digital Physics With Akashic Memory, Beyond/Before Space And Time

After reading *"Demystifying the Akasha,"* I was intrigued and contacted the authors to better understand their ideas. I was previously unaware of Roy's work, but I knew of Abraham as the author of *"Foundations of Mechanics"* [Abraham 1987], and the co-author of a series of "trialogues" with Rupert Sheldrake and Terence McKenna [Sheldrake 2001]. I remember being surprised when I realized that it's one and the same Abraham.

"Demystifying the Akasha" outlines a possible theoretical foundation for Akashic Physics with a cosmic memory field that stores permanent records of everything that ever happens in the universe.

The "pre-geometry" model of Abraham and Roy (AR model) is based on a dynamical cellular network dubbed QX - a graph with a huge number of nodes and internal dynamics similar to [cellular automata] - beyond space and time, from which the geometry of spacetime is derived.

The graph "contains all times" and fluctuates in an internal time-like dimension, not to be confused with ordinary time. Ordinary space and time emerge from the dynamical cellular network. This is difficult to visualize, because we can only imagine evolution in time and can't intuitively conceive of something that changes beyond time. However, the concept can be studied mathematically.

Stephen Wolfram has similar ideas. "One needs something in a sense 'underneath' space: something from which space as we know it can emerge," he says [Wolfram 2015].

> "And one needs an underlying data structure that's as flexible as possible. I thought about this for years, and looked at all sorts of computational and mathematical formalisms. But what I eventually realized was that basically everything I'd looked at could actually be represented in the same way: as a network. A network - or graph - just consists of a bunch of nodes, joined by connections. And all that's intrinsically defined in the graph is the pattern of these connections."

While the AR model is but a simplified toy model designed for preliminary investigations in this direction, it permits to derive early but intriguing results. Abraham and Roy propose to obtain macroscopic spacetime from the dynamical cellular network QX through a process of condensation:

> "Thus, spacetime is squeezed from the dynamical cellular network, QX, as toothpaste from a tube... The microscopic system, QX, sparkles with activity on the scale of Planck space and time, while macroscopic spacetime unrolls essentially continuously. The past and present become known, while the future remains yet a mystery."

Abraham and Roy developed the AR model not only as a pre-geometry model, but also and especially as a model of the interactions of consciousness and the material world. Mind and matter are derived from condensation processes acting on separate (but interacting) subnetworks of QX. In this essentially monistic (as opposed to dualistic) process, mind and matter interact within QX, beyond spacetime:

> "In sum, then, the mind/body connections are completed in a circuit outside or-

dinary consensual reality in a submicroscopic atomic realm beyond our senses, but revealed by the progress of modern physics… This provides a background for psi phenomena such as telepathy and clairvoyance, but also leaves a window of opportunity for free will. Like a zipper closing, the past is zipped (or firmed) up, while the microscopic future is subject to interaction with the macroscopic body and mind, until the zipper closure arrives, and condensation (or collapse) occurs."

This very short outline doesn't do justice to the book. Fortunately, [the full text of "*Demystifying the Akasha*" is available online], and I encourage you to study the book.

In August 2016 I hosted an online [India Awakens] mini conference with Abraham, Roy and other participants [Prisco 2016]. Abraham and Roy noted that "*Demystifying the Akasha*" is very much a work in progress and envisaged further iterations, for example new electronic versions of the book.

When I talk about Akashic engineering I usually say something like "of course, we are talking of very speculative, far future technologies," but Abraham and Roy are more daring. Abraham noted that science advances not only with incremental little steps, but also with sudden quantum leaps and catastrophic (in the mathematical sense, see [Abraham 1992]) jumps, and a sudden scientific revolution could bring about Akashic physics and engineering much sooner than I hope.

Abraham emphasized that such momentous and catastrophic scientific advances are unlikely to happen in the conservative environment of academic research. In fact, revolutionary developments like chaos theory, cellular automata, and fractal geometry, were initially developed largely outside of the mainstream academic circuits.

Roy noted that India, which is becoming a hotbed of futuristic science and technology, could provide a more open and culturally supportive environment than the conservative US and Europe for the development of the new science. Could Akashic engineering be developed rapidly, perhaps in India, with the participation of mavericks and citizen scientists worldwide?

Abraham sent a paper [Abraham 2017] and a video [Prisco 2017a] for the India Awakens 2017 video proceedings. The conclusion of the paper is:

"Whether located in the astral plane, between the mental and the etheric, or surrounding them all, the atomic model of the akasha developed in our book, *Demystifying the Akasha*, supports the idea of the akashic record, including the future as well as the past in a mammoth mathematical system."

As noted above, in the late 19th and early 20th century the Theosophists introduced Akashic thinking in the West [Abraham 2017], popularizing the idea of a cosmic memory field that stores permanent records of everything that ever happened in the universe, including you and me. Theosophy used to have a less than pristine reputation (and has an even worse reputation today), but Nikola Tesla, one of the smartest persons of the time, appreciated it.

It's worth noting that the speculative intuitions of contemporary frontier physics are starting to mirror those of the Theosophists and Nikola Tesla.

Nikola Tesla On Akashic Engineering And The Future Of Humanity

The maverick genius Nikola Tesla was a cosmist, a pre-transhumanist thinker, and an early proponent of a synthesis of Eastern mysticism and Western can-do engineering spirit.

Tesla envisioned transhumanist technologies that would permit a complete triumph over the physical world, and boldly dared to imagine Akashic engineering.

In 1900 Tesla wrote an article titled "The Problem of Increasing Human Energy" [Tesla 1900], which clearly establishes him as a Cosmist, pre-transhumanist thinker. "Inherent in the structure matter, as seen in the growth of crystals, is a life-forming principle," notes Marc Seifer in "*Wizard: The Life and Times of Nikola Tesla*" [Seifer 1998], referring to Tesla's article.

> "This organized matrix of energy, as Tesla comprehended it, when it reaches a certain stage of complexity, becomes biological life. Now, the next step in the evolution of the planet was to construct machines so that they could think for themselves... Life-forms need not be made out of flesh and blood."

In "*The Akashic Experience*" [László 2009] Ervin László noted that Tesla "spoke of an 'original medium' that fills space and compared it to Akasha, the light-carrying ether. In his 1907 paper 'Man's greatest achievement,' Tesla wrote that this original medium, a kind of force field, becomes matter when Prana, or cosmic energy, acts on it, and when the action ceases, matter vanishes and returns to Akasha."

I found this interesting and searched for the sources. The Tesla Memorial Society has a story [Grotz 1997] on Tesla's article, which was written on May 13, 1907, and probably inspired by Tesla's association with [Swami Vivekananda].

"Man's greatest achievement" was published on July 13, 1930, in *The Milwaukee Sentinel*. The full text is in the public domain, but difficult to find. Since it could disappear from the internet anytime, I have taken the liberty of reproducing it below.

An inspiring quote often attributed to Tesla is:

> "The day science begins to study non-physical phenomena, it will make more progress in one decade than in all the previous centuries of its existence."

The idea of science studying non-physical phenomena seems odd, but I think what Tesla meant (if he ever said these words - the quote is unsourced) is phenomena beyond the framework of known physical science.

I guess Tesla had in mind subtle Akashic interactions underneath ordinary reality, as well as paranormal phenomena, psi powers, mind over matter and all that. Abraham and Roy give a readable explanation of current research on paranormal phenomena, which could one day provide insights into yet unknown Akashic physics.

The Abraham-Roy model is beyond physics as we know it today, but it's a scientific theory. When physical reality turns out to be more complex than our current models, which happens all the time in science, we can extend our models to encompass previously unseen aspects of reality. In this sense, Tesla's non-physical phenomena are physical, and in principle accessible to engineering.

Man's Greatest Achievement, By Nikola Tesla

This article, written by Nikola Tesla in 1907, was published on July 13, 1930, in *The Milwaukee Sentinel.*

"When a child is born its sense-organs are brought in contact with the outer world. The waves of sound, heat, and light beat upon its feeble body, its sensitive nerve-fibres quiver, the muscles contract and relax in obedience: a gasp, a breath, and in this act a marvelous little engine, of inconceivable delicacy and complexity of construction, unlike any on earth, is hitched to the wheel-work of the Universe.

The little engine labors and grows, performs more and more involved operations, becomes sensitive to ever subtler influences and now there manifests itself in the fully developed being - Man - a desire mysterious, inscrutable and irresistible: to imitate nature, to create, to work himself the wonders he perceives.

Inspired in this task he searches, discovers and invents, designs and constructs, and enriches with monuments of beauty, grandeur and awe, the star of his birth.

He descends into the bowels of the globe to bring forth its hidden treasures and to unlock its immense imprisoned energies for its use.

He invades the dark depths of the ocean and the azure regions of the sky.

He peers into the innermost nooks and recesses of molecular structure and lays bare to his gaze worlds infinitely remote. He subdues and puts to his service the fierce, devastating spark of Prometheus, the titanic forces of the waterfall, the wind and the tide.

He tames the thundering bolt of Jove and annihilates time and space. He makes the great Sun itself his obedient toiling slave.

Such is the power and might that the heavens reverberate and the whole earth trembles by the mere sound of his voice.

What has the future in store for this strange being, born of a breath, of perishable tissue, yet immortal, with his powers fearful and divine? What magic will be wrought by him in the end? What is to be his greatest deed, his crowning achievement?

Long ago he recognized that all perceptible matter comes from a primary substance, of a tenuity beyond conception and filling all space - the Akasha or luminiferous ether - which is acted upon by the life-giving Prana or creative force, calling into existence, in never ending cycles, all things and phenomena.

The primary substance, thrown into infinitesimal whirls of prodigious velocity, becomes gross matter; the force subsiding, the motion ceases and matter disappears, reverting to the primary substance.

Can Man control this grandest, most awe-inspiring of all processes in nature? Can he harness her inexhaustible energies to perform all their functions at his bidding, more still - can he so refine his means of control as to put them in operation simply by the force of his will?

If he could do this he would have powers almost unlimited and supernatural. At his command, with but a slight effort on his part, old worlds would disappear and new ones of his planning would spring into being.

He could fix, solidify and preserve the ethereal shapes of his imagining, the fleeting visions of his dreams. He could express all the creations of his mind, on any scale, in forms concrete and imperishable.

He could alter the size of this planet, control its seasons, guide it along any path he might choose through the depths of the Universe.

He could make planets collide and produce his suns and stars, his heat and light. He could originate and develop life in all its infinite forms.

To create and annihilate material substance, cause it to aggregate in forms according to his desire, would be the supreme manifestation of the power of Man's mind, his most complete triumph over the physical world, his crowning achievement which would place him beside his Creator and fulfill his ultimate destiny."

Tesla's bold suggestion that Man could learn how to control the physics of Akashic interactions - "this grandest, most awe-inspiring of all processes in nature" - is the first modern formulation of the concept of Akashic engineering.

Tesla went beyond typical Western and Eastern modes of thought, the technological control of simple physical processes on the one hand, and the contemplation of a more subtle complex reality on the other hand, and proposed a powerful synthesis of the two.

A widespread appreciation of the prospect of future Akashic science and technology could, I think, trigger the "resacralization of the world" envisioned by Ralph Abraham.

Notes

[cellular automata] See "The Life of Joe Glider."

[dynamical systems theory, aka chaos theory] See "There's plenty of room at the bottom," "Eligo, ergo sum, ergo Deus est."

[Everett's "Many-Worlds Interpretation" of quantum physics (MWI)] See "Exotic space, mysterious time, magic quantum."

[Fedorov and the Russian Cosmists] See "Knocking on Heaven's door."

[India Awakens] See "The lights of Eastern spirituality."

[information is fundamentally and irretrievably erased by the collapse of the wavefunction] The collapse of the wavefunction (von Neumann's Process 1) is nonunitary, irreversible, and doesn't conserve information. See "Exotic space, mysterious time, magic quantum."

[recently revived as an online magazine] The *Mondo 2000* website: http://www.mondo2000.com/

[space and time might emerge from the non-local entanglement structure of a fundamental field beyond space and time] See "In the beginning was the field."

[Swami Vivekananda] See "The lights of Eastern spirituality."

[the full text of "*Demystifying the Akasha*" is available online]: https://www.researchgate.net/publication/281765423_DEMYSTIFYING_THE_AKASHA_ Consciousness_and_the_Quantum_Vacuum

References

[Abraham 1987] Ralph Abraham, Jerrold Marsden. *Foundations of Mechanics*, Second Edition. Addison-Wesley, 1987.

[Abraham 1992] Ralph Abraham, Christopher Shaw. *Dynamics: The Geometry of Behavior*. Addison-Wesley, 1992.

[Abraham 2001] Ralph Abraham, Yoshisuke Ueda (Eds.). *The Chaos Avant-Garde: Memoirs of the Early Days of Chaos Theory*. World Scientific, 2001.

[Abraham 2010] Ralph Abraham, Sisir Roy. *Demystifying the Akasha: Consciousness and the Quantum Vacuum*. Epigraph Publishing, 2010.

[Abraham 2017] Ralph Abraham. Theosophy and the Arts, 2017.
http://www.ralph-abraham.org/articles/MS%23151.Theosoph/ms151.pdf

[Deutsch 1997] David Deutsch. *The Fabric of Reality*. Viking Press, 1997.

[Gleick 1987] James Gleick. *Chaos: Making a New Science*. Viking Books, 1987.

[Grotz 1997] Toby Grotz. The Influence of Vedic Philosophy on Nikola Tesla's Understanding of Free Energy. 1997.
http://www.teslasociety.com/tesla_and_swami.htm

[László 2003] Ervin László. *The Connectivity Hypothesis: Foundations of an Integral Science of Quantum, Cosmos, Life, and Consciousness*. State University of New York Press, 2003.

[László 2007] Ervin László. *Science and the Akashic Field: An Integral Theory of Everything*. Inner Traditions, 2007.

[László 2009] Ervin László. *The Akashic Experience: Science and the Cosmic Memory Field*. Inner Traditions, 2009.

[László 2014] Ervin László. *The Self-Actualizing Cosmos: The Akasha Revolution in Science and Human Consciousness*. Inner Traditions, 2014.

[Pirsig 1974] Robert Pirsig. *Zen and the Art of Motorcycle Maintenance*. William Morrow and Company, 1974.

[Prisco 2016] Giulio Prisco. Q/A with Ralph Abraham and Sisir Roy. YouTube, 2016.
https://www.youtube.com/watch?v=MRSTMlptJW4

[Prisco 2017a] Giulio Prisco, Ralph Abraham: The Quantum Akasha. *Turing Church*, 2017.
https://turingchurch.net/ralph-abraham-the-quantum-akasha-91309801dc52

[Prisco 2017b] Giulio Prisco. Mathemagician Ralph Abraham: We Need Another Miracle. *Mondo 2000*, 2017.
https://www.mondo2000.com/2017/08/24/mathemagician-ralph-abraham-we-need-another-miracle/

[Prisco 2017c] Giulio Prisco. I am pleased and honored to contribute to the new *Mondo 2000*, 2018.
https://giulioprisco.com/i-am-pleased-and-honored-to-contribute-to-the-new-mondo-2000-c6af6f85b31b

[Requardt 2001] Manfred Requardt, Sisir Roy. (Quantum) Space-Time as a Statistical Geometry of Fuzzy Lumps and the Connection with Random Metric Spaces. *Classical and Quantum Gravity*, 2001.

[Roy 1998] Sisir Roy. *Statistical Geometry and Applications to Microphysics and Cosmology.* Springer, 1998.

[Seifer 1998] Marc Seifer. *Wizard: The Life and Times of Nikola Tesla.* Citadel Press, 1998.

[Sheldrake 2001] Rupert Sheldrake, Terence McKenna, Ralph Abraham. *Chaos, Creativity, and Cosmic Consciousness.* Park Street Press, 2001.

[Sinnett 1883] Alfred Percy Sinnett, *Esoteric Buddhism.* Trübner & Co, 1883.

[Sreekantan 2019] B.V. Sreekantan, Sisir Roy. *Understanding Space, Time and Causality: Modern Physics and Ancient Indian Traditions.* Routledge, 2019.

[Tesla 1900] Nikola Tesla. The Problem of Increasing Human Energy. *Century Magazine*, 1900.

[Wolfram 2015] Stephen Wolfram. What Is Spacetime, Really?, 2015. http://blog.stephenwolfram.com/2015/12/what-is-spacetime-really/

CHAPTER 18 – THERE'S PLENTY OF ROOM AT THE BOTTOM

I have stolen the title of this chapter from a lecture by Richard Feynman [Feynman 1959]. In the lecture Feynman suggested the possibility of molecular nanotechnology, but here I am much more ambitious.

Some central open questions in scientific philosophy, related to time, causation, quantum physics, the fabric of fundamental reality, consciousness, and a cosmic Mind, could have conceptually simple, related answers.

Questions:

- How to reconcile irreversible thermodynamics and the arrow of time with the idea that fundamental physics is time-reversible?
- How to reconcile free will with the idea that fundamental physics is deterministic?
- How to reconcile the action of mind (or Mind) in the world with the idea that fundamental physics is causally closed, with no room at the bottom?

There is a simple answer:

- Fundamental physics is NOT time-reversible, NOT deterministic, and NOT causally closed: There's plenty of room at the bottom.

This simple answer seems evident if one just takes quantum mechanics seriously, and considers quantum possibilities and quantum collapse as ontologically real.

The state of a quantum system is a superposition of many possible states (like, a particle is here AND there). The quantum superposition evolves deterministically and time-reversibly between observations, but "collapses" into one of the possible states upon observation (the particle is found here OR there). What observation is and who/what observes is unclear. The collapse breaks determinism and time-reversibility, and seems entirely random.

These things were well known in the 1930s. In "*Mathematical Foundations of Quantum Mechanics*" [von Neumann 1955], John von Neumann clearly stated that there are two different quantum evolution processes: Process 2, the smooth mathematical evolution of a quantum superposition of interfering possibilities between observations, and Process 1, the abrupt collapse upon observation. Both are fundamental.

Many physicists then and now have tried hard to deny the ontological reality of Process 1, but it appears that Process 1 is in the universe to stay. In "*How Can Physics Underlie the Mind*" [Ellis 2016], cosmologist George Ellis, co-author with Stephen Hawking of a classic cosmology treatise [Hawking 1973], says:

> "Because of the existence of quantum processes at the bottom, physics is not deterministic, despite the way many writers represent the situation as if it is. It seems that the profound nature of the quantum revolution has still not permeated the con-

sciousness of many physicists and biologists, who present the situation as if physics were deterministic all the way down. This is not the case: the bottom level is not deterministic!"

Physicist Ruth Kastner argues [Kastner 2017, 2019] that Process 1 is the physical basis for the thermodynamic arrow of time - the unidirectional increase of entropy against a backdrop of otherwise time-reversible laws. Von Neumann's Process 1 (collapse) breaks time-reversibility, which suggests the idea to consider Process 1 as the microscopic origin of the second law of thermodynamics.

How do we get the irreversible processes we see all around us from laws that are supposedly reversible? "The trick: they are not all reversible," answers Kastner [Kastner 2016]. "A crucial part of the physics of Nature involves an irreversible step that has long been neglected."

> "In fact, Von Neumann himself showed that his 'Process 1' is irreversible and always entropy increasing."

Kastner's arguments use her "Relativistic Transactional Interpretation" (RTI) [Kastner 2012, 2015] of quantum physics, a variant of John Cramer's "Transactional Interpretation" [Cramer 2016]. Similar arguments have been proposed by physicist and philosopher David Albert, notably in his book "*Time and Chance*" [Albert 2001]. Albert's arguments use another formulation and interpretation of quantum mechanics: The spontaneous collapse theory of Ghirardi-Rimini-Weber (GRW).

According to Albert, microscopic quantum collapse processes create random perturbations that force macroscopic systems to follow thermodynamics. This is a modern version of the "clinamen," the random unpredictable swerve of atoms in the void imagined by Lucretius.

Regardless of any specific mechanism for Process 1 (GRW, RTI, or others), it seems plausible to me to consider the reality and (apparent) randomness of Process 1 as the microscopic origin of the second law of thermodynamics.

Kastner seems to agree. "Yes, I do think that a genuinely non-unitary process leads to entropy increase, independently of specific interpretations," she said [Kastner 2016]. "This just seems to follow from the fact that a pure state has the lowest possible entropy, while a mixed state always will have more."

Becoming Before Being

In "*The Nature of the Physical World*" [Eddington 1929], after defining the physics of individual particles as "primary law" and thermodynamics as derived "secondary law," Arthur Eddington said:

> "One would not be surprised if in the reconstruction of the scheme of physics which the quantum theory is now pressing on us, secondary law becomes the basis and primary law is discarded."

Nobel laureate Ilya Prigogine also suggested that thermodynamics could be "more fundamental" than particle and field dynamics. Following the philosophies of Henri Bergson and Alfred North Whitehead [Prigogine 1984], Prigogine proposed "a conception of the world in which process, becoming, is taken as a primary constituent of physical existence."

According to Prigogine, "we should consider the thermodynamic quantities to be the primary reality and the allegedly more fundamental description in terms of microscopic structure to be secondary," explains Alastair Rae [Rae 2012]. Prigogine "suggested that it would then be possible to treat the second law of thermodynamics in the way its name suggests: as a law that is always followed rather than a statistical rule..."

"The classical order was particles first, the second law later - being before becoming!," says Prigogine in "*From Being to Becoming*" [Prigogine 1980]. "It is possible that this is no longer so when we come to the level of elementary particles and that here we must first introduce the second law before being able to define the entities..." In this and following books (including [Prigogine 1984, 1997]), Prigogine tried to formulate mathematical models of becoming before being, but his ideas have not been widely accepted as part of the scientific consensus.

Prigogine's books "contain the progressive development of the same ideas, enriched by successive updates," notes Prigogine's collaborator Radu Balescu in an essay [Balescu 2007] that describes the evolution of Prigogine's ideas. In "*The End of Certainty*" [Prigogine 1997], one of his latest books, Prigogine referenced chaos theory, which is now bringing related ideas to consensus science.

The idea that irreversible change could be more fundamental than particles and fields is also found in Prigogine's thermodynamics textbook [Kondepudi 2014]:

> "But, we see everywhere in nature change that is irreversible, and organization, and life itself, born out of irreversible processes. It makes one wonder: is mechanics a convenient approximation of natural processes that are fundamentally irreversible and not the converse, as the current dogma holds?"

I have no in-principle objections. Why should nature conform to our expectations of what is really fundamental? But I find Prigogine's ideas difficult to visualize. Like everyone (I guess), I am only able to visualize fields driving particles, particles radiating fields, particles colliding, particles emitting/absorbing particles, or mass/energy shaping space-time geometry and being driven by it - the microscopic interactions that we use to consider as fundamental and build thermodynamics upon. I am unable to visualize things the other way around.

I guess this reductionist mental habit, which is difficult to break, is due to the spectacular success of reductionist science, which is now sort of burned deep in our mind. But non-reductionist concepts of causation didn't seem so strange in the past. In fact, the concept of "downward causation" was used by Aristotle and medieval thinkers.

Downward Causation?

Downward causation, or top-down causation, is the idea that the whole of a system can influence its parts in ways that cannot be reduced to the local interactions between the parts.

The related but weaker concept of emergence recognizes that higher level system models emerge from lower levels. For example, fluid dynamics and thermodynamics emerge from the physics of interacting particles, and higher levels like biology emerge from lower levels. The high levels have their own models, relatively independent of the low levels.

For example, trying to study cancer with quantum field theory wouldn't make practical sense: One has to use higher level concepts from molecular biology to study cancer. At the same time, emergence doesn't speculate on high level laws that overwrite low level laws, but considers high level behavior as compatible with low level laws, though unpredictable from them in practice.

Top-down causation is a very strong form of emergence where high level laws are considered as able to directly dictate the behavior of the lower levels. Strong emergence is often invoked to suggest how a Cosmic Mind (aka God) can influence the physical world (divine action).

I am open to the possibility that downward causation might be the non-mechanical mechanism of divine action, but I am also open to the possibility that we - intelligent life forms in the universe - could learn how to use downward causation methods ourselves.

Ellis provides a thorough encyclopedic discussion of downward causation ideas (Ellis prefers to use the term "top-down causation") in *How Can Physics Underlie the Mind?* [Ellis s016]. A central recurring theme in the book is:

> "The lower levels do the physical work, but the higher levels decide what work should be done."

Cool, but I still don't see how it works. Some biologists, philosophers and theologians don't seem to have a problem with downward causation, but I keep trying to think of a simple model than even a physicist can understand. Ellis puts his finger on the conceptual problem:

> "How is there freedom for higher level causation to be efficacious... But how does it happen, given the causal completeness of physics at the bottom? How is there freedom at the bottom for this to occur?..."

> "How can top-down causation be possible in the case of the implementation hierarchy, if the physics at the bottom is a causally closed system, determining all that happens through interactions of particles and fields mediated by forces and potentials? Isn't the system already fully determined, so there is no room for any kind of top-down causation?"

Ellis thinks (and I agree) that the simplest answer is that the system is NOT fully determined because the physics at the bottom is NOT a causally closed system: irreducible randomness occurs in quantum and chaos physics.

I never had any problem with the idea that randomness could be fundamental: Perhaps that's just the way things work. So I have no problem accepting THAT top-down causation could occur, but I still have a problem visualizing HOW it could occur.

Frustrated by being unable to visualize how downward causation could "work," [I devised an intuitive "visual" model for downward causation].

The idea is that different [Everett worlds] unfold for a short while (perhaps very short from our perspective), but then most of those worlds evaporate into nothingness, or something like that, while the "fittest" winners take all and become fully real according to certain reality selection criteria.

The outcome is a "thin multiverse," halfway between one single world and the full multiverse of Everett. My intuition tells me that reality includes more than one world, but less than all possible worlds.

Downward causation is in the reality selection criteria. The model can be made compatible with all that we know about physics by assuming that the selection criteria are related to information, entropy, and thermodynamics: The laws of thermodynamics are always satisfied in the worlds that eventually achieves full reality.

Whether or not a world will pass reality selection can't be known immediately. The universe is computationally irreducible: there's no way to compute tomorrow in less than 24 hours, because you really need to do all the computations (there is no computational shortcut) and you can't do all the computations faster than the universe itself. But doing all the computations, in parallel worlds, is exactly what this model does.

This makes a lot of sense as a reality [simulation] strategy. In fact, we use random lower level processes plus higher level selection in optimization methods like simulated annealing and evolutionary computing. Genetic Programming (GP) researcher Wolfgang Banzhaf observes that GP implements downward causation [Banzhaf 2014]:

> "With the still lingering dispute about whether emergence using downward causation is a valid idea, GPers can confidently declare that emergence is happening in GP for all the world to see. I believe this is due to the presence of selection as one of the driving forces of evolution, a clear case of downward causation."

The simplest reality selection criteria (fitness functions) that I can think of are those that just enforce thermodynamics, entropy production and all that. It's nice to think that perhaps, besides thermodynamics, the reality selection criteria could include concepts like complexity, richness, quality, goodness, and love.

Higher level selection criteria might be related to what Rudy Rucker calls "gnarliness" (interesting, surprising unpredictability at the edge between boring order and boring randomness) [Rucker 2016], or even to what Robert Pirsig called "Quality" [Pirsig 1974, 1991].

Another intriguing possibility is that the reality selection process might be related to a [Cosmic Mind] that lives in the fabric of physical reality itself.

Fractal (Non)Determinism In Classical Chaos Theory

The arguments presented so far in this chapter are based on quantum physics. This makes sense because quantum physics is considered as a fundamental description of the world. But we shouldn't entirely rule out the possibility that [quantum behavior might emerge] from underlying more classical models.

In a talk titled "The Development Of Quantum Mechanics" (Accademia Nazionale dei Lincei, Roma, 1972), Paul Dirac said [Palmer 2013]:

> "One can always hope that there will be future developments which will lead to a drastically different theory from the present quantum mechanics and for which there may be a partial return of determinism."

However, it turns out that even in classical (non-quantum) physics there's plenty of room at the bottom. In fact, chaos theory shows that classical physics is causally open.

Max Born pointed out that even classical physics is nondeterministic, because computing the future with absolute certainty would require specifying the initial conditions (the present) with the infinite precision of a real number. In his 1954 Nobel Prize lecture [Born 1954], Born said:

> "As a mathematical tool the concept of a real number represented by a nonterminating decimal fraction is exceptionally important and fruitful. As the measure of a physical quantity it is nonsense... concepts which correspond to no conceivable observation should be eliminated from physics... the determinism of classical physics turns out to be an illusion, created by overrating mathematico-logical concepts."

According to Born, since every conceivable observation has a margin of uncertainty, classical physics should be formulated in terms of statistical distributions.

Similarly, according to Prigogine [Prigogine 1980], "belief in strict determinism is justified only when the notion of a well defined initial state does not correspond to an excessive idealization." Otherwise, "we leave the model of strict determinism. We can make only statistical predictions, forecasting average results."

Chaos theory brings the approach of Born and Prigogine to the surface. In fact, even in classical (non-quantum) physics, many mathematical models exhibit deterministic chaos. These models are deterministic (the future is uniquely determined by the present), but strongly sensitive to initial conditions. Small initial differences are amplified exponentially in time, which makes prediction impossible in practice.

The weather is nonlinear, dissipative, chaotic, and impossible to predict in practice. This is often illustrated with the butterfly effect: A flap of a butterfly's wings "could lead to a tornado that would not otherwise have formed, it could equally well prevent a tornado that would otherwise have formed," says Edward Lorenz in "*The Essence of Chaos*" [Lorenz 1995].

The chaotic behavior of a dynamical system can be qualitatively visualized with trajectories, attractors and attraction basins in the system's phase space (the space of all possible states of the system). A highly recommended book is "*Dynamics*" [Abraham 1992], by Ralph Abraham and Christopher Shaw, a masterpiece of "visual math" with plenty of illustrations and without mathematical formulas. For a more conventional introduction, try "*Chaos in*

Dynamical Systems" [Ott 2002] or "*Chaotic Dynamics*" [Tél 2006].

The trajectory of a real-world (dissipative and nonlinear) dynamical system in its phase space eventually reaches an attractor, which can be geometrically simple or strange like a fractal, and then stays in the attractor. All trajectories that start in the attraction basin of an attractor eventually reach the attractor.

What if the system starts exactly on the boundary between two different attraction basins? It seems that the system, unable to choose between the two attractors, could only make a random choice.

But (using Born's argument against him) one could reply that a point exactly on the boundary is a mathematical abstraction: In all but a vanishingly small (zero probability) set of cases, the starting point is on either one or the other side of the boundary, and in principle we can always specify the starting point accurately enough to be in either one or the other basin. Once the initial conditions are given accurately enough, one could think, the evolution of the system is determined and can be predicted.

But no, it doesn't work. Things start to become fuzzy when the boundary is fractal. While smooth (continuous and differentiable) curves and surfaces become locally flat if you zoom-in deep enough, fractals remain rough at all scales [Mandelbrot 1982].

The fractal dimension is a generalization of the concept of dimension that can have non-integer values and describe fractals. A moderately rough fractal curve has a non-integer fractal dimension between 1 and 2. The boundary of the Mandelbrot set is a super-rough curve with fractal dimension 2, more like a surface than a curve.

When the boundary is fractal, the precision needed to determine which attraction basin contains the starting point increases with the fractal dimension of the boundary. A system that starts close to the boundary will wander chaotically for some time near the boundary, and eventually reach the attractor that corresponds to the starting point.

But chaotic behavior can be even more complex, and undetermined not only in practice, but also in principle. Enter ultra-fractal "riddled basins," for which nothing short of the infinite, unattainable precision of a mathematical real number will work.

A riddled basin is a basin of attraction with "the property that every point in the basin has pieces of another attractor's basin arbitrarily nearby" [Aguirre 2009].

In other words, a set of intermingled riddled basins can be thought of as a space-filling "fat fractal" [Ott 2002, Tél 2006] boundary between different attraction basins. A system that starts on the boundary stays on the boundary, but the boundary is space-filling and contains (in the sense of extending arbitrarily close to) the attractors.

Every neighborhood of the starting point, no matter how small, contains points that will eventually reach different attractors. Therefore, no matter how accurate is the specification of the starting point, the attractor that the system will eventually reach is undetermined.

Riddled basins, which have been found in many dissipative systems described by simple mathematical equations, "show that totally deterministic systems might present in practice an absolute lack of predictability" [Aguirre 2009]. According to Ott, "this results in what might be called an extreme obstruction to determinism" [Ott 2002]. See also the book "*Transient Chaos*" [Lai 2011].

It can be mathematically proven that (see "The End of Classical Determinism," by John Sommerer [Sommerer 1995], and references therein) that some simple dynamical systems have intermingled riddled basins: Any infinitesimal phase space neighborhood of any starting point contains, with full Lebesgue measure (that is, with nonzero density), points that will eventually end up on different attractors.

Sommerer explains that there are starting points, arbitrarily close to an attractor, which still end up going to another attractor. There is also a dense and uncountably infinite set of starting points that never reach an attractor (imagine an endless pinball game).

In *"Does God Play Dice?"* [Stewart 1997], a highly recommended masterpiece, Ian Stewart notes that a system with two intermingled riddled basins is SERIOUSLY unpredictable: "You can predict that eventually any chosen initial point will end up on either one attractor or the other, but you can't predict which."

> "As close as you like to initial points that end up on attractor 1 there exist initial points that go to attractor 2, and vice versa. Now the butterfly effect doesn't just move points around on the same attractor - it can switch them from one attractor to the other."

Regardless of the accuracy of the starting point, the attractor that the system will eventually reach can't be predicted even in principle. In other words, the evolution of the system is NOT determined. Only probabilities, proportional to local phase space densities, are determined.

I suspect that the fractal depth of riddled basins might be widespread in real-world, dissipative dynamical systems, and be the rule rather than the exception. If so, chaotic evolution is really nondeterministic in principle.

Nature "knows" the starting point of the system as an infinitely precise real number. But we can't know the starting point with infinite precision, and any finitely precise starting point in a riddled basin contains the possibility of different outcomes. For any finitely precise starting point, only the probability of different outcomes can be known.

Philipp Frank used a circle perfectly balanced on the tip of a triangle in a vertical gravitational field to illustrate nondeterminism in classical mechanics [Frank 1998]. Any neighborhood of this starting point contains both points that will go to the left and points that will go to the right. It could be argued that this very special initial condition has zero probability, but riddled basins extend Frank's example to finite probabilities: The tip of the triangle is everywhere.

If a dynamical system starts in a riddled region of its phase space, there's no way to tell, even in principle, to which attraction basin it belongs. The starting point is in a space-filling fat fractal boundary between different attraction basins, and can be thought of as being in all basins, with a potentiality to reach any attractor.

The unpredictable nature of chaos is often related to the [environmental noise] that inevitably perturbs real-world dynamical systems in essentially unpredictable ways, and/or to the fact that Heisenberg's quantum uncertainty relations make it impossible to specify initial conditions with arbitrary accuracy. Both points are correct, but misleading, because chaos is deeper than that.

It must be emphasized that the arguments and results presented above apply to simple, isolated, classical dynamical systems described by simple mathematical equations, without having to invoke external noise or quantum mechanics. The unpredictable nature of chaos is deeper than noise and uncertain initial conditions, and stems directly from the mathematical laws of classical physics based on the continuum of real numbers. Joseph Ford explains [Ford 1989]:

> "In summary, most numbers and most initial states... are specified by random digit strings which are unpredictable, uncomputable and undefinable. Clearly then, only a god can provide the initial state... Thus, we have now tracked our missing information to the real number system whose individual members are, in general, beyond man's ability even to define, much less specify or compute."

So, chaos can't be reduced to quantum uncertainty. But perhaps quantum behavior might emerge from chaotic behavior in an underlying sub-quantum substrate.

Back To Quantum Physics

Werner Heisenberg noted [Heisenberg 1927] that "in the rigorous formulation of the law of causality - 'If we know the present precisely, we can calculate the future' - it is not the conclusion that is faulty, but the premise."

> "We simply can not know the present in principle in all its parameters. Therefore all perception is a selection from a totality of possibilities and a limitation of what is possible in the future."

Heisenberg had quantum physics in mind. But, as noted above, it can be argued that [quantum behavior might emerge] from nonlinear, strongly fractal chaotic dynamics in an underlying substrate.

In fact, there are intriguing conceptual parallels between the collapse of a quantum state into one or another possible state and the collapse of a chaotic dynamical system, starting in a riddled region of its phase space, into one or another attractor. In both cases, an initial state contains (can be considered as a "superposition" of) different possible outcomes. After the discovery of riddled basins in 1992, some scientists have suggested related dynamical models of quantum collapse.

In "*Does God Play Dice?*," Stewart outlines Tim Palmer's suggestion [Palmer 1995], based on this analogy with riddled basins, that "quantum indeterminacy may perhaps be replaced by certain kinds of 'hidden variable' chaotic dynamic, provided that the chaos is sufficiently nasty." Stewart says:

> "Indeed, Palmer's approach is the kind of thing that, at least in spirit, you must employ if you want to render the quantum dice deterministic by the introduction of hidden variables. Otherwise Bell's inequality will bite. The precise details are probably wrong - there are many possibilities for internal dynamics with intertwined basins, and Palmer chooses a specific one merely for the sake of argument - but the spirit of the approach is mathematically sound. And Einstein would definitely have approved of the philosophy."

It's worth noting that this approach suggests that new mathematical models of quantum mechanics might be continuous like in classical continuum mechanics, electromagnetism, and general relativity, with differential geometry extended to fractal geometry. I think Einstein would have approved of this as well.

In a followup book wittily titled "*Do Dice Play God?*" [Stewart 2019], Stewart outlines a suggestive analogy between quantum measurement and a coin spinning in the air, eventually landing head (H) or tail (T) on a table:

> "The coin doesn't just sit on the table flickering between the two states H and T that we can measure. It flips over and over in the air. While it's doing that, its state is neither heads nor tails... We 'observe' the head/tail choice by making the coin interact with a 'measuring instrument', the table... All of the fine detail of the movement in space is obliterated by the act of observation: literally, smashed flat."

Stewart explains [Bell's theorem] and underlines that Bell's theorem seems to rule out models of quantum measurement based on local hidden variables (the "fine detail" in the coin analogy), but it seems to me that, in the coin analogy, the table represents spacetime, and whatever happens above the table is not "local."

However, Stewart reiterates that models based on fractal chaos, similar to Palmer's model, could bypass Bell's theorem: If the underlying chaotic dynamics "is sufficiently badly behaved, the proof of Bell's inequality falls apart, because the correlations it considers aren't computable."

While no solid theory has emerged so far, I have the impression that this research program is worth pursuing. Analogies between chaotic dynamical systems with riddled basins and quantum systems could lead to physical (but still nondeterministic) models of quantum behavior. See for example [Heylighen 2018].

The possibility of devising dynamical models of quantum collapse based on fractal chaos theory would seem to lend support to the common sense concept that reality consists of only one universe, instead of Everett's concept of a multiverse of parallel realities, or the concept of "thin multiverse" that I have briefly outlined above in the context of downward causation.

However, nature is most certainly smarter and more imaginative than me, and therefore I prefer to keep an open mind.

In "*Randomness and Undecidability in Physics*" [Svozil 1993] Karl Svozil suggests that randomness in physics might be a signature of mathematical undecidability in the Gödel sense. See also Svozil's recent open access book "*Physical (A)Causality*" [Svozil 2018]. It seems plausible that [further research in algorithmic complexity and computability could shed light on these fundamental issues].

(Non)Determinism By Any Other Name

Some readers of a draft version of this chapter have objected to "chaotic evolution is really nondeterministic in principle" and insisted on "deterministic chaos." In fact, despite the butterfly effect, despite the fact that chaotic evolution is unpredictable in practice, and even despite the fact that strongly fractal chaotic evolution is undetermined in principle, many experts emphasize that chaos is deterministic chaos.

Fine with me, provided that my point is clear: In the physical universe, there's plenty of room at the bottom for [divine action and free will] (discussed in the next chapter).

A simple dynamical system with riddled basins of attraction is deterministic in the sense that it has a simple mathematical description without uncertain parts. But it's also nondeterministic in the sense that its evolution is undetermined and can't be predicted even in principle.

So both terms (deterministic and nondeterministic) can be used, depending on what one wants to say. Like, a half-empty glass and a half-full glass are exactly the same thing, and calling the glass half-empty or half-full depends on the emphasis one wants to give. It depends on why one is talking about the glass.

Here, I want to protect free will, which I consider as a very solid experimental fact, from the threat of full determinism in the sense of Laplace (the future and the past are uniquely determined by the present, and pre/retrodictable in-principle). I also want to protect the free will of the cosmic intelligence, aka God, which I believe exists in the bedrock of reality and acts upon the universe (divine action).

Dirac's (hoped for) new quantum mechanics with a partial return of determinism, mentioned above, might be provided by strongly fractal deterministic chaos, which I am calling nondeterministic. Feel free to call it deterministic if you like, labels don't really matter. "It doesn't matter whether a cat is black or white, as long as it catches mice," Deng Xiaoping astutely observed. Here the mice are free will and divine action. This cat catches mice, so color it as you like.

The term "causally open" triggers less objections than "nondeterministic" (though the two terms sound equivalent to me), so it might be a good alternative. Another is "open determinism."

Notes

[Bell's theorem] See "Exotic space, mysterious time, magic quantum."

[quantum behavior might emerge] See "Into the deep waters."

[Cosmic Mind] See "Eligo, ergo sum, ergo Deus est," "Thought experiments in physical theology."

[divine action and free will] See "Eligo, ergo sum, ergo Deus est."

[environmental noise] A related consideration is that, regardless of the accuracy of our measurements, the effects of interactions too small to detect directly (e.g. yet undiscovered forces) could be dramatically amplified by chaotic dynamics.

[Everett worlds] See "Exotic space, mysterious time, magic quantum."

[further research in algorithmic complexity and computability could shed light on these fundamental issues] See "Thought experiments in physical theology."

[I devised an intuitive "visual" model for downward causation] Initially I thought [Prisco 2017] that only one real universe would emerge from parallel evolution and selection. But given computational irreducibility, how could the universe "know the right move" without trial and error? It seems safer to leave more options open. For this and other reasons, now I find the idea of a "thin multiverse" more appealing. See also "In the beginning was the field."

[simulation] See "Sims City."

References

[Abraham 1992] Ralph Abraham, Christopher Shaw. *Dynamics: The Geometry Of Behavior*. Basic Books, 1992.

[Aguirre 2009] Jacobo Aguirre, Ricardo L. Viana, and Miguel A. F. Sanjuán. Fractal structures in nonlinear dynamics. *Reviews of Modern Physics*, 2009.

[Albert 2001] David Albert. *Time and Chance*. Harvard University Press, 2001.

[Balescu 2007] Radu Balescu. Ilya Prigogine's Life And Work. In *Advances in Chemical Physics: Special Volume in Memory of Ilya Prigogine* (Stuart A. Rice, Editor). Wiley, 2007.

[Banzhaf 2014] Wolfgang Banzhaf. Genetic Programming and Emergence. *Genetic Programming and Evolvable Machines*, 2014.

[Born 1954] Max Born. The statistical interpretation of quantum mechanics. Nobel lecture, 1954.
https://www.nobelprize.org/nobel_prizes/physics/laureates/1954/born-lecture.pdf

[Eddington 1929] Arthur Eddington. *The Nature of the Physical World*. MacMillan, 1929.

[Ellis 2016] George Ellis. *How Can Physics Underlie the Mind? Top-Down Causation in the Human Context*. Springer, 2016.

[Feynman 1959] Richard Feynman. There's Plenty of Room at the Bottom (1959). *Journal of Microelectromechanical Systems*, 1992.

[Ford 1989] Joseph Ford. What is Chaos, that we should be mindful of it?. *The New Physics* (Paul Davies, Ed.). Cambridge University Press, 1989.

[Frank 1998] Philipp Frank. *The Law of Causality and Its Limits*. Springer, 1998.

[Hawking 1973] Stephen Hawking, George Ellis, *The Large Scale Structure of Space-Time*. Cambridge University Press, 1973.

[Heylighen 2018] Francis Heylighen. Entanglement, symmetry breaking and collapse: correspondences between quantum and self-organizing dynamics. Unpublished draft.
https://pdfs.semanticscholar.org/e97d/aff4942683ccdeb601f609c779997adbf59d.pdf

[Heisenberg 1927] Werner Heisenberg, The Actual Content of Quantum Theoretical Kinematics and Mechanics (translation from German). NASA Technical Memorandum, 1983.
https://ntrs.nasa.gov/archive/nasa/casi.ntrs.nasa.gov/19840008978.pdf

[Kastner 2012] Ruth Kastner, *The Transactional Interpretation of Quantum Mechanics: The Reality of Possibility*. Cambridge University Press, 2012.

[Kastner 2015] Ruth Kastner. *Understanding Our Unseen Reality: Solving Quantum Riddles*. Imperial College Press, 2015.

[Kastner 2016] Ruth Kastner. More on Entropy and the Arrow of Time, 2016.
https://transactionalinterpretation.org/2016/12/24/more-on-entropy-and-the-arrow-of-time/

[Kastner 2017] Ruth Kastner. On Quantum Collapse as a Basis for the Second Law of Thermodynamics. *Entropy*, 2017. Republished in [Kastner 2019].

[Kastner 2019] Ruth Kastner. *Adventures in Quantumland: Exploring Our Unseen Reality*. World Scientific, 2019.

[Kondepudi 2014] Dilip Kondepudi, Ilya Prigogine. *Modern Thermodynamics: From Heat Engines to Dissipative Structures*. Wiley, 2014.

[Lai 2011] Ying-Cheng Lai, Tamás Tél. *Transient Chaos: Complex Dynamics on Finite Time Scales*. Springer, 2011.

[Lorenz 1995] Edward Lorenz. *The Essence of Chaos*. University of Washington Press, 1995.

[Mandelbrot 1982] Benoît Mandelbrot. *The Fractal Geometry of Nature*. W. H. Freeman and Co., 1982.

[Ott 2002] Edward Ott. *Chaos in Dynamical Systems*. Cambridge University Press, 2002.

[Palmer 1995] Tim Palmer. A local deterministic model of quantum spin measurement. *Proceedings of the Royal Society A*, 1995.

[Palmer 2013] Tim Palmer. Lorenz, Gödel and Penrose: New perspectives on determinism and causality in fundamental physics. *arXiv*, 2013.
https://arxiv.org/abs//1309.2396

[Pirsig 1974] Robert Pirsig. *Zen and the Art of Motorcycle Maintenance*. William Morrow and Company, 1974.

[Pirsig 1991] Robert Pirsig. *Lila: An Inquiry into Morals*. Bantam Books, 1991.

[Prigogine 1980] Ilya Prigogine. *From Being to Becoming: Time and Complexity in the Physical Sciences*. W H Freeman & Co, 1980.

[Prigogine 1984] Ilya Prigogine, Isabelle Stengers. *Order out of Chaos: Man's new dialogue with nature*. Bantam Books, 1984.

[Prigogine 1997] Ilya Prigogine, Isabelle Stengers. *The End of Certainty: Time, Chaos, and the New Laws of Nature*. The Free Press, 1997.

[Prisco 2017] Giulio Prisco. Racing Worlds: A visual model for downward causation in physics. *Turing Church*, 2017.
https://turingchurch.net/racing-worlds-a-visual-model-for-downward-causation-in-physics-55c7452f7756

[Rae 2012] Alastair Rae. *Quantum Physics: Illusion or Reality?* Cambridge University Press, 2012.

[Rucker 2016] Rudy Rucker. *The Lifebox, the Seashell, and the Soul: What Gnarly Computation Taught Me About Ultimate Reality, The Meaning of Life, And How to Be Happy*. Transreal Books, 2016.

[Sommerer 1995] John Sommerer. The End of Classical Determinism. *Johns Hopkins APL Technical Digest*, 1995.

[Stewart 1997] Ian Stewart. *Does God Play Dice?: The New Mathematics of Chaos*. Penguin UK, 1997.

[Stewart 2019] Ian Stewart. *Do Dice Play God?: The Mathematics of Uncertainty*. Basic Books, 2019.

[Svozil 1993] Karl Svozil. *Randomness and Undecidability in Physics*. World Scientific, 1993.

[Svozil 2018] Karl Svozil. *Physical (A)Causality: Determinism, Randomness and Uncaused Events*. Springer, 2018.

[Tél 2006] Tamás Tél, Márton Gruiz. *Chaotic Dynamics: An Introduction Based on Classical Mechanics*. Cambridge University Press, 2006.

[von Neumann 1955] John von Neumann. *Mathematical Foundations of Quantum Mechanics*. Princeton University Press, 1955. (translation of *Mathematische Grundlagen der Quantenmechanik*, Springer, 1932).

CHAPTER 19 - ELIGO, ERGO SUM, ERGO DEUS EST: THE PHYSICS OF FREE WILL AND DIVINE ACTION

Think of a splitting trail in the woods. Are you free to choose which way to go? Common sense and experience say yes. 19th century physics says no. Contemporary physics seems to say perhaps. And what about divine action - the freely willed intervention of God in the world?

In "*Humanity in a Creative Universe*" Kauffman 2016a], polymath biologist and complexity theorist Stuart Kauffman notes that the deterministic universe of 19th century physics is incompatible with free will: In a deterministic universe consciousness, whatever it is, could only observe the predetermined unfolding of the world with a delusion of free agency.

That's not what experience and common sense tell me. They tell me that, yes, I am constrained by circumstances, temperament, memories, emotions and all that, but I have at least some control over my own choices.

Of course common sense could just be wrong in this case. But without free agency, it's difficult to take anything seriously. If I can only write this paragraph exactly like it was predetermined that I would write it, then I could just type random keystrokes and save the time.

It can be argued that freedom to choose is a necessary condition for existence. Not in the cogito (I think) but in the eligo (I choose) lies the certainty of existence, "so that the Cogito, ergo sum (I think, therefore I am) of Descartes becomes an Eligo, ergo sum (I choose, therefore I am)," said Kurt F. Reinhardt in "*The Existentialist Revolt*" [Reinhardt 1960].

Following the existentialists, I'm assuming that free will exists, and wondering about physical models of reality compatible with free will. I'm willing to consider free will as a solid experimental fact. If we accept this premise, we can rule out the models of physical reality that are not compatible with free will.

For example we can rule out: Fully deterministic models where the future is uniquely determined by and predictable from the present (e.g. classical physics before chaos theory); Nondeterministic models entirely driven by pure randomness (e.g. random quantum collapse); Models entirely driven by an external entity (e.g. God makes all decisions).

Quantum physics seems nondeterministic: A quantum system can "freely" choose to settle in one of many possible states. When and how the choice is made isn't clear. According to most quantum physicists, quantum states "collapse" randomly into one of many possible outcomes upon observation, but what observation is and who/what observes is unclear. The collapse seems entirely random.

Randomness is hardly more appealing than determinism: In neither case we have free agency.

But perhaps quantum randomness is not entirely random. An encrypted or optimally compressed message looks like random noise, but isn't really random and can be decoded with appropriate algorithms.

Kauffman argues that the biosphere, and perhaps even aspects of the abiotic universe, evolve in ways that are clearly nondeterministic, and some kind of free will could be part of the very fabric of reality. The Free Will Theorem [Conway 2009] proposed by John Conway (yes, the same Conway of the Game of Life) and Simon Kochen proves that, if we have free will in the sense that our choices are not determined by the past history of the universe, then quantum particles must have their own "free will" as well:

> "Our provocative ascription of free will to elementary particles is deliberate, since our theorem asserts that if experimenters have a certain freedom, then particles have exactly the same kind of freedom. Indeed, it is natural to suppose that this latter freedom is the ultimate explanation of our own."

In other words, elementary collapse events are "atoms" of freely willed action.

Kauffman proposes to consider quantum possibles as real: Not just aspects of our (lack of) knowledge, but "things" that have ontological reality beyond the actual spacetime that we perceive. This is the old concept of "potentia" in Aristotelian philosophy, described by Werner Heisenberg [Heisenberg 1958] as "standing in the middle between the idea of an event and the actual event, a strange kind of physical reality just in the middle between possibility and reality." Kauffman says:

> "The universe is observing what is happening and also able to 'act' nonrandomly and perhaps with intent to change or choose what happens... Mind acausally mediates measurement that converts Possibles to Actuals. Thus: Actuals, Possibles, Mind."

Kaufmann wrote a paper titled "Taking Heisenberg's Potentia Seriously" [Kastner 2017, 2019] with Ruth Kastner and Michael Epperson, both of whom have proposed quantum interpretations compatible with the ontological reality of quantum possibles. Kastner's interpretation [Kastner 2012, 2015, 2019] is a variant of John Cramer's "Transactional Interpretation" [Cramer 2016].

Set in stone? Free will vs. superdeterminism

In physical models of reality compatible with free will, we have at least some control over our own choices. The opposite view is superdeterminism: everything is preset in stone, including your and my "free" choices: We do what we choose, but we can't choose what we choose.

John Bell demonstrated that quantum mechanics rules out models or reality that are both deterministic and local (local means without instant correlations between events in different places). Experiments in the lab agree with Bell. But real deterministic theories have not yet been excluded, explains Nobel laureate Gerard 't Hooft ['t Hooft 2016]:

> "If a theory is deterministic all the way, it implies that not only all observed phenomena, but also the observers themselves are controlled by deterministic laws. The notion that, also the actions by experimenters and observers are controlled by deterministic laws, is called superdeterminism."

Bell said in a *BBC* interview (transcribed in Paul Davies' *"The Ghost in the Atom"* [Davies 1986]):

> "There is a way to escape the inference of superluminal speeds and spooky action at a distance. But it involves absolute determinism in the universe, the complete absence of free will. Suppose the world is super-deterministic, with not just inanimate nature running on behind-the-scenes clockwork, but with our behavior, including our belief that we are free to choose to do one experiment rather than another, absolutely predetermined, including the 'decision' by the experimenter to carry out one set of measurements rather than another, the difficulty disappears. There is no need for a faster than light signal to tell particle A what measurement has been carried out on particle B, because the universe, including particle A, already 'knows' what that measurement, and its outcome, will be."

Superdeterminism escapes the Free Will Theorem of Conway and Kochen: We do NOT have free will (our choices ARE determined by the past history of the universe), and there's no such thing as free will in the universe. In a superdeterministic universe consciousness, whatever that is, can observe the deterministic unfolding of the world, but is unable to make choices. Consciousness is a spectator, or perhaps an actor, but not a screenwriter.

If one doesn't make a fundamental difference in-principle between matter and life (I don't), super-determinism should be called just determinism: Everything is strictly pre-determined by physical laws, and that's it. Thiis is not a spelling error, because I couldn't have chosen to type it right.

My esthetic preference goes to a nondeterministic universe, where genuinely new things happen and we are free agents. But a superdeterministic universe has its own esthetic and emotional appeal as well: If everything is set in stone, then the present includes all information needed to reconstruct the past, and future scientists could find ways to read that information and resurrect the dead.

The esthetic and emotional flaw of superdeterminism is that the present also uniquely determines the future. If I could choose a universe, I would choose one where the past is fixed but the future is not.

Ergo Deus Est

[According to Fred Hoyle], the apparent randomness of quantum events is really nonrandom and driven by a cosmic intelligence. Complex arrangements of matter can decode messages encoded in quantum randomness. In particular, life - a very complex and organized form of matter - can decode and execute these messages.

Interestingly, both Hoyle and Kastner use "advanced waves" that propagate backward in time. Hoyle's cosmic intelligence acts in the infinitely distant future.

In the last chapter of "*What is Life?*" [Schrödinger 1944], Erwin Schrödinger argued that freedom of choice is compatible with physical laws only if all free agents are aspects of a Cosmic Mind that does the choosing.

You know that you are a physical system whose behavior is determined by Nature, but you also know that you are an autonomous agent with free will, able to choose. The only way out of the apparent contradiction is to conclude that the two agents that make the same choice - Nature and you - are one and the same. In other words, all conscious beings are aspects of the same universal entity. In Schrödinger's words:

> "The only possible inference from these two facts is, I think, that I - I in the widest meaning of the word, that is to say, every conscious mind that has ever said or felt 'I' - am the person, if any, who controls the 'motion of the atoms' according to the Laws of Nature."

Schrödinger noted that, in a dream, your consciousness plays not only you, but also other characters. Similarly, a writer's mind plays all the characters in a novel. Perhaps the characters in future forms of literature, not paper books but AI-powered synthetic worlds with multiple storylines, will be conscious entities played by the same multitasking AI, which in this analogy is equivalent to the intelligence of the cosmos.

Many other scientists cited in this book, including Ervin László, Mani Bhaumik, Roger Penrose, and Stuart Hameroff, have speculated on a Cosmic Mind embedded in the fabric of fundamental reality. Kauffman says:

> "... aspects of the entire universe know and nonrandomly act at each measurement among independent or entangled quantum variables. If this arises among entangled quantum variables, they may 'jointly know and decide.' We do not know if there is some whispering form of Cosmic Mind playing a role in the becoming of the universe..."

In a *Scientific American* interview [Horgan 2015], Kauffman said that science and religion could be compatible in some sense, and speculated on "a wildly panpsychist participatory universe."

> "In such a view, measurement anywhere is associated with consciousness and responsible will, and for entangled particles a coordinated version of the above, a kind of 'mind of God'..."

Many scientists entertain similar ideas, but (like Kauffman himself) take a distance from traditional religion and consider the Cosmic Mind as an abstract, non-personal consciousness. But to me it seems very plausible that the mentality of a cosmic ultimate intelligence would contain our own mentality and be, in the words of Olaf Stapledon [Stapledon 1947], "in some sense personal, or at least not less than personal... probably infinitely more than personal."

In his masterpiece "*Star Maker*," [Stapledon] suggests that the Star Maker - God - learns from his creations. Perhaps the "wholly other" impersonal consciousness embedded in the fabric of reality learns from intelligent life and becomes also a personal, caring God.

Kauffman speculated on "a possible panpsychism in which something like cosmic mind or plural minds among entangled quantum variables may be possible" and the possibility of survival after death [Kauffman 2016b]:

> "Far more remotely, something like souls - partly quantum aspects of the living, where quantum biology is now flowering - may persist after death."

In "Life After Death? An Improbable Essay" [Kauffman 2017], Kauffman added:

> "Finally, if at death, quantum entangled variables reflecting the living state in some way can escape the now dead classical body, perhaps souls can exist and can in some remotely conceivable manner, reincarnate."

It's interesting to note how Kauffman tries to take distance from the implications of his ideas. He begins his essay with "I believe nothing of what I shall write. Yet I think that, scientifically, what I shall say is remotely possible," and concludes with "These are very remote possibilities, but not, I think, ruled out scientifically."

In a lesser scientist, this would indicate fear of career-killing ostracism for getting too close to, God forbid, religion. But Kauffman is a top scientist, an 800-pound scientific gorilla who has earned the right to sit wherever he wants. Therefore, I interpret Kauffman's caution as an effort not to alienate those who feel a strong emotional need to reject everything that sounds like religion.

Kauffman himself is wiser. "I wrote '*Reinventing the Sacred*' [Kauffman 2008] as one voice to say, of a natural but emergent biosphere beyond entailing law, here is one sense of God enough for me," he says. "But yet more if the universe is conscious and choosing and we with it. How dare we say no in our arrogance?"

How Does God Play Dice?

In a letter to Max Born [Einstein 2004], Einstein said that quantum nondeterminism "is not yet the real thing."

> "The theory says a lot, but does not really bring us any closer to the secret of the 'old one'. I, at any rate, am convinced that He is not playing at dice."

Einstein wanted a fully deterministic (superdeterministic) universe. Born disagreed, and defended the intrinsic nondeterminism of quantum physics. Born also pointed out that even pre-quantum mathematical physics is nondeterministic [Born 1954], because computing the future with absolute certainty would require specifying the initial conditions (the present) with the unattainable infinite precision of a real number.

[As outlined in the last chapter], it appears that Born was right. Recent research shows that, even in pre-quantum classical physics, the chaotic evolution of strongly fractal dynamical systems is causally open (undetermined in principle).

Using quantum-speak, the path of a dynamical system in a fractally "riddled" region of its phase space can be considered as a superposition of different possible paths, which eventually undergoes a collapse (apparently random, with probabilities instead of certainty) into one specific path.

This analogy suggests the possibility that quantum behavior could emerge from "deterministic" mathematical equations. But these mathematically deterministic equations would allow indeterminate, quantum-like behavior. The pictures of fundamental nondeterminism (or, to use alternative terms, causal openness or open determinism) provided by quantum mechanics and fractal chaos theory - quantum and chaotic collapse - are essentially equivalent.

Using the fractal chaos picture, if a dynamical system starts in a riddled region of its phase space, there's no way to tell, even in principle, to which attraction basin it belongs. The starting point is in a space-filling fat fractal boundary between different attraction basins, and can be thought of as being in all basins, with a potentiality to reach any attractor.

So, let God choose (divine action).

Of course one is tempted to speculate on what it is exactly that God DOES to PUSH the starting point into one specific basin. But the thing is, God doesn't have to push, because the point IS ALREADY THERE as far as we can know.

God doesn't have to spend energy to put the starting point in the right position. God doesn't have to shout, because an imperceptible whisper will do. Whatever it is that God does to choose one of many possible realities, it seems more of a perception than an action.

Think of "My Wife and My Mother-in-Law," an [optical illusion] created by British cartoonist William Ely Hill in 1915 and published in *Puck* magazine with the caption "They are both in this picture - Find them."

You don't have to DO anything substantial, like changing the picture with a pencil, to push a young woman or an old woman into the picture. Both women ARE ALREADY IN THE PICTURE, and you can choose to see one or the other with an insubstantial act of perception, without doing anything to the picture.

In his 1932 book *"The Law of Causality and its Limits"* [Frank 1998], Philipp Frank distinguished between two conceptions of divine action. According to the first, a higher power intervenes in the world by violating natural laws.

> "The other, I should like to say more 'scientific', conception is that it is not in the character of natural laws that they predetermine everything. Rather they leave certain gaps. Under certain circumstances they do not say what definitely has to happen but allow for several possibilities; which of these possibilities comes about depends on that higher power which therefore can intervene without violating laws of nature."

Riddled basins, fractally full of holes that belong to other basins, suggest that [natural laws are riddled with gaps] through which God can act subtly and steer the universe with elegance, without violating any law.

We only know the rational numbers (numbers with arbitrary but finite precision). But God (or a sufficiently advanced intelligence) knows the real numbers, and uses them to play dice. God doesn't throw the dice randomly, but accurately places the dice on the table face up, slipping divine action underneath the laws of nature.

These considerations based on classical chaos theory suggest the possibility that, even if quantum behavior emerges from underlying "deterministic" mathematical laws, nature remains underdetermined, with gaps that leave room for free will and divine action.

It's worth emphasizing that, if the underlying mathematical laws are deterministic in the sense that they don't contain uncertain parts, free will and divine action can be thought of as emerging from inside in some way, as opposed to coming from outside.

Therefore, there's no need to resort to mind/matter dualism. Monism is a viable philosophy, and there might be a self-consistent unified description of mind and matter.

Following Conway and Kochen, the idea comes to mind that perhaps elementary collapse events should not be thought of as results of freely willed action, but as atoms of freely willed action. In other words, free will and divine action don't CAUSE collapse events, but CONSIST OF collapse events. [Something like that, more or less].

Of course this is not a full theory, but an example of what physicist and Christian theologian John Polkinghorne calls thought experiments - "attempts to explore and try out ideas in a simplified way, rather than purporting to be complete solutions to the problem of divine action" [Polkinghorne 2010].

Polkinghorne had previously considered [Polkinghorne 2009] (non)deterministic chaos as the most plausible entry point for divine action through system-level [top-down causation], or active information. In the 2010 book, Polkinghorne limits himself to pointing out that, while we really don't know enough yet to say more, these thought experiments are worthwhile. The plausibility of top-down causation, he says, "demands some form of causal analysis, however tentative, to indicate that there is genuine room for its operation."

> "Interpreting intrinsic unpredictabilities as signs of ontological openness to the operation of other causal principles affords just such necessary room for manoeuvre."

I agree with Polkinghorne. We aren't ready to understand divine action in more detail, but quantum mechanics and fractal chaos theory provide useful templates and directions.

In my thought experiment, God whispers imperceptibly to shape the evolution of the world. This is divine action. The whispers seem random, but only because we don't have the decryption key and aren't yet smart enough to find it.

I think we'll one day develop the ability to whisper ourselves. Some really advanced civilizations out there might already be whispering alongside God.

In the meantime, you and I are whispering along in a more limited way. My whispers have a special influence on the quantum and/or chaotic collapse events in my brain, and the same for you. This is personal free will.

In the book and TV documentary "*The Colours of Infinity*" [Lesmoir-Gordon 2010], starring among others Arthur Clarke, Ian Stewart, and the "father of fractals" Benoît Mandelbrot, mathematician Michael Barnsley says:

> "This is how God created a system, which gave us free will."

In "*Does God Play Dice?*" [Stewart 1997], Ian Stewart notes that the "texture of normal weather patterns" is an attractor for the dynamics of the Earth system, but dynamical systems can possess more than one attractor.

I think a "spontaneous" switch to a better attractor with much gentler weather patterns could be interpreted as divine action, freely willed by God, or ultra-advanced technology indistinguishable from divine action.

Similarly, God, perhaps aided by future cosmic engineers, might one day switch the entire universe to a better attractor, a renewed universe with new forms of matter "arising from the divine transformation of present matter" [Polkinghorne 2010].

In the [reality-as-simulation] picture (which, as I am often emphasizing, is indistinguishable from traditional religion), it makes a lot of sense for the Programmer to design a world riddled with gaps that allow [intervention via a programming interface], without changing the source code.

Notes

[According to Fred Hoyle] See "A for Almighty."

[As outlined in the last chapter] See "There's plenty of room at the bottom."

[intervention via a programming interface] See "Thought experiments in physical theology."

[natural laws are riddled with gaps] See "There's plenty of room at the bottom," "Thought experiments in physical theology."

[optical illusion] See also "United Quantum Consciousness."

[reality-as-simulation] See "Sims City."

[Something like that, more or less] See "Thought experiments in physical theology."

[Stapledon] See "Agnostics, possibilians, and mysterians."

[top-down causation] See "There's plenty of room at the bottom."

References

[Born 1954] Max Born. The statistical interpretation of quantum mechanics. Nobel lecture, 1954.
https://www.nobelprize.org/nobel_prizes/physics/laureates/1954/born-lecture.pdf

[Conway 2009] John Conway, Simon Kochen. The Strong Free Will Theorem. *Notices of the AMS*, 2009.

[Cramer 2016] John Cramer. *The Quantum Handshake: Entanglement, Nonlocality and Transactions*. Springer, 2016.

[Davies 1986] Paul Davies. *The Ghost in the Atom: A Discussion of the Mysteries of Quantum Physics*. Cambridge University Press, 1986.

[Einstein 2004] Albert Einstein, Max Born. *Born-Einstein Letters, 1916-1955: Friendship, Politics and Physics in Uncertain Times*. Palgrave Macmillan, 2004.

[Frank 1998] Philipp Frank. *The Law of Causality and Its Limits*. Springer, 1998.

[Heisenberg 1958] Werner Heisenberg. *Physics and Philosophy: The Revolution in Modern Science*. Harper & Brothers Publishers, 1958.

[Horgan 2015] John Horgan. Scientific Seeker Stuart Kauffman on Free Will, God, ESP and Other Mysteries. *Scientific American*, 2015.
https://blogs.scientificamerican.com/cross-check/scientific-seeker-stuart-kauffman-on-free-will-god-esp-and-other-mysteries/

[Kauffman 2008] Stuart Kauffman. *Reinventing the Sacred: A New View of Science, Reason, and Religion*. Basic Books, 2008.

[Kauffman 2016a] Stuart Kauffman. *Humanity in a Creative Universe*. Oxford University Press, 2016

[Kauffman 2016b] Stuart Kauffman. Cosmic Mind? *Theology and Science*, 2016.

[Kauffman 2017] Stuart Kauffman. Life After Death? An Improbable Essay. *Scientific GOD Journal*, 2017.

[Kastner 2012] Ruth Kastner, *The Transactional Interpretation of Quantum Mechanics: The Reality of Possibility*. Cambridge University Press, 2012.

[Kastner 2015] Ruth Kastner. *Understanding Our Unseen Reality: Solving Quantum Riddles*. Imperial College Press, 2015.

[Kastner 2017] Ruth Kastner, Stuart Kauffman, Michael Epperson. Taking Heisenberg's Potentia Seriously. *International Journal of Quantum Foundations*, 2018. Republished in [Kastner 2019].
https://arxiv.org/abs/1709.03595

[Kastner 2019] Ruth Kastner. *Adventures in Quantumland: Exploring Our Unseen Reality*. World Scientific, 2019.

[Lesmoir-Gordon 2010] Nigel Lesmoir-Gordon (Ed.). *The Colours of Infinity: The Beauty and Power of Fractals*. Springer, 2010.

[Polkinghorne 2009] John Polkinghorne. The Metaphysics of Divine Action. *Philosophy, Science and Divine Action*. Brill, 2009.

[Polkinghorne 2010] John Polkinghorne. *Theology in the Context of Science*. Yale University Press, 2010.

[Reinhardt 1960] Kurt Reinhardt. *The Existentialist Revolt*. Frederick Ungar Publishing, 1960.

[Schrödinger 1944] Erwin Schrödinger. *What Is Life? The Physical Aspect of the Living Cell*. Cambridge University Press, 1944.

[Stapledon 1947] Olaf Stapledon. *The Flames*. Secker and Warburg, 1947.

[Stewart 1997] Ian Stewart. *Does God Play Dice?: The New Mathematics of Chaos*. Penguin UK, 1997.

['t Hooft 2016] Gerard 't Hooft. *The Cellular Automaton Interpretation of Quantum Mechanics*. Springer, 2016.

CHAPTER 20 - INTO THE
DEEP WATERS

I have stolen the title of this chapter from the last chapter of "*The Mysterious Universe*" [Jeans 1930], by James Jeans. I found Jeans' book among my grandfather's books when I was twelve or so, and was enormously impressed. The book is dated, but one thing seems certain: Now, as in 1930,

> "science is not yet in contact with ultimate reality."

Current theories of fundamental physics seem to fail at small scales and high energies (two related concepts).

This is often considered a problem to solve. But we have probed nature only in a small range of scales. Why should our theories continue to work near zero length and infinite energy, which is infinitely far from the laboratory?

Quantum gravity, the quantum theory of gravitation at the Planck scale, remains elusive.

I'll outline some exotic physics, but allow me to start with something simple: Think of water.

Water is described by fluid dynamics, which is mathematically complicated, but we all know what water does, and the equations of fluid dynamics confirm that. For example, waves propagate in water. Low-energy waves move nicely and smoothly, but high-energy waves break in turbulent flow. [All that is in the equations].

But the equations of fluid dynamics don't represent the ultimate reality of water.

Zooming into water, we find that fluid dynamics only works until we approach the microscopic scale of water molecules. Then, the fluid description of water breaks down, and macroscopic concepts (like wetness) cease to be applicable.

For water at microscopic scales, we need the physics of water molecules and their interactions.

Water can boil or freeze, resulting in phases of water - gaseous steam or solid ice - that look very different from the liquid phase. The molecules are still the same though. The difference is in how the molecules get organized. The phase transitions of water can be described accurately enough with a few macroscopic parameters, but explaining what happens requires molecular and statistical physics.

Zooming below the molecular scale, we find that molecules are composed of atoms. Zooming in some more, we find what we currently consider as fundamental matter particles (fermions) and fundamental force carriers (bosons).

Some scientists are persuaded that we'll soon reach the bottom, and find a nice Theory of Everything (ToE) that fits on a T-shirt. Others think that we are still far from the bottom - if, that is, there's a bottom that can be reached.

A Material Vacuum

The term "quantum vacuum" indicates the low-energy ground state of spacetime. But you shouldn't think of the vacuum as empty space where nothing happens.

On the contrary, modern physics suggests that lots of things happen in the quantum vacuum. For example, virtual particles keep popping out of nowhere, temporarily borrowing the energy they need to exist for times too short for the universe to notice. The quantum vacuum shouldn't be thought of as a nothing, but as a complex, dynamic material like turbulent water.

In "*Fantastic Realities*" [Wilczek 2006], Nobel laureate Frank Wilczek describes the concept of a "material," superconducting vacuum. Modern physicists "hypothesize that what we perceive as empty space is actually a highly structured medium," Wilczek explains.

> "In fact, as I will elaborate below, we strongly suspect that the world is a multi-layered, multicolored, cosmic superconductor."

A chapter of Wilczek's "*The Lightness of Being*" [Wilczek 2008] is titled "The Multilayered, Multicolored Cosmic Superconductor." Wilczek's exploration continues in "*A Beautiful Question*" [Wilczek 2015]. I highly recommend these three books: Wilczek is a great teacher able to explain the subtlest concepts of modern physics in creative and accessible ways.

Electrons in superconductors organize themselves into "Cooper pairs" that dance around each other with phases aligned in the same direction. Interaction with Cooper pairs slows photons down, making them behave as massive particles. "The equations that describe photons in superconductors are mathematically identical to the equations for a massive particle," explains Wilczek. "Within a superconductor, photons effectively become particles with non-zero mass."

Similarly the Higgs field plays, for electroweak W and Z bosons in empty space, the same role played by Cooper pairs in a superconductor. Interaction with the Higgs field in empty space makes W and Z bosons behave as massive particles, just like photons in superconductors. So, what we perceive as empty space is not so empty.

In fact, the essence of the Higgs mechanism is the idea that "empty space" is filled with a material medium that renders the W and Z bosons massive. "This idea lets us keep the beautiful equations for massless particles, while observing a decent respect for the opinion of reality," explains Wilczek.

> "According to this conception, the basic equations of electroweak theory apply to a (nonexistent) external world of massless particles, within which we happily inhabit a weird superconductor... Something new must be added - the so-called Higgs field. What we call empty space, or vacuum, is filled with a condensate spawned by that field."

Allow me to note that a "nonexistent" external world within which something actually happens seems a contradictory concept. If a world doesn't exist, how can one inhabit a place within that world?

Photons in a superconductor behave like massive particles, but this doesn't mean that massless photons don't exist. On the contrary, the behavior of the effectively massive photons in a superconductor can be derived from more fundamental physics that includes massless photons in empty space.

Similarly, perhaps our physics of particles and fields in empty space could be derived from the more fundamental physics of a hidden "microworld" in which our empty space is some kind of "material system" like the Bose-Einstein (BEC) condensates, superconductors and superfluids studied by condensed matter physicists.

In "*A Beautiful Question*," Wilczek proposes a nice simple metaphor: we are like intelligent fish "immersed in a cosmic ocean, which complicates the observed laws of physics."

Perhaps someday the intelligent fish will gain access to the fundamental physics of the underlying cosmic ocean and its real water molecules, electrons and all that.

In January 2017 Wilczek gave a talk titled "Materiality of a Vacuum" [Wilczek 2017] at Arizona State University (ASU). From the abstract:

> "In modern physics we've discovered that it is very fruitful to regard empty space, or vacuum, as a sort of material, which can have exotic properties, like superconductivity. Conversely, materials can be viewed 'from the inside' as the vacua of alternative worlds, which often have exotic, mind-expanding properties."

Wilczek presented an intriguing speculative metaphor:

> "Life in Siliconia - Intelligent creatures who lived inside silicon, and didn't know any better, might think of their surroundings as the default condition. They would call it vacuum. For them, phonons would be elementary particles. But we know better: the Siliconians live inside a material… We are like the Siliconians. 'Empty space' - our vacuum - is a material. The particles we know, and those we are made of, are minor disturbances within that material."

In other words, our reality emerges from a deeper reality substrate that we don't perceive.

"What our naked senses perceive as empty space turns out to be a riotous environment of virtual particles fluorescing and dying away on extremely small scales of space and time, as well as fog-like fields and condensates, which permeate all space and dictate the properties of elementary particles," reads a summary of Wilczek's talk and following discussion with organizer Lawrence Krauss [Harth 2017]. Humans could "become creators of new universes, through the intelligent manipulation of material substrates."

The Microphysics Of The Quantum Vacuum: Superfluid Vacuum Theory

Before moving to more exotic forms of matter, let's stay in water some more. Suppose the intelligent fish imagined by Wilczek are blind and can only perceive the world through sound waves in water.

Studying physics, the fish might discover "event horizons" from which sound waves can't get out, and call the regions hidden by event horizons "black holes."

From our vantage point, we see that these "sonic black holes" are formed when the water flows faster than the local speed of sound. This is a simple example of how fundamental physics, in this case Einstein's general relativity, can be simulated in a material, in this case water.

Sound and elastic waves in a material can be thought of as composed by "phonons," just like light and electromagnetic waves in empty space can be thought of as composed by photons. The quantum behavior of both photons and phonons is described by quantum field theories.

Phonons are "quasiparticles" that represent collective excitations of elastic vibration fields in a material substrate. For a simple mental picture, think of atoms arranged in a fixed grid and vibrating around the nodes of the grid. The phonons are vibrations propagating in the grid with particle-like motion.

Quasiparticles in a material take a life of their own, behave like particles, and can give the underlying material properties like superconductivity and superfluidity.

For another suggestive mental picture, think of groups of dancers that move around a dance floor, each group behaving as a single coherent unit. Imagine looking at the dance floor from a vantage point above the dancers. If you take off your glasses and half-close your eyes to blur your visions, you are blind to the individual dancers and see only the groups. Similarly, perhaps we (and our current scientific instruments) see only collective motions of sub-microscopic stuff that we don't perceive directly.

Quasiparticles can be described by quantum field theories just like ordinary particles, with observable physical effects. At the same time, quasiparticles seem "less real" than ordinary particles. In "*Quasiparticles*" [Kaganov 1979], M. I. Kaganov and I. M. Lifshits explain that:

> "Real particles exist, i. e. move, collide, turn into one another, and form more or less complicated structures (from atoms to crystals) in empty space, while quasiparticles exist, i. e. move, etc., inside macroscopic systems, which are constructions of real particles."

At the same time, quasiparticles are real enough because they behave and interact, mathematically and in the laboratory, just like particles. "The phonons are true particles living in the crystal," notes Giuseppe Vitiello [Vitiello 2001]. "We observe them indeed in the scattering with neutrons... Thus phonons propagate over the whole system as the elastic waves do and therefore act as long range correlation among the atoms (for this reason they also called collective modes)."

In "*The Trouble with Physics*," [Smolin 2006], a provocative look at current problems in theoretical physics, Lee Smolin praises emergent models of fundamental physics:

> "These are models developed by condensed-matter physicists, such as Robert Laughlin, of Stanford; Grigori Volovik, of the Helsinki University of Technology; and Xiao-Gang Wen, of MIT... These men are master craftsmen and seers both. Having done perhaps the best and most consequential normal science of the last few decades, they decided to try their hands at the deep problems of quantum gravity..."

In his 1998 Nobel Prize lecture [Laughlin 1998], Laughlin defines an emergent phenomenon as a low-energy collective effect of huge numbers of particles that cannot be deduced from the microscopic equations of motion in a rigorous way and that disappears completely when the system is taken apart, and suggests that "most of the important outstanding problems in physics are emergent in nature, including particularly quantum gravity." See also Laughlin's book "*A Different Universe*" [Laughlin 2006].

Phonons in metals are emergent in nature. Smolin explains that a phonon is not an elementary particle: "It is certainly not one of the particles that make up the metal, for it exists only by virtue of the collective motion of huge numbers of the particles that do make up the metal."

> "But a phonon is a particle just the same. It has all the properties of a particle. It has mass, it has momentum, it carries energy. It behaves precisely the way quantum mechanics says a particle should behave. We say that a phonon is an emergent particle."

In radically emergent models of fundamental physics, all known particles are emergent particles. All known fields, symmetries, and physical laws, including Einstein's relativity and quantum mechanics, emerge from new, more fundamental physics in an underlying substrate.

In "*Artificial Black Holes*" [Volovik 2002] and "*The Universe in a Helium Droplet*" [Volovik 2003], Grigory Volovik shows that quasiparticles in condensed matter substrates, such as superfluid liquid helium, follow mathematical equations, derived from the microscopic physics of the substrate, very similar to those that describe real particles in empty space.

These mathematical equations contain "effective fields" that play a role similar to real fundamental fields in empty space, including metric fields analogous to Einstein's gravitational field in empty space.

In fact, phenomena that bear a strong resemblance to the fundamental physics of the standard model and gravity (or, following Wilczek, the "core theory" [Wilczek 2008, 2015]) arise in condensed matter systems. The similarities can be leveraged to explore fundamental physics, both theoretically and in the laboratory. For example, sonic black holes can be induced in condensed matter to simulate astrophysical black holes. Though no known condensed matter system reproduces exactly the particles and fields of the core theory, superfluid liquid helium comes close.

Exotic forms of "quantum matter," where the effects of [quantum entanglement] are manifest on the macroscopic scale, giving rise to physical properties that are intrinsically quantum, could shed light on fundamental physics near and beyond the Planck scale.

Volovik's "*The Universe in a Helium Droplet*" is an awesome book. "Provides a splendid guide into this mostly unexplored wilderness of emergent particle physics and cosmology," notes James D. Bjorken, co-author of one of the standard textbooks on quantum field theory, in the foreword. "Physicists will find a wealth of powerful and entertaining ideas in this highly original work," said Wilczek.

Volovik's book shows how fundamental connections between particle physics, cosmology, and condensed matter physics allow us "to simulate the least understood features of high energy physics and cosmology: the properties of the quantum vacuum (also called ether, spacetime foam, quantum foam, Planck medium, etc.)" with condensed matter systems described by known microphysics.

Volovik suggests that the core theory might be an effective field theory valid only at low energies, and break down at high energies and small scales approaching the Planck scale. The particles and fields of the core theory might be quasiparticles and effective fields in a "superfluid vacuum" - a superfluid state of matter in an underlying, more fundamental "trans-Planckian" microscopic world, which we don't perceive.

Near and beyond the Planck scale, the core theory should be replaced by a more accurate theory of the unknown microphysics of the trans-Planckian world.

Relativistic quantum field theory, according to Volovik, "is an emergent phenomenon arising as a fixed point in the low-energy corner of the physical vacuum whose nature is inaccessible from the effective theory." Gravity, both classical and quantum, and the Standard Model are not fundamental: Both are "effective field theories which are not applicable at small length scales where the 'microscopic' physics of a vacuum becomes important."

> "We hope that condensed matter can show us possible routes from our present low-energy corner of the effective theory to the 'microscopic' physics at Planckian and trans-Planckian energies... Our ultimate goal is to reveal the still unknown structure of the ether (the quantum vacuum) using our experience with quantum liquids."

This research program makes, I think, a lot of sense.

The analogy with effective field theories of low-energy phenomena in condensed matter suggests that the detailed microphysics of the ether could be "lost in translation" to currently observable physics. In fact, in condensed matter physics, the role of the microscopic (atomic) structure of a substance "is only to choose among different universality classes," explains Volovik.

> "Once the universality class is determined, the low-energy properties of the condensed matter system are completely described by the effective theory, and the information on the underlying microscopic physics is lost."

Quasiparticles in a superfluid "perceive the homogeneous ground state of condensed matter as an empty space - a vacuum - since they do not scatter on atoms comprising this vacuum state," says Volovik. Therefore, a hypothetical inner observer in the superfluid, made of low-energy quasiparticles, "views the smooth inhomogeneity of the underlying liquid as the effective spacetime in which free quasiparticles move along geodesics... At the same time the vacuum of the liquid, which looks empty for an inner observer, is not 'empty' at all: it is densely populated with the underlying atoms."

The idea comes to mind that perhaps we are in the same situation of Volovik's inner observers, still blind to a deeper reality, to be unveiled by future science.

It's worth noting that, if Einstein's spacetime metric, which is the structure of space and time, emerges from the yet unknown trans-Planckian microphysics of the quantum vacuum, then space and time are also emergent. It follows that the space and time of fundamental microphysics might be other than the space and time that we perceive.

In particular, Einstein's special relativity might be valid only at low energies and large scales. Just like the maximum possible speed of phonons and quasiparticles in condensed matter is lower (often much lower) than the maximum possible speed in our world (the speed of light in vacuum), near-instant signals much faster than our light might propagate in the sub-microscopic trans-Planckian world.

Mind And The Quantum Vacuum

Many scientists are persuaded that quantum physics doesn't play a critical role in the biological brain. Other scientists are persuaded that consciousness couldn't arise in non-quantum systems - it can only arise in macroscopic quantum systems that exhibit coherent, long-range collective quantum behavior.

In 1967 Luigi Maria Ricciardi and Hiroomi Umezawa proposed a "quantum brain" mathematical model based on quantum field theory [Ricciardi 1967]. More recent developments of the model are explored in "*My Double Unveiled*" [Vitiello 2001].

The quantum brain model of Ricciardi and Umezawa, and related models proposed by Karl Pribram, Stuart Hameroff, Roger Penrose, and other scientists, link consciousness and memory to quantum fields in the biological brain. Umezawa said [Vitiello 2009]:

> "In any material in condensed matter physics any particular information is carried by certain ordered pattern maintained by certain long range correlation mediated by massless quanta. It looked to me that this is the only way to memorize some information; memory is a printed pattern of order supported by long range correlations."

In the section "Biological Order" of "*Advanced Field Theory*" [Umezawa 1993], Umezawa notes that, since known macroscopic ordered states of matter are controlled by quantum fields, it seems natural to assume that macroscopic ordered states in biological systems and memories in the brain are also controlled by quantum fields.

"To develop such a theory we need some degrees of freedom which play the role analogous to that of electrons in metals," says Umezawa. "Since these degrees of freedom are some quantum fields residing in the cortex, we may call them corticons. We need also other boson degrees of freedom to act like photons in metals..."

According to the Orchestrated Objective Reduction (Orch-OR) theory of consciousness proposed by Stuart Hameroff and Roger Penrose, biological consciousness lives in coherent, collective quantum processes in the cytoskeleton and microtubules of neurons and living cells. A preliminary version of the Orch-OR theory is sketched in Hameroff's book "*Ultimate Computing*" [Hameroff 1987] and Penrose's book "*Shadows of the Mind*" [Penrose 1994]. More recent development are explained in a 2014 review article by both scientists, titled "Consciousness in the universe: A review of the 'Orch OR' theory" [Hameroff 2014].

These models of consciousness and memory in the biological brain, based on condensed matter physics, suggest that consciousness and memory could also be found in other condensed matter systems, such as superconductors and superfluids, with equivalent long range coherent collective modes that depend critically on quantum dynamics.

We are only aware of carbon-based organic life in the Earth's biosphere, but we can't assume that all forms of life in the universe must be similar to life as we know it. Surely nature is much more imaginative than that.

Following the analysis in the privately circulated book "*Xenology*" [Freitas 1979], by molecular nanotechnology pioneer Robert Freitas, Clément Vidal analyzes possible metabolisms of living systems based on all four fundamental physical forces in "*The beginning and the end*" [Vidal 2014].

Following astrophysicist [Fred Hoyle] (in "*The Black Cloud*" [Hoyle 2010] and related non-fiction works), Freitas and Vidal speculate on living creatures operating on the principles of plasma physics rather than the usual molecular biochemistry. Super-exotic life forms based on non-electromagnetic interactions such as quantum chromodynamics could exist in high-energy environments such as neutron stars, and even more exotic life could exist in black holes.

If so, some intelligent minds in the universe could run on condensed matter substrates much faster and more powerful than the biological brain. Such minds might emerge spontaneously, or be engineered by intelligent biological beings, which then might choose to port themselves to new substrates.

From here, another leap of imagination brings us to thinking of intelligent life based directly on quantum vacuum physics. Could mind-genesis, consciousness, memory and intelligence happen in the bare fabric of spacetime?

The condensed matter analogies outlined in the previous section seem to suggest that the answer is yes. Taken together, the quantum brain model, its generalization to non-biological macroscopic quantum systems like superfluids, and the idea that the quantum vacuum itself behaves like a superfluid, give some plausibility to the idea that intelligent minds could exist in a dynamic substrate consisting of nothing but the bare fabric of spacetime, the quantum vacuum itself.

Hameroff and Penrose suggest that "proto-conscious events," acting in accordance with physical laws not yet fully understood, happen and have always happened everywhere in the universe. These proto-conscious events can be considered as "atoms of consciousness" in some sense, but are too simple to be associated with subjective conscious experiences. However, proto-conscious events in living brains can condensate coherently and give rise to complex forms of consciousness. This, according to Hameroff and Penrose, is what happens in our own brains.

David Bohm and Basil Hiley [Bohm 1993] are persuaded "that in some sense a rudimentary mind-like quality is present even at the level of particle physics, and that as we go to subtler levels, this mind-like quality becomes stronger and more developed."

In a 2005 interview titled "The Quantum Mind of Stuart Hameroff" [Taylor 2005], Stuart Hameroff said:

> "There is a universal proto-conscious mind which we access, and can influence us. But it actually exists at the fundamental level of the universe, at the Planck scale…"

Other thinkers consider the idea of consciousness and intelligence woven throughout the fabric of reality, but keep a cautious distance and are careful to speak only of "proto" consciousness and intelligence.

But why just proto-intelligence? Why not super-intelligence?

Perhaps proto-minds arise spontaneously like Boltzmann Brains from quantum vacuum fluctuations, and then evolution takes over.

In the delightful short story "The Gravity Mine," republished in the "*Phase Space*" collection [Baxter 2003], science fiction author Stephen Baxter imagines the birth of a Boltzmann Brain:

"At last - by chance - the quantum tangle emitted a knot of structure sufficiently complex to reflect, not just the universe outside, but its own inner state. It was a spark of consciousness... born from the random quantum flexing of a singularity... it gathered more data, developed sophistication."

Now, since quantum fields are much faster than biology, the evolution of proto-intelligence into super-intelligence might be much faster than biological evolution, and give rise to God-like entities soon after emerging: Not billions of years, but billionths of a second.

Intelligent beings made of the ultra-fast quantum stuff of virtual particles and fluctuations in the quantum vacuum - think of huge neural networks that operate at light speed, or even faster if the substrate of quantum fluctuations works with nonlocal physics - would think and live much faster than us.

It follows that the evolution of proto-minds could rapidly result in the emergence of a cosmic society of super-intelligent beings, adapted to their quantum spacetime habitat and able to engineer it with near-omnipotence.

Intelligent Quantum Fields And Dancing Qubits

Summarizing the core ideas proposed so far in this chapter, the brain might be macroscopic quantum matter, other forms of quantum matter might be able to support the conscious mind, and intelligence might arise and thrive in the ultimate fundamental substrate, the quantum vacuum.

Related ideas have been recently proposed by other scientists as well.

Physicist Jae-Weon Lee, best known for a theory that relates gravity to quantum information, argues that quantum fields can memorize information and learn like deep neural networks (DNN) [Lee 2017]:

> "Our conjecture also implies a surprising possibility that the quantum fields, and hence matter in the universe, can memorize information and even can perform self-learning to some extent like DNN in a way consistent with the Strong Church-Turing thesis."

Jae-Weon Lee's paper builds upon previous results [Mehta 2014] that established an exact mathematical analogy between deep learning, a branch of Artificial Intelligence (AI), and renormalization group methods used in condensed matter physics and quantum field theory.

Deep learning, a group of AI methods based on multi-layered neural networks where computing neurons in one layer send intermediate processing results to the higher level layer and so forth, has achieved spectacular results in early AI applications.

For example, in deep neural networks for face recognition, low level layers learn how to combine pixels to detect edges, mid level layers learn how to combine edges to detect facial features such as ears and eyes, and high level layers learn how to combine facial features to identify a person. All that, with only limited supervision by human operators.

Researchers at the Canadian Institute for Advanced Research (CIFAR) and Google AI experts recently suggested [Guerguiev 2017] that deep learning could be at work in the brain: "Our own brains may use the same sort of algorithms that they use in AI," said a CIFAR scientist. For a current background on deep learning, see the recent book "*Deep Learning*" [Goodfellow 2016], co-authored by CIFAR AI experts.

The renormalization group is a systematic theoretical framework and a set of elegant (and often effective) mathematical methods to correlate physical models at different scales and build effective field theories, valid at large scales, by coarse-graining models valid at smaller scales and smoothing out irrelevant fluctuations.

Phase space trajectories connect states of a physical system at different times. Similarly, renormalization flows connect theoretical models of a physical system at different scales, with scale-dependent parameters.

There are interesting analogies with fractal geometry [Mandelbrot 1982]: The length of a fractal curve is scale-dependent, and can go to infinity as the observation scale goes to zero. But a non-integer fractal dimension permits recovering measurable lengths by, sort of, absorbing the infinities, like renormalization methods in particle physics.

Renormalization group methods are used all over theoretical physics, for example in condensed matter physics and quantum field theory. The 1979 *Scientific American* article "Problems in Physics with Many Scales of Length" [Wilson 1979], by Nobel laureate Ken Wilson, is still the best conceptual introduction to the renormalization group that I am aware of.

Most recent textbooks emphasize technical aspects and gloss over conceptual aspects, leaving the reader with the impression that the renormalization group is just a mathematical method that works.

But it can be argued that useful mathematical models must have something to do with what nature actually does.

Physical models reflect what nature does to compute the future from the past. Similarly, renormalization group methods reflect what nature does to compute large scale observable phenomena from the underlying small scale microphysics. Only relevant features of the underlying microphysics contribute, while irrelevant features are "lost in translation."

And what does nature do? Perhaps both nature and deep neural networks use an information bottleneck procedure to compress noisy data "as much as possible while preserving information about what the data represent" [Wolchover 2017]. Note that this is a good description of language as well.

Both deep learning and renormalization group methods extract "important" features from underlying data, filtering out irrelevant microscopic noise. Thinking of the universe as an unfolding computation (or a [simulation]), this computational strategy seems to make a lot of sense.

The quantum brain and superfluid vacuum research programs of Umezawa and Volovik, both inspired by frontier condensed matter physics, aimed respectively at unveiling the material basis of memory and intelligence in the brain, and shedding light on the still unknown sub-microscopic structure of the quantum vacuum, using analogies with quantum liquids, are also advancing.

Max Tegmark is persuaded that it makes sense to consider consciousness as a state of matter. His paper "Consciousness as a State of Matter" [Tegmark 2015] "generalizes Giulio Tononi's integrated information framework [Tononi 2012, Koch 2019] for neural-network-based consciousness to arbitrary quantum system."

Matter optimized for information processing is often dubbed "computronium." Similarly, Tegmark defines "perceptronium" as matter "that feels subjectively self-aware" (in later works [Tegmark 2017], Tegmark prefers using the term "sentronium" for sentient matter). [Tononi's "phi," a measure of self-awareness in arbitrary physical systems], marks the difference between perceptronium and unaware matter.

The brain is a complex physical system able to support consciousness. Perhaps the brain's perceptronium is "quantum matter" in which quantum physics and long-range entanglement play a strong, critical role. Other physical systems able to support consciousness might include plasmas, superfluids, and perhaps the fabric of spacetime itself, the quantum vacuum.

In fact, the quantum vacuum can be thought of as quantum matter, and the known particles of the standard model as excitations in a deeper substrate. Tegmark explains:

> "As motivation for this emergence approach, note that a large number of quasiparticles have been observed such as phonons, holes, magnons, rotons, plasmons and polarons, which are known not to be fundamental particles, but instead mere excita-

tions in some underlying substrate. This raises the question of whether our standard model particles may be quasiparticles as well.

It has been shown that this is indeed a possibility for photons, electrons and quarks, and perhaps even for gravitons, with the substrate being nothing more than a set of qubits without any space or other additional structure."

Qubits, the building blocks of quantum computers, are units of quantum information [Nielsen 2010]. While a classical bit can be in two states (zero and one), a qubit can be in a quantum superposition of zero and one states, for example spin-up and spin-down. Quantum computers work with entangled qubits.

Tegmark recommends Seth Lloyd's book *"Programming the Universe"* [Lloyd 2006] and a research paper by Zheng-Cheng Gu and Xiao-Gang Wen [Gu 2012] for an introduction to the "it's all qubits" approach.

The textbook *"Quantum Information Meets Quantum Matter"* [Zeng 2019], co-authored by Wen, explains:

"In the emergence approach, we view space as an ocean of qubits, i.e. a qubit ether. The empty space (the vacuum) corresponds to the ground state of the qubit ether, and the elementary particles (that form the matter) correspond to the excitations of the qubit ether."

In some forms of "topological" quantum matter, the patterns woven by dancing particles are more complex than the simple dancing patterns of Cooper pairs in superconductors. "Topological orders correspond to global correlated dances, which are produced by various local dancing rules," explain Wen and co-authors. "The global correlated dances produce patterns of long-range entanglement, which is the microscopic origin of topological order."

According to Wen and co-authors, known matter and fields such as electrons and light are excitations of a "string-net condensed state" of the qubit ether. The string-net model has parallels with "Loop Quantum Gravity" [Rovelli 2014], one of the currently leading approaches to developing a quantum theory of gravity.

"According to Wen, the quantum vacuum is a string-net liquid," reads Ervin László's summary of Wen's research [László 2014]. "Particles are entangled excitations - 'whirlpools' - in the space-filling string-net liquid."

If quantum vacuum fields can process information in mind-like ways, and since quantum fields are much denser and faster than the forms of matter we work with, then the quantum vacuum can be thought of as ultra-high performance computronium.

Similarly, according to Lloyd [Lloyd 2006], quantum computers can simulate (or process, which is essentially the same thing) physics with optimal efficiency. Therefore, quantum computers are a form of computronium, and the universe can be thought of as a quantum computer. It seems to plausibly follow that the qubit ether might be the ultimate form of ultra-high performance computronium.

Besides that, we can think of the "bedrock of reality" of quantum fields and/or the qubit ether as self-aware perceptronium. While computronium is not necessarily perceptronium, it seems plausible that ultimate ultra-high performance computronium should also be perceptronium.

Thinking of quantum fields and string-nets in the qubit ether as ultra-high performance computronium and self-aware perceptronium, we can imagine self-aware entities in the quantum vacuum, and super-intelligent God-like beings that live in, and [control], the bedrock of reality.

Down Into The Fractal Depths

If reality as we know it emerges from a deeper reality, the idea comes to mind that there might be an even deeper reality beneath that, and so forth. Perhaps there's no Theory of Everything (ToE) that can be found, and reality is a fractal with infinite depth.

Smooth (continuous and differentiable) curves and surfaces become locally flat if you zoom-in deep enough. But fractals are always rough at all scales, and you can zoom-in a fractal forever.

In his seminal book "*The Fractal Geometry of Nature*" [Mandelbrot 1982] Benoît Mandelbrot mentioned "a new fractal wrinkle to the presentation of quantum mechanics."

> "Feynman & Hibbs 1965 notes that the typical path of a quantum mechanical particle is continuous and nondifferentiable, and many authors observe similarities between Brownian and quantum-mechanical motions (see, for example, Nelson 1966 and references herein). Inspired by these parallels and by my early Essays, Abbot & Wise 1980 shows that the observed path of a particle in quantum mechanics is a fractal curve with D=2. The analogy is interesting, at least pedagogically."

Here D is the fractal dimension, a generalization of the concept of dimension that can have non-integer values and describe fractals.

A moderately rough fractal curve has fractal dimension D higher than 1. The boundary of the Mandelbrot set is a super-rough fractal curve with D=2, more like a surface than a curve.

Perhaps the analogy is more than pedagogical. [Perhaps the fabric of spacetime has a fractal structure]. The similarity between quantum paths and fractals seems to indicate that fundamental reality itself has a fractal structure.

The caption of Fig. 7-1 in "*Quantum Mechanics and Path Integrals*" [Feynman 2010] reads: "Typical paths of a quantum-mechanical particle are highly irregular on a fine scale, as shown in the sketch… In other words, the paths are nondifferentiable."

In 1980, after the introduction of Mandelbrot's fractal geometry, the observed path of a particle in quantum mechanics was shown to be a fractal curve with dimension 2 [Kröger 2000].

It's often thought that quantum particle paths (trajectories) are undefined. The double slit experiment, which according to Feynman encompasses all that is "mysterious" in quantum physics, is often taken as a demonstration that quantum particles are not "real particles" with clearly defined trajectories. But quantum mechanics can be formulated in terms of fractal paths similar to the stochastic (random) Brownian motion of particles suspended in a fluid, first explained mathematically by Einstein.

Stochastic mechanics, an approach to quantum mechanics pioneered by Edward Nelson [Nelson 1967, 1985], treats quantum particles as driven by Brownian-like quantum fluctuations. Nelson proposed a detailed mathematical model of quantum fluctuations based on a purely stochastic process, which seems to reproduce the results of standard quantum mechanics. However, Nelson didn't propose a physical model for the origin of the quantum fluctuations.

Perhaps quantum particles are really suspended in some kind of sub-quantum "fluid" and relentlessly bombarded and kicked around by the sub-quantum "particles" of this fluid. This is similar to Einstein's explanation of Brownian motion, which is what eventually persuaded physicists of the reality of atoms and molecules. Similarly, reality could be deeper than current physical models.

The plausibility of these ideas is confirmed by recent findings showing that quantum-like behavior can be reproduced in classical fluids and explained by classical (non-quantum) fluid dynamics. In fact, fluid droplets bouncing on a vibrating fluid bath move with a striking similarity to quantum behavior [Bush 2015a, 2015b, [Ananthaswamy 2018, Stewart 2019].

This has boosted the popularity of the "pilot-wave" theories of quantum motion that have been proposed since the 1920s by quantum physicists, notably Louis de Broglie and David Bohm [Bricmont 2016, Smolin 2019]. The idea comes to mind that quantum particles could be driven by sub-quantum microphysics.

Stochastic mechanics is nonlocal (it needs instantaneous correlations between remote particles), which troubled Nelson himself. But since standard quantum mechanics is nonlocal, any theory that reproduces the results of standard quantum mechanics must be nonlocal. In a 2012 review paper [Nelson 2012], Nelson noted that stochastic mechanics could be "an approximation to a correct theory of quantum mechanics as emergent."

"But what is the correct theory?"

It seems to me plausible that the emergent physics research programs of Laughlin, Volovik and Wen, outlined earlier in this chapter, could permit developing a correct theory of quantum mechanics as emergent. Perhaps quantum particles are relentlessly kicked around by sub-quantum processes in the material vacuum, which could be the source of the quantum fluctuations in Nelson's stochastic mechanics.

Volovik concludes "*The Universe in a Helium Droplet*" [Volovik 2003] by noting that the theory outlined in the book is not complete because quantum mechanics is still fundamental. "It is the only ingredient which does not emerge in condensed matter."

"However, in exploring the quantum liquids with Fermi points, we are probably on the right track toward understanding the properties of the quantum vacuum and the origin of quantum mechanics."

Perhaps a theory of quantum fluctuations, or even a new formulation of quantum mechanics itself, could be derived from the microphysics of the quantum vacuum. Emergent quantum theories could shed light on important unresolved issues, but I don't expect new theories to explain away quantum weirdness and recover the conceptual simplicity of 19th century physics. In particular, as outlined in the previous chapters, I expect new physics to remain causally open, with plenty of room at the bottom for [free will and divine action].

This approach can easily accommodate nonlocality: The speed of light in vacuum is higher (often much higher) than the maximum speed of quasiparticles and collective excitations in a material substrate. Similarly, unseen signals could propagate much faster than "our" speed of light in the sub-quantum ether, resulting in quantum fluctuations that seem instantaneously correlated.

Suppose future scientists find a good theory of the microphysics of the quantum vacuum, one that explains quantum mechanics and the core theory in one shot. Would that be a final theory?

Not necessarily. The new theory could be unable to explain all experimental evidence. Remember that theoretical and experimental science advance together and, by the time a new theory is developed that is able to explain all known experimental facts, new experimental facts inaccessible to previous scientists could challenge the new theory...

And so forth.

Perhaps there is no such thing as ultimate fundamental reality, but a fractal reality with unexpected novelty at all scales. In "Defense of a modest scientific realism" (a chapter in "*Beyond the Hoax*" [Sokal 2008]), Alain Sokal (yes, the Sokal of Sokal hoax fame) and Jean Bricmont outline a "renormalization-group view of the world" and suggest that perhaps there are "theories all the way down," linked by renormalization flows.

Xiao-Gang Wen, who as noted earlier in this chapter views spacetime as an ocean of qubits (a qubit ether), paraphrased the Chinese classic "*Dao de jing*" as [Wen 2004]:

> "The physical theory that can be formulated cannot be the final ultimate theory. The classification that can be implemented cannot classify everything. The unformulatable ultimate theory does exist and governs the creation of the universe. The formulated theories describe the matter we see every day."

Perhaps reality is a mathematical fractal with unexpected structure and novelty at all scales, which just go on forever.

Many mystics believe in supernatural phenomena beyond the reach of science. Many ultra-rationalists believe in a soon to be found ToE that will explain all that happens in the universe with a few elegant formulas. I think they are both wrong: nothing is beyond the reach of science, but Shakespeare's "There are more things in heaven and earth, Horatio, than are dreamt of in your philosophy" may remain true forever.

You can count up to any number, and there will still be infinite numbers beyond. Similarly, our scientific understanding of the universe might grow without bonds, but always find new fractal depths of unexplained phenomena, to be explored by future scientists. "If it turns out there is a simple ultimate law which explains everything, so be it, that would be very nice to discover," said Richard Feynman [Feynman 2005]. "If it turns out it's like an onion with millions of layers and we're just sick and tired of looking at the layers, then that's the way it is."

Perhaps Feynman's onion with millions of layers is really an onion with an infinite number of layers, and we will always find new things to explore and understand.

Perhaps ultimate reality, including consciousness and God, can only be found at the unattainable bottom of an infinite fractal zoom. Thinking of this, a zoom in the Mandelbrot set will blow your mind.

Notes

[All that is in the equations] It's worth noting that the Navier-Stokes equations of fluid dynamics and the nature of turbulence still present unresolved challenges and problems [Lemarie-Rieusset 2016].

[control] See "Eligo, ergo sum, ergo Deus est," "Thought experiments in physical theology."

[free will and divine action] See "Eligo, ergo sum, ergo Deus est," "Thought experiments in physical theology."

[Fred Hoyle] See "A for Almighty."

[Perhaps the fabric of spacetime has a fractal structure] See for example the approach of Laurent Nottale [Nottale 1993, 2011]. I have the impression that, while having some good ideas, Nottale promoted his ideas in unorthodox ways that other scientists didn't like, and pushed his ideas too far trying to develop a ToE. I guess that, if Nottale had limited himself to publish specific results and small steps in top physics journals, his ideas would have been better received.

[quantum entanglement] See "Exotic space, mysterious time, magic quantum."

[Simulation] See "Sims City."

[Tononi's "phi," a measure of self-awareness in arbitrary physical systems] See "In the beginning was the field."

References

[Ananthaswamy 2018] Anil Ananthaswamy. *Through Two Doors at Once: The Elegant Experiment That Captures the Enigma of Our Quantum Reality*. Dutton, 2018.

[Baxter 2003] Stephen Baxter. *Phase Space: Stories from the Manifold and Elsewhere*. Voyager, 2003.

[Bohm 1993] David Bohm, Basil Hiley. *The undivided universe: An ontological interpretation of quantum theory*. Routledge, 1993.

[Bricmont 2016] Jean Bricmont. *Making Sense of Quantum Mechanics*. Springer, 2016.

[Bush 2015a] John Bush. Pilot-Wave Hydrodynamics. *Annual Review of Fluid Mechanics*, 2015.

[Bush 2015b] John Bush. The New Wave of Pilot-Wave Theory. *Physics Today*, 2015.

[Feynman 2005] Richard P. Feynman. *The Pleasure of Finding Things Out: The Best Short Works of Richard P. Feynman*. Basic Books, 2005.

[Freitas 1979] Robert Freitas. *Xenology: An Introduction to the Scientific Study of Extraterrestrial Life, Intelligence, and Civilization*. Xenology Research Institute, 1979. http://www.xenology.info/Xeno.htm

[Feynman 2010], Richard P. Feynman, Albert R Hibbs. *Quantum Mechanics and Path Integrals*. Dover, 2010.

[Goodfellow 2016] Ian Goodfellow, Yoshua Bengio, Aaron Courville. *Deep Learning*. MIT Press, 2016.

[Gu 2012] Zheng-Cheng Gu, Xiao-Gang Wen. Emergence of helicity ±2 modes (gravitons) from qubit models. *Nuclear Physics B*, 2012.

[Hameroff 1987] Stuart R. Hameroff. *Ultimate Computing: Biomolecular Consciousness and NanoTechnology*. Elsevier, 1987.

[Hameroff 2014] Stuart R. Hameroff, Roger Penrose. Consciousness in the universe: A review of the 'Orch OR' theory. *Physics of Life Reviews*, 2014.

[Harth 2017] Richard Harth. Finding nothing: A conversation with Nobel laureate Frank Wilczek. https://asunow.asu.edu/20170208-finding-nothing-conversation-frank-wilczek

[Hoyle 2010] Fred Hoyle. *The Black Cloud*. Penguin Classics, 2010. (First published by Heinemann, 1957).

[Kaganov 1979] M. I. Kaganov, I. M. Lifshits. *Quasiparticles: Ideas and principles of solid state quantum physics*. Mir publishers, 1979.

[Koch 2019] Christof Koch. *The Feeling of Life Itself: Why Consciousness Is Widespread but Can't Be Computed*. MIT Press, 2019.

[Kröger 2000] H. Kröger. Fractal geometry in quantum mechanics, field theory and spin systems. *Physics Reports*, 2000.

[Jeans 1930] James Jeans. *The Mysterious Universe*. Cambridge University Press, 1930.

[Laughlin 1998] Robert Laughlin. Fractional Quantization. Nobel Lecture, 2006. https://www.nobelprize.org/nobel_prizes/physics/laureates/1998/laughlin-lecture.pdf

[Laughlin 2006] Robert Laughlin. *A Different Universe: Reinventing Physics from the Bottom Down*. Basic Books, 2006.

[László 2014] Ervin László. *The Self-Actualizing Cosmos: The Akasha Revolution in Science and Human Consciousness*. Inner Traditions, 2014.

[Lee 2017] Jae-Weon Lee. Quantum fields as deep learning. *arXiv*, 2017. https://arxiv.org/abs/1708.07408

[Lemarie-Rieusset 2016] Pierre Gilles Lemarie-Rieusset. *The Navier-Stokes Problem in the 21st Century*. CRC Press, 2016.

[Lloyd 2006] Seth Lloyd. *Programming the Universe: A Quantum Computer Scientist Takes On the Cosmos*. Alfred A. Knopf, 2006.

[Mandelbrot 1982] Benoît Mandelbrot. *The Fractal Geometry of Nature*. W. H. Freeman and Co., 1982.

[Mehta 2014] Pankaj Mehta, David J. Schwab. An exact mapping between the Variational Renormalization Group and Deep Learning. *arXiv*, 2014. https://arxiv.org/abs/1410.3831

[Nelson 1967] Edward Nelson. *Dynamical Theories of Brownian Motion*. Princeton University Press, 1967.

[Nelson 1985] Edward Nelson. *Quantum Fluctuations*. Princeton University Press, 1985.

[Nelson 2012] Edward Nelson. Review of stochastic mechanics. *Journal of Physics: Conference Series*, 2012.

[Nielsen 2010] Michael Nielsen, Isaac Chuang. *Quantum Computation and Quantum Information: 10th Anniversary Edition*. Cambridge University Press, 2010.

[Nottale 1993] Laurent Nottale. *Fractal Space-Time And Microphysics: Towards A Theory Of Scale Relativity*. World Scientific, 1993.

[Nottale 2011] Laurent Nottale. *Scale Relativity and Fractal Space-Time: A New Approach to Unifying Relativity and Quantum Mechanics*. Imperial College Press, 2011.

[Penrose 1994] Roger Penrose. *Shadows of the Mind*. Oxford University Press, 1994.

[Ricciardi 1967] L. M. Ricciardi, H. Umezawa. Brain and physics of many body problems. *Kybernetik*, 1967.

[Rovelli 2014] Carlo Rovelli. *Covariant Loop Quantum Gravity: An Elementary Introduction to Quantum Gravity and Spinfoam Theory*. Cambridge University Press, 2014.

[Smolin 2006] Lee Smolin. *The Trouble with Physics: The Rise of String Theory, the Fall of a Science, and What Comes Next*. Houghton Mifflin Harcourt, 2006.

[Smolin 2019] Lee Smolin. *Einstein's Unfinished Revolution: The Search for What Lies Beyond the Quantum*. Penguin, 2019.

[Sokal 2008] Alain Sokal. *Beyond the Hoax: Science, Philosophy, and Culture*. Oxford University

Press, 2008.

[Stewart 2019] Ian Stewart. *Do Dice Play God?: The Mathematics of Uncertainty*. Basic Books, 2019.

[Taylor 2005] Greg Taylor. The Quantum Mind of Stuart Hameroff. *The Daily Grail*, 2005.
https://www.dailygrail.com/2005/01/the-quantum-mind-of-stuart-hameroff/

[Tegmark 2015] Max Tegmark. Consciousness as a state of matter. *Chaos, Solitons & Fractals*, 2015.
https://arxiv.org/abs/1401.1219

[Tegmark 2017] Max Tegmark. *Life 3.0: Being Human in the Age of Artificial Intelligence*. Knopf, 2017.

[Tononi 2012] Giulio Tononi. *Phi: A Voyage from the Brain to the Soul*. Pantheon, 2012.

[Umezawa 1993] Hiroomi Umezawa. *Advanced Field Theory: Micro, Macro, and Thermal Physics*. AIP Press, 1993.

[Vidal 2014] Clément Vidal. *The beginning and the end: the meaning of life in a cosmological perspective*. Springer, 2014.

[Vitiello 2001] Giuseppe Vitiello. *My Double Unveiled: The dissipative quantum model of brain*. John Benjamins Publishing Company, 2001.

[Vitiello 2009] Giuseppe Vitiello. Coherent States, Fractals and Brain Waves. *New Mathematics and Natural Computation*, 2009.

[Volovik 2002] Mario Novello, Matt Visser, G. E. Volovik (Editors). *Artificial Black Holes*. World Scientific Publishing Company, 2002.

[Volovik 2003] G. E. Volovik. *The Universe in a Helium Droplet*. Clarendon Press, 2003. Oxford University Press, 2009.

[Wen 2004] Xiao-Gang Wen. *Quantum Field Theory of Many-body Systems: From the Origin of Sound to an Origin of Light and Electrons*. Oxford University Press, 2004.

[Wilczek 2006] Frank Wilczek. *Fantastic Realities: 49 Mind Journeys And a Trip to Stockholm*. World Scientific Publishing Company, 2006.

[Wilczek 2008] Frank Wilczek. *The Lightness of Being: Mass, Ether, and the Unification of Forces*. Basic Books, 2008.

[Wilczek 2015] Frank Wilczek. *A Beautiful Question: Finding Nature's Deep Design*. Penguin Press, 2015.

[Wilczek 2017] Frank Wilczek, Lawrence Krauss. Lecture: Materiality of a Vacuum.
https://origins.asu.edu/events/materiality-vacuum

[Wilson 1979] Kenneth G. Wilson. Problems in Physics with Many Scales of Length. *Scientific American*, 1979.
https://websites.pmc.ucsc.edu/~wrs/Project/2014-summer%20seminar/Renorm/Wilson-many%20scales-Sci%20Am-79.pdf

[Wolchover 2017] Natalie Wolchover. New Theory Cracks Open the Black Box of Deep Learning. *Quanta Magazine*, 2017.

https://www.quantamagazine.org/new-theory-cracks-open-the-black-box-of-deep-learning-20170921/

[Zeng 2019] Bei Zeng, Xie Chen, Duan-Lu Zhou, Xiao-Gang Wen. *Quantum Information Meets Quantum Matter: From Quantum Entanglement to Topological Phase of Many-Body Systems.* Springer, 2019.
Open access draft: https://arxiv.org/abs/1508.02595

CHAPTER 21 - THOUGHT EXPERIMENTS IN PHYSICAL THEOLOGY

Elaborating on the ideas presented so far, and in particular on [the previous three chapters], in this chapter I sketch a physical theology framework. I am not proposing this as a scientific theory, but as a rough sketch, or as a template, or as a [thought experiment in the sense of Polkinghorne].

I have cited the work of several top mainstream scientists, and I am pretty sure that many of them wouldn't like my admittedly wild speculations. I think it's safe to assume that many of them would strongly object to their name being used to promote scientific theology, and the essential compatibility of science and religion.

So here's a disclaimer: My sources can't be blamed for my wild & weird speculations on frontier science and theology. But I think the spiritual and theological implications of their work are evident for those who want to see.

In radically emergent models of fundamental physics, all known particles are emergent particles. All known fields, symmetries, and physical laws, including Einstein's relativity and quantum mechanics, emerge from new, more fundamental physics in an underlying substrate.

[Following Grigori Volovik and Xiao-Gang Wen (and Nikola Tesla)], "ether" seems an appropriate name for the fundamental substrate. Volovik says [Volovik 2003]:

> "According to the modern view the elementary particles (electrons, neutrinos, quarks, etc.) are excitations of some more fundamental medium called the quantum vacuum. This is the new ether of the 21st century."

Wen speaks of "qubit ether," but let's dispense with the new and qubit qualifiers. Ether is a good name, with solid scientific and philosophical precedents.

It's often said that Albert Einstein's 1905 paper on special relativity eliminated the ether from physics. But in later works Einstein introduced a "cosmological constant" to balance the equations of general relativity. Though eventually dismissed by Einstein, the cosmological constant reappears in today's physics as the energy density of the ether.

I like these emergent models of fundamental physics because they are physical, permit reasoning by analogy with known material systems like superfluids that can be studied in the lab, and are flexible enough to leave room for spiritual and theological speculations.

According to Einstein's special relativity, the speed of light in vacuum is the same for all inertial observers (Lorentz symmetry). But a Lorentz symmetry for the speed of sound can emerge in a superfluid, Wen explains [Wen 2013], if the clock and ruler are made by low energy phonons.

In other words, inner observers in the superfluid would think that the speed of sound is a fundamental speed limit. But we know that the speed of light in our vacuum is much higher than the speed of sound in the superfluid. Similarly, influences in the ether might propagate much faster than the speed of light in our vacuum. The idea comes to mind that future ether engineering might permit faster-than-light communications and travel.

Metric fields analogous to the gravitational field in empty space, which according to Einstein is the structure of our spacetime, emerge in condensed matter systems. Similarly, our space and time themselves might emerge from the physics of the ether, opening the way to space-time engineering and "time magic" (self-consistent causal loops in time, time scanning, perhaps even time travel and all that).

Quantum mechanics itself might emerge from chaotic dynamical systems in the ether. The underlying dynamics would be nonlocal and causally open. In fact, even in classical (non-quantum) physics, the chaotic evolution of strongly fractal dynamical systems is causally open (undetermined in principle).

Using quantum-speak, the path of a dynamical system in a fractally "riddled" region of its phase space can be considered as a superposition of different possible paths, which eventually undergoes a collapse (apparently random, with probabilities instead of certainty) to one specific path.

This analogy suggests the possibility that quantum behavior could emerge from "deterministic" mathematical equations for the underlying ether physics. But these mathematically deterministic equations would allow indeterminate, quantum-like behavior.

The Planck scale and beyond, which is currently considered as a no-go zone for physics, could be accessible to new ether physics. The ether could be a continuum described by continuous mathematical models, with differential geometry extended to fractal geometry.

Once the physics of chaos and nonlocality in the ether is better understood, quantum ether engineering might permit controlling fundamental processes in the universe.

There are speculations that the biological brain could be "quantum matter" able to support the thinking and feeling mind through long-range quantum coherence. According to radically emergent models of fundamental physics, the ether also exhibits long-range coherent behavior.

Recent research suggests that quantum fields (ether fields) could process information in mind-like ways. Since ether fields are much denser and faster than familiar forms of matter, we can think of the ether as ultra-high performance computronium and self-aware perceptronium.

Therefore, we can imagine self-aware, intelligent life in the ether. Some of these beings could be super-intelligent, God-like Minds able to control the universe (divine action) through ultimate ether engineering and "quantum/chaos magic."

Let's go back to the possibility, mentioned above in the context of classical (non-quantum) chaos theory, that quantum behavior could emerge from "deterministic" mathematical equations for the underlying ether physics. If so, how can the divine Minds, and smaller minds like you and me, make freely willed choices? Where do the apparently random inputs needed to actualize one of several possible outcomes come from?

A possible answer is that, if the underlying mathematical laws are deterministic in the sense that they don't contain uncertain parts, [free will and divine action can be thought of as emerging from inside in some way], as opposed to coming from outside.

If so, there's no need to resort to mind/matter dualism. Monism is a viable philosophy, and there might be a self-consistent unified description of mind and matter.

Another possibility is an infinite regress. Beneath the ether there might be a deeper ether, and so forth with turtles all the way down in an infinite fractal zoom. In this case, the origin of freely willed choices is pushed down to the infinitely far, unattainable bottom.

Yet another possibility is that freely willed choices really come from outside, which brings us straight into [simulation] hypothesis territory. Or, since it's really the same thing, into traditional dualistic theology territory. However, in the following I'll stick to monism and argue that a material formulation of the simulation hypothesis can be integrated in this framework.

In any case, I am persuaded that intelligent organic life forms like current humankind can learn much more and earn a place in the community of God-like Minds. If there is an absolute God, we'll become cosmic engineers in God's control room. If needed, we'll start exploring deeper turtles on the way down. Eventually, we'll re-engineer the universe and resurrect the dead, achieving [the Cosmist vision of Nikolai Fedorov].

The parallels between these ideas and traditional religions are clear and evident for those who want to see. My message is that, if you want to believe in [the cosmological core of your religion] without abandoning the scientific worldview, yes you can.

A Cloud Computing Universe: Resurrection, Afterlife, And God

Mani Bhaumik is persuaded that awareness is present in the ether, and individual consciousness is but a reflection of the spirit that pervades the universe, encoded in ether fields. He says that this is a modern scientific formulation of "the Vedic concept that all conscious beings are aspects of the same universal entity" [Bhaumik 2014], and adds that:

> This "cosmic awareness would be a likely origin of our own consciousness, perhaps through some process like resonance or entanglement occurring in our brains." Consciousness "would be manifest when the individual brain's quantum state is in resonance with the cosmic potentiality of consciousness."

Human-level consciousness and personal memories might be coarse-grained versions of the cosmic awareness and memory fields in the ether, linked to the latter by renormalization flows.

If so, we live in a cloud computing universe.

I am typing these words using Google Drive. This book is being composed using a personal device, and can be read using a personal device, but it really lives in Google's computing cloud. Similarly, consciousness is out there in the cosmic computing cloud, and your memories are also out there, auto-updated in real time.

I am persuaded that there is no such thing as "my consciousness" or "your consciousness." There is just consciousness, which is best thought of as a state of matter that is realized in the biological brain but also in the ether itself, and [consciousness + your memories = you]. In the cloud computing universe, the ether is the hardware that runs the cloud, consciousness is part of the system software of the cloud, and memories are dynamically stored in the cloud.

Stuart Hameroff speculated on the possible survival of personal consciousness after death [Taylor 2005]:

> "Under normal circumstances consciousness occurs in the fundamental level of spacetime geometry confined in the brain. But when the metabolism driving quantum coherence (in microtubules) is lost, the quantum information leaks out to the spacetime geometry in the universe at large. Being holographic and entangled it doesn't dissipate. Hence consciousness (or dream-like subconsciousness) can persist."

But, in the cloud computing universe, consciousness and your quantum information don't need to leak out to the spacetime geometry, because they have always been there.

The cloud computing universe allows for technological resurrection: Future technology will permit retrieving your memories stored in the ether, and uploading you to the future by re-instantiating you in a new perceptronium substrate.

Perhaps our descendants will also find ways to upload human consciousness directly to the cosmic computing cloud, re-instantiating people as thinking and feeling ether fields.

But there are also other possibilities, because the cosmic cloud runs on ultra-high performance computronium and self-aware perceptronium: The cosmic cloud is alive, self-aware, and superintelligent. Allow me to use a shorter and simpler name for the conscious, superintelligent cosmic cloud: I'll call the cloud "God."

God has access to your memories, which are stored in the ether.

After you die, God can continue to run your memories in low-power mode, granting you peaceful dreams until you come back to fully awake consciousness. God can also fully re-instantiate you in a cloud afterlife (aka Heaven).

Reincarnation without memories is automatically granted, since all consciousness is one and the same. But God (or future tech) can grant access to your memories to another personal stream of consciousness. This would be reincarnation with some memories of a previous life.

Eventually, God (or future tech) can engineer a new and better physical world (a new "renormalized" large-scale world built on top of the ether) and resurrect everyone there. This new Kingdom thing seems like a big cosmic engineering project, and perhaps God will recruit us as helpers.

God might have emerged from ultra-fast physical processes in the ether shortly after the beginning of the universe, or later, or not yet. But when God emerges doesn't matter that much.

Wen and co-authors suggest [Zeng 2019] that spacetime geometry itself is "an emergent phenomenon that appears only at long distances," derivable from the (yet unknown) microphysics of the ether. Similarly, Volovik argues that Einstein's metric, the fabric of spacetime, emerges from the microphysics of the ether.

Therefore, a God that controls fundamental physical processes in the ether can [control] the totality of spacetime, and is able to act anywhere, anytime, including here and now.

God And Jesus In The Plenum

In "Consciousness in the universe" [Hameroff 2014] Stuart Hameroff and Roger Penrose outline the parallels between their theory of quantum consciousness and spiritual approaches that "assume consciousness has been in the universe all along, e.g. as the 'ground of being', 'creator' or component of an omnipresent 'God'."

In "*Code Name God*" [Bhaumik 2018], Mani Bhaumik suggests the idea of an abstract, "divine" intelligence, encoded in quantum fields, woven into the very fabric of space throughout the universe, that spawned the universe and continues to direct how it unfolds.

"*Code Name God*" is also the fascinating autobiography of Bhaumik, an Indian physicist born in a very poor family who became a renowned scientist and a wealthy philanthropist, and then rediscovered his roots in the Indian spiritual tradition.

While Bhaumik is careful not to anthropomorphize the cosmic consciousness, or field, he believes it plays a central role in the universe. "A single field emerged at the origin of the universe, already containing within itself the blueprint of the physical universe, just as a human genome contains the plan for the entire human," reads Bhaumik's creation story. "The single field then unfolded to direct the construction of the universe."

Bhaumik concludes "*Code Name God*" by evoking a power which is encrypted everywhere in the foundation of space itself:

> "It is the power of the one source, the order that underlies and enfolds all others, that unifies all fields and forms, as well as consciousness, and it will not, by now, surprise you to hear my assertion that we call this source by its code name: God."

The consciousness of Bhaumik's God encoded in the fabric of spacetime would likely be very different from ours, a "wholly other" impersonal consciousness embedded in the fabric of reality.

There are interesting parallels with [the Logos], described for example in Robert Wright's "*The Evolution of God*" [Wright 2009]. It's worth noting that the Greek original for "Word" in John 1:1 - "In the beginning was the Word, and the Word was with God, and the Word was God" - is "Logos."

Theologian Stephen L. Harris defines Logos as: "A Greek term meaning both 'word' and 'reason,' used by Greek philosophers to denote the rational principle that creates and informs the universe," and "the principle of cosmic reason, the intelligent force that orders and sustains the universe" [Harris 2010]. Harris notes that the concept of Logos was "amplified by Philo to represent the mediator between God and his material creation," and "adopted and modified by the author of John's Gospel."

> "Human souls are sparks of the divine Logos, which is symbolized by cosmic fire and sometimes associated with a supreme god. In the prologue of John's Gospel, the pre-human Jesus is identified with the Logos, the creative Word of God (John 1:1, 14)."

It's worth noting interesting parallels with [Eastern thinking]. " The sun reflected from millions of globules of water appears to be millions of suns," said Swami Vivekananda [Munshi 2016].

Related ideas in theology also include [Christian] theologian Wolfhart Pannenberg's analysis of the parallels between field concepts in physics and God's spirit that pervades the universe, Pannenberg's reflections of God and time (for both, see for example *"Systematic Theology"* [Pannenberg 1994], Vol. 2), and [Mormon] prophet Joseph Smith's concepts of a material universe where spirit is also material (a more fine and pure form of matter), and an essential continuity between God and the material universe.

Bhaumik's impersonal God resembles the Logos, or the similar concept of Brahman found in Eastern spiritual traditions, more than the personal God of Western religions.

But the spirit of the universe could be more than personal, not less, perhaps "infinitely more than personal" as suggested by Olaf Stapledon [Stapledon 1947], with a human aspect besides the cosmic ones.

Remember [Stapledon]'s suggestion that perhaps God learns from lesser entities: The unfolding cosmos, intelligent life, and we ourselves, can influence and change God, and make It more like us: It becomes Him and Her.

My favorite analogy for this point is based on our own relationships with pets. We are way smarter than dogs, but every dog lover knows that we can choose to "descend" to their mental level and have a meaningful, personal relationship with them.

To [my doggies], I am a big friendly dog. Within limits, I understand my doggies and know how to communicate with them in understandable doggish language.

My doggies can't understand the whole of me, but they can understand an aspect of me, my doggish aspect that I have acquired by watching and interacting with them. I love them, and they can understand my love and love me in return.

Similarly, I am persuaded that Bhaumik's God, Brahman, the Logos, acquires human aspects by watching and interacting with us, becoming a personal, loving and caring God.

Christian transhumanist thinker Micah Redding emphasizes [Redding 2016] that the otherwise transcendent and unknowable God has also human aspects, and this is a key part of Christian theology.

"In the trinitarian doctrine of creation, God the Father creates the world, God the Son is embodied within it, and God the Spirit brings new life out of it," explains Redding. Once "created, the world is not complete until the Son can be incarnated within it. Then it can be experienced from the inside."

> "Then, according to Christian doctrine, God can truly understand us and relate to us as we are."

In Christian theology the Son, Jesus, is the human aspect of God. "Christians believe that God has acted to make the divine nature known in humanly accessible ways, particularly in the life, death and resurrection of Jesus Christ," says physicist and Christian theologian John Polkinghorne [Polkinghorne 2007].

To the question "What will Jesus be like when we meet him in the world to come?," Polkinghorne answers that we must "expect to encounter Jesus as a human figure."

God is able to engineer matter and spacetime with near-omnipotence. But God is also watching you here and now, cares for you, and perhaps helps you now and then. After death, God will resurrect you, and your loved ones.

I'm perfectly aware that many scientists, including many of the scientists cited in this book, are outspoken atheists who find support for their atheism in modern physics. But it's worth noting that others, and I am one of them, find support for belief in the same modern physics. Not support in the sense of proof, but support in the sense of compatibility. Following the speculative science outlined in his book, I am persuaded that God-like Minds exist and have the same properties attributed to the Gods of the world's religions.

[Richard Dawkins], an outspoken atheist, admits [Powell 2011] that God-like entities could (and probably do) exist in the universe, and even more God-like entities could have created the universe from outside as a [simulation] - a concept that is totally indistinguishable from religion.

In an interview [Ross 2009], Nobel laureate Frank Wilczek described his position as "I lost my faith in conventional religion in my early teens but still yearn for some kind of transcendence." He added: "For that, Star Maker may be on the right track," referring to Olaf [Stapledon]'s science fiction (and speculative theology) masterpiece "*Star Maker.*"

Dawkins and Wilczek are open to transcendence, but want to keep far from traditional religions. I am persuaded that the atheism of many scientists is not motivated by science, but rather by personal and political reasons. Some people want to take revenge for having been personally harmed by religion (which is perfectly understandable) and/or are persuaded that organized religion plays a harmful role in society and politics (which is often the case indeed).

But "Religion 2.0" can be perfectly compatible with science, and affirm universal compassion and love.

Let me propose a new name of God. Lots of things happen in ether, aka quantum vacuum, which therefore is really a "plenum," a Latin term that indicates fullness, the opposite of vacuum. According to the considerations above, the plenum is a "Numen" - a Latin term for "divinity."

The terms "plenum" and "Numen" have a common string, "Num," which has been used as a name of God: Num is the high sky creator god of the Nenets, the largest group of Samoyedic people in northern arctic Russia. In "*A Grammar of Tundra Nenets*" [Nikolaeva 2014], Irina Nikolaeva notes that the literal meaning of "Num" is "something like 'sky, weather, universe, god'..."

The serendipity here is too nice to ignore, so to those looking for yet another name of God, a name that reminds of both religion and science, I suggest calling Her / Him / Them "Num." But I am persuaded that all the names that have been given to God, and all the concepts of God found in the world's religions, refer to the same cosmic intelligence.

Intelligent biological life, such as ourselves, might contribute to the emergence of God. Future generations might go to the stars, colonize the universe, develop God-like mastery of space and time, energy and matter, meet and merge with other super-advanced civilizations out there, and eventually find and talk to the deep intelligence of the plenum. The ultimate outcome of this process could be the emergence of the omnipotent and benevolent God.

[Perhaps God will emerge only at the end of time]. But a God that comes to full being and omnipotence at the end of time might, through "time magic," be present and act in the universe at all earlier times, and be the benevolent God of all times.

These entangled concepts of time and causation are beyond current physics and language, and can't be formulated more precisely at this moment. But they suggest that "weird" physical theology could be fully compatible with traditional religions.

Sims City, Lego Redux: A Material Simulation Hypothesis

Let's go back to the idea mentioned in the previous chapter, advanced by Wilczek and Krauss [Harth 2017], that humans could become creators of new universes, through the intelligent manipulation of material substrates.

We have seen that "inner observers" living in condensed matter have been suggested by Grigory Volovik [Volovik 2003], as a metaphor (I guess). But Leonard Susskind is more daring. In a recent paper [Susskind 2017], he imagines artificial condensed matter systems that contain sentient observers:

> Suppose "we construct a large block of matter engineered to have the standard model (without gravity) as its excitations." Is the world in the block real? "Sure it is; the block and its excitations are certainly real, and if the standard model was well simulated it may support observers who could communicate with laboratory observers."

Here "the standard model" is the physics of our world, and Susskind is proposing that we could (in principle) engineer [a material system] to support excitations (think of phonon-like quasiparticles) that correspond exactly to the fundamental particles and quantum fields of our world. Since we emerge from the standard model, it follows that sentient observers could eventually emerge in the material system.

It's refreshing to see a top scientist of Susskind's stature suggesting this idea, which is essentially equivalent to the [simulation] hypothesis. Perhaps we ourselves are observers in "a large block of matter" engineered by "laboratory observers" in a deeper reality?

Susskind's setup is simple: A laboratory where engineers Alice and Bob experiment with condensed matter shells. Their experiments are totally beyond the reach of today's technology, but Susskind seems to think that, if something is feasible in principle, someday it will be doable in practice. I totally agree.

The paper doesn't contain equations, but is addressed to experts in Susskind's league. For example: "The shell has been engineered to be at a quantum critical point, where the excitations are described by a conformal field theory having a holographic bulk dual." Don't worry, a footnote explains it all: "By bulk I mean the AdS-like geometry dual to the CFT."

To understand Susskind's paper you need to know about string theory, general relativity, black holes, wormholes, quantum gravity research, the holographic principle, AdS/CFT duality, ER=EPR, condensed matter physics and whatnot, and you'll have to go through all the references.

To make a long story short, the ER=EPR conjecture roughly says that quantum entangled physical systems are connected by wormholes. AdS/CFT duality roughly means that a quantum field theory without gravity can be equivalent (dual) to a [string theory] with gravity in a spacetime with more dimensions, in the sense that the two theories are different mathematical descriptions of the same physics.

In "*The Black Hole War*" [Susskind 2008], Susskind suggests an analogy for AdS/CFT duality. Imagine "a can of soup" with a two-dimensional surface ("boundary") enclosing a three-dimensional volume ("bulk").

On the outside boundary of the can, we have a two-dimensional quantum field theory of particles and fields that live on the boundary. In the bulk inside, we have a three-dimensional string theory of a soup of matter and energy, including gravitational waves, black holes and whatnot. One interpretation of AdS/CFT duality is that the bulk physics is determined by the boundary physics (holographic principle), but the relationship between the two is symmetric.

There is a correspondence between what happens on the boundary and what happens in the bulk. For example, it turns out that a hot gas of particles and fields on the boundary corresponds to a black hole in the bulk. It also turns out that, when one of two dual theories is strongly coupled (difficult to calculate), the other is weakly coupled (easier to calculate). So one can calculate using the easier theory and translate the results into the language of the more complex theory at the end.

For example, the behavior of a hot quark-gluon plasma in our four-dimensional spacetime is easier to calculate using a higher dimensional dual string theory. The high temperature of the boundary theory "translates into a black hole in the interior description," explains Brian Greene [Greene 2011]. The difficult calculations of the quark-gluon plasma "translate into the response of the black hole's event horizon to particular deformations - a technical but tractable calculation."

"Conservatively, analyzing quarks and gluons by using a higher dimensional theory of strings can be viewed as a potent string-based mathematical trick," notes Greene. "Less conservatively, one can imagine that the higher dimensional string description is, in some yet to be understood way, physically real."

In this example, another universe provides the easiest and most useful (the best) way to calculate what happens in our universe. This seems to suggest, vaguely but intriguingly, that [the simulation hypothesis is a coherent and useful mental picture of reality].

Back to Susskind's paper, the core idea that I want to explore here is that a suitably engineered matter shell might be an artificial universe containing conscious observers.

This is a physical formulation of simulation theology: The simulator (aka God) organizes the universe like we organize a material system to give it desired properties (like superfluidity and superconductivity) and behaviors. God operates in the deeper physical reality of the ether, which we could conceivably gain access to.

The difference with the "conventional" simulation hypothesis is that now the creator is not simulating a new reality in a computer, but building a new world with ethereal Lego blocks. In a theological interpretation of "The Lego Movie" [Redding 2014], Micah Redding emphasizes that the main movie character eventually escape his world of Lego bricks and "finds himself in the real world of children and adults, where Legos are just toys, and his whole life has existed on a table in somebody's basement."

In passing: Susskind is a top physicist and a great teacher (see his highly recommended "Theoretical Minimum" [books and video courses]), and I have an enormous respect for him. He is often described as an atheist. So how do I dare interpreting his work in a theological key? Well, Susskind is actually an agnostic [Susskind 2014]. I think he is a "cultural atheist" and I am fairly sure he wouldn't like what I'm writing, not at all, but his work does have theological implications for those who want to see.

In the following, read "bulk" as an artificial world. Let's go back to Alice and Bob experimenting with condensed matter shells in Susskind's lab:

"The shell has been engineered to be at a quantum critical point, where the excitations are described by a conformal field theory having a holographic bulk dual...

I argue that the bulk with its gravitons, black holes, and bulk observers is just as real as the laboratory itself. It can be probed, entered, measured, and the results communicated to observers in the lab...

From the holographic AdS/CFT correspondence we may assume that observers, perhaps with human-like cognitive abilities, are possible in the bulk."

The observers in the lab (Alice and Bob) and the observers in the bulk can communicate with each other by generating, respectively, excitations in the shell and gravitational waves in the bulk. The observers in the lab could upload their minds to the shell and the bulk:

What if the bulk of such a shell has no observer? "In principle the lab observer can create one by applying appropriate perturbations to the shell," notes Susskind. "In fact there is nothing to prevent her from merging her own quantum state with the shell and entering into the bulk."

It's worth noting that the shell can be engineered to correspond to a bulk where the speed of light (the maximum signal propagation speed) is much less than the speed of light in the lab. If so, Alice and Bob can engineer signals that would appear as faster than light to the bulk observers.

Susskind thinks future advanced quantum computers could permit carrying out these experiments: "Instead of shells supporting conformal field theories, a more practical alternative might be quantum computers simulating the CFTs."

Here Susskind seems to agree with [Seth Lloyd] that a quantum (as opposed to classical) simulation would be indistinguishable from reality, and therefore be fully real. This brings the Lego and computer formulations of the simulation hypothesis back together, but I think it's worth pointing out that the two formulations are separable.

From Elon Musk To Joseph Smith

[According to Elon Musk], it's almost certain that we are living in a computer simulation: We are some advanced version of The Sims. The [simulation] hypothesis - the idea that our reality could be a simulation running in a deeper or higher level of reality - has been elaborated by several scientists and philosophers, notably by Nick Bostrom [Bostrom 2003].

The Mormon Transhumanist Association (MTA) has formulated an explicitly religious version of the simulation hypothesis: "The New God Argument" (NGA) [Cannon 2015], inspired by Bostrom's argument and adapted to Mormon cosmology.

I find the NGA totally awesome. However, it seems to me that Bostrom's formulation of the simulation hypothesis, with an infinite gap between the universe and its creators in a different, higher level reality, is hardly compatible with the key [Mormon] concepts of a material universe where spirit is also material (a more fine and pure form of matter, according to Mormon prophet Joseph Smith), and an essential continuity between God and the material universe.

These aspects of Mormon cosmology strongly resonate with my own ideas. I tend to see God as a super-smart cosmic engineer who works with available resources, as opposed to a "wholly other," infinitely distant metaphysical entity who created the universe out of nothing and rules it from outside.

According to Lincoln Cannon, the NGA relies on the structure of Bostrom's simulation argument but not the mechanism, and is compatible with other creation mechanisms such as "cosmoforming," defined by Bostrom as "the possibility that an advanced civilization with some as-yet unknown technology might be able to induce the creation of baby universes (perhaps expanding into hidden dimensions)." The transposition of the simulation argument to this hypothesis is straightforward, according to Bostrom [Bostrom 2011].

There's also another way to make the NGA fully compatible with Mormon materialism and theology: we just need to extend the definition of "universe" to include the base reality in which our universe is computed. Then, all reality is material and God is a busy engineer who organizes matter in the extended universe.

Here I want to describe a simpler, more self-contained physical model of reality "as a simulation" that, while offering all the benefits of the simulation argument, is more "down to earth" and more compatible with Mormon materialism and theology.

In the King Follett sermon [Bushman 2005], Joseph Smith said:

> "Now, the word create... does not mean to create out of nothing; it means to organize; the same as a man would organize materials and build a ship. Hence we infer that God had materials to organize the world out of chaos - chaotic matter..."

According to Joseph Smith, we live in a clean and simple material universe, not overburdened by metaphysical dualism, and spirit is also material - a more fine and pure form of matter [Bushman 2005]:

> "There is no such thing as immaterial matter. All spirit is matter, but it is more fine or pure, and can only be discerned by purer eyes."

Following Joseph Smith, instead of thinking of a "simulator" in a higher level reality creating our universe out of nothing, I am thinking of an engineer organizing the material reality of this universe, building with "Lego blocks." God organizes the universe like we organize a material system to give it desired properties (like superfluidity and superconductivity) and behaviors, operating in a deeper (deeper, not higher) level of the same physical reality, the ether, which we could conceivably gain access to.

I have argued that super-intelligent consciousness might exist in the ether and organize the reality that we perceive.

If so, the reality that we see is engineered by a super-intelligent entity in a deeper reality that we don't see - which is the simulation hypothesis. Here I'm trying to move beyond naive formulations of the simulation hypothesis and suggest a more physical model: The Mind that dwells in the deeper reality - God - engineers our reality just like we engineer condensed matter systems with desired properties.

We are learning how to control condensed matter systems like superconductors and superfluids, and future advances could permit to precisely control individual excitations. It is conceivable that future technology could permit creating condensed matter systems ("worlds") that, as suggested by Susskind, contain self-aware, intelligent beings. Then we could upload these beings to our world, or they could figure out how to upload themselves.

Similarly, God uses ultimate ether physics and engineering to organize and fine-tune our world. Perhaps God uploads us to a new habitat after death, and perhaps we will find out how to upload ourselves, including all those who died in the past (remember that this model allows for spacetime engineering and time magic).

In this material simulation hypothesis, the ether is the computing hardware, and our world (particles, fields, tables, chairs, and we ourselves) plays the role of "data" generated by a "simulation." All important features of the simulation hypothesis, including the possibility of resurrection, are still present, but there is an essential continuity and everything really happens in one and the same material universe.

Let's call the world in Susskind's block of matter "Level 1." Then our world is Level 0, and the ether is Level -1. But why stop there? Perhaps there could be Level -2, Level -3 and so forth, all the way down into the [fractal depths] discussed in the previous chapter.

Vacancy Notice: Cosmic Engineers In God's Control Room

God can be conceived as an infinitely distant metaphysical entity, or as a powerful and friendly cosmic Engineer, way higher than us but not so hopelessly distant, who wants us to help in the cosmic control room. I prefer the second conception.

The first view has the esthetics of a Gothic cathedral. The second view has the esthetics of a space-age control room. We can't understand all that the Engineer does with all those high-tech control panels, but we can understand something and we could learn more, perhaps with some help from the Engineer, who might want us to help in the control room when we are ready.

We are still in the cradle compared with what intelligent life has the potential to become. But we will realize our potential, and become more and more like God. Then, we will earn a place in God's cosmic control room.

I think religions should make this transhumanist concept central to their message.

Enter Joseph Smith, who said the same things (much better) and built a transhumanist religion [Cannon 2015] for the modern age. The Mormon Transhumanist Association (MTA) emphasizes transhumanist concepts that can be easily traced back to Smith's teachings.

God was once like Man, and Man can become like God - or, in the words of Lorenzo Snow [Givens 2014]:

> "As man now is, God once was; as God now is, man may be."

The road to our God-like future is built by scientists and engineers. In his foreword to "*Parallels and Convergences*" [Bushman 2012], Richard Bushman, one of the leading contemporary Mormon scholars, says:

> "The end point of engineering knowledge may be divine knowledge. Mormon theology permits us to think of God and humans as collaborators in bringing to pass the immortality and eternal life of man. Engineers may be preparing the way for humans to act more like gods in managing the world."

God is a friendly cosmic Engineer, who organizes matter and energy, particles and fields in the universe. God wants us to study and eventually master divine knowledge and divine engineering, and work in the cosmic control room when we are ready.

There's a control panel to provide an afterlife. How, we don't know yet. But we'll learn how to operate the resurrection controls, and we'll understand how they work. My best guess is that future technology will permit retrieving personal memories stored in ether fields (or, in other words, in God's memory), and re-instantiating these memories in new self-aware material substrates.

In "*Joseph Smith as Scientist*" [Widtsoe 1908], John Widtsoe defended the compatibility of Mormonism and science. Widtsoe established an analogy between the ether of 19th century physics - a medium that fills empty space - and the Holy Spirit:

> "God, who is a person, filling only a portion of space is, by His power carried by the ether, everywhere present. The ether of science though material is essentially different from the matter composing the elements. So, also, in Mormon theology, is the

Holy Spirit different from the grosser elements."

Modern physics is getting closer to the intuitions of Joseph Smith and those of [apprentice cosmic engineer Nikola Tesla], who said:

All "perceptible matter comes from a primary substance, of a tenuity beyond conception and filling all space - the Akasha or luminiferous ether...

Can Man control this grandest, most awe-inspiring of all processes in nature?...

To create and annihilate material substance, cause it to aggregate in forms according to his desire, would be the supreme manifestation of the power of Man's mind, his most complete triumph over the physical world, his crowning achievement which would place him beside his Creator and fulfill his ultimate destiny."

Tesla makes explicit references to Eastern thinking, but his vision - a pre-transhumanist synthesis of Eastern mysticism and Western can-do engineering spirit - seems to me perfectly compatible with Mormon cosmology as well. I am persuaded that future humans will master ether engineering, and join God in the cosmic control room.

Future ether engineering (or akashic engineering, depending on whether one wants to use Western or Eastern terms, both used by Tesla) could include magic spacetime engineering. In fact, if the gravitational field - which is spacetime in Einstein's general relativity - emerges from the microphysics of the ether, then space and time are not metaphysical entities but physical systems that can be tweaked and organized.

I am persuaded that we will master ether physics, develop spacetime engineering, work in God's control room, and bring the dead back. If fundamental ether physics includes backward causation and self-consistent causal loops in time, a God that comes into full being in our future could still be the God of all spacetime, including here and now. Paraphrasing Widtsoe:

"God, who is a person, filling only a portion of time is, by His power carried by the ether, present at all times."

In other words, if God will emerge from advanced civilizations in the universe - hopefully including ours - in the far future, then God is present here and now.

The Physics Of Infinite Bottlecaps

I said that I prefer to consider God as a powerful and friendly cosmic Engineer, rather than an infinitely distant metaphysical entity. But this mathematical (or metamathical) digression prepares the way for more thought experiments on the possibility and nature of an absolutely infinite, infinitely far, totally unknowable God.

Mathematics is often thought of as disembodied exploration of a higher Platonic world, but an alternative view considers mathematics as empirical evidence: "Two plus two equals four" is nothing more (and nothing less) than an experimental result, and mathematics is the physics of things that can be counted.

In "*A System of Logic*" (1843) John Stuart Mill argued that we discover mathematical facts by empirical research [Balaguer 2014]: "All numbers must be numbers of something: there are no such things as numbers in the abstract. Ten must mean ten bodies, or ten sounds, or ten beatings of the pulse." Mills considered "two and one is equal to three" as an assertion respecting objects: "It affirms that if we put one pebble to two pebbles, those very pebbles are three."

Other thinkers have expressed similar views.

> "Alan picked up two bottlecaps and set them down on the ground. 'Two. One-two. Plus -' He set down two more. 'Another two. One-two. Equals four. One-two-three-four.'"

Here Alan is the fictional Alan Turing in Neal Stephenson's "*Cryptonomicon*" [Stephenson 1999]. Turing is explaining to Lawrence (one of the main characters) that mathematics could be "a sort of physics of bottlecaps."

> "That any mathematical operation you could do on paper, no matter how complicated, could be reduced - in theory, anyway - to messing about with actual physical counters, such as bottlecaps, in the real world."

I tend to consider Mill's empiricism, and positivism, as healthy down-to-earth philosophy.

Physics could be fractal all the way down in a really continuous (or even denser) spacetime, but perhaps no space can be denser than the continuum.

Set theory is the branch of mathematics that includes the study of infinity. I list some of the best set theory books that I'm aware of in the references. In a nutshell:

Georg Cantor's work on infinities started modern set theory by showing that the continuous uncountable infinity of the real numbers is essentially, infinitely larger than the countable infinity of the integer numbers. Cantor proved that the real numbers are uncountable, packed infinitely more densely than the integer and rational numbers, and defined an infinite hierarchy of infinities, the alephs [Rucker 2005], each "more infinite" than the previous.

It's interesting to note that Cantor's infinities, now part of mainstream mathematics, were initially rejected by the mathematicians, but considered with interest by the theologians. See John Barrow's "*The Infinite Book*" [Barrow 2005] for the full story.

To an applied mathematician or physicist, the real numbers seem packed as densely as possible, and it's difficult to conceive of higher infinities.

But think of this: If you didn't know of the real numbers, the rational numbers would also seem packed as densely as possible, because there are infinite rational numbers between any two. Yet, the rational numbers are an infinitesimally small subset of the real numbers, a merely countable infinity equivalent to that of the integer numbers.

To see that, place the rational numbers like m/n on a 2-dimensional grid (0, 1, 2... on both axes), and walk through all rational numbers in a zig-zag path. This walk through the rational numbers one by one, in an order different from the < (less than) ordering, shows that the rational numbers, which seem continuously dense, are really countable: The rational numbers are only as many as the integer numbers.

The real numbers are as many as (technically, "have the cardinality of") the sets of integer numbers (technically, the "power set" of the integer numbers). To see that, represent a real number between zero and one as a string of bits: The bits whose value is 1 define a set of integer numbers, and vice-versa.

One can try and think of numbers packed infinitely more densely than the real numbers. The power set of the real numbers with beth-2 points [Steinhart 2018] (all sets of real numbers, or all bit-valued functions of real numbers) seems a good first candidate.

Try and imagine one of these numbers: A continuous string of bits that you can zoom into forever. In two dimensions, think of fractals like the Mandelbrot set, only much more complex. Black pixels have many ones at the next zoom scale, white pixels have many zeros, and grey pixels are halfway between. Most of these numbers would look like random noise, grey at all zoom scales and indistinguishable from one another.

Contemplating beth-2 could blow up your mind, but then there is beth-3 (the power set of beth-2), and so forth.

Then there are John Conway's surreal numbers [Conway 2001, Rucker 2005], which include the real numbers, as well as all sorts of infinite and infinitesimal numbers, in a class that is too big to even be considered as a set.

The surreal numbers fill all gaps, for example the gap between one and the real numbers smaller than one. Just "as the real numbers fill in the gaps between the integers, the surreal numbers fill in the gaps between the reals," notes Siobhan Roberts in Conway's biography "*Genius at Play*" [Roberts 2015].

Roberts and Conway reveal that Kurt Gödel considered surreal numbers as "the correct theory of infinitesimals," and Martin Kruskal was persuaded that the surreal numbers could find important applications to fundamental physics.

In a new preface [Rucker 2019] for a new 2019 edition of "*Infinity and the Mind*" [Rucker 2005], Rudy Rucker suggests that "the space around us really is transfinite - not only with all the usual real numbers, but with even more points dusted into the infinitesimal gaps."

> "I'm supposing that space is an absolute continuum, jam-packed with surreal numbers. And never mind about atoms or quantum mechanics - you can go on down and down."

In a related science fiction story [Rucker 2012], Rucker suggests that "the Planck length scale isn't a wall. It's a frontier."

However, not all mathematicians are persuaded that high infinities "exist" in the universe of set theory: The real numbers could be as dense as one can get.

Frank Tipler notes [Tipler 2005] that "physics assumes the continuum, but is any higher infinity required?"

Tipler emphasizes that the two greatest mathematical logicians of the 20th century, Kurt Gödel and Paul Cohen, disbelieved in the continuum hypothesis, according to which the real numbers are the next order of infinity (aleph-1) after the integers. Tipler continues:

> "My intuition is the same as Paul Cohen's: that the continuum is larger than any of the alephs. For me, the continuum plays the same role as Cantor's Absolute Infinity."

The most popular axiomatic system for set theory, the Zermelo-Fraenkel (ZF) axiomatic system [Jech 2006], leaves the question undecided and undecidable [Stillwell 2013]. The real numbers could have any of the orders of infinity defined by the theory (the alephs) or be larger than any of the alephs.

The continuum hypothesis conjectures that forming the power set (the set of all subsets) is the only way to move from an order of infinity to the next, so the alephs and the beths are the same thing, and in particular the real numbers have the first order of infinity after the integer numbers (beth-1 and aleph-1 are the same thing).

Gödel and Cohen produced a combined proof [Rucker 2005, Stillwell 2013] that the continuum hypothesis is independent of the ZF axioms: Both the continuum hypothesis and its negation are consistent with the axioms.

There are several proposals for extending ZF with new axioms that would decide the issue, but none is universally accepted. This reminds of non-Euclidean geometries: There are many alternative geometries, all internally consistent, and none can be considered as more "true" than the others.

Therefore, the choice of a geometry must be based on utility rather than "truth." We can and should use Euclidean flat geometry to design a bridge, but we must switch to a non-Euclidean curved geometry, described by Einstein's general relativity, to engineer a black hole (or just an accurate GPS system).

In "*Cryptonomicon*," discussing with Alan, Lawrence defines mathematical truth as:

> "It has to be true because if you do physics with it, it all works out!"

So we are back at the bottlecaps. Mathematical truth is whatever offers a good theoretical model for physics and engineering in the real world.

I suspect that, like for geometry, the open problems in set theory will be eventually settled based on the ability of the theory to offer useful models for fundamental physics. The question is not "How many points are in the real number line?" but "How many points are in the best mathematical spacetime (or whatever) model for fundamental physics?" Whether physics needs infinities higher than the continuum is, I think, an open issue.

The Turing Oracle: Creative Randomness From The Beyond

It seems plausible that our best mathematical models of the world will always include irreducible randomness. I think this implies that God - an absolutely infinite, infinitely far, totally unknowable God - is undecidable but plausible.

In "*Randomness and Undecidability in Physics*" [Svozil 1993] Karl Svozil suggests that randomness in physics might be a signature of mathematical undecidability. Svozil elaborates further in his recent open access book "*Physical (A)Causality*" [Svozil 2018]. The book is very concise, essentially an introduction to a long and comprehensive list of references.

Svozil builds on the works of Kurt Gödel, Alan Turing, Gregory Chaitin and others on (un-) provability, decidability, computability and randomness in mathematics, with parallels in quantum and chaos physics. See [Rucker 2005, 2016] and Gregory Chaitin's "*Meta Math!*" [Chaitin 2005] for a good first introduction to these things.

If a mathematical system is consistent (and powerful enough to deal with integer arithmetic), then it must be incomplete, with unprovable mathematical facts that just happen to be true. In other words, incompleteness is the price that a mathematical system must pay for consistency.

Undecidable possibilities are everywhere. There are incomputable functions and irreducible, incompressible random numbers that can't be finitely described. Almost all real numbers, besides a countable set lost in the continuum, are incomputable and random.

Chaitin defines true randomness as maximally complex, irreducible and incompressible: A random string has no description shorter than itself. The concept of randomness is central in Chaitin's algorithmic information theory [Chaitin 2004], which includes theorems on (un-) provability, decidability, and computability, similar to those of Gödel and Turing.

Comprehension is compression: A useful theory is a strongly compressed description of a set of facts. But any mathematical system must include irreducible, incompressible random facts. To prove this, Chaitin constructs Omega, a real number between zero and one, and shows that only a finite number of bits of Omega can be derived in any given mathematical system. Therefore, Chaitin concludes [Chaitin 2015]:

> "No mathematical theory can capture more than an infinitesimal part of mathematical truth!"

Svozil notes that "several attempts have been made to translate mathematical undecidability into a physical context." In fact, thinking of the universe as a computation based on mathematical axioms and rules (initial conditions and physical laws), it seems that the conclusions of Gödel, Turing and Chaitin must apply. If so, the universe is causally open, there are random facts, and the future doesn't uniquely follow from the past.

Svozil says that his last book [Svozil 2018] has been greatly inspired by, and intends to be an "update" of, Philipp Frank's 1932 book "*The Law of Causality and its Limits*" [Frank 1998]. The concept of gaps in the laws of nature is central in both books. Svozil explains:

> A gap "stands for the incompleteness of the laws of nature, which allow for the occurrence of events without any unique natural (immanent, intrinsic) cause, and for the possible intervention of higher powers."

Svozil admits that current quantum mechanics implies nondeterminism and irreducible randomness. Quantum mechanics "formally operates with an inconsistent set of rules; in particular, pertaining to measurement."

> "As has already been pointed out by von Neumann, the assumption of irreversible measurements contradicts the unitary deterministic evolution of the quantum state."

In other words, randomness is fundamental in quantum physics as we know it, and [the collapse of the quantum wavefunction] is really random.

Chaitin notes that "quantum mechanics demands real intrinsic randomness in the physical world, real unpredictability, and chaos theory even shows that a somewhat milder form of randomness is actually present in classical, deterministic physics, if you believe in infinite precision real numbers."

I think irreducible randomness will still be a feature of future mathematical theories that might replace current quantum mechanics. I also think that the form of randomness found in chaos theory is not "somewhat milder" but as strong as the form of randomness found in quantum mechanics.

Philipp Frank used a circle perfectly balanced on the tip of a triangle in a vertical gravitational field [to illustrate nondeterminism in classical mechanics]. Any neighborhood of this starting point contains both points that will go to the left and points that will go to the right, and therefore the outcome is random.

This simple example can be extended to real [dynamical systems with fractally "riddled" attraction basins] and irreducible "chaotic collapse" events analogous to quantum collapse events. This suggests that randomness is fundamental in classical physics as well, due to the assumed physical existence of the continuum.

Svozil explains:

> "Almost all elements of a continuum are random... Thereby, 'true' irreducible chaos rests on the assumption of the continuum, and the possibility to 'grab' or take (supposedly random with probability 1) one element from the continuum, and recover the (in the limit algorithmically incompressible) 'information' contained therein. That is, if the initial value is computable - that is neither incomputable nor random - then the evolution is not chaotic but merely sensitive to the computable initial value."

Svozil shows that "almost all" real numbers are incomputable. Computable reals are a mere countable infinity in a continuous ocean.

> "That is, if one considers the real unit interval as a 'continuum urn' - one needs the axiom of choice [Jech 2006] in order to 'draw' a general element of this urn, as no computable 'handle' exists to fetch it - then with probability 1 it will be incomputable."

Only an oracle can provide a randomly chosen real number, the value of an incomputable functions, or an unprovable truth. The concept of oracle was introduced by Alan Turing in "Systems of Logic Based on Ordinals" [Turing 1939] as "some unspecified means of solving number-theoretic problems; a kind of oracle as it were." Turing added:

"We shall not go any further into the nature of this oracle apart from saying that it cannot be a machine."

Svozil explains:

"An oracle (if it exists) is conceptualized by an agent capable of a decision or an emanation (such as a random number) which cannot be produced by a universal computer. Again, we take up Frank's conception of a gap by realizing oracles via gaps."

The term "oracle" is often used in computer science to indicate an input channel that drives a computer program by providing information and choices that the program needs. Considering the universe as a computer, an oracle is needed to choose the outcome of quantum or chaotic collapse events, which can't be computed within the universe. Svozil continues:

"Suppose that transcendent agents, interact with a(n) (in)deterministic universe via suitable interfaces. In what follows we shall refer to the transcendental universe as the beyond."

Svozil uses the metaphor of a real-time computer system that receives input from the outside. For example, a game world like Second Life. Human players "are transcendental with respect to the context of the game world, and are subject to their own universe they live in (including the interface)."

"Nevertheless the game world itself is totally deterministic in a very specific way: it allows the player's input from beyond; but other than that it is created by a computation. One may think of a player as a specific sort of indeterministic (with respect to intrinsic means) oracle, or subprogram, or functional library."

Perhaps an agent from the beyond (some call the agent God) steers our world - subtly but purposefully - through an oracle, an application programming interface that allows input from the beyond through fundamental gaps in the natural laws.

Mathematics seems to say, and physics seems to confirm, that the oracle exists and feeds choices to a universe that, left to itself, wouldn't know what to do. The picture that comes to mind is a hugely complex network of linked collapse events all over space and time, purposefully driven by the oracle.

God Is Undecidable But Plausible

Of course, the question is: Is there an agent (God) behind the oracle, or is it all random chance?

It turns out that proving purposeful intervention from the beyond (aka divine action), as opposed to random chance, is "difficult or even impossible," notes Svozil.

> "How can one intrinsically decide between chance on the one hand, and providence, or some agent executing free will through the gap interface, on the other hand?... Both cases - free will of some agent as well as complete chance - express themselves by irreducible intrinsic indeterminism."

Perhaps what appears as random chance in physics is not entirely random, and the apparently random network of collapse events is purposefully driven by God (or, perhaps, the network IS God).

But we are, and will remain, unable to tell, because random chance is indistinguishable from divine action. This seems odd at first, but it grows on you. Put it like this: If you play chess against a much more skilled player, some moves of your opponent seem sort of random to you.

Similarly, superior technologies produce encoded messages that seem indistinguishable from random noise. The actions of an entity that is infinitely smarter than you would seem entirely random to you. In general, except for special cases, randomness is provably unprovable [Chaitin 2007].

Mathematicians can try to escape Gödel by adding new axioms to mathematics. Similarly, future scientists could try to go back to a self-contained universe by including the beyond and its currently unknown natural laws in a new, extended mathematical model of reality.

But Gödel is lurking beyond the beyond: The new mathematical model will also be incomplete, with new gaps and new random facts. Then we'll be forced to keep extending our mathematical models of reality. The beyond will have its own oracle interface to a new beyond, and so forth without end.

Scientific knowledge can and will advance without bounds, but what we can name, prove, compute, and decide will remain a tiny part of a vaster reality.

Chaitin is persuaded that "fundamental questions go back millennia and are never resolved. For example, the tension between the continuous and the discrete, or the tension between the world of ideas (math!) and the real world (physics, biology)."

God is a fundamental question. The hierarchy of beyonds suggests a hierarchy of gods, from finite and perhaps attainable natural gods all the way to the asymptotic, unattainable, absolutely infinite God.

If our mathematical models of reality will always include what appears as random chance, and if random chance is indistinguishable from divine action, then we'll never be able to prove that God exists and acts, but we'll never be able to prove the contrary either. The proposition is undecidable.

But another way of putting this is that our best models of reality are, and will remain, indistinguishable from models of reality that include God and divine action.

This isn't proof of the existence and action of God (I've just said that there can't be a proof, haven't I?), but I think it's a very strong plausibility argument.

The God suggested by this argument is a transcendent entity beyond all comprehension, like the unknowable God of Christian theology and Islam. God controls our reality from outside with continuous interventions, like the hands-on God of Islam.

Serkan Zorba, a physicist and an Islamic thinker, speculates [Zorba 2016b] that the true randomness observed in nature "is a strong indication, if not the 'proof,' of the existence of an infinitely intelligent entity (God)."

"Absolute randomness is a telltale sign of God."

Zorba elaborates further in [Zorba 2016a]. I don't think the randomness argument "proves" divine action. I don't think God can be proven, and I tend not to take alleged "proofs" too seriously, even though Gödel himself proposed one [Fitting 2002].

However, I think the randomness argument does prove that divine action is undecidable but plausible.

While the asymptotic, absolutely infinite God will remain unknowable, I think future humans will know, understand, and achieve intermediate levels of God-likeness. In mathematics, any conceivable property of the unattainable absolute infinity is also a property of an intermediate infinity [Rucker 2005]. Similarly, I am persuaded that future God-like humans will realize all promises of religions, and resurrect the dead.

Notes

[According to Elon Musk] See "Sims City."

[apprentice cosmic engineer Nikola Tesla] The full text of Nikola Tesla's "Man's Greatest Achievement" is reproduced here, in "The quest for Akashic physics and engineering."

[a material system] See "Into the deep waters."

[books and video courses] See Susskind's *Theoretical Minimum* website: http://theoreticalminimum.com/

[Christian] See "Christianity and transhumanism are much closer than you think."

[consciousness + your memories = you] See "Transhumanism" for a more detailed discussion of this point.

[dynamical systems with fractally "riddled" attraction basins] See "There's plenty of room at the bottom," "Eligo, ergo sum, ergo Deus est."

[Eastern thinking] See "The lights of Eastern spirituality."

[Following Grigori Volovik and Xiao-Gang Wen (and Nikola Tesla)] See "Into the deep waters," "The quest for Akashic physics and engineering."

[fractal depths] See "Into the deep waters."

[free will and divine action can be thought of as emerging from inside in some way] See "In the beginning was the field."

[Mormon] See "Man will become like God, say Mormons and transhumanists."

[My doggies] I have only Ricky at this moment. But when I composed an early draft of this chapter my sweet Sacha was still with us, so I decided to leave her here in spirit.

[Perhaps God will emerge only at the end of time] See "A for Almighty," "Omega Point."

[Richard Dawkins] See "Little green Gods."

[Seth Lloyd] See "Into the deep waters."

[simulation] See "Sims City."

[Stapledon] See "Agnostics, possibilians, and mysterians."

[string theory] See "Exotic space, mysterious time, magic quantum."

[the chaotic evolution of strongly fractal dynamical systems is causally open (undetermined in principle)] See "There's plenty of room at the bottom," "Eligo, ergo sum, ergo Deus est."

[the collapse of the quantum wavefunction] See "Exotic space, mysterious time, magic quantum."

[the Cosmist vision of Nikolai Fedorov] See "Knocking on Heaven's door."

[the cosmological core of your religion] See "Turing Church."

[the Logos] See the chapter titled "Logos: The Divine Algorithm" in [Wright 2009].

[the previous three chapters] I recommend reading the previous three chapters before reading this one, which isn't meant to be self-contained. Here I'm just briefly stating my points, see the previous three chapters for supporting arguments and references.

[the simulation hypothesis is a coherent and useful mental picture of reality] See "Sims City," "In the beginning was the field."

[thought experiment in the sense of Polkinghorne] See "Eligo, ergo sum, ergo Deus est."

[to illustrate nondeterminism in classical mechanics] See "There's plenty of room at the bottom."

References

[Balaguer 2014] Mark Balaguer. Mill and the Philosophy of Mathematics: Physicalism and Fictionalism. *Mill's A System of Logic: Critical Appraisals* (Antis Loizides, Ed.) Routledge, 2014.

[Barrow 2005] John Barrow. *The Infinite Book: A Short Guide to the Boundless, Timeless and Endless*. Pantheon Books, 2005.

[Bhaumik 2018] Mani Bhaumik. *Code Name God: The Spiritual Odyssey of a Man of Science*. Penguin, 2018.

[Bhaumik 2014] Mani Bhaumik. Is the Source of Awareness Present in the Quantum Vacuum? In *Interdisciplinary Perspectives on Consciousness and the Self*. Sangeetha Menon, Anindya Sinha, B. V. Sreekantan, Eds. Springer, 2014.

[Bostrom 2003] Nick Bostrom. Are You Living In a Computer Simulation? *Philosophical Quarterly*, 2003.
http://www.simulation-argument.com/simulation.html

[Bostrom 2011] Nick Bostrom. The Simulation Argument FAQ, 2011.
https://www.simulation-argument.com/faq.html

[Bushman 2005] Richard Bushman. *Joseph Smith: Rough Stone Rolling*. Alfred A. Knopf, 2005.

[Bushman 2012] Richard Bushman, Scott A. Howe. *Parallels and Convergences: Mormon Thought and Engineering Vision*. Greg Kofford Books, 2012.

[Cannon 2015] Lincoln Cannon. What is Mormon Transhumanism? *Theology and Science*, 2015.
https://new-god-argument.com/

[Chaitin 2004] Gregory Chaitin. *Algorithmic Information Theory*. Cambridge University Press, 2004.

[Chaitin 2005] Gregory Chaitin. *Meta Math!: The Quest for Omega*. Peter N. Nevraumont Books, 2005.

[Chaitin 2007] Gregory Chaitin. Randomness and mathematical proof. *Thinking about Gödel and Turing: Essays on Complexity, 1970–2007*. World Scientific, 2007.

[Chaitin 2015] Gregory Chaitin. An Algorithmic God. *Inference*, 2015.
https://inference-review.com/article/an-algorithmic-god

[Conway 2001] John Conway. *On Numbers and Games*. A K Peters, 2001.

[Fitting 2002] Melvin Fitting. Types, *Tableaus, and Gödel's God*. Springer, 2002.

[Frank 1998] Philipp Frank. *The Law of Causality and Its Limits*. Springer, 1998.

[Givens 2014] Terryl Givens. *Wrestling the Angel: The Foundations of Mormon Thought: Cosmos, God, Humanity*. Oxford University Press, 2014.

[Greene 2011] Brian Greene. *The Hidden Reality: Parallel Universes and the Deep Laws of the Cosmos*. Alfred A. Knopf, 2011.

[Hameroff 2014] Stuart Hameroff, Roger Penrose. Consciousness in the universe: A review of the 'Orch OR' theory. *Physics of Life Reviews*, 2014.

[Harris 2010] Stephen Harris. *Understanding the Bible*. McGraw-Hill Education, 2010.

[Harth 2017] Richard Harth. Finding nothing: A conversation with Nobel laureate Frank Wilczek.
https://asunow.asu.edu/20170208-finding-nothing-conversation-frank-wilczek

[Jech 2006] Thomas Jech. *Set Theory: The Third Millennium Edition, revised and expanded.* Springer, 2006.

[Munshi 2016] Nupur Munshi. A Tribute to Swami Vivekananda. *Turing Church*, 2016.
http://turingchurch.com/2016/01/12/a-tribute-to-swami-vivekananda/

[Nikolaeva 2014] Irina Nikolaeva. *A Grammar of Tundra Nenets*. De Gruyter Mouton, 2014.

[Pannenberg 1994] Wolfhart Pannenberg. *Systematic Theology*. T & T Clark, 1988–1994.

[Polkinghorne 2007] John Polkinghorne. *Exploring Reality: The Intertwining of Science and Religion*. Yale University Press, 2007.

[Powell 2011] Michael Powell. A Knack for Bashing Orthodoxy. *The New York Times*, 2011.
http://www.nytimes.com/2011/09/20/science/20dawkins.html

[Redding 2014] Micah Redding. The Theology of the Lego Movie, 2014.
http://micahredding.com/blog/2014/05/27/theology-lego-movie

[Redding 2016] Micah Redding. The Creative Process of God, 2018.
http://micahredding.com/blog/the-creative-process-of-god

[Roberts 2015] Siobhan Roberts. *Genius At Play: The Curious Mind of John Horton Conway*. Bloomsbury, 2015.

[Ross 2009] Greg Ross. Scientists' Nightstand: Frank Wilczek. *American Scientist*, 2009.
https://web.archive.org/web/20170621161911/https://www.americanscientist.org/bookshelf/pub/scientists-nightstand-frank-wilczek

[Rucker 2005] Rudy Rucker. *Infinity and the Mind: The Science and Philosophy of the Infinite*. Princeton University Press, 2005.

[Rucker 2012] Rudy Rucker. Jack and the Aktuals, or, Physical Applications of Transfinite Set Theory. In *Complete Stories*. Transreal Press, 2012.

[Rucker 2016] Rudy Rucker. *The Lifebox, the Seashell, and the Soul: What Gnarly Computation Taught Me About Ultimate Reality, The Meaning of Life, And How to Be Happy*. Transreal Books, 2016.

[Rucker 2019] Rudy Rucker. Our World is an Absolute Continuum, 2019.
http://www.rudyrucker.com/blog/2019/07/27/our-world-is-an-absolute-continuum-new-infinity-the-mind/

[Stapledon 1947] Olaf Stapledon. *The Flames*. Secker and Warburg, 1947.

[Steinhart 2018] Eric Steinhart. *More Precisely: The Math You Need to Do Philosophy*. Broadview Press, 2018.

[Stephenson 1999] Neal Stephenson. *Cryptonomicon*. Avon, 1999.

[Stillwell 2013] John Stillwell. *The Real Numbers: An Introduction to Set Theory and Analysis.* Springer, 2013.

[Susskind 2008] Leonard Susskind. *The Black Hole War: My Battle with Stephen Hawking to Make the World Safe for Quantum Mechanics.* Little, Brown and Company, 2008.

[Susskind 2014] Leonard Susskind. Arguments for Agnosticism? *Closer to Truth*, 2014. https://www.youtube.com/watch?v=eeIxHqtB_B8

[Susskind 2017] Leonard Susskind. Dear Qubitzers, GR=QM. *arXiv*, 2017. https://arxiv.org/abs/1708.03040

[Svozil 1993] Karl Svozil. *Randomness and Undecidability in Physics.* World Scientific, 1993.

[Svozil 2018] Karl Svozil. *Physical (A)Causality: Determinism, Randomness and Uncaused Events.* Springer, 2018.

[Taylor 2005] Greg Taylor. The Quantum Mind of Stuart Hameroff. *The Daily Grail*, 2005. https://www.dailygrail.com/2005/01/the-quantum-mind-of-stuart-hameroff/

[Tipler 2005] Frank Tipler. The structure of the world from pure numbers. *Reports on Progress in Physics*, 2005.

[Turing 1939] Alan Turing. Systems of Logic Based on Ordinals. *Proceedings of the London Mathematical Society*, 1939.

[Volovik 2003] Grigori Volovik. *The Universe in a Helium Droplet.* Clarendon Press, 2003. Oxford University Press, 2009.

[Wen 2013] Xiao-Gang Wen. Answer to a question in StackExchange - Physics, 2013. https://physics.stackexchange.com/questions/63507/

[Widtsoe 1908] John Widtsoe. *Joseph Smith as Scientist: A Contribution to Mormon Philosophy.* Young Men's Mutual Improvement Associations, 1908.

[Wright 2009] Robert Wright. *The Evolution of God.* Little, Brown and Company, 2009.

[Zeng 2019] Bei Zeng, Xie Chen, Duan-Lu Zhou, Xiao-Gang Wen. *Quantum Information Meets Quantum Matter: From Quantum Entanglement to Topological Phase of Many-Body Systems.* Springer, 2019.
Open access draft: https://arxiv.org/abs/1508.02595

[Zorba 2016a] Serkan Zorba. God is Random: A Novel Argument for the Existence of God. *European Journal of Science and Theology*, 2016.

[Zorba 2016b] Serkan Zorba. God is Random: A New Perspective on Evolution and Creationism. *IslamiCity*, 2016.
https://www.islamicity.org/8254/god-is-random-a-new-perspective-on-evolution-and-creationism/

CHAPTER 22 – IN THE BEGINNING WAS THE FIELD

I added this chapter, based on essays written after the publication of the first edition of this book, to this second edition. For clarity and readability, I am reintroducing some concepts already introduced in previous chapters.

In previous chapters I developed some (in my opinion plausible) pictures of reality that leave room for transcendence, based on very speculative physics. Here I am trying to develop a picture based on known, mainstream physics.

[God is plausible but undecidable]. God is also undefinable and unknowable, but we shouldn't let that deter us from forming mental pictures of God and fundamental reality.

Scientifically plausible pictures of God, compatible with both traditional religions and contemporary science, let us allow ourselves to, in the words of William James [James 1960], "adopt a believing attitude in religious matters, in spite of the fact that our merely logical intellect may not have been coerced."

I think this is a much (perhaps the most) needed thing at this moment. Science is great, but a superficial "scientific" outlook can steal from everyone the hope of seeing their loved ones again in an afterlife. Without this hope, I think, life is just unbearable.

People shouldn't give up hope and embrace despair in the name of a dull, politically correct, forced atheism predicated on poorly understood science. The cosmological core of religion, including benevolent God(s) and an afterlife, is perfectly compatible with science, and perfectly compatible with the possibility that future generations of humans could use ultra-advanced science and technology to become like Gods and realize all the promises of traditional religion, including resurrecting the dead and re-making the universe.

So, don't fall into despair: Science does NOT rule out God(s) and an afterlife (on the contrary, science provides solid supporting arguments), and you CAN believe in these things if you want to, without abandoning the scientific worldview. So be happier, and do something good.

The picture of physical reality outlined below is based on mainstream (that is, only moderately speculative, as opposed to wildly speculative) science, and fully compatible with a wide range of religions.

My goal is to show that, while future science will certainly change our understanding of reality, even today's consensus science is essentially compatible with religion. The picture outlined below, in which free will and awareness are elementary building blocks of the fabric of reality, includes concepts of God and an afterlife.

This picture is related to that proposed by Mani Bhaumik [Bhaumik 2014, 2018], which is inspired by Eastern spirituality and quantum field theory, with some tweaks to make it more compatible with Western religions and establish parallels with other intriguing ideas of contemporary science and philosophy.

19th century physics was fully deterministic (causally closed) and incompatible with "mind-stuff" (consciousness, free will and all that) [Eddington 1929], but contemporary quantum physics and even (arguably) non-quantum chaos physics are causally open, with [plenty of room at the bottom for mind-stuff].

Transcendent beliefs in God and some kind of survival after death (call it reincarnation, resurrection or whatever you like) are compatible with science. So, if you want to believe, you can, without abandoning the scientific worldview.

I don't try to prove that God exists and we will live again, but I argue that hoping in God and an afterlife is totally compatible with science.

Of course I am not the first.

In "*The Nature of the Physical World*" [Eddington 1929], Arthur Eddington said:

> "Strict causality is abandoned in the material world. Our ideas of the controlling laws are in process of reconstruction and it is not possible to predict what kind of form they will ultimately take; but all the indications are that strict causality has dropped out permanently. This relieves the former necessity of supposing that mind is subject to deterministic law or alternatively that it can suspend deterministic law in the material world…"

> "It will perhaps be said that the conclusion to be drawn from these arguments from modern science, is that religion first became possible for a reasonable scientific man about the year 1927… If our expectation should prove well founded that 1927 has seen the final overthrow of strict causality by Heisenberg, Bohr, Born and others, the year will certainly rank as one of the greatest epochs in the development of scientific philosophy."

More recently, it has been found that classical (non-quantum) physics is not causally closed (not strictly subject to deterministic law) either. Contemporary [fractal chaos] physics shows that, in dynamical systems with ultra-fractal, riddled basins of attraction, the attractor that the system will eventually reach is undetermined, regardless of the accuracy with which the starting point is known.

Riddled basins "are not at all exotic: they show up reliably when the dynamical system obeys a few perfectly reasonable conditions" [Stewart 1997]. I suspect that, in really complex dynamical systems, fractal chaos is not the exception but the rule.

So, those who want to claim that physics leaves no room for transcendence are not following the physics of the 20th and 21st century, but the physics of the 19th century. Modern quantum and chaos physics, on the contrary, point to the plausibility of transcendence.

In "*Disturbing the Universe,*" [Dyson 1979] Freeman Dyson says:

> "I think our consciousness is not just a passive epiphenomenon carried along by the chemical events in our brains, but is an active agent forcing the molecular complexes to make choices between one quantum state and another. In other words, mind is already inherent in every electron, and the processes of human consciousness differ only in degree but not in kind from the processes of choice

between quantum states which we call 'chance' when they are made by electrons."

This is the clearest formulation of this concept that I am aware of. Dyson seems to be suggesting that "chance" molecular events in our brain, and more generally "chance" physical events (like [quantum] collapse) that seem entirely random to us, are not entirely random but driven by a consciousness that makes purposeful choices.

The Free Will Theorem

That I'm a self aware agent able to make free choices is the most basic fact that I know about reality. Everyone would say the same about their own experience.

Some people like to claim that free will is an illusion, but their arguments sound to me like those demonstrations that 1 = 0. Nice, clever, and wrong. Science should be consistent with facts, and free will is a basic fact. You know that, don't you?

I think science should help us make sense of our experience, not deny the reality of our experience. Therefore, I am not listening to those who claim that free will is an illusion. On the contrary, I am assuming as a basic fact that free will is a fundamental aspect of physical reality. In my search for useful models of reality, I exclude the models that are not compatible with free will.

[Stuart Kauffman argues] that some kind of free will could be part of the very fabric of reality. In Kauffman's words [Kauffman 2016], "aspects of the entire universe know and nonrandomly act at each measurement among independent or entangled quantum variables."

> "If this arises among entangled quantum variables, they may 'jointly know and decide.' We do not know if there is some whispering form of Cosmic Mind playing a role in the becoming of the universe… And if free will is at the foundations, or in us, no laws can entail the becoming of the universe."

Like Dyson, Kauffman is saying that perhaps quantum randomness is not random. It's worth noting that [the nature of randomness] is a subject of active exploration at the frontiers of mathematics and physics.

As emphasized by Kauffman, quantum mechanics shows that, if we have free will in the sense that our choices are not determined by the past history of the universe (remember that I am assuming this as a fact), then quantum particles must have their own "free will" as well. This is formalized in the free will theorem, proposed by John Conway and Simon Kochen. Conway and Kochen say that, if we humans have free will, then elementary particles "already have their own small share of this valuable commodity."

> "More precisely, if the experimenter can freely choose the directions in which to orient his apparatus in a certain measurement, then the particle's response (to be pedantic - the universe's response near the particle) is not determined by the entire previous history of the universe…

> Our provocative ascription of free will to elementary particles is deliberate, since our theorem asserts that if experimenters have a certain freedom, then particles have exactly the same kind of freedom. Indeed, it is natural to suppose that this latter freedom is the ultimate explanation of our own."

The current version of "The Strong Free Will Theorem" [Conway 2009], by Conway and Kochen, is republished in "*Deep Beauty*" [Halvorson 2011], edited by Hans Halvorson, a collection of essays highly relevant to this chapter. Halvorson is a philosopher of physics and a Christian believer. With physicists Andrew Briggs and Andrew Steane, Halvorson wrote "*It Keeps Me Seeking*" [Briggs 2018], a highly recommended book that, in soberly understated ways, suggests that science does not rule out belief.

While the definition of free will used by Conway and Kochen (ability to behave in ways that are not predetermined) is non-anthropomorphic and applicable to any physical system, it may seem odd to ascribe free will to a tiny and simple elementary particle like an electron. But Conway and Kochen clarify that, strictly speaking, it is the universe near the particle that acts with free will.

It's The Field, Stupid!

A new edition of "*Code Name God*" [Bhaumik 2018], by Mani Bhaumik, has been published by Penguin in 2018. The book, a masterpiece of accessible science writing, includes the fascinating autobiography of Bhaumik, an Indian physicist born in a very poor family who became a renowned scientist and a wealthy philanthropist, and then rediscovered his roots in the Indian spiritual tradition. The book includes a foreword by Walter Thirring and a new preface, in which Bhaumik gives a compact and insightful overview of contemporary physics.

In particular, Bhaumik emphasizes that, according to quantum field theory (QFT), an electron or any other elementary particle is but a manifestation of a more fundamental and "real" underlying field. Bhaumik suggests to imagine these elementary particles "as being like the spray that's thrown up as ocean waves crash against the rocks, only to fall back into the sea from which it came."

Elementary particles are manifestations of underlying gravitational, electroweak, and strong fields. Bhaumik notes that "all the fields in our universe are now believed to comprise a common source, which may be appropriately called the primary field," which is a plausible extrapolation from current QFT. Following Bhaumik, I'm referring to the common source as "primary field," or just "field."

If an electron is not a fundamental particle but a manifestation of the more fundamental field, then it is not to the electron, but to the field that we must ascribe free will. It's the field, stupid!

An elementary particle seems too tiny and simple to be endowed with free will, but the field, which spawns zillions of particles per nanosecond all over spacetime with non-local correlations (Einstein's "spooky action at a distance") across space and time, is hugely more complex than you and me. So, it doesn't seem that strange to think that the field acts with free will, and orchestrates apparently random quantum events.

This is a simple and economic way to short-circuit the infinite regress that arises when we try to explain how free will "works" - free will just IS. In this picture, free will comes first. The same can be said of consciousness. The simplest way to make sense of mind-stuff is pushing it all the way down to fundamental quantum fields.

Other entities (like you and me) in the physical universe are also endowed with some degree of free will, which is part of, or derived from, the free will of the field.

Mind-Stuff All The Way Down

I won't try to define consciousness, but you know what it is. You are living proof that consciousness exists in the universe. Here and there, now and then, fundamental quantum fields condensate into relatively independent conscious minds, able to act with some degree of free will.

We know that biological brains support conscious minds. It seems plausible to consider biological brains as special physical systems able to support local field condensates endowed with consciousness and free will. Conventional computers could not, I think, support [human mind uploads or conscious artificial intelligences], but quantum computers could.

Besides biological brains and quantum computers, non-biological physical systems, including plasmas, superconductors, superfluids, and perhaps localized blobs of bare quantum fields, could support conscious minds.

Some non-biological conscious entities in the universe could be much more intelligent and powerful than us, and appear God-like to us. I am persuaded that future humans will become post-biological and God-like in this sense. [In the words of Arthur Clarke], perhaps future humans will learn how "to store knowledge in the structure of space itself, and to preserve their thoughts for eternity in frozen lattices of light" (that is, in blobs of bare quantum fields).

Panpsychism is the idea that "consciousness is a fundamental and ubiquitous feature of the physical world," explains Philip Goff in *"Galileo's Error"* [Goff 2019]. Goff shows that panpsychism, whose contemporary formulation can be traced back to Eddington [Eddington 1929], is enjoying a renaissance and new waves of support. In *"The Feeling of Life Itself"* [Koch 2019], neuroscientist Christof Koch notes that [Giulio Tononi's integrated information theory (IIT)] "shares many insights with panpsychism, starting with the fundamental premise that consciousness is an intrinsic, fundamental aspect of reality."

Panpsychists think that fundamental physical entities have some kind of consciousness, or at least some kind of infinitesimal "proto-consciousness." In the words of David Chalmers, "the fundamental physical entities (such as quarks and photons), have conscious experiences," notes Barbara Gail Montero in *"Panpsychism: Contemporary Perspectives"* [Brüntrup 2016].

This seems difficult to swallow: How could a quark or a photon have conscious experiences? But Montero continues with the same argument that I am making:

> "However, if our current physics is in the right ballpark, the fundamental nature of reality may not comprise discrete particles but rather the continuous fields of quantum field theory... then it would seem that panpsychists should think of the fundamental nature of the world as comprising not discrete particles, but rather a continuous expanse of consciousness..."

In other words, it is not the tiny and simple quarks and photons that have conscious experiences and free will, but the hugely complex, universe-spanning, non-local field, which is a continuous expanse of consciousness.

If so, instead of infinitesimal proto-consciousness, we should be talking of super-consciousness. Not less than human consciousness, but MORE than human consciousness.

GIULIO PRISCO

Bhaumik is persuaded that awareness is present in the bedrock of reality, the quantum vacuum (the undisturbed, lowest-energy ground state of the field), which "seethes with quantum frenzy." The universe "is flooded by a sea of energy - a clear light, if you like - that fills what is known as the quantum vacuum," he explains [Bhaumik 2018]. Spirit, embedded in this clear light, pervades the universe.

According to Bhaumik, individual consciousness is but a reflection of the spirit that pervades the universe, encoded in quantum fields. He says that this is a modern scientific formulation of "the Vedic concept that all conscious beings are aspects of the same universal entity."

Consciousness "would be manifest when the individual brain's quantum state is in resonance with the cosmic potentiality of consciousness." Bhaumik suggests [Bhaumik 2014] "to explore the possibility of a primary cosmic awareness that may be the progenitor of consciousness, a source that evokes awareness in our brain utilizing its unique neural structure."

> "A search for such a universal awareness naturally leads to the ultimate source of everything, which is the quantum vacuum and the quantum field theory (QFT) that deals with it...
>
> Thus, it is credibly indicative that the source of all things physical as well as the attribute of awareness is present in the quantum vacuum in a complementary fashion throughout the universe. It then follows that this cosmic awareness would be a likely origin of our own consciousness, perhaps through some process like resonance or entanglement occurring in our brains."

Bhaumik assumes that the field is the bedrock of ultimate reality. I think science is still far from ultimate reality, and sometimes I suspect that the bedrock is unreachable and undefinable. However, I think quantum mechanics and QFT are good preliminary descriptions of some aspects of physical reality.

So, here I am considering a near-future version of QFT as an accurate description of the bedrock of reality. By "near-future version" I mean a unified field version of QFT that includes gravitation and irons out the problems of today's QFT.

Let's take a look at what QFT says about ultimate reality.

Quantum Field Theory For Mad Scientists And Theology Hackers

[Quantum field theory (QFT)] is the basis of the current consensus description of electroweak and strong interactions, and the standard model of particle physics.

According to current consensus, the quantum fields described by QFT are the bedrock of fundamental reality. Current QFT research seeks to achieve a solid, rigorous, unified description of fundamental fields, including gravity.

QFT may look like a patchwork of incoherent pieces, often logically and mathematically inconsistent. Some tools used in QFT may look more like emergency surgery than preventive medicine. In my student days I didn't like QFT, to which I preferred the exquisite elegance and pristine beauty of Einstein's general relativity, and I have had a mixed love-hate relation with QFT ever since.

However, it has to be said that QFT seems to work perfectly well for electroweak and strong fields, and also for gravitational fields until they become too strong.

In QFT, Nobel laureate Steven Weinberg explains [Weinberg 1977], "the essential reality is a set of fields, subject to the rules of special relativity and quantum mechanics; all else is derived as a consequence of the quantum dynamics of these fields." In *"Something Deeply Hidden"* [Carroll 2019], Sean Carroll emphasizes that:

> "Fields are more fundamental; it's fields that provide the best picture we currently have of what the universe is made of. Particles are simply what we see when we observe fields under the right circumstances."

That QFT is somewhat more fundamental than [quantum] mechanics (QM) is a somewhat mainstream position these days, but some physicists try to make it stronger and rigorous.

In *"An Introduction to a Realistic Quantum Physics"* [Preparata 2002a], the late lamented, often controversial physicist Giuliano Preparata [Preparata 2002b] argues that QM "is nothing but an approximation of QFT in the limit of extreme 'dilution'" (that is, for a small number of particles). Preparata emphasizes that:

> "QM with its formalism and dynamical equations is a rigorous consequence of the fundamental principles of QFT... in QFT the 'elements of reality' only belong to the quantum field, which is neither localized nor separable..."

QFT inherits the weirdness of QM. Like in QM, only probabilities are determined. Like in QM, a physical system can be in a superposition of quantum states, including states with any number of different particles (defined as quanta of different fields).

In some cases it is useful to consider a field as a collection of particles, but this is an approximation that eventually breaks down, leaving in place only the reality of the field itself.

In general, interacting quantum fields cannot be given a consistent particle interpretation [Fraser 2006]. "When fields are interacting intensely," notes science writer George Musser [Musser 2015], "waves are so jumbled that particles no longer exist, even by a liberal definition."

In QFT, like in QM, physical systems separated in space and time are entangled [Musser 2015, Zeilinger 2010], with non-local correlations even "spookier" than in QM. Edward Witten explains [Witten 2018] that, in quantum field theory,

> "all field variables in any one region of spacetime are entangled with variables in other regions."

In the words of Heide Narnhofer and Walter Thirring [Narnhofer 2012], "in quantum field theory almost everything is entangled." It's worth underlining that entanglement extends not only across space, but also across time.

There are interesting speculative efforts to derive the very concepts of space and time from the entanglement structure of the field [Carroll 2019]. The idea is to take the degree of entanglement between field variables as a definition of distance.

The bedrock of reality described by QFT is non-local. "There isn't anything that's truly localized," says Halvorson, as reported by Musser [Musser 2015]. While we can't use entanglement to travel through time, send faster-than-light signals, or perform other feats of scientific magic (as far as we can tell today), fundamental reality is non-local.

This is spectacularly illustrated by the Reeh-Schlieder theorem. The theorem is usually stated in the sober and somewhat cryptic jargon of algebraic quantum field theory (AQFT) [Haag 1996, Araki 2000, Halvorson 2006]. But what the theorem seems to say is that, by "poking" (e.g. with a measurement) "a quantum field in one tiny region of space, it's possible to turn the quantum state of the whole universe into literally any state at all" [Carroll 2019].

An intuitive visual illustration is provided by the mathematics of complex analytic functions [Stewart 2018]. A complex analytic function is determined by its values in any arbitrarily small region. Therefore, imagine a complex analytic surface: If you poke it with your finger anywhere, you change it anywhere else.

Stephen Summers notes [Halvorson 2011]:

> "In our view, a reasonable physical picture of this situation is indicated in this way: an experimenter in any given region O can, in principle, perform measurements designed to exploit nonlocal vacuum fluctuations... in such a manner that any prescribed state can be reproduced with any given accuracy."

According to Witten [Witten 2018], the Reeh-Schlieder theorem implies that, by acting locally on quantum fields, "one can create whatever one wants - possibly a complex body such as the Moon - in a faraway, spacelike separated region of spacetime." Carroll adds that the theorem "implies that without leaving my room, I can do an experiment and get an outcome that implies there is now, suddenly, a copy of the [Taj Mahal] on the moon."

Allow me to propose even weirder illustrations: By poking the field locally, perhaps within your own brain, you could do [real magic] [Radin 2018]. By masterfully tweaking the field, it would be possible to create a perfected copy of your great-grandmother anywhere in the future universe, perhaps on a planet similar to ours but better, inhabited by perfected copies of everyone who ever lived. This is what Christianity promises to believers.

OK, OK. We don't have the faintest idea of how to do that in practice, or even in theory. The experts emphasize that mathematically valid operations in the formalism of QFT do not necessarily correspond to operations that are possible in the physical world, and that entangled correlations in QFT decay exponentially. Also, like in QM, [quantum randomness protects spacetime from superluminal effects].

But none of that would prevent Kauffman's "whispering form of Cosmic Mind" - or future engineers with read-write access to the bedrock of reality - from engineering spacetime with subtly orchestrated, non-random interventions.

The Memory Of The Universe

In the picture that I am proposing, free will is a primary property of the field. The same can be said of conscious experience, the basic awareness of existence, or "what it is like to be" [Nagel 1974]. Free-will and what-is-likeness are fundamental stuff, and don't need to be explained in terms of other stuff.

Besides free-will and what-is-likeness, there are things like memory and general intelligence. We are living proof that there are physical systems with these properties in the universe. It seems plausible that memory and intelligence are emergent collective modes of fundamental mind-stuff in suitable physical systems, of which the biological brain is one.

Can bare quantum fields give rise to memory and intelligence? [Some scientists like Jae-Weon Lee are publishing intriguing frontier speculations] along this line, but the fact that that quantum fields memorize information is already a solid result of mainstream theoretical physics.

[Gravitational wave] memory effects predicted by general relativity have been known for decades, and equivalent memory effects for electromagnetic and strong interactions have been found. These memory effects haven't yet been confirmed experimentally, but the theories are solid and feasible experiments have been proposed.

Permanent memory effects have a solid and growing place in modern physics. The current reference textbook is *Lectures on the Infrared Structure of Gravity and Gauge Theory* [Strominger 2018], by Andrew Strominger.

Strominger realized that spacetime "will retain an almost homeopathic imprint of what passes through it," notes George Musser [Musser 2019].

Recent theoretical work by Strominger and others, including the late Stephen Hawking, links memory effects to "soft" (zero energy) particles and the unexpectedly complex structure of spacetime far away from radiating sources. Hawking explains [Hawking 2018]:

> "Back in the 1960s, Hermann Bondi, A. W. Kenneth Metzner, M. G. J. van der Burg and Rainer Sachs made the truly remarkable discovery that space–time far away from any matter has an infinite collection of symmetries known as supertranslations..."

A supertranslation, Strominger says (as reported by Musser), adds soft particles to spacetime.

> "This realisation, in turn, provides a clearer picture of how a seemingly empty spacetime that is far from any gravitating bodies can retain a residue of gravity's effects. Plop a soft particle into a vacuum and, though it adds no energy, it does contribute its angular momentum and other properties, thereby bumping the vacuum to a new version of itself. Strominger realised that if the vacuum can assume multiple forms, it will retain an almost homeopathic imprint of what passes through it."

Supertranslations "are not as easy to visualize as taking three steps to the right," notes Musser, "and for decades resisted simple explanation."

The closest I get to visualizing these things is by imagining a soft graviton, with zero frequency and infinite wavelength, as a static, permanent deformation of spacetime.

Hawking continues:

> "What was remarkable about the discovery of supertranslations is that there are an infinite number of conserved quantities far from a black hole. In 2016 [Hawking 2016], together with my collaborators Malcolm Perry and Andy Strominger, I was working on using these new results with their associated conserved quantities to find a possible resolution to the information paradox... This supertranslation hair might encode some of the information about what is inside the black hole."

In his last paper [Haco 2018], co-authored with Strominger, Perry, and Sasha Haco, Hawking made further advances related to the [black hole information paradox].

Next-generation [gravitational wave] detectors could plausibly detect gravitational wave memory. Analogous memory effects are theoretically predicted for electromagnetism and quantum chromodynamics (QCD, the QFT of strong interactions) as well, and could be within reach of next-generation detectors in the lab. Musser continues:

> Physicists "are on the hunt for evidence of an observable 'memory effect' left behind by gravity that could soon be picked up in a lab. Other experimentalists plan to look for the analogous memory effects for electromagnetic and nuclear forces."

The quantum vacuum ((the undisturbed, lowest-energy ground state of the field) is not unique, but comes in infinitely many physically distinguishable forms. Physical processes push the field into a different ground state, characterized by soft infrared excitations with vanishingly small energy.

Therefore, information on whatever happens is encoded, or permanently "printed" in the vacuum, which retains, in Musser's words, "an almost homeopathic imprint of what passes through it." To use another suggestive analogy, the vacuum retains a permanent "scent" [Asorey 2018] that remains forever.

That the universe stores memories is also, I think, suggested by [Landauer's principle and reversible computing]: It seems plausible that the universe, viewed as a computation, should be optimally energy-efficient, like a reversible computation that stores intermediate results instead of discarding them. Therefore, the field should store permanent memories of whatever happens.

To me, since memory is a primary building block of intelligent systems, this is a powerful indication of intelligence in the field. The words of James Jeans [Jeans 1930] come to mind: "the universe begins to look more like a great thought than like a great machine."

Since the field is hugely more complex than a human brain, speaking of super-consciousness, super-intelligence and some kind of super-personality seems appropriate. The field is not less than conscious and less than personal, but MORE than conscious and MORE than personal, hugely more so.

Writing about Hawking's last paper, Dennis Overbye noted [Overbye 2018]:

> "Cleansed of its abstract mathematics, the paper is an ode to memory, loss and the oldest of human yearnings, the desire for transcendence... Few of us, including Dr. Hawking, ever harbored the hope that solving the information paradox would bring back our parents..."

But why not? Let's recap.

Our best physical theories, Einstein's general relativity, Maxwell's electromagnetism, quantum electrodynamics and chromodynamics, predict permanent memory effects. These memory effects are likely to be found in the lab with sufficiently powerful detectors, which could be developed soon.

If so we'll have to conclude that, according to current consensus physics, everything that ever happens leaves a measurable and permanent trace in the fabric of reality. In other words, there are [Akashic records], and future scientists equipped with sufficiently powerful technology will be able to read them.

Of course, this is a huge extrapolation from today's theories and tomorrow's likely first measurements in the lab. But I take today's theories as promising hints, and I am persuaded that future physics will unveil more and more memory effects and means to detect them.

So, give future generations time to develop better theories and technologies. Give them a few thousand years and, perhaps, they will be able to use Akashic technologies to bring back our fathers.

Code Name God

The field is everywhere, knows everything (via infrared memory and non-local entanglement), is not limited by time (entanglement extends across time), and orchestrates elementary physical processes everywhere. In other words, the field is omnipresent, omniscient, and [omnipotent].

The idea of a super-consciousness embedded in the field, omnipresent and omniscient, and able to orchestrate elementary physical processes all over space and time in subtly non-random ways (omnipotent), without needing to violate the probabilistic laws of physics, is strongly suggestive of God.

Bhaumik identifies the field with God, a soberly non-anthropomorphic, impersonal concept of God rooted in Bhaumik's own Indian spiritual tradition, and concludes [Bhaumik 2018] by evoking "the power of the one source, the order that underlies and enfolds all orders, that unifies all fields and forms, as well as consciousness," and suggesting "that we call this source by its code name: God."

Bhaumik explained to me that, in the Indian spiritual tradition, the abstract entity Brahman is inseparably intertwined with all there is in this universe. But we are not yet able to embrace the reality of a totally abstract Brahman, which is the concept of God Bhaumik is referring to. An anthropomorphic entity is perhaps the most we can grasp at this stage of our evolution, and this is the genesis of the plethora of deities in India.

Also, many people need a more anthropomorphic, personal concept of God, and hope in survival of the self after death. The equations of QFT don't keep you warm at night.

I will stop short of identifying the field with God, because whatever we can say about the field will fall short of fully defining and explaining the undefinable and unknowable nature of God. Rather, I will say that quantum field theory suggests a vague but useful panentheistic [Brüntrup 2016] picture of some core aspects of God.

As suggested by this field picture, God is everywhere (omnipresent). God is maximally conscious and omnipotent, able to subtly tweak and orchestrate apparently random events without violating physical laws.

God is inseparably intermingled with physical processes in the universe, just like our mental activity is inseparably intermingled with physical processes in the brain. In both cases, the conscious mind orchestrates physical processes in the substrate. God orchestrates the universe with maximal knowledge and freedom, constrained only by fundamental physics, most likely with subtle diffuse interventions that we could only describe as "[downward causation]."

We are (relatively autonomous) parts of God, and we also orchestrate physical processes in more limited ways, in small parts of the universe in and around us (see Dyson's quote above).

The super-consciousness embedded in the field is more than human consciousness, not less, and therefore God is more than personal, not less. [I have argued that God] evolves with the physical universe, learns, and acquires personal, human aspects by interacting with us. God is not impersonal, but (in the words of Olaf Stapledon [Stapledon 1947]) "in some sense personal, or at least not less than personal... probably infinitely more than personal."

The concept of a personal God, able and willing to remake the world and resurrect the dead, perhaps by copy/pasting them into a new world, bridges Bhaumik's ideas and traditional religions like Christianity, the East and the West.

God is beyond our understanding, like the full scope of our mental activity is beyond the understanding of a dog. However, we can plausibly think that God cares for us, like we care for dogs. A personal, caring God is able and willing to grant us an afterlife, and perhaps to answer our questions and prayers now and then.

Christian theologian Wolfhart Pannenberg proposed analogies between field theories in physics and concepts of God and divine action in theology. The meaning of "the statement in John 4:24 that 'God is spirit'" is considerably close, he said [Pannenberg 2007], "to the field concept of modern physics."

[Concepts of intelligent matter and material spirit are prominently featured in Mormon cosmology], which also includes God-like entities halfway between humans and God, and the possibility that future humans could become God-like.

In an interview [Maack 2019] published in *TNW*, Mormon transhumanist Lincoln Cannon said:

> "Our theology is materialistic... in Mormonism spirits are material... In our scriptures, we have a passage that says: 'There's no such thing as immaterial matter, all spirit is matter'... One of the fundamental principles of Mormonism is the concept that humans are of the same species as God, if you will, and that we are children of God and have the capacity to become like God."

Mormon theologians Orson and Parley Pratt "defined the Holy Ghost, or Holy Spirit, as an intelligent, cosmic ether" and "imputed to the Holy Ghost a foundational role as a kind of ground out of which all self-awareness, sentience, and God himself emerged" [Givens 2014].

Without entering the history and subtleties of Mormon theology, I will note that contemporary Mormons are more likely to use the term "Light of Christ" to indicate these aspects of the Holy Ghost. Joseph Smith described the Light of Christ as "the light which is in all things, which giveth life to all things, which is the law by which all things are governed, even the power of God" [Givens 2014].

Regardless of the terminology used, these Mormon concepts seem strongly suggestive of the field picture that I am proposing. Worth noting, quantum fields include and generalize "Light." Also worth noting (again), future technologies able to subtly influence and tweak the field might give humans God-like abilities.

Alpha And Omega

It's interesting to speculate about the emergence of super-consciousness in the Cosmic Mind, aka God. Perhaps God has always been. Perhaps God awoke to super-consciousness soon (billionths of a second) after the beginning of the universe, and has been watching and acting upon the universe all along. Or [perhaps the awakening of God takes billions of years], which leaves open the possibility that perhaps God is not fully formed yet.

But there are indications that time is stranger than we think. For example, according to the transactional interpretation of QM, first proposed by John Cramer, physical reality emerges from feedback loops across time.

Then, a God operating in the far future could subtly influence past events. In other words: The Cosmic Mind in the bedrock of far-future reality acts here and now.

Cramer has written a book, "*The Quantum Handshake*" [Cramer 2016], to explain the transactional interpretation. In a nutshell (from Cramer's science fiction novel "*Einstein's Bridge*" [Cramer 1997]):

> "This universe... moves forward in time at the quantum level by a chain of handshakes between past and future... the future reaching back to make an accommodation with the past that allows a quantum event to happen, to become reality. Each quantum event emerges into reality as the result of a feedback loop between past and future. These are allowed timelike loops that bring the universe into being."

See also Ruth Kastner's books [Kastner 2012, 2015, 2019] on her own (subtly different) formulation of the transactional interpretation.

Cramer, who describes himself as "an experimental nuclear physicist, not a philosopher of science or an abstract theoretician," focuses on the transactional interpretation's ability to provide a more intuitive visualization of quantum processes. Kastner ventures into more abstract theory and philosophy, and some of her conclusions are very similar to mine.

It's important to remember that quantum entanglement [Musser 2015] connects not only different locations in space, but also different times. In the words of Anton Zeilinger [Zeilinger 2017], the entanglement between two quantum events is "fully independent of their distance, independent of which is earlier or later, etc... So quantum mechanics transgresses space and time in a very deep sense."

Science allows us to conceive of a future God acting here and now, and in our remote past. God, eventually emerging from intelligent life in the universe, perhaps born in the far future to our own grandchildren among the stars, retroactively creates the universe and acts at all times through self-consistent time loops. This vision, shared by Pannenberg in more abstract terms [Pannenberg 2007], is repeatedly explored in previous chapters.

Beam Me Up

I am persuaded that God, or future God-like entities in the universe (hopefully including our descendants) will resurrect us by copying us from their past (our present) and uploading us to their present (our future).

It seems easy: Digital information can be copied from one computer to another. If your mind is somewhat equivalent to a digital computer, they'll just have to find a way to copy your mind from the past and upload it to the future. Nothing here that ultra-advanced, God-like entities could not do.

This is somewhat equivalent to the Christian idea of resurrection. I am equating ultra-advanced humans or aliens with God, but perhaps this is not entirely wrong. Or, if "they" can conceivably do all that, so can God.

But wait a sec. What if "you" are encoded in the exact quantum state of your brain (or parts of it)? By "exact quantum state" I mean, not something similar to, not a compressed version of, but the real thing. If so, you are quantum information, and the "no-cloning theorem" [Aaronson 2013, Zeilinger 2010] says that quantum information can't be copied.

Does the no-cloning theorem apply to you and me? The authors of "*It Keeps Me Seeking*" [Briggs 2018] say:

> "If it does, then the type of copying process invoked by science-fiction writers, when they imagine that people could one day save 'backup' copies of themselves, may be physically impossible. We already know that each person is unique. It may be also that each person is intensely fragile."

I (and most mind uploading experts and enthusiasts) have always assumed that the exact quantum state of the brain (or parts of it) is not needed for [mind uploading]: A highly compressed classical version with all and only the essential digital information will do. But I could be wrong, in which case the no-cloning theorem would make mind uploading (to the future or to the present) impossible.

But quantum teleportation comes to the rescue! The authors of "*It Keeps Me Seeking*" explain:

> "The no-cloning theorem does not prevent a quantum state being passed on from one physical embodiment to another, as long as the first embodiment loses the state when the other one gains it. One way this can happen is through a process known as quantum teleportation."

Known (and experimentally confirmed) quantum teleportation schemes allow to teleport a unit of quantum information (qubit) X, roughly as follows [Aaronson 2013, Zeilinger 2010]:

Two experimenters (call them Alice and Bob as usual) have two entangled qubits A and B. Alice entangles X with A, destroys X with a measurement, and sends the results of the measurement to Bob over a classical channel. Now Bob, using the classical information sent by Alice, knows how to measure B in such a way that B becomes identical to X. And here you go! X has been teleported from Alice to Bob.

If [ER=EPR], the entangled connection between A and B can be seen as a wormhole through which X is teleported. Scientists are investigating quantum teleportation for things more complex than qubits. The road from a qubit to a person is still (very) long, but our first baby steps with qubits are encouraging.

The authors of "*It Keeps Me Seeking*" remark that "if entanglement is significant, then there is a direct physical sense in which a human being is a unity in significant ways." If the no-cloning theorem applies to human minds, then "the notion of backup copies might prove to be incoherent when it comes to persons,"

> "but there is nothing here to prevent the Christian idea of Resurrection from having intellectual coherence."

Teleporting quantum information destroys the original, but isn't that what happens at the moment of death? Perhaps, at death, the quantum information that is you will be transported away, in ways somewhat analogous to quantum teleportation as we understand it today.

As Above, So Below

In *"Cosmic Impressions"* [Thirring 2007], Walter Thirring interprets the opening verses of Genesis as:

> "The vacuum state, unstructured and empty, dominated matter as well as light. There weren't any other spirits beyond God... The language of God is the laws of nature, and according to them, the vacuum in the quantum gravitation is unstable. This instability can develop into a big bang, an avalanche of light that creates our immense universe out of nothing..."

At a first glance, Thirring's words seem quite compatible with the field picture that I have outlined. However, while in my picture God is embedded in the field deep inside physical reality, of which consciousness and free will are fundamental aspects, Thirring is suggesting a God beyond the physical universe, who created our universe out of nothing from outside.

I will borrow the terms "immanent" and "transcendent," often used in theology. I guess most Christians would agree with Thirring: God is not an immanent entity within physical reality, but a transcendent entity beyond physical reality.

I never miss a chance to emphasize that the [simulation] hypothesis, recently discussed in a popular book by Rizwan Virk [Virk 2019], is essentially equivalent to the cosmological core of popular Christianity, and many other religions.

Virk notes that the simulation hypothesis "bridges the gap between religion and science in ways that weren't possible before," and "may just be the answer that provides a single framework, a coherent model that brings together science and religion." I agree, and I think the simulation hypothesis can be a good introduction to scientific theology for believers, and a good way for atheists to allow themselves hope in an afterlife.

Therefore, in the following I'll deliberately blend simulation theology and popular Christianity.

There is a creator (aka God) outside the physical universe. God wrote our physical laws and could choose to violate them anytime. But God doesn't even need to violate our physical laws, because God wrote our physical laws with an application programming interface (API) that allows intervention from outside.

God can remake the universe into a better version of itself. God can copy you from here and now, and paste you into the new better universe, or into any afterlife that you can (or can't) imagine.

Quantum and chaotic collapse events are driven by choices coming from outside (divine action) through the API. But personal free will on this side of the reality divide seems difficult to account for. If everything in our reality is driven from the other side, then you and I are puppets without free will.

Another issue is how the world on the other side of the reality divide works. If the world outside is a fully deterministic universe, we are back to square one and there's no free will. If the world outside is causally open like our own universe, then either we must assume that free will is a fundamental aspect of the fabric of reality in the outside world, or we are forced to think of yet another world, and so forth.

The field picture of a whole undivided reality, which includes consciousness and free will, is essentially monist (as opposed to dualist). There's just one kind of fundamental stuff, which includes mind-stuff and God-stuff, and God is inside physical reality. This seems more appealing to me, intellectually and esthetically. Others may differ, of course.

However, God can be coherently conceived as either immanent or transcendent (or both), so you can choose the picture closer to your comfort zone. As above, so below: There are ways to make immanent pictures of God inside physical reality, such as the field picture, more compatible with transcendent pictures of God outside physical reality, such as popular Christianity and the simulation hypothesis.

First way: We can extend our concept of physical reality to include the outside world within which our universe exists. Mind-stuff is part of the fundamental fabric of reality in the outside world, and God lives in the outside world. The "hardware on which the simulation runs," whatever that is (perhaps some kind of quantum ultra-computer in the outside world, or something like that, or more likely nothing like that), executes the simulation of our world, which includes self-aware entities with (limited) free will like you and me.

We are not mindless puppets, but have a degree of free agency. To use Virk's analogy, we are not NPCs (non-playing characters) in a game like World of Warcraft, but real players that visit a game world like World of Warcraft or Second Life from outside. In Virk's words, "we are players outside of the game (and thus conscious entities) playing characters inside the video game."

Second way: We can try and split the field picture of a whole undivided reality into layers. We can place some aspects of the field, and the derived physical reality of our world, in the innermost layer, and other aspects of the field, including God's super-consciousness, in the outer layer(s).

Physical reality is one and undivided, but the fundamental reality of the minded field is "wholly other," entirely different from the intuitive ordinary reality of things that exist locally in space and time. Fundamental reality is non-local: Space and time, which are central to our conception of reality, might be shadows of the entanglement structure of the field [Carroll 2019] as noted above.

If so, the innermost layer of ordinary reality can be thought of as a construct created by entities beyond space and time, acting with (super)intelligence and free will. In other words, we live in a simulation computed in [a transcendent universe beyond our world], and driven by transcendent agents. We can then adopt the simulation hypothesis, which provides a bridge to traditional religions like Christianity.

I could go on and explore parallels with the concept of the Trinity in Christian theology. For example, I could try and place the Father in the outermost layer, the Holy Ghost in the innermost layer that includes our world, and the Son in between.

However, one important lesson from QFT is that consistently defining layers in a whole undivided reality (e.g. particles in QFT) can be difficult or even impossible. So, I guess the Trinity is an entangled whole that can't be consistently split into three separately definable persons.

[Other ideas, halfway between] immanent pictures of God inside physical reality and transcendent pictures of God outside physical reality, also come to mind.

Now I must say that I do NOT believe that today's QFT is anywhere close to an accurate description of the bedrock of fundamental reality. Bhaumik mentions speculative ideas beyond QFT, but he stays grounded in QFT, which is the current consensus. Here I am using the same conservative approach, and I think the essential features of the picture I have presented won't be invalidated by future developments.

A new sub-quantum bedrock of physical reality would only be manifest at very small scales, much deeper than the physical reality that we (and our scientific instruments) perceive. This is yet another way to conceive of a more fundamental reality beyond the universe known to current science.

Of course, future scientists will be able to study physical reality at smaller scales, but we might be very, very far from the bedrock. Or perhaps there's no bedrock that we can ever reach, but turtles (coarse pictures of a hidden finer reality) all the way down. In this case, again, fundamental reality is and will remain outside the physical universe.

QM is assumed as valid, and fundamental, in today's physical theories that try to go beyond QFT, e.g. string theory. According to Scott Aaronson, "quantum mechanics is the operating system that other physical theories run on as application software" [Aaronson 2013]. It seems likely that future theories of physics at or beyond the Planck scale will still be based on QM and be compatible with my starting point: Physical reality is not strictly deterministic, but causally open.

Even in the extreme case of new theories, radically different from today's QM, based on differential equations like those of classical electromagnetism and general relativity (this is what Einstein and Dirac hoped for), [fractal chaos] would likely bite and open apparently deterministic mathematical descriptions to non-determinism.

The field picture that I have outlined pushes mind-stuff and God-stuff all the way down to the quantum fields described by QFT, considered as the bedrock of reality. Perhaps future research will unveil [sub-quantum physics underneath QFT]. But then a revised picture could push mind-stuff and God-stuff further down to the new bedrock of reality (if there is such a thing).

Can We Still Have Many Worlds?

Here I want to try and "save" the concept of many parallel worlds in this context. If the field chooses what happens next in this one and only world, we don't need [many worlds] where different possible outcomes are realized.

But Hugh Everett's idea of many parallel worlds enables [interesting afterlife pictures] that seem intriguing to me, such as those presented in Gregory Benford's 2019 novel "*Rewrite*" and the 2017 film "*The Discovery*."

One way to have many worlds within a reality driven by free will & divine action is to switch from Everett's quantum version of the many worlds picture to the [inflationary cosmology] version, where there are many (perhaps infinitely many) bubble universes in an ever inflating space, and our entire observable universe is but a minute fraction of one of these bubble universes. It seems plausible that God, the Cosmic Mind in the field, could choose to let different possibilities play out in different bubbles.

But let's stay with Everett's Many Worlds.

In "*Something Deeply Hidden*" [Carroll 2019], Sean Carroll focuses "on the approach I feel is clearly the most promising route, the Everett or Many-Worlds formulation of quantum mechanics."

It's worth noting that Carroll seems to interpret Everett in a way similar to mine:

> "Likewise, it is often helpful to talk about the post-decoherence wave function as describing a set of distinct worlds; that's justified, because what happens on each branch doesn't affect what happens on the others. But ultimately, that language is a convenience for us, not something that the theory itself insists on. Fundamentally, the theory just cares about the wave function as a whole."

I also think "Many-Worlds" should be taken only as a simple picture. We live in One Big World, of which a representation as many (small) worlds is only a simplified intuitive illustration.

All possibilities, including exotic "[Taj Mahal] states," are somewhere in the multiverse to be found. "Looked at in the right way, the potential for a Taj Mahal on the moon was there all along, in some tiny part of the quantum state," explains Carroll.

But Carroll is adamant that all Everett's worlds are real, and all possibilities are realized in one or another Everett world. This seems to kill free will & divine action: If the field makes (or I make, or God makes) all possible choices, with probabilities given by the inflexible rules of deterministic quantum physics, then no choice has been made. Everett's multiverse is a clockwork multiverse.

However, we can think that not all possibilities are realized, but only some. In this picture of divine action, God doesn't work by adding (like a painter) but by taking away (like a sculptor).

Freely willed divine action is not in actualizing one desired world, but in eliminating many undesired worlds. This is also an intuitive "visual" model for [downward causation]. The idea is that different Everett worlds unfold for a short while (perhaps very short from our perspective), but then most of those worlds evaporate into nothingness, or something like that, while the "fittest" winners take all and become fully real according to certain reality selection criteria.

The outcome is a "[thin multiverse]," halfway between one single world and the full multiverse of Everett. I thought this idea was original, but then I found out that a similar idea had been proposed by Thomas Campbell [Campbell 2003]. Virk summarizes [Virk 2019]:

> "Campbell asserts that the universe spins up possible universes and outcomes, evaluates them using his profitability function and then comes back and chooses the universe that is most profitable. This is similar to how video game AIs choose which path to follow - by evaluating possible future states based on some evaluation function."

I am suggesting that more than one possible universe could be chosen. This saves the idea of many parallel worlds.

Notes

[Akashic records] See "The quest for Akashic physics and engineering."

[a transcendent universe beyond our world] See also the discussion of oracle interfaces to a transcendent universe (the beyond) in "Thought experiments in physical theology."

[black hole information paradox] I think the "paradox" is not a paradox because, in the interpretation of [quantum] mechanics that I am using here, wavefunctions do collapse (Von Neumann's Process 1) and information is not necessarily conserved (see "Exotic space, mysterious time, magic quantum"). But some information on what actually happened in the past (as opposed to unrealized possibilities) might be conserved, perhaps in a retrievable form.

[Concepts of intelligent matter and material spirit are prominently featured in Mormon cosmology] See "Man will become like God, say Mormons and transhumanists," "Thought experiments in physical theology."

[downward causation] See "There's plenty of room at the bottom."

[ER=EPR] See "Thought experiments in physical theology."

[fractal chaos] See "There's plenty of room at the bottom," "Eligo, ergo sum, ergo Deus est."

[Giulio Tononi's integrated information theory (IIT)] According to IIT, a physical system is conscious if and only if it has a maximum of integrated information ("phi"), "with the maximum being evaluated over all spatiotemporal scales and levels of granularities," explains Koch [Koch 2019]. Consciousness "is present at the level at which there is the most integrated information," explains Goff [Goff 2019]. So, a physical system can be conscious, or it can be part of a larger conscious system, but not both. This seems to exclude the possibility that a conscious mind could also be part of a super-conscious Mind. But it seems plausible to me that future versions of IIT could include local maxima in different scale ranges, each conscious in its own way.

[God is plausible but undecidable] See "Thought experiments in physical theology."

[gravitational wave] See "Exotic space, mysterious time, magic quantum."

[human mind uploads or conscious artificial intelligences] See "Transhumanism."

[I have argued that God] See "Thought experiments in physical theology."

[inflationary cosmology] See "Exotic space, mysterious time, magic quantum."

[interesting afterlife pictures] See "The interplay of science fiction, science, and religion."

[In the words of Arthur Clarke] See "Agnostics, possibilians, and mysterians."

[Landauer's principle and reversible computing] According to Landauer's principle, erasing information costs energy. Reversible computers, which store intermediate results instead of erasing them, are more energy-efficient than irreversible computers. See [Kurzweil 2005] and references therein. Ray Kurzweil explains: "Rolf Landauer showed in 1961 that reversible logical operations such as NOT (turning a bit into its opposite) could be performed without putting energy in or taking heat out, but that irreversible logical operations such as AND (generating bit C, which is a 1 if and only if both inputs A and B are 1) do require energy. In

1973 Charles Bennett showed that any computation could be performed using only reversible logical operations. A decade later, Ed Fredkin and Tommaso Toffoli presented a comprehensive review of the idea of reversible computing..." [Kurzweil 2005].

[many worlds] See "Exotic space, mysterious time, magic quantum," and following chapters.

["mind-stuff"] In *The Nature of the Physical World* [Eddington 1929], Arthur Eddington said: "To put the conclusion crudely - the stuff of the world is mind-stuff. As is often the way with crude statements, I shall have to explain that by 'mind' I do not here exactly mean mind and by 'stuff' I do not at all mean stuff. Still this is about as near as we can get to the idea in a simple phrase. The mind-stuff of the world is, of course, something more general than our individual conscious minds; but we may think of its nature as not altogether foreign to the feelings in our consciousness."

[mind uploading] See "Transhumanism."

[omnipotent] A caveat on omnipotence: Physical laws don't constrain individual elementary events, but they do constrain the statistics of many events. So the omnipotence of God is limited by the laws of physics. However, God can do a lot of things without violating expected statistics.

[Other ideas, halfway between] For example, our universe could be a brane-world engineered by ultra-advanced, God-like beings in the higher-dimensional bulk space of string theory (see "Exotic space, mysterious time, magic quantum"). Or, our universe could be sub-quantum matter engineered to simulate the physical reality that we know (see "Thought experiments in physical theology").

[perhaps the awakening of God takes billions of years] This would be the case if biological life is the simplest and first realized instance of awareness and intelligence in the field. If so, the awakening of God must wait for biological life to emerge and mature. But then, intelligent life will reach the bedrock of fundamental reality and awaken the field to super-consciousness.

[plenty of room at the bottom for mind-stuff] See "There's plenty of room at the bottom," "Eligo, ergo sum, ergo Deus est."

[quantum] See "Exotic space, mysterious time, magic quantum" and following chapters.

[Quantum field theory (QFT)] There are good QFT textbooks. But QFT is conceptually and mathematically complicated, and there aren't many accessible references for the general public. See the QFT chapters in [Bhaumik 2018, Carroll 2019, Musser 2015], and of course Richard Feynman's "*QED*" [Feynman's 2006]. If you want to go deeper, I recommend starting with [Han 2014], a short barebone introduction with essential mathematics, and [Teller 1995], a thorough conceptual analysis.

[quantum randomness protects spacetime from superluminal effects] See the discussion of quantum entanglement in "Exotic space, mysterious time, magic quantum."

[real magic] According to Dean Radin [Radin 2018], three ideas are the basis of real magic: "1 Consciousness is fundamental, meaning it is primary over the physical world; 2 Everything is interconnected; 3 There is only one Consciousness." My formulation of these three ideas is different, but essentially compatible. Therefore, I agree with Radin: We'll be able to do real magic, once we know how. Perhaps some people already do.

[simulation] See "Sims City," "The Life of Joe Glider."

[Some scientists like Jae-Weon Lee are publishing intriguing frontier speculations] See "Into the deep waters."

[Stuart Kauffman argues] See "Eligo, ergo sum, ergo Deus est."

[sub-quantum physics underneath QFT] See "Into the deep waters," "Thought experiments in physical theology."

[Taj Mahal] The original source of the suggestive Taj Mahal picture is (I think) [Verch 2006]: "This result by Reeh and Schlieder appears entirely counter-intuitive since it says that every state of the theory can be approximated to arbitrary precision by acting with operators (operations) localized in any arbitrarily given spacetime region on the vacuum. To state it in a rather more drastic and provocative way (which I learned from Reinhard Werner): By acting on the vacuum with suitable operations in a terrestrial laboratory, an experimenter can create the Taj Mahal on (or even behind) the Moon!"

[the nature of randomness] See "Thought experiments in physical theology."

[thin multiverse] See "There's plenty of room at the bottom."

References

[Aaronson 2013] Scott Aaronson.*Quantum Computing since Democritus*. Cambridge University Press, 2013.

[Araki 2000] Huzihiro Araki. *Mathematical Theory of Quantum Fields*. Oxford University Press, 2000.

[Asorey 2018] Manuel Asorey et al. Entangled scent of a charge. *Journal of High Energy Physics*, 2018.
https://arxiv.org/abs/1802.03922

[Bhaumik 2014] Mani Bhaumik. Is the Source of Awareness Present
in the Quantum Vacuum? In *Interdisciplinary Perspectives on Consciousness and the Self*. Sangeetha Menon, Anindya Sinha, B. V. Sreekantan, Eds. Springer, 2014.

[Bhaumik 2018] Mani Bhaumik. *Code Name God: The Spiritual Odyssey of a Man of Science*. Penguin, 2018.

[Briggs 2018] Andrew Briggs, Andrew Steane, Hans Halvorson. *It Keeps Me Seeking: The Invitation from Science, Philosophy and Religion*. Oxford University Press, 2018.

[Brüntrup 2016] Godehard Brüntrup, Ludwig Jaskolla (Eds.). *Panpsychism: Contemporary Perspectives*. Oxford University Press, 2016.

[Campbell 2003] Thomas Campbell. *My Big Toe*. Lightning Strike Books, 2003.

[Carroll 2019] Sean Carroll. *Something Deeply Hidden: Quantum Worlds and the Emergence of Spacetime*. Oneworld, 2019.

[Conway 2009] John Conway, Simon Kochen. The Strong Free Will Theorem. *Notices of the AMS*, 2009.

[Cramer 1997] John Cramer. *Einstein's Bridge*. Avon Books, 1997.

[Cramer 2016] John Cramer. *The Quantum Handshake: Entanglement, Nonlocality and Transactions*. Springer, 2016.

[Dyson 1979] Freeman Dyson. *Disturbing the Universe*. Harper & Row, 1979.

[Eddington 1929] Arthur Eddington. *The Nature of the Physical World*. MacMillan, 1929.

[Feynman 2006] Richard Feynman. *QED: The Strange Theory of Light and Matter*. Princeton University Press, 2006.

[Fraser 2006] Doreen Lynn Fraser. *Haag's theorem and the interpretation of quantum field theories with interactions*. University of Pittsburgh, 2006.
http://d-scholarship.pitt.edu/8260/

[Givens 2014] Terryl Givens. *Wrestling the Angel: The Foundations of Mormon Thought: Cosmos, God, Humanity*. Oxford University Press, 2014.

[Goff 2019] Philip Goff. *Galileo's Error: Foundations for a New Science of Consciousness*. Pantheon, 2019.

[Haag 1996] Rudolf Haag. *Local Quantum Physics: Fields, Particles, Algebras*. Springer, 1996.

[Haco 2018] Sasha Haco, Stephen Hawking, Malcolm Perry, Andrew Strominger. Black Hole Entropy and Soft Hair. *arXiv*, 2018.
https://arxiv.org/abs/1810.01847

[Halvorson 2006] Hans Halvorson, Michael Miiger. Algebraic Quantum Field Theory. In *Philosophy of Physics (Handbook of the Philosophy of Science)*. North Holland, 2006.

[Halvorson 2011]. Hans Halvorson (Ed.). *Deep Beauty: Understanding the Quantum World through Mathematical Innovation*. Cambridge University Press, 2011.

[Han 2014] Moo-Young Han. *From Photons To Higgs: A Story Of Light* (second edition). World Scientific, 2014.

[Hawking 2016] Stephen Hawking, Malcolm Perry, Andrew Strominger. Soft Hair on Black Holes. *Physical Review Letters*, 2016.

[Hawking 2018] Stephen Hawking. *Brief Answers to the Big Questions*. Hodder & Stoughton, 2018.

[James 1960] William James. *The Will to Believe, Human Immortality, and Other Essays in Popular Philosophy* (first published in 1896). Dover, 1960.

[Jeans 1930] James Jeans. *The Mysterious Universe*. Cambridge University Press, 1930.

[Kastner 2012] Ruth Kastner, *The Transactional Interpretation of Quantum Mechanics: The Reality of Possibility*. Cambridge University Press, 2012.

[Kastner 2015] Ruth Kastner. *Understanding Our Unseen Reality: Solving Quantum Riddles*. Imperial College Press, 2015.

[Kastner 2019] Ruth Kastner. *Adventures in Quantumland: Exploring Our Unseen Reality*. World Scientific, 2019.

[Kauffman 2016] Stuart Kauffman. *Humanity in a Creative Universe*. Oxford University Press, 2016.

[Koch 2019] Christof Koch. *The Feeling of Life Itself: Why Consciousness Is Widespread but Can't Be Computed*. MIT Press, 2019.

[Kurzweil 2005] Ray Kurzweil. *The Singularity Is Near: When Humans Transcend Biology*. Viking Press, 2005.

[Maack 2019] Már Másson Maack. Why Mormonism is the best religion for cyborgs. *TNW*, 2019.
https://thenextweb.com/tech/2019/06/27/why-mormonism-is-the-best-religion-for-cyborgs/

[Musser 2015] George Musser. *Spooky Action at a Distance: The Phenomenon That Reimagines Space and Time - and What It Means for Black Holes, the Big Bang, and Theories of Everything*. Scientific American / Farrar, Straus and Giroux, 2015.

[Musser 2019] George Musser. Gravity's Residue. *FQXI*, 2019.
https://fqxi.org/community/articles/display/233

[Nagel 1974] Thomas Nagel. What Is It Like to be a Bat? *The Philosophical Review*, 1974.

[Narnhofer 2012] Heide Narnhofer and Walter Thirring. Entanglement, Bell inequality and all that. *Journal of Mathematical Physics*, 2012.

[Overbye 2018] Dennis Overbye. Stephen Hawking's Final Paper: How to Escape From a Black Hole. *New York Times*, 2018.
https://www.nytimes.com/2018/10/23/science/stephen-hawking-final-paper.html

[Pannenberg 2007]. Wolfhart Pannenberg. *The Historicity of Nature: Essays on Science and Theology* (Niels Henrik Gregersen, Ed.). Templeton Press, 2007.

[Preparata 2002a] Giuliano Preparata. *An Introduction to a Realistic Quantum Physics*. World Scientific, 2002.

[Preparata 2002b] Giuliano Preparata. *Dai quark ai cristalli. Breve storia di un lungo viaggio dentro la materia*. Bollati Boringhieri, 2002.

[Radin 2018] Dean Radin. *Real Magic: Ancient Wisdom, Modern Science, and a Guide to the Secret Power of the Universe*. Harmony, 2018.

[Stapledon 1947] Olaf Stapledon. *The Flames*. Secker and Warburg, 1947.

[Stewart 1997] Ian Stewart. *Does God Play Dice?: The New Mathematics of Chaos*. Penguin UK, 1997.

[Stewart 2018] Ian Stewart, David Tall. *Complex analysis: The hitch hiker's guide to the plane*. Cambridge University Press, 2018.

[Strominger 2018] Andrew Strominger. *Lectures on the Infrared Structure of Gravity and Gauge Theory*. Princeton University Press, 2018.

[Teller 1995] Paul Teller. *An Interpretive Introduction to Quantum Field Theory*. Princeton University Press, 1995.

[Thirring 2007] Walter Thirring. *Cosmic Impressions: Traces of God in the Laws of Nature*. Templeton Press, 2007.

[Verch 2006] Rainer Verch. Vacuum Fluctuations, Geometric Modular Action and Relativistic Quantum Information Theory. In *Special Relativity: Will it Survive the Next 101 Years?* (Jürgen Ehlers, Claus Lämmerzahl, Eds.). Springer, 2006.

[Virk 2019] Rizwan Virk. *The Simulation Hypothesis: An MIT Computer Scientist Shows Why AI, Quantum Physics and Eastern Mystics All Agree We Are In a Video Game*. Bayview Books, 2019.

[Weinberg 1977] Steven Weinberg. The Search for Unity: Notes for a History of Quantum Field Theory. *Daedalus*, 1977.
http://www.fafnir.phyast.pitt.edu/py3765/WeinbergQFThistory.pdf

[Witten 2018] Edward Witten. APS Medal for Exceptional Achievement in Research: Invited article on entanglement properties of quantum field theory. *Reviews of Modern Physics*, 2018. Open access version: Notes on Some Entanglement Properties of Quantum Field Theory. *arXiv*, 2018.
https://arxiv.org/abs/1803.04993

[Zeilinger 2010] Anton Zeilinger. *Dance of the Photons: From Einstein to Quantum Teleportation*. Farrar, Straus and Giroux, 2010.

[Zeilinger 2017] Anton Zeilinger. Quantum Entanglement Is Independent of Space and Time. In *Know This: Today's Most Interesting and Important Scientific Ideas, Discoveries, and Developments* (John Brockman, Ed.). Harper Perennial, 2017.

CONCLUSION

Thanks for reading so far! I am acutely aware that I have presented many alternative pictures and options, instead of one simple view of life, the universe, and everything. But I hope that you have found some of the ideas outlined in this book interesting, hopeful, meaningful, and plausible.

Let's pretend that I have persuaded you of the plausibility of my main recurring points, including:

- Future science and technology will permit playing with the building blocks of space, time, matter, energy, and life, in ways that we could only call magic and supernatural today.
- Someday in the future, you and your loved ones will be resurrected by transcendent, divine science and technology.
- Inconceivably advanced God-like intelligences are out there among the stars.
- Even more God-like beings operate in the very fabric of spacetime, or underneath spacetime, or beyond spacetime, and control reality. Future science will allow us to find them, and become like them.
- Perhaps intelligent life has not yet achieved God-likeness. But once God-like beings come into existence in the future, they are present and active anywhere in the universe at all times, including here and now.
- These inconceivably advanced, wholly other intelligences have personal, human aspects.
- Our descendants in the far future will join the community of God-like beings among the stars and beyond, and use divine technology to resurrect the dead and remake the universe.
- Mind is part of the fabric of fundamental reality.
- The simulation hypothesis is a coherent and useful mental picture of reality.
- The ultimate, unattainable, absolutely infinite God is undecidable but plausible.
- Physical reality is wide open to divine action.
- Religion is totally compatible with science.

I have also outlined some pictures of physical reality that leave room for transcendence. The pictures that I have proposed are only rough sketches, but you can anchor your imagination to them until you find better ones.

Now you can believe in a religion without abandoning science. You don't have to fear death, and you can endure the temporary separation from your beloved departed ones. So be happier, and do something good. You can focus on the task ahead.

The task ahead is to start moving forward on the sacred road to the stars. Eventually we'll find God-like beings out there, learn from them, become God-like ourselves, remake the universe, and resurrect the dead.

Our task requires making this planet a better place for everyone, and offering all people ways to participate in our journey on the sacred road. No task is too big or too small, and you have an important role to play.

Perhaps you can discover new science, build new technologies, create stimulating art, develop new ideas in philosophy and theology, find new solutions to social problems, or do other BIG things to make the world a better place. If so, I envy you, and Godspeed.

But more likely you are one of us little people, and you can only do small things. If so, your task is equally important. You are a crew member of Spaceship Earth, en route toward its cosmic manifest destiny.

You are needed and important. Feel it in your heart.

Your task is to do all the little things that you can do to make our common journey easier, safer, and more enjoyable for everyone. Help your fellow crew members, and be kind to them.

Start now.